Praise for

Immigration and Canada: Global and Transnational Perspectives

"This is the most comprehensive book I have read on international migration. The author argues that contemporary Canadian society cannot be de-coupled from history and the global system. The presentation of ideas and analysis in this book are born out of sound pedagogy from an experienced scholar."
— Charles Adeyanju, Department of Sociology,
Brandon University

"This volume will serve as a very useful book. The major strengths are its breadth and its Canadian focus. This book is a welcome addition to the literature on international migration."
— Tanya Basok, Director, Centre for Studies in Social Justice,
University of Windsor

"This book is a well-organized, comprehensive overview of issues of transnational migration. It reflects a very thorough coverage of objective evidence on migration and integration issues. It promises to be a useful compilation with a particular focus on implications for Canada."
— Sylvia Hale, Chair, Department of Sociology,
St. Thomas University

"This book, written by one of Canada's more recognized authorities, addresses the historical and contemporary dimensions of incorporation and exclusion."
— Sean P. Hier, Department of Sociology,
University of Victoria

"This book will certainly fill an important vacuum.
The author clearly indicates mastery over the subject."
— R. Cheran, Department of Sociology and Anthropology,
University of Windsor

"The transnational emphasis is both welcome and appropriate to this original treatment of immigration to Canada."
— David Ley, Department of Geography,
University of British Columbia

D0521685

Immigration and Canada

Global and Transnational Perspectives

Alan B. Simmons

Critical Issues in Contemporary Sociology,
under the direction of Vic Satzewich

Canadian Scholars' Press Inc.
Toronto

Immigration and Canada: Global and Transnational Perspectives
by Alan B. Simmons

First published in 2010 by
Canadian Scholars' Press Inc.
180 Bloor Street West, Suite 801
Toronto, Ontario
M5S 2V6

www.cspi.org

Canadian Scholars' Press Inc. gratefully acknowledges financial support for our publishing activities from the Government of Canada through the Book Publishing Industry Development Program (BPIDP) and the Government of Ontario through the Ontario Book Publishing Tax Credit Program.

Library and Archives Canada Cataloguing in Publication

Simmons, Alan
    Immigration and Canada : global and transnational perspectives / Alan B. Simmons.

(Critical issues in contemporary sociology) Includes bibliographical references and index.
ISBN 978-1-55130-362-8

    1. Canada—Emigration and immigration. 2. Canada—Emigration and immigration—Government policy. 3. Emigration and immigration. 4. Immigrants—Canada—Social conditions. 5. Immigrants—Canada—Economic conditions. I. Title. II. Series: Critical issues in contemporary sociology

JV7220.S45 2009   325.71   C2009-905769-7

Text design and layout by Brad Horning and Stewart Moracen
Cover by John Kicksee/KIX BY DESIGN

Printed and bound in Canada

Canada

MIX
Paper from
responsible sources
FSC **FSC® C004071**

Table of Contents

Preface

Since there are already a number of excellent books on Canadian immigration, ethnicity, and multiculturalism, one might ask why I wrote this one. The answer is fairly simple. After going through other books, I concluded that the existing literature leaves considerable room for a new volume on Canadian immigration from the perspective of being in a globalized and transnational world. Stated briefly, the book builds on the well-known argument that Canadian immigration is a key element in an often internally contradictory nation-building process that is oriented outward with regard to attracting immigrant workers to strengthen trade competitiveness and inward with regard to creating a peaceful, prosperous, multicultural society. The fact that this nation-building model does not entirely achieve these ideals provides the foundation for an existing body of critical studies of Canadian immigration. My objective is to contribute to this established body of writing by adding arguments and examining evidence on the nation-building process at different levels: global, the nation-state, ethnic and home associations of immigrants, and institutions formed by native-born Canadians that variably include immigrants and ethnic minorities.

The key questions addressed in the book are: What historical and institutional forces explain Canadian immigration? Who benefits from it, and how? And, most importantly, do the outcomes for Canada, the immigrants, and others correspond to what was imagined and hoped for, and if not, what can be done? I am hesitant to put the approach taken to these questions into a single category. The book draws on frameworks and concepts in political economy, economic sociology, critical geography, anthropology, demography, cultural change, social psychology, and family relations. It reviews selected studies from these fields as well as works done by demographers and historians. Throughout, the goal of the book is to understand Canadian immigration as a multi-level historical process with systemic features that generate periods of relative stability between moments of change and transition. The focus is on the contemporary period from the 1980s to the present, understood in terms of its emergence out of earlier developments. The dynamics involve ongoing struggles over who constitutes the nation and how different parts of its bilingual, multi-ethnic, multicultural, immigrant-transnational, regionalized, and localized structure fit into different imagined futures of Canada. I acknowledge that the breadth in this perspective creates a challenge. At the same time it provides an opportunity to look for underlying patterns and forces that cut across complex realities and that can be summarized in the form of simplifying models and frameworks. It is my hope that my application of concepts such as *imagined national futures* to review and integrate the current research literature will add to knowledge and debate in the field.

My indebtedness to other researchers will be evident throughout the book in my citation of their works. A good number of those cited are former teachers, current colleagues, and past students. I owe them special thanks for the pleasures of working with them and what I have learned from them. Readers of the book will note that my theoretical inclinations are broadly in the direction of hegemonic analysis of state and political-economic structures and social resistance to these structures. This orientation, and my particular approach to it in terms of international migration "regimes," "historical systems," "transnational social spaces," and the "politics of identity," developed over several years of research and teaching on developing regions, social change, and international migration affecting Canada and immigrant-origin countries. As I reflected on my evolving understanding of these themes, I realized that contributions to my thinking came not only from my work with colleagues and students in Canada, but also from collaborative work with many others outside Canada. My interests have for many years covered development issues in Latin America and the Caribbean, and to some extent in West Africa and Southeast Asia. They have also concerned Canadian immigration issues and the study of Canadian population dynamics. These diverse interests come together in this book. I view Canada and the countries with which it trades and those from which it receives immigrants as places that are undergoing a dynamic joint transformation through their direct and indirect interactions in a global and transnational world. The welfare and harmony within these nations depend on the interactive relations between them. Immigration to Canada is a Canadian issue and a global and transnational one as well. These views and the detailed research issues they raise, which I discuss in this book, developed in working closely with many people over the years. I owe a great debt of gratitude to them and I thank them all.

Certain institutions and people who have played key roles in this book deserve particular thanks. Two research centres at York University — namely, the Centre for Research on Latin America and the Caribbean and the Centre for Refugee Studies — provided support for my research on international refugee and development issues over many years as well as stimulation and encouragement for the ideas that are developed in this book. The Centre for Excellence on Immigrant Settlement (CERIS) in Toronto funded some of the research reported in this book and provided access to useful data. Vic Satzewich, as editor of the series in which this book appears, deserves a particular note of thanks for encouraging me to take on this writing project. He contributed through helpful advice on matters related to the structure of this book and even more so as a scholar whose works provided inspiration for my reflections on racism and transnationalism. I also add a special thanks to Megan Mueller at Canadian Scholars' Press Inc. for her strong support of this project from the beginning to the end.

My deepest thanks are reserved for Jean Turner, my spouse, research collaborator on several happy occasions, and a constant source of encouragement for my writing. As she has done in the past on other projects, she provided insightful and detailed feedback on my drafts of the chapters in this book and stimulated my efforts to improve them. That she took time from her own research and teaching to do this is particularly appreciated.

Alan Simmons
September 2009

CHAPTER 1
Introduction

Understanding migration as a transnational process, and that people will simultaneously belong to this country and their homelands for the long haul, reveals several important things. For one, sometimes migration is as much about the people who stay behind as it is about people who move. (Levitt 2007: 23)

Canadian immigration is a broad topic. The goal of this chapter is to introduce and clarify the topic and the goals of this book in three ways. First, I will give an overview of several different useful definitions of what constitutes Canadian immigration. Secondly, I will outline a general approach to the topic and illustrate this with selected examples. Thirdly, in a longer section that is most important for comprehending the scope and perspective of the book, I will examine a number of concepts that are used in the book to analyze and understand Canadian immigration. The chapter ends with a brief review of the themes and issues to be addressed in and across other chapters.

Canadian Immigration

Canada is a geographically large territory with somewhat more than 33 million inhabitants who are settled mainly across the southern edge of the nation. Nearly a fifth of the inhabitants were born in other countries. With the exception of Native peoples who currently comprise less than 5 percent of the population, all the rest are descendants of immigrants. In some cases the foreign ancestors of native-born Canadians arrived long ago. Some are descended from early French settlers who arrived in the 16th and 17th century. Following the establishment of British colonial governance in 1763, new "settlement" projects brought in new influxes of European-origin immigrants, including some 40,000 United Empire Loyalists from the United States. This was Canada's first refugee inflow. The mass-immigration flows that established Canada as a multi-ethnic nation began slowly after Confederation in 1867, then swelled to huge waves of immigration in the late 1800s and early 1900s, reaching a peak of 400,000 immigrants in one year just before the First World War. Immigration then largely closed down for the two Great Wars and the 1930s Depression. It then resumed at a high level after the Second World War. In the contemporary period since 1989, immigration levels have stayed relatively high, with immigrants coming largely from Africa, Asia, the Caribbean, and Latin America. The nation, which has been multicultural for a long time, is becoming far more ethnically diverse. Currently, immi-

gration is the main contributor to Canadian population growth, the key determinant of growing ethnocultural diversity, and the main reason why population and labour force decline due to below-replacement fertility will be postponed.

One can define Canadian immigration in several ways. To begin with, we can define it as *a field concerned with immigration policy with respect to numbers, origins, and settlement patterns of immigrants*. This is the main orientation of books on the history of Canadian immigration such as those by Kelley and Trebilcock (2000) and Knowles (1992). In addition, we can define Canadian immigration as *a field covering the impacts of immigration on Canadian social, economic, cultural, and political development*. This is the main focus of books on Canadian immigration by economists, demographers, geographers, sociologists, and political scientists, including the recent volumes by Biles, Burstein, and Frideres (2008); Carment and Bercuson (2008); Satzewich and Liodakis (2007); Fong (2006); Beach, Green, and Reitz (2003), and Reitz (1998). These two preceding definitions constitute the main ones found in the field. Increasingly, however, there is an interest in defining Canadian immigration more broadly as *a political-economic and cultural process linked to global and transnational forces*. The global forces include Canadian trade patterns and how they affect the demand for immigrant workers. The transnational forces include the social links between migrants and their home communities, which draw in new immigrants. This global-transnational concern can be found to some extent in the works listed above, but the transnational aspects are developed far more thoroughly in edited volumes by Satzewich and Wong (2006) and Goldring and Krishnamurti (2007). In this book, I examine immigration from a perspective that highlights both globalizing and transnationalizing processes in relation to Canadian nation-building.

All three of the above definitions can be found in the present book. The focus of the book is contemporary, from the 1980s to the present. At the same time, prior historical developments are highlighted because they illuminate the contemporary era. They do so by making clearer the continuities from the past, and also by drawing attention to ways in which the present is distinctive. Perhaps most importantly, the approach highlights Canada's position in a global and transnational world. The word "position" is used with careful intent: Canada is part of the global and transnational world, so it both contributes to and is affected by transformations taking place in this world. The goal of the book is to better understand how global-transnational forces and Canadian immigration and settlement patterns are related to each other within the same field.

Another way of understanding Canadian immigration is to ask: Who are the actors involved in it? These actors may be conceptualized at various levels. At the global level, the actors include *powerful nation-states* that set the agenda for trade, immigration, migrant worker programs, and ethnocultural relations for other nations. Within this global context, *the Canadian state* sets national goals through establishing immigration targets and related trade, visa workers and multicultural policies. *Immigrants* set their own goals when they decide to migrate. Less obvious and sometimes forgotten is that the *family members of immigrants in home communities* also enter into the process. They may encourage the decision of family members to move abroad in the hopes that the migrants will become more affluent elsewhere and will send money home or sponsor the immigration of other family members at a later date. Interactions at this level provide the core of immigrant transnational social engage-

ments and networks. Finally, *non-migrants in the host society* clearly have objectives that enter into the process. Their goals may lead them to welcome immigrants or to marginalize them as outsiders. Either way, their goals and practices will affect how immigrants settle. They will also affect state immigration policies. Thus, the field of social action that shapes Canadian immigration not only includes many actors with different access to resources and power, but these actors may not always agree on what is best. As a result, the field is characterized by a mixture of overlapping goals, harmony, tensions, and deep divisions. From the perspective of actors and their goals, Canadian immigration can be defined in a fourth way *as a field of study focusing on immigration and immigrant settlement as key elements of Canadian nation-building and social transformation brought about by the interactions of actors outside and inside the nation*. This last definition, while a bit long, effectively combines the earlier three definitions. It needs to be fleshed out to distinguish more clearly the diverse objectives of the actors, the resources they have to achieve their interests, and how their access to resources and power determines who "wins" and who "loses" in relative terms. This, in fact, is the project of the book.

Immigration as a Systemic Process

Viewing immigration as a complex field of action involving many actors at different levels is both a challenge and an opportunity. The challenge is that the broad scope and complexity of the field do not readily fall into any simple, narrow theory. The opportunity is that we may be able to overcome the challenge in part by developing frameworks that will allow us to cut through the breadth and complexity and find patterns of coherence and explanations for change. Previous research provides insights into the ways in which immigration has been structured into relatively coherent patterns or migration systems within specific contexts. These systems then change when the context and/or internal dynamics lead to transition points. Models of such patterns can provide a foundation for developing perspectives on Canadian immigration. Consider the following two contrasting examples of migration systems founded on completely different ideological principles. Following Weber's (1949: 89–95) "ideal-type" methodology, these two examples are put forward as analytic "types" or constructs to draw attention to causes, internal coherence, and consequences of the two migration system types of interest.

The first type is a *utopian migration system*, founded on liberal principles, in which poor people in less developed countries want to move to wealthy nations; wealthy nations want to admit at least some of these individuals because they need their work; the immigrants find good jobs and feel at home so that they stay; the economy of the wealthy nation expands in part through the contributions of immigrant workers; the immigrants send money, gifts, and support for local development projects in their home countries such that the lives of their family members remaining there are improved, and the whole world becomes a happier and better-off place. Coherence comes about through a "win-win" situation in which the goals of many actors are realized at least in part within the context of supportive political-economic and cultural processes.

The second model is a *dystopian migration system*, founded on colonial and authoritarian principles, in which a few actors gain and many lose. In an extreme case, very poor people are forced to move to wealthy states in order to survive;

wealthy states offer them low wages and insist that they reside in ethno-racially segregated slums; when the migrants are old, worn out, and not so productive, they are sent back to their home countries; and given that the migrants were never paid well and could not send much money back to their families, their families remain poor. In this scenario coherence comes about through domination and the exercise of power. The wealthy nation and particularly its wealthiest and most powerful members "win," while others "lose" and the system overall suffers from a potential for violent racial, ethnic, and class conflict.

What do the above observations suggest for understanding Canadian immigration? Canada is a nation with a long history of immigrant settlement premised broadly on liberal values and nation-building principles. These values and principles were first expressed within an ethnocentric White Canada framework in effect up until 1962, and subsequently within a non-racist, multicultural framework. It is therefore not surprising that contemporary state immigration and multicultural policies are founded on a rhetoric in which immigration is a promoted as a "good idea" because all key actors — immigrants and everyone who lives in Canada — are assumed to gain. Looking back to earlier times, we can see that this was not always the case. Canada has not always assumed that immigration was a good idea for Canadians. In addition, on occasion the state assumed that immigration was good for Canada, but that certain racialized categories of immigrants should not benefit. During the 1930s Depression years, immigrants were viewed as threats to employment, political stability, and, in some cases, national values and culture. During the Depression, the state's focus shifted from welcoming immigrants to excluding and deporting them. In the years after Confederation in 1867, Chinese immigrants were allowed to enter freely for a period, but later they were excluded and those who remained, plus the few new Chinese immigrants who were admitted, were largely men confined to doing hard, dangerous, and poorly paid railway construction and coal mining. These historical episodes are discussed more fully in Chapter 3 on historical perspectives.

Policy rhetoric is not the same as actual policy. We may first ask: What is immigration policy? The answer is not simple. Immigration policy is the sum of many different policies and administrative processes. The basket of what we call immigration policies includes the arguments and rationales that support immigration legislation. I have referred to this as policy rhetoric, but this is not to make it less important or to suggest that it is "empty rhetoric." Quite to the contrary, the language used to frame legislated policy is a fundamentally important element of what we understand policy to be. The main items in the immigration policy "basket" include laws and policies on the selection of economic immigrants whom that state wished to attract for their work skills; other official procedures for deciding who will be admitted as a refugee; additional regulations concerning the acceptance of business proposals from foreign entrepreneurs who want to relocate in Canada as residents and future citizens; still other official procedures governing family reunification; and, last but not least, policies on which temporary migrant workers can convert their status to that of an immigrant. Each of these policies involves its own criteria, specialized application form, and administrative procedures. For example, refugee admissions includes a large quasi-judicial organization known as the Immigration and Refugee Board of Canada (IRB) with offices and staff in major urban centres across the country devoted to adjudicating thousands of claims each year from foreigners who

have travelled to Canada to request asylum (see IRB 2009). Immigration officials are occasionally asked to carry out very specific border-control tasks, such as to determine whether a Canadian's marriage to a foreign person is "real" or "fraudulent" so they can decide if the foreign spouse can be admitted as an immigrant.

The immigration policies package normally includes immigrant settlement programs. Such programs cover specific language training and orientation efforts set up to help immigrants shortly after they arrive. Policies concerning multiculturalism, anti-discrimination, hate crimes, and human rights are not immigrant settlement policies, yet they play such an important role in supporting the settlement of newcomers that it is useful to include them within a wider definition of "policies relevant to the settlement of immigrants." These various pieces of policy never fill the potential of all that could be done to meet the rhetoric of Canada as a "peaceful, multicultural, nation of immigrants" (see Chapters 4 and 5). Nor does what we call immigration policy cover other policy areas such as trade, migrant worker, and educational policies that indirectly and directly affect immigration and immigrant settlement. In sum, immigration policy is one among many fields of policies and other forces that determine who will enter Canada and the reception they will receive when they arrive. What actually happens depends on all these policies and many other influences.

An Analytic Approach, with Examples

From the above, we can see that understanding Canadian immigration requires that we answer at least the following three broad questions: (1) What historical and institutional forces explain Canadian immigration? (2) Who benefits from it, and how? (3) How do ideologies, cultural beliefs, and economic forces lend coherence to its operation in any given historical period? In addressing these questions in this book, I frequently draw on Weberian "ideal type" analysis. This analysis involves creating constructs to represent distilled or summary versions of social institutions and processes found in particular places or times. The construct is intended to draw attention to key features of the institutions or processes and how they function. The utopian and dystopian ideal types of migration systems examined earlier provide examples of ideal types. Throughout the book, I use this approach to analysis in order to understand the evolution of Canadian immigration policies and the nation-building assumptions associated with them. As immigration, trade, and cultural policies change, I look for break points in the overall package of policies and ways to distill the main features of each package and present them in ideal type constructs. The constructs can then be compared with one another to gain insights on causation and historical change. They can also be used to examine whether reality comes close to fitting the ideal type of policy objectives observed in the same place and time period.

The following analysis involves use of the ideal type approach. It begins with a sketch of what Canada might look like to Canadians or others favourably disposed to Canada. The view is on the utopian side and accentuates national strengths and accomplishments. I then move from this image to consider two contrasting examples of immigrants and their settlement. One corresponds to or perhaps exceeds the utopian image; the other provides a counter case. This is an analytic exercise to see what can be learned and where this takes us with regard to questions and concepts that can be used in reviewing the research literature.

Speaking positively about Canada, one might say that it is widely viewed as a lucky nation for many reasons. Canada is a member of the G8 club of the eight most economically developed and influential nations of the world. The other G8 members are France, Germany, Italy, Japan, Russia, the United Kingdom, and the United States. Canada falls among the top countries in the United Nations Human Development Index (UNDP 2006). Montreal, Ottawa, Toronto, Calgary, and Vancouver are rated among the top 25 best cities in the world as places to live with respect to political stability, crime, law enforcement, banking services, censorship and limitations on personal freedom, hospital quality, schooling quality, public services, recreation, and the natural environment (Mercer 2008). Canadian citizens and residents are protected by a contemporary Charter of Rights and Freedoms (Justice Canada 1982). Canadians benefit from state programs supporting education, health, unemployment insurance, and post-retirement social security that are similar to those of other wealthy nations.

Not least of the various features of the country that are celebrated, Canada is a multicultural nation that welcomes large numbers of immigrants every year from diverse countries around the world. From 2000 to 2005, between a fifth and a quarter of a million new immigrants arrived in Canada each year (CIC 2008c). It is widely said that Canada is a "nation of immigrants," a statement that is intended to draw positive attention to the large number of foreign-born in Canada today and the fact that many Canadian-born citizens are the children or grandchildren of immigrants, and hence have a living memory of their immigrant past. The 2006 census reported that nearly a fifth of all current Canadian residents are foreign-born, an unusually high percentage compared with most other countries (Statistics Canada

2007c). Under current trends, the proportion of immigrants in Canadian society will rise, as will the level of diversity of backgrounds among these newcomers. For the past three decades, Canadian immigrants have come predominantly from Asia, yet significant streams of immigrants have come from all regions of the globe, such that Canada is becoming one of the most ethnically diverse nations in the world (Bélanger and Caron Malenfant 2005).

What is the relationship between Canada's advanced development and its immigration experience? Public pronouncements by Canadian leaders frequently praise current and past immigrants for their important contributions to the development of Canada's economy, political institutions, and its multi-ethnic society. Relatively high levels of current immigration and the selection of immigrants on the basis of their advanced levels of schooling are part of a government policy that seeks to maximize future contributions from immigrants to the Canadian economy as skilled workers, affluent consumers, and well-off taxpayers. Not surprisingly, state immigration policy gives priority to the need for highly skilled immigrants to fill gaps in the labour supply, to raise the skill level of workers, to increase productivity, and to enhance Canada's export capacity (CIC 2002). In the view of many, current below-replacement birth rates in Canada will continue to generate future shortages of workers that will encourage new immigration (see Chapter 10).

This distilled image of Canada is that of a wealthy multicultural nation that invites large numbers of immigrants to settle permanently to promote economic growth and pluralist values. This then could be contrasted with other nations in the world that do not fit such a model. One of the clearest contrasts would be with Japan. Its distilled image might be that of a wealthy monocultural nation that admits very few immigrants and instead uses robots to replace workers and relocates its manufacturing plants to other countries where the work is done by foreign labour. Going around the globe leads to other types that cover European and other nations (Simmons 1999b).

Now let us use the Canadian ideal type model as a benchmark against which to assess actual experiences of immigrants. We may begin with a thumbnail sketch of a case that not only fits the distilled positive model of immigration and Canada as a welcoming country to immigrants, but exceeds it. Then we will consider a counter example in which things did not work out so well. Both are stories of Jamaican immigrants. Contrasting examples can be found among immigrants from every national and cultural origin. I use the two Jamaican stories because I became aware of them through my own research and collaboration with others, as the sources below will indicate. In addition, I find the contrast useful because it corresponds to findings that the Caribbean immigrant community in Toronto, the location of the largest concentration of immigrants from that region and Jamaicans as the largest part of the Caribbean community in Canada, is socially divided in many ways, one being a division between a more affluent professional class and a less affluent non-professional class. These groups live largely separately and interact only in certain contexts and on specific occasions (Simmons and Plaza 2006).

The high success story is that of Michael Lee-Chin, who came from Jamaica to Canada initially as a university student in 1970. Some years later, after he became very successful and wealthy, he added to his accomplishments by becoming a major investor and benefactor in the Caribbean (see Box 1.1). Perhaps as a tribute to his relatively humble roots, the Jamaica National Commercial Bank (JNCB), which he controls, has set up financial services to

Box 1.1: A Very Successful Immigrant: Michael Lee-Chin

Dr. Peter George, President of McMaster University, Dr. Vishwanath Baba, former dean of the DeGroote School of Business, and Mr. Michael Lee-Chin at the official opening of the AIC Institute at McMaster University.

Michael Lee-Chin is a Jamaican-born Canadian investor. He is the founder and chairman of Portland Holdings Inc., which owns a diversified portfolio in media, tourism, health care telecommunications, and financial services. He is currently executive chairman of AIC Limited (a Canadian mutual fund), and the National Commercial Bank of Jamaica. *Canadian Business* has named him one of the richest people in Canada. He is also a philanthropist. In 2003, he made headlines when he donated $30 million to the Royal Ontario Museum for the new Crystal building addition, now named after him. He is also a founding donor to the AIC Institute at McMaster University (see photo above). He has been remarkably open about his family background and business ventures. Below is a brief resumé from Canadian and Caribbean sources.

Lee-Chin was born in Port Antonio, Jamaica, in 1951. Both his parents were biracial, Black and Chinese, Jamaicans. His mother held down jobs as a bookkeeper at a hotel, as an Avon cosmetics sales representative, and as a *Reader's Digest* salesperson. His father sold Singer sewing machines and worked as a grocery clerk. Only later did his father open a modest grocery store, Super Plus, which is now one of Jamaica's largest grocery chains. Lee-Chin's first job came in 1965, working as part of the landscaping team at the Frenchman's Cove Hotel. In 1966 he got a summer job working on the *Jamaica Queen* cruise ship, cleaning the engine room.

In 1970 he came to Canada with his own savings and a scholarship sponsored by the Jamaican government to study civil engineering at McMaster University. Graduating in 1974, he describes his career as follows:

> I sent out 100 resumés for jobs in the engineering field and got 100 negative responses. But I got three non-engineering options: a soap salesman, a truck driver, and a financial adviser with Investors Group. I opted for the third.
>
> I was 26, I had one week of training, and had to go out and sell.... I knew no one with money, so I had no prospects. It was May 1977 and my mom was coming to visit me. Her flight was delayed by two hours, so I decided to drive around the neighbourhood. It suddenly hit me that the people tending their gardens were my

prospects. So I plucked up the courage to stop and approach the next person I saw. Out of six such contacts, I got five appointments, and after the first month in the business, I made $10,000.

I thought cold-calling could be profitable, so I decided to venture further afield to hone my skills at prospecting. I drove from Hamilton to Tillsonburg—rural Ontario tobacco-farming country. Each farmer I approached told me to see their accountant A.W. Judd. I met him, told him about my product, and he said it was the same one they had been told to recommend to the farmers at a conference he just attended. He gathered the other accountants and invited me to make a presentation to them....

I was an aggressive investor and in 1983, after five years in the business, I had another pivotal point. I decided to invest in businesses that I understood, so that year I borrowed $500,000 to invest in McKenzie Financial Corporation.... I bought the stock at $1.00 per share and four years later it was $7.00, and five years later, $500,000 became $35 million.

Sources: Mr. Lee-Chin's current positions and contribution to the Royal Ontario Museum can be found at [www.rom.on.ca/about/newsroom/pdf/leechin.pdf].
The interview extract is from an interview by Barbara Ellington, published in the *Jamaican Gleener* [http://www.jamaica-gleaner.com/gleaner/20060313/business/business1.htm].
CP Photo/Adrian Wyld [http://www.forbes.com/lists/2008/10/billionaires08_Michael-Lee-Chin_7TE8.html]

provide a low-cost way for Jamaicans in Canada to transfer monetary remittances to family members in Jamaica (Simmons, Plaza, and Piché 2005). The precise reasons for Mr. Lee-Chin's phenomenal success can only be guessed at from his biographic statements and what has been written about him in media and business reports. That he is a person of exceptional talent is widely recognized. His family background may also have been a benefit. His mother is reported to have had a modest job as a salesperson for Avon beauty products, a clue that suggests a job involving connections and practices very different than those of a *higgler*, the Jamaican name for people who live from informal trading and street vending. His father started off as a small store owner, but eventually built up his business to a major enterprise. Entering Canada as a young university student was also likely a crucial step. While a student at Queen's University, Mr. Lee-Chin gained high-level credentials and may also have established useful contacts with other stu-

dents for a business career in finance at a moment in the late 1970s and early 1980s when investments and financial institutions were about to undergo an important period of growth in Canada.

The other case is the Anderson family (a fictitious name), described by Turner (1991) in an analysis from the perspective of a family therapist. An extract from Turner's account of the family's situation is shown in Box 1.2. Her analysis, based on this account, examines the transnational context and dynamics of the family. She observes the following:

> Recent Caribbean immigration to North America is marked by several noteworthy features. One aspect is that a significant part of the movement appears to be female-led. In the case of Canada, for example, young adult women were the leaders who later sponsored their children to come to study, and their own mothers to

Box 1.2: The "Anderson" Family

Like most stories that are brought to therapists, this one was told from a point of view structured by the clients' emotional pain and frustration as they faced a major crisis situation. In that sense, it is an abridged version of their longer, more complex life story, which would also encompass themes related more to survival and success.

The Andersons (fictitious name) were a Black, Jamaican-Canadian family of four, living in Montreal, Canada. The family was seen at a mental health institution after referral by a school teacher who was concerned about their 11-year-old son, George. The teacher expressed concern about the boy's increasing withdrawal and depression. Included in the referral package was a handwritten note from George, which indicated a plea for help and a wish to return to a happier time and place.

The family, in the beginning sessions, focused on their concern about George as a troubled child who appeared to be alternately angry and depressed. Eventually his story became part of a broader text that included many other problem themes, particularly those related to migration, family connectedness, and loss. The history of the Anderson family was one of chain migration and circular movement similar to that of other Caribbean immigrants. George's mother, Pauline, recalled how years earlier, as a young woman in Jamaica, her own mother had urged her to follow her sister who had already made the pioneering move to Canada alone. The sister, living in Alberta, also provided encouragement, though later she proved to be too caught up in her own new life to help Pauline. Leaving George, who was a baby at the time, in the care of his grandmother, Pauline migrated to work as a maid/housekeeper. She was met with racial prejudice, low wages, loneliness, and the hardship of the cold, Canadian prairie climate.

On a return visit to Jamaica, she asked Anthony, George's father and her former visiting-partner, to come to join her in Canada. By this time she had moved to Montreal and found better avenues of employment. There were lengthy long-distance telephone discussions and another extended visit of several months with Anthony in Jamaica before he was ready to make his decision. Pauline's invitation included a proposal of marriage—this would allow Anthony to enter Canada as a sponsored family member eligible to seek employment.

Eventually Anthony migrated to join Pauline, knowing that he could return at any time to Jamaica without losing much, because his already narrowing job opportunities were unlikely to get much worse while he was gone. After establishing themselves economically by both working at factory jobs for a couple of years, they sent for their son. By that time George had been living for almost 6 years with his maternal grandmother; he thought of his parents as visitors who arrived at Jamaica from time to time. With childish protest, he left his "in-fact" mother behind and joined his real parents in a strange new place. Everyone recalled how difficult the adjustment had been.

Both the maternal and paternal grandmothers visited Montreal one after the other to help Pauline and her husband care for George and his new baby sister who arrived within the next year. For different reasons, neither grandmother took up the invitation to stay for an extended period, a fact that greatly disappointed George and his parents. Over this entire period in their family life, those in Canada and those remaining in Jamaica shared, by way of phone calls and visits, their common concerns, including how George and his sister should be cared for and how financial commitments should be carried out between the two home settings.

With a change in import regulations, the bottom fell out of the garment industry. Both parents were laid off even though they were by then among the most skilled machine operators. Pauline was able to return to at least part-time work cleaning private homes, but Anthony had no other employment that was acceptable to him. He began to sense more strongly that his race and ethnic background were barriers to finding good jobs in other sectors. Feeling hopeless about his own situation, Anthony began to insist that they all return to Jamaica, but Pauline could not agree. She foresaw losing her potential economic independence, giving up the dream of "making good," and sacrificing the children's chance for a Canadian education.

The marital discord, reciprocal blaming, and financial stresses that followed had fed George's idea that he belonged back with his grandmother. He demonstrated his anger through silent resistance at home, which led his father to punish him harshly and then feel terribly sad and guilty. By the time the family met with the therapist, they all felt frozen by indecision and could see no escape from anger and despair.

Source: Turner, Jean. 1991. "Migrants and Their Therapists: A Trans-context Approach." *Family Process* 30:407–419. The text has been slightly abridged by the author to select and highlight certain points.

help care for the children/grand-children. Many men also come, but they and children often come later.

A second aspect of the migration process reflects West Indian family culture. Family ties are maintained through extensive visiting, child-fostering by kin, the sending of remittances (financial support) to kin at home, and the use of telephone calls and letters to provide emotional support. The result is a "transnational family" in which there is a bi-directional flow of ideas, support, and commitment.... (Turner 1991: 409)

In a related but separate paper, Simmons and Turner (1993) provide the context for the above and other families. They note that the garment industry, which had been solid in the 1970s, was downsizing by the 1980s as low-cost imported clothing from Asia and other less developed regions undercut sales of more expensive Canadian-made apparel. The employers had the option of relocating their manufacturing to low-wage countries and they did so. The immigrant workers who found themselves out of jobs were in a more difficult situation. They had already made a commitment to Canada. Relatives abroad were counting on them to be a success in Canada to provide greater security for the family as a whole. Going back to Jamaica was an option for only a few for these reasons plus the fact that Jamaica, during the period they had been in Canada, had also undergone industrial downsizing and was in a deep economic slump. In the process, the family members in Jamaica and those in Canada did what they could to help one another and to jointly figure out what to do next. Neither Jamaica nor Canada was happy about the losses in jobs in their respective nations as global trade patterns forced plant closures in both countries. They had to reimagine their futures under circumstances not of their own choosing.

Few immigrants will become multi-millionaires like Mr. Lee-Chin and, hopefully, most immigrants will not face such deeply troubling periods in their lives as the Andersons. However, many do have serious struggles, and the optimism of many is buoyed up by the hope that their children will do well. The extreme illustrations provided above serve as a first step to clarify the range of outcomes, and to help us understand the many different forces that together determine who comes to Canada, the motives of immigrants, their connections to families and home, and how settlement works out differently, depending on circumstances. In contextualizing the stories of immigrants, we can see how Canadian trade, immigration, and cultural patterns and policies affect what happens. The Canadian state encouraged immigration from the Caribbean in the 1960s and 1970s to meet labour needs in various sectors, including the textiles and garment sector, which in that period employed many workers. The state imagined that Caribbean immigrants would find jobs in this and other sectors and a new home in Canadian society. The imagined future of the nation underlying state policies was that of an industrially expanding, immigrant-welcoming, multicultural nation. When, as a result of new trade policies and the importation to Canada of very inexpensive clothing from Asia, the Canadian garment industry "headed south" with factories closing down in Canada and jobs being relocated to low-wage countries, Canadian immigration officials did not entirely drop the old imagined future. Rather, they transformed it into a new one. The new imagined future placed its hopes on knowledge industries and on immigrants with very high levels of education suited to work in them. The Anderson family and Mr. Lee-Chin arrived in Canada about the same time, but under different circumstances in the context of trade and other changes that would lead to dramatic differences for how the immigration decisions worked out for them.

Immigrants come with their own hopes or imagined futures. The period when immigrants arrive and the skills they bring with them, or acquire soon after, make a huge difference to their individual outcomes, as the preceding contrasting cases suggest. In the chain of connections, the outcomes for these Jamaican immigrants affected their family members and others in home countries. Note, for example, the ways in which members of the Anderson family in Jamaica and in Canada tried to help one another, and how Mr. Lee-Chin later became involved in investments and philanthropy in the Caribbean. As well, others in Canada were affected by the outcome for the immigrants. Thus, Mr. Lee-Chin's accomplishments contributed to Canadian corporate success, while the Anderson family's struggles became one segment of a larger story of how Afro-Caribbean immigrants have been resilient in the face of prejudice and other obstacles and have eventually become successful in Canada by working hard and maintaining hope. These stories are incomplete fragments, leaving a great deal that is unknown. At the same time, they provide an initial grounding from which to more clearly identify the issues of concern in this book.

Very few Canadians, immigrants included, have extremely high levels of work or business success. Many more Canadians, including immigrants, suffer from periods of unemployment and dislocation as certain sectors of the economy decline and others rise. What, then, is the range of outcomes that describes the jobs, income, and social incorporation of immigrants, and how does this compare to the same outcomes for native-born Canadians, including those of ethnic minority status? This is the main analytic question in the literature and a key focus in this book. Findings from diverse studies provide mounting evidence that actual immigrant settlement patterns do not correspond in many ways to hoped-for goals and images of successful incorporation. The discrepancies include very low earnings among immigrants; problems that immigrants face in obtaining recognition of their credentials; evidence that visible minority immigrants experience racism; high levels of residential concentration associated with poverty among recent immigrants; and patterns of individual and collective identity formation that reveal the rising importance of transnational ethnic and cultural connections. The reasons for these trends are not fully understood. These puzzles are the central focus of the book. It seems that many immigrants are caught in a double bind: They are trying against the odds to do well in Canada and to support themselves and their family members here, and they are hoping to have enough time and money to contribute emotional and financial support to family members in their home countries. They turn to their friends, networks, and ethnic communities in Canada for contacts and information to help them solve these joint problems. The help they receive is often positive for feeling culturally more at home in Canada, but it may not help so much in finding a better job or getting a business started (Chapters 7 and 8). These circumstances affect outcomes related to immigrant and minority ethnic groups' sense of belonging and associated "identity politics" at the individual and collective level (Chapter 9).

Among researchers and immigration policy officials there is considerable debate on the importance we should attach to evidence that the immigration system is not working well with respect to its assumptions and policy goals. In the late 1980s and early 1990s, a number of observers and policy analysts blamed the problem on selection of what they perceived to be poor-quality immigrants. They pointed in particular to the problem of the high proportion of family-class immigrants, who had less education, and argued that the state should admit more highly skilled workers under the points system, a proposal that the state subsequently implemented (see Chapter 5). However, it seems that the criticism of immigrants who did not have particularly high levels of schooling was unfair since subsequent research has shown that family-class immigrants do as well as—if not better than—those with very high levels of schooling (see Chapter 7). Some researchers conclude that Canada can carry on by tweaking the current system of admitting and settling immigrants to make it more efficient and effective. Others suggest the need to change Canadian immigration in more fundamental ways, yet just what these new directions might be has not yet been identified, although the challenges they need to address are increasingly clear (Chapter 11). How informed observers and researchers view these matters depends a great deal on the concepts and frameworks they use to read the evidence across diverse studies that involve different data sources and measures of outcomes. The following section examines the main concepts underlying the analysis in the present book.

Concepts and Frameworks

Canadian immigration is susceptible to analysis using many different concepts and related frameworks. In my review of the available findings from other studies and analysis of data from secondary sources, I rely on certain concepts and frameworks related to Canadian nation-building and ethnic belonging in a globalized, transnational era. I view these selected concepts as malleable tools. They can be further developed and added to as the review of findings proceeds. What follows is an introduction to the most central concepts used in this book.

Nation-Building, Imagined Communities, and Belonging

Nation-building is a concept that applies particularly well to settler societies such as Canada and Australia because they were first planned from the outside, as colonies, and then adopted what I will call self-colonizing practices in the form of immigration and immigrant-settlement policies, along with economic and cultural strategies designed to make effective use of and peacefully settle immigrant workers. Nation-building is therefore a historical process guided by political leaders through their implementation of relatively coherent policy packages covering economic growth, trade, immigration, and cultural goals and strategies, as well as other related matters. For example, in the 1880s Canadian leaders imagined the future nation in terms of an ethnically European farming and grain-exporting nation in the Americas. By the 1960s leaders imagined the future of Canada as a multicultural nation that would bring in skilled immigrant workers to produce industrial goods for national consumption. By the 1990s the imagined future promoted by national political and economic elites proposed that Canada was or soon would be a post-industrial nation in need of immigrants from all corners of the world to generate a knowledge economy and production efficiencies to ensure Canada's competitiveness in exports and international trade. Each imagined future led to a different mix of trade, immigration, and cultural policies. The objective in analyzing these changing historical patterns is to understand why Canadian immigration policy changed when and how it did based on the hypothesis that changes were anything but random. Rather, the changes came about due to shifting world conditions and internal transformation within Canada. The external and internal forces are both cultural and economic, covering such matters as the rise of anti-racism in the world and Canada's participation in this mobilization, and changes in the kinds of workers Canada needed to succeed in its economic and trade pursuits.

Imagined Communities

The concept of an "imagined community" is very useful in examining the emergence of nations and their evolution over time. The term is credited to Anderson (see Box 1.3), who put forward the problem as follows:

> Nations, nationality, nationalism—all have been notoriously difficult to define, let alone to analyze…. My point of departure is that nationality, or as one might prefer to put it in view of that word's multiple significations, nation-ness, as well as nationalism, are cultural artifacts of a particular kind. To understand them properly we need to consider carefully how they have come into historical being, in what ways their meanings have changed over time, and why, today, they command such profound emotional legitimacy. (Anderson 1991: 3–4)

Anderson's answer was to focus on the process by which the concepts of nation and nationality came into being. His examination of various cases of the emergence of nations historically around the world, with particular attention to Indonesia and other post-colonial nations, led him to look at strategies used by political and economic elites to gain power by organizing areas that were politically, economically, and cultural fragmented or weakly integrated. He noted that the process involved creating a situation in which all citizens of the nation-state felt that they belonged to a common community. The large national community could not exist as a "real community" of individuals who personally knew and interacted with each other member, so it had to be imagined. It is, in this sense, that nation-states are largely "cultural artifacts" with early origins in religious communities and political dynasties and more recent origins in elite-led nation-building processes facilitated by the spread of printed documents and the growth of mass media. In the wider scheme of national development in various places, Anderson observes that English-speaking Canada is an anomaly in that it was not absorbed by the United States due to the Americans' "failure" to realize a territorial dream that included Canada (p. 64). He also notes that Canada in the 1930s still showed strong evidence of a community being constructed around the legacy of ethnocentrism and racist exclusions arising from its history as a colony within the British Empire (p. 93). These are relevant observations for the historical evolution of Canadian immigration policy. They provide a context for Canada's energetic efforts to colonize the Western provinces by mass-immigration in the late 1800s. A key goal was to retain the Western territories and provinces within Canada. This led, for example, to opposition to the formation of a Métis nation in Manitoba and the offer of a national railway to entice British Columbia to join the Confederation. These and other steps were taken to block U.S. imperial ambitions with regard to largely vacant Western lands (Kelley and Trebilcock 2000: 65–98; Knowles 1992: 44–45). The framework of imagined national futures also explains why this colonization and all subsequent immigration for a long time after, up to 1962, was overwhelmingly oriented to attracting British and other European immigrants. Canada had been

---

Box 1.3: Benedict Anderson's Concept of Imagined Communities

In his book *Imagined Communities*, Benedict Anderson persuasively argued that nation-states as diverse as Brazil and Japan were constructed through a process that involved the spread of a sense of *belonging* in an *imagined community*. He argued that this was not an accident. The community came about through the rise of literacy, the spread of newspapers, improved communication and travel within nation territory, and the use of media by national elites. State schools and other institutions were also frequently involved in creating imagined communities. The community that was created this way is imagined because people cannot possibly personally know everyone else in it. However, if they accept the idea of the imagined community, they will tend to feel a greater bond, solidarity, and identity with others in it.

Anderson argued that state actors and national elites have access to powerful tools — such as national newspapers, school curricula, and the building of national telephone and railway systems — to create a sense of nationhood and nationalism. He also observed that the imagined community is often an attempt to gloss over, cover up, and ignore ethnic, religious, and regional identities that exist in the nation-state due to colonization or other historical circumstances.

Source: The author, based on Anderson, Benedict. 1991. *Imagined Communities: Reflections on the Origin and Spread of Nationalism.* London: Verso. See particularly the introduction of this book for Anderson's concept of "imagined community" and Chapter 3, "The Origins of National Consciousness," for his views on the role of printed media in nation-building.

initially constructed within British colonial practices as a European nation, and it continued to use this imagined future to implement self-colonization as a self-governing nation for a long period after.

From the 1930s to the early 1950s, the Canadian political economist Harold Innis (1956) put forward an approach to Canadian nation-building that has several ideas similar to those later independently developed by Anderson. Innis saw Canada as a country with an outward-looking and opportunistic viewpoint. He argued that this viewpoint stemmed from the nation's early colonial history and its development over time as a place where the role of settlers was to gather or grow staples—such as furs, fish, lumber, and grains—for export markets. Initially, when the economy was dependent on furs and fish, few settlers were required. Furs were obtained through trade with Native peoples. Fish were obtained by European fishermen who came and returned in their own boats. As the country developed and exports of lumber, agricultural products, and minerals became more important, large numbers of settlers were required to generate profits for foreign investors and a growing national economic elite. What began as a simple staples economy expanded into a much more complex one based on the leadership of outward-looking national elites who were eager to use foreign capital and export markets in combination with immigrant and national labour to build a particular kind of nation. Innis observed that control of the media was an important tool in elite nation-building control and practices, and in this regard his insights predate but parallel those of Anderson. Innis did not focus on immigration per se, and he died in 1954 when the post-Second World War recovery of large-scale Canadian immigration was just getting underway, so he did not observe this new phase of nation-building. However, his

ideas are very relevant for developing an analytic framework on how immigration can be best understood from a political-economic perspective on nation-building. In Chapter 3, these insights are used to better understand Canadian nation-building in several historical stages, beginning with a process in which the nation imagined itself as a "European nation in the Americas" (up to 1962) through to the contemporary period when it imagines itself as a "multicultural nation on the world stage" (from 1989 on). In each nation-building period, Canadian policies in the areas of trade, immigration, and cultural development were rationalized and promoted by images of what the future of the nation would look like if all these policies were successful. Harold Innis's ideas are examined further in Chapter 2.

In the spirit of the frameworks advanced by Anderson and Innis, I propose adding the term "imagined futures" to the set of concepts that relate to nation-building. An imagined future is a dynamic element in an imagined community. When a nation comes into existence, it will be composed of different interest groups that view the future of the collective body from different perspectives, and that propose actions or policies in accord with these diverse interests. As Anderson has argued, the formation of nations involves the emergence of *imagined communities*. However, the basic framework can be usefully developed somewhat further. Political proposals for nations to adapt to changing circumstances or to move in certain directions involve *imagined futures*. The concept of an imagined future is particularly useful for understanding immigration policies. Policies concerning the entry and settlement of immigrants in a proactive, immigrant-seeking country like Canada are not put forward in isolation from other elements that together constitute what the nation hopes to accomplish. Rather, immigration policy is put forward as part of a package of policy proposals that the state understands to have internal coherence and to support one another in achieving a larger goal. It is useful to understand the overall package as an imagined future with various components. The discourse of political and economic leaders supports such a step in analysis. For example, over the 1990s and continuing at present, Canadian policy-makers imagined the future of the nation in terms of its emerging post-industrial capacity as a knowledge-based society and economy that was able to maintain a high standard of living through efficiencies created by highly educated workers and the nation's ability to compete in global trade. In the area of immigration, this image was then applied to the understanding that Canada would find highly skilled immigrants from around the world, and would use its multicultural policies and history of accommodating immigrants with diverse cultural backgrounds as assets to attract and peacefully settle new immigrants. In effect, the imagined future had several linked components: efficient workers including immigrant workers; successful trade strategies; cultural diversity; and successful immigration and settlement strategies. Each historical period of Canadian nation-building had its own imagined future (Chapter 3); in every case, including the present, the issue arises as to how well the imagined future actually corresponds to what is or was taking place (see the overview on this point in Chapter 11). The contrasting cases of Mr. Lee-Chin and the Anderson family remind us that desired futures and actual outcomes can be quite different.

Belonging and identity politics: Imagined communities arise in the context of struggles between elites and others over what the nation is to be and who is to be included. The national community that emerges

may then be understood in various ways. Anderson (1991) draws attention to it as a cultural artifact; that is, a set of beliefs, values, and practices that allow those who feel they belong in a particular community to confirm that this is justified through day-to-day interactions with others who also understand that they belong in the same imagined community. This process can include interactions with others they have never met previously. Language, dress, expressed values, and other indicators are enough to generate reciprocal recognition and to support relating in culturally appropriate ways. National culture can also be understood as being an ideology: to belong is to accept the culture; to reject the core values and understandings could lead to exclusion. Imagined futures also operate this way. Individuals who are out of step with the dominant future image may face censure. This creates a potential predicament for immigrants. To return to the case of Caribbean immigrants in Canada, when they are so poor that they cannot send money and gifts home, or when they find it a hardship to entertain visitors from the home country who expect that they are wealthy, they feel deeply troubled (Simmons, Plaza, and Piché 2005). Caribbean men, who migrated to the United Kingdom in the expectation that they would return home wealthy to retire, did not return home at all when they felt ashamed of their failure, with implications for all members of their families (Plaza 2000). The "culture of migration" in the Caribbean is based on notions of success and mobility through migration; messages that do not fit this image may get suppressed as a result of what may be viewed as the ideological dimension of imagined communities and their imagined futures (see Chapter 9).

Ethnic belonging and identity politics: Anderson (1991) argued that over the course of the late 19th century, loosely bonded but fragmented regions such as Italy and Germany that were developing into nations did not have a set model for the process or a fixed image to promote as to what the result would look like, so what took place involved "spontaneous" crossings of historical forces. However, once such nations had emerged, "they became 'modular' and capable of being transplanted, with varying degrees of self-consciousness, to a great variety of social terrains" (Anderson 1991: 4). Such pro-cesses are understood to have developed out of the ethno-linguistic and religious formations that preceded them. It is often felt that these earlier "ethnic" formations needed no model, for they were primordial forms "based on blood, speech, custom and so on" (Rex 1986: 26–27) that were seemingly "pre-social, almost instinctual, something one is born into" (Castles and Miller 2003: 34). However, this is not the way ethnic identity appears in Canadian research or to researchers who have studied the phenomenon elsewhere. The research-based view of ethnicity corresponds more to Max Weber's ([1922] 1978: 342) perspec-tive that ethnicity is one of several ways that a "group" seeks "social closure" in order to gain some advantage. Ethnicity from this perspective is "political," "fluid," and "con-textual." It is more a process than a fixed outcome. A mixed-race Canadian—when asked "Where are you from?"—may choose to reveal his or her complex place of birth and ethnic ancestry or to avoid the possible hidden agenda of the person who asked the question by responding, "Canada" (see Chapter 9). What constitutes ethnic identity, the subjective meaning attached to such labels by those who use them to define themselves, and what others make of them remain among the more challenging ques-tions addressed in this book. However, the processes are fundamental to understand-ing Canadian immigration and Canada.

The "Big Picture": Globalization and Transnationalism

Given that Canadian immigration can be best understood as a reflection of Canada's place in the global and transnational world, the big picture for analyzing Canadian immigration is global, international, and transnational in scope. Various global and transnational forces set the obstacles and opportunities in relation to which Canadian nation-building policies are established, immigration takes place, and immigrants retain links to their home fami-lies and communities, even as they adjust to life in Canada. To conclude our review of useful concepts, I briefly introduce glo-balization and transnationalism as complex constructs or frameworks. Before entering into details, I should make clear that global-ization and transnationalism are not new processes. Both have long histories associ-ated with the rise of Western expansion, colonialism, and the growth of worldwide trade, migration, and communications. The review of these processes below draws attention to their intensity and scope in the contemporary era.

Globalization: Globalization may be under-stood in three different but equally impor-tant ways. Firstly, it may be understood as *time-space compression* in which more frequent and intense economic, social, and political links form among places, institu-tions, and people that were previously isolated or, at best, loosely connected to one another (Harvey 1992: Part III). Expanding trade, travel, and telecommunications are understood to be at the core of globaliza-tion. The physical space between people shrinks as they can communicate in real time by telephone, travel by airplanes to visit one another, and experience the same news or sports event on television at the same time as family or friends elsewhere in the world, then email their reactions to them.

Secondly, globalization has also been understood as a *state of mind*: Individuals have a different view of themselves and their interconnected place in the world with others when they look at a satellite photo taken of Earth showing it as a small blue marble-like orb (Robertson 1992). Waters (1995: 3) puts the ideas of time-space compression and a transformed subjectivity into one definition. He says that globalization is: "A social process in which the constraints of geography on social and cultural arrangements recede and in which people become increasingly aware that they are receding."

Thirdly, globalization may be understood as an *ideology* and related set of normative state practices that generate imagined futures for nation-states in the international system. Globalization ideology is promoted by major international banks and trade and financial institutions, such as the World Bank, the International Monetary Fund, and the World Trade Organization (Gill 2003). These institutions receive their support from the wealthiest nations that on the whole, despite debates, have viewed globalization as the springboard for worldwide economic and political co-operation for human progress. The logic of globalization ideology is that trade increases well-being and peace in the world. Nations compete through exports, not through war. In the process, they focus their economies on what they can produce more efficiently and export at lower costs than other nations can. Efficiency increases among all trading nations, and they all become wealthier over time in a process in which they also become more interdependent.

From the perspective of our focus on Canadian immigration, globalization may be understood as having impact related to each of the dimensions outlined above. As an ideology, contemporary globalization directs Canada's outward gaze toward global trade and competition and in particular toward the need to have an efficient economy in order to maintain an affluent society. Canadians and national economic and political leaders are drawn to the future image of Canada as a place in which sophisticated technology, communications, and knowledge industries and services create the desired efficiencies and affluence. Immigrants are to be welcomed in relatively large numbers as important contributors to this imagined future, but they must meet new entry criteria that require high levels of education, among other attributes. People with such characteristics who are not well paid and happy where they are located are more likely found in certain countries around the world than others. This variation in well-being has implications for the countries from which they come (Chapter 6) and how they become incorporated into Canadian society (Chapters 7 and 8).

From the perspective of Canadian workers, new immigration flows in the context of global trade potentially generate two reactions. One is to welcome the new immigrants as workers who will strengthen the Canadian economy and create more jobs for everyone. The other is to fear that, in the context of job competition, the immigrants will take away jobs. National populations vary in how these two reactions to immigration under conditions of globalization play out. Canadian attitudes to immigration have been biased on the positive side, but show considerable ambivalence (Chapters 8 and 9).

It is noteworthy that globalization ideology does not include a strong normative proposal on international migration. The ideology focuses almost exclusively on the advantages of unrestricted flows of investment capital and trade among nations. What each nation decides to do with respect to international migration is its own sovereign business. It can close borders, allow temporary migrants only, promote immigration, or combine those elements so that borders are closed to many people, open to others who enter as temporary migrants, and open only to a select few to enter as immigrants or permanent settlers. Waters (1995: 94) argues that globalization assumes that *eventually* all nations will become wealthy, with the result that labour will circulate freely from one country to another. However, we are very far from this point. As noted above, globalization currently has several effects: It promotes the desire of people in poor countries to move; it leads wealthy nations to control immigration; and it leads workers and citizens in wealthy nations to be more concerned about the impacts of large numbers of immigrants (Simmons 2002). Wealthy nations that have porous borders with large poor countries, as is the case for Europe and the United States, are preoccupied with border controls. Canada does not have such borders, but nevertheless undocumented migration and border controls are important concerns (Chapter 4). We may conclude that globalization both promotes international migration and leads to increased controls on who can move, with the result that these opposing forces are increasingly in tension with one another.

Transnationalism: The concept *transnational* provides a particular way of dividing and examining global space. The word breaks down into "trans" and "national." "Trans" derives from Latin to signify something that extends across or beyond or falls on the opposite side of something else. The Trans-Canada Highway stretches across the country from one side to the other. The term "transsexual" applies to people who reject the gender or sexual orientation that was assigned to them at birth; their new identity is outside or beyond that original assignment. In the field of migration stud-

ies, transnational combines the notion of across, beyond, and something new. *Transnational space* covers *transnational institutions, transnational actions/actors,* and *transnational flows* taking place across and outside the control of nation-states and across them to connect people and institutions within them.

International migrants are viewed as key transnational actors connecting themselves and their community abroad to family members, friends, and others in their home countries. Transnationalism, once initiated by immigrants, tends to be self-reinforcing under certain conditions. For example, communication promotes remittances; remittances promote engagement in family decision making; engagement in family decision making can lead to efforts to sponsor the migration of relatives; and so on until over time and through a change in circumstances, the transnational flows come to an end. As Vertovec (1999: 455) has pointed out, transnationalism has multiple meanings and levels. It can be understood as a way in which its participants reproduce their own culture; as a base for their political action; and also as a philosophy, a point of view, and a state of consciousness.

It is important to note that while the world is increasingly shaped by transnational social relations, not every international migrant or person associated with an international migrant is necessarily deeply engaged in transnational flows, communities, or ideologies. Some immigrants leave their home country and never look back. Others carry memories, but have no close friends, family members, or other forms of belonging in their home country. Still others have family and friends with whom they stay in close touch and support in every way they can. Those most deeply involved in transnationalism own property, do work, and are politically active in communities in two different nations (see

Chapter 8). In sum, following the caution offered by Castles and Miller (2003: 30), we must take care not to "inflate" the concept of transnational migrant or transnational community to include everyone. There is wide variation in transnational practices and affiliations. We are just beginning to learn about this variation and its implications.

The Joint Transformation of Global, Transnational, and National Spheres

Global time-space compression, expanding transnational social spaces, and nation-building processes have developed jointly over time. Within the span of recorded history, global space became more compressed. Smaller communities and the occasional empire or large kingdom formed into larger units and established boundaries or rules with neighbouring units about mutually beneficial defence and trade relations. As nation-states emerged, they gradually and increasingly came to control their borders with respect to trade, defence, and international migration. They also began to control the inhabitants of their national territories by seeking to unify them, often around a common language and culture. However, a great deal was left outside the control of nation-states. For a brief summary of what came to fall within nation-state control and what did not, we may collapse the complex history of nation-state formation into three steps.

Step one was the emergence of an idea of a nation-state. The invention of the idea is widely attributed to the Treaty of Westphalia (1648). The signatory states of this treaty, consisting of the kingdoms of Spain, France, and Sweden; the Dutch Republic; and various smaller principalities within the Holy Roman Empire, agreed that a balance of power among nations can be established and maintained for their mutual benefit by defining each nation as a sovereign entity occupying a territory with clear borders agreed to by all member states. Nations so established would control their own borders with respect to trade and defence. This agreement brought to an end three decades of terrible and costly wars affecting these countries. However, the treaty left completely unclear how future territories would establish themselves as nation-states. As a result, the practice of forming nation-states did not spread much until roughly 200 years later.

Step two was the spread and evolution of the nation-state system, starting in the late 18th century and continuing on through the 19th century. This took place mainly in Europe and the United States, but also in South America (following the secession of various nations from Spain and, in the case of Brazil, from Portugal), Japan, and partially in "European" colonies such as Canada and Australia, which were beginning a peaceful evolution toward full nationhood. In many instances, the new nation-states were formed out of territories that included high levels of ethnic and linguistic diversity as well as regions that had well-established local cultures and identities. Hobsbawm (1992) notes that at the time of the 1789 French Revolution, only half of the French people spoke some French. In Italy at the time of national reunification, the percentage speaking Italian was even lower. While an international system of nations emerged prior to the First World War, it was shattered by the two great wars and emerged at the end with a mix of problems, including in particular the fact that many states contained minorities who did not identify with the states in which they found themselves.

Step three was the decolonization movement following the Second World War in which European colonies around the world either gained their independence through struggle or were granted independence by their colonizers. These nations often had arbitrary borders that had been drawn over and through linguistic and cultural territories by the colonizers. Unfortunately, some of these nations, such as Rwanda and Sri Lanka, later erupted in vicious struggles between groups regarding control of the new nations. The post-Second World War era also coincided with new international migration patterns from the former colonized regions of the world to other countries. Whereas the colonial nations of Europe had previously sent their administrators and settlers to colonies elsewhere, people in these colonies began to move to Europe and other regions, such as Australia, Canada, and the United States, which had been colonized largely by Europeans. This so-called "reverse" migration transformed the ethnic composition of the former colonial powers and led to new transnational social, cultural, and ethnic links between them and their ex-colonies. In the colonial era, the transnational links were from Europeans in Europe to European settlements in the colonized nations. In the post-colonial era, these links were between ex-colonized peoples in their home countries and migrants from the same countries living in the former colonizing nations. In addition, people from formerly colonized nations began to move to other parts of the world. The oil wealth of the Gulf states attracted immigrant labour from South and East Asia; rapid development in Malaysia and Thailand attracted migrant workers from neighbouring countries, and so on. Last but not least, the world was faced with large-scale refugee flows. These were mostly from weak states in the formerly colonized regions of the world. The refugees mostly fled to neighbouring countries within the same regions, but significant numbers also fled outside their regions to wealthier and more politically stable countries in Europe, North America, and Oceania.

From the above it is clear that global or world space has now been filled by nation-states, but that these nation-states have within them and between them large spheres of transnational action that they do not control. Many nation-states throughout the world have ethnic, religious, and "national" minority communities within them that do not feel they belong to the nation in which they are located. This often leads these minorities to mobilize within the transnational sphere and seek external support wherever they can find it. Many of these minorities are spread across different nation-states, yet they each retain, to a greater or lesser degree, a historically established culture and identity. Their dispersion and relocation came about through diverse historical events. These include the delineation by force of borders they did not agree with, dislocations due to war and genocide, and migration to other parts of the world for better jobs and futures. Those minority ethnic groups found in different nation-states are key actors in the transnational sphere. They play a major role as "brokers" in international migration by providing information and support for new migrant flows. Their cultural and ethnic institutions — which are both national and transnational at the same time — transform the nations in which they live and the relationships across nations within their transnational sphere.

Putting the Pieces Together: Round One

I have thought of different ways of representing the various actors and field of action examined in this chapter. Figure 1.1 is one way of doing this. It is not a theoretical model so much as a map showing the relationships of the fields of action affecting Canadian immigration to each other. Elsewhere in the book I present other

Figure 1.1: Global-Transnational Actors and Fields of Action

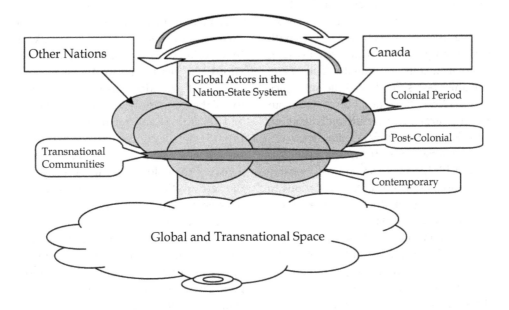

Note: The arrows at the top of the diagram show flows of trade goods, information, finance capital, remittances, and (im)migrants between nations and societies. Nations are shown as emerging or transforming over different historical periods within an also developing international system of nation-states. As these processes take place, globalization compresses the space between nations and societies and they move closer together. Some begin to overlap in new supra-national trade and political economic blocs. Transnational communities are present at all historical periods and always extend beyond the bounds of the nation-state system. They become stronger in the contemporary era through time-space compression. The various hypotheses and arguments on immigration policy and settlement outcomes constitute a global transnational systems model.

charts to express and highlight additional features of what is shown more generally here. For example, the global-transnational systems model in Chapter 2 is based on the same actors, but shifts the focus to the flows of capital, goods, migrants, and communications among nations within a global-transnational field. This said, Figure 1.1 is an easier place to begin and corresponds to the focus of this introductory chapter.

Readers may wish to draw their own charts and diagrams to clarify relationships and processes related to Canadian immigration. All efforts will reflect qualified hypotheses. For example, my inclination is to show nations coming closer together and becoming more interdependent in a global-

izing world. However, this does not agree with all perspectives. Huntington (1996) has argued that globalization brings people and nations into closer contact, but this does not necessarily make their encounters more interdependent. According to his view, the threat of greater proximity generates a "clash of civilizations" of the kind evident in conflicts between certain Muslim states and the West. Others have argued that the coming together is primarily in the areas of consumerism, as revealed in the spread of a "McWorld" of fast-food outlets to all corners of the globe, a development opposed by those who wish to maintain "authentic" national and ethnic cultures free from Western consumerism (Barber 1996). Still others have argued that nations and peoples are indeed coming together more closely through economic exchange and technologically driven time/space compression, but that the system is held together with a fractured postmodern culture consisting of transient collages of media images and consumer tastes that have little substance (Harvey 1992). It has also been pointed out that the surge of economic globalization, with rising international capital flows and trade, that took place from around 1885 to around 1914, came to an end with terrible wars and a depression that led nations to recoil from one another and enter into a period of relative isolation before the same globalization forces resumed their march forward. The same could happen again. These observations all suggest qualifications and possible additions to what the chart shows, but then one cannot show everything in one simple frame. The chart attempts to reflect patterns of nations' ever closer relations with one another as the international system of nation-states develops, global actors come to play more encompassing and powerfully integrative roles, and transnational communities become more dynamic and spread across nations. International migration flows are deeply embedded in these developments. This provides the foundational perspective followed throughout this book.

Chapter Topics

Each chapter in this book builds on the chapters that precede it. At the same time, readers who have gone through this introduction should be able to read any other chapter as a free-standing piece. This makes it possible for readers to skip forward and backward in the book, if they desire. Chapter 2, migration theory, should be read early in the sequence because it provides a useful foundation for all the chapters in the book. Chapters 3 and 4 examine Canadian immigration and provide details concerning the historical perspective taken in the book. Chapter 3 covers the colonial period through to the Second World War and sets forth the historical periods that help us to understand how the present is linked to the past and also how it is different from the past. Chapter 4 covers more recent developments, from the 1950s to the present, giving particular attention to major policy changes in 1962 and from 1989 onward. Chapters 5 through 10 address specific analytic themes in the contemporary period, dating largely from the 1980s or 1990s forward. These themes are who gets in (Chapter 5), immigrant national and ethnic origins (Chapter 6), immigrant jobs and earnings (Chapter 7), transnational belonging (Chapter 8), ethnic identity politics (Chapter 9), and future projections of Canada's labour force under different immigration and demographic scenarios (Chapter 10). The final chapter (Chapter 11) covers the overall conclusions reached and how they relate to emerging policy issues and developments on such matters as migrant worker programs and immigration policy.

CHAPTER 2
Theoretical Issues

Introduction

Evidence that we will examine in greater detail in subsequent chapters indicates an alarming trend. Each cohort of new immigrants arriving in Canada since 1980 has experienced lower job outcomes and earnings than the cohort that arrived previously (Chapter 7). Over time, new immigrants have become relatively poorer. It also seems that those who arrived since 1980 are taking longer to achieve the level of earnings found among similarly educated Canadian-born workers. As a result, recent immigrants remain relatively poor and live together in lower-cost housing areas of major cities. These disturbing trends give rise to puzzling questions. Why do many highly trained immigrants continue to come to Canada in the face of these devel-

opments? Given the economic problems faced by recent immigrants and evidence of this emerging trend over the past 20 years or more, why is it that Canadian immigration targets have not changed much in this period?

When we think seriously about puzzling features of Canadian immigration, we need to delve deeply, and look for ways of reframing reality in terms of underlying processes expressed as theoretical constructs and abstract frameworks. Examining reality without theoretical constructs leads, as William James said many years ago, to "a 'bloomin buzzin' confusion." From this perspective, it has frequently been repeated that nothing is more useful than a good theory, yet what constitutes a good theory is often in dispute. This is certainly the case in the field of international migration where a number of models and approaches have been put forward.

The objective of this chapter is to examine the best-known theoretical models of international migration and then to extract from them ideas for understanding the Canadian case. More specifically, the chapter addresses frameworks for understanding the motives of migrants; the processes that generate and control the international movement of peoples, including immigrants and temporary foreign workers; and the diverse settlement and identity outcomes that emerge for immigrants and native-born Canadians. These issues are examined in three sections. The first section picks up themes from Chapter 1 regarding nation-building through imagined futures and uses this political economic framework as a backdrop for assessing migration-specific theories and models. The second section examines the evolution of migration theory through several steps up to the "migration system" approach, which was also introduced briefly in Chapter 1. The third section provides a "round two" synthesis of theoretical arguments on Canadian immigration using migration systems and nation-building frameworks.

Theory for What?

While the objective of this chapter is to understand migration theory and identify concepts and frameworks for understanding Canadian immigration, I will argue that the most useful general theoretical framework is not migration specific; rather, it is a model of nation-building. More specifically, it is a model of Canadian nation-building known both as the staples framework and as the Canadian school of political economy. The model dates from research by Harold Innis, the founder of staples theory, from the mid-1930s to the early 1950s (Acland and Buxton 1999;

Drache and Clement 1985). The fact that Innis carried out his research more than a half-century ago should not be of concern. As is often the case, the best foundation for a contemporary analysis can be found in good ideas from earlier studies.

Innis observed that Canada was not a large country in terms of its population, but it was a resource-rich nation spread across a vast expanse of land. In various books and articles he argued that three conditions—a relatively small population, rich natural resources (minerals, grains, lumber, and other such staples), and a vast territory—set the foundation for the long-term political and economic orientation of the nation (Innis 1930, 1940, 1952, 1956). In his view, Canada was and would likely remain outward-oriented to the sources of investment capital, trade opportunities, and immigrant labour on which it depended. In addition, Canada was and would likely remain a country concerned with communication across large distances, such that "space-binding media" (his term for radio and newspapers) and the owners of these media would play large roles in how the nation developed. Those who controlled these media, in his view, were likely to act in a self-interested way to help form a nation-state that would benefit them and others who owned and managed capital, natural resources, and commerce. This framework suggests that a particular political-economic orientation would adapt to changing circumstances and lead, over time, to evolving trade, immigration, and other policies. As the package of nation-building strategies evolved, so too would the imagined future of the nation, and vice versa in an interdependent pattern.

Innis was most interested in trade and communications and had little to say specifically on international migration, yet immigration was an important element in his understanding of Canada's political economy and culture. He understood that

Canada was well placed to generate economic growth by bringing in immigrants to strengthen its labour force and promote exports. Although he did not express it in these terms, the thrust of his arguments suggested that Canada, operating within a staples framework, had developed a deep hunger for international migrants. Given that he did not explore how this hunger might be satisfied in the future, many developments in international migration to Canada since his death in 1952 would have perhaps surprised him, but he probably would have had little difficulty fitting them in as additions consistent with his framework. He viewed Canada as part of an international system of trading nations, not as a country operating on its own. The distinctiveness of Canada's own political economy arose from the niche that it occupied in relation to a wider system of international investment flows, trade, and migration. He might not have guessed that Europe would dry up as the main source of Canadian immigration in the 1960s nor that Asia would subsequently become the main new source of immigrants. However, he would have understood Canada's continuing hunger for immigrants as part of a historically embedded appetite, and that Canada would shift to new source countries to find immigrants if old source countries dried up. He might also have been surprised to see that labour unions' opposition to immigration, so common in his era, has weakened (if not disappeared) and that workers, like other citizens in Canada, have come to increasingly accept the view that immigrants are also job-generators through their productive work, professional skills, business experience, and investments. Lastly, as a scholar who had a deep interest in issues of power and communication, Innis would have been intrigued by the emergence of the Internet and modern low-cost telephone services. He would have wondered how they

empowered international migrants and their families in home countries.

The Canadian political economy framework addressed issues of struggle and conflict, particularly between Canada and the United States over trade policy, and between the provinces and the federal state with respect to resource control, transportation subsidies, and a variety of other matters. Innis's perspective also addressed social class conflict between owners/investors and labour (workers). Other writers have subsequently noted the implications of his perspective for understanding potential labour-capital conflict in the area of immigration policy (Stafford and McMillan 1988). Furthermore, Innis did not consider gender and race/ethnic inequalities in international migration and settlement, but others who have carried forward research with approaches within or compatible with a Canadian political economy framework have done so (see, for example, Li 1996: chapters 1, 4, and 6; Luxton 2006: 9; Stasiulis 1997).

While the Canadian political economy perspective provides a promising foundation on which to build an approach to understanding international migration in the transformation and development of Canada, it is insufficient in its original form to meet our needs. The foundation requires additional elements to address major developments over recent decades. These developments include significant shifts in immigrant-origin countries; transformations in selection procedures to privilege highly educated immigrants; the emergence of low-cost telephone and Internet communications to link immigrants more closely than in the past to their home countries; the rise of multiculturalism; and the emergence of transnationalism as a force connecting immigrants in Canada with their families and ethnic communities elsewhere. Our efforts to see how the Innis framework can be used to understand both historical and contemporary Canadian immigration will involve two steps. First, we will examine major theoretical models of migration. Then, from this review, we will elaborate more fully an approach to Canadian immigration that combines insights from Innis, related contributions from Anderson and others with respect to the formation of nations, and an understanding of specific features of international migration systems as they apply to the Canadian case.

Theoretical Approaches to International Migration

International migration is shaped by many forces, including state immigration and border-control policies; income differences among countries; labour demand and supply in migrant origin and destination nations; civil wars; and cultural, ethnic, and religious ties among nations. Not only is migration shaped by many forces, but these forces interact with one another over time and lead to constant changes in the origins, destinations, and characteristics of global migrant streams. Figure 2.1 provides an approximate snapshot of contemporary international migrant origin-destination flows. Asia is the main global source of migrants, but Mexico, the Caribbean, West Africa, and the Horn of Africa are also major sources. Very large movements across countries that were part of the former Union of Soviet Socialist Republics, after its breakup in 1989, are represented by a two-headed arrow across that region. The main destinations are wealthy regions and nations: Australia, Europe, and North America. The scale of the map does not permit many specific flows to be shown. Some that could be shown on a larger map with more space to show details would include, for example, the large flows within southern Africa to South Africa. There is also a

small but significant flow of ethnic Japanese from Brazil to Japan. Brazil is one of the few places outside Japan that has a large ethnic Japanese population. In fact, there are 1.5 million ethnic Japanese in Brazil. They are descendants of Japanese settlers who went to Brazil mostly between the two world wars and just after the Second World War. Japan has an affinity for ethnic Japanese migrant workers and immigrants, and it is a wealthy nation, so these two factors account for the movement. However, not all Brazilians of Japanese ethnicity have felt comfortable in Japan and many of those who moved to live and work in Japan have subsequently returned to Brazil (Hotaka Roth 2002). Turning to the major flows that are represented, Africans move primarily to Europe, yet large numbers also move to North America. While Latin American and Caribbean peoples move primarily to North America, many also move to Europe. Mexicans move overwhelmingly to the United States, although smaller flows to Canada and Europe are also evident. Spain has been a major recipient of migrants from countries such as Ecuador and Peru over the early 2000s, but the future of this has been in question following the 2008 slowdown of construction and other economic activity employing immigrants in Spain. Overall global patterns of international migration are constantly changing. Significant and ongoing changes in the national and ethnic origins of immigrant flows to Canada are examined in Chapter 6.

One challenge to theory is that migration falls into several broad types. Some migration is forced and takes the form of displacement and refugee flight. Other migration is voluntary but short-term, as in the case of the coming and going of visa workers. Still other migration involves permanent resettlement in another country. The causes of these different patterns are often overlapping, yet they are not entirely the same. A second challenge to

Figure 2.1: Global Migration Flows

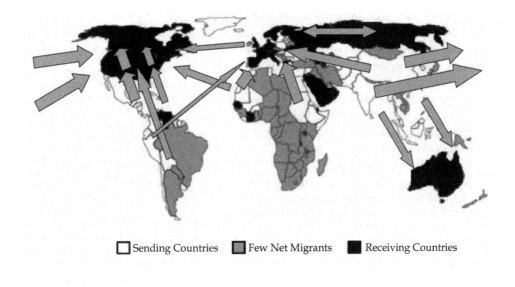

Sending Countries ☐ Few Net Migrants ▧ Receiving Countries ■

theory is that migrant streams and their causation involve different elements. People move from one nation to another when three favourable conditions come together: (1) they are motivated to; (2) they have the credentials and attributes that meet official entry criteria in the receiving nation; and (3) they possess the necessary resources to travel and cover initial settlement costs. Each of these conditions may have its own independent determinants. In sum, international migration includes different types of movement and a range of determinants that vary from place to place and from one historical moment to another. Even though this complexity creates a major challenge to theory, considerable progress has been made in finding broad frameworks to understand international migration.

Several of the best-known models of international migration are summarized in Box 2.1. These models are often referred to as "theories of migration," but this is a potentially misleading label. To label them

this way could suggest that each approach is an all-inclusive perspective that can explain all or many aspects of international migration. Listing them separately could also suggest that the various approaches do not overlap with one another. These assumptions are *not* correct. These so-called theories are better viewed as alternative conceptual frameworks that are capable of examining the same phenomenon from different angles. As such their arguments are not necessarily contradictory. In some cases they lead to complementary understandings.

Three Generations of Theory and Research

The three generations of migration theory listed in Box 2.1 did not emerge exactly in a top-to-bottom historical sequence, though it is correct to say that developments from the simplest model (push-pull) to the most complex model (transnational migrant sys-

Box 2.1: Selected "Theories" of Migration

Generation I: Models Focusing on Migrant Motivation
Approaches that address migration motivation while leaving aside issues of border controls and immigration policies vary in complexity, from simple push-pull models that are now outdated to more complex household decision-making and survival models that are still useful, although limited due to their focus on a narrow range of outcomes and inattention to questions of border controls.

Push-pull is a now outdated simple mechanical model in which people move from areas of lesser opportunity to areas of greater opportunity. Outcomes and border controls are not considered.

Household survival strategies is a more complex, systemic model in which households make migration decisions to maximize the collective opportunities of all members while minimizing their risks from new ventures. Outcomes (at the household level only) are considered, but border controls are not.

Generation II: Models That Address Migrant Motivation and Border Controls
Approaches in this class fall broadly into two categories: (1) those such as the trade and migration model that view migration as contributing to human welfare and economic development, and (2) those such as the labour reserves and global cities models that view migration as improving the welfare and economic conditions of some while suppressing or limiting positive outcomes for others.

Trade and migration is a dynamic model with feedback and attention to borders. It assumes that free-trading nations with different economic resources—financial capital, export possibilities, and supplies of workers—will establish programs in which workers move voluntarily from one country to the other in response to the contribution that their efforts will make to economic efficiency and growth in the system as a whole.

Labour reserves is a model of migration under conditions where a migrant origin country is subject to the political-economic domination of the migrant destination nation. In a classic case, South Africa, during the era of apartheid, conspired to arrange circumstances that led rural workers and their families in Mozambique to become dependent on contract jobs in South African mines. It has been argued that domestic workers and foreign farm workers in Canada may provide an illustration of similar principles in operation. *Global cities* is a variation on the labour reserves model. See the text for details.

Generation III: Transnational Migration Systems
Approaches in this class view migration as emerging within specific historical, cultural, imperial/colonial, and global systems. They give particular attention to transnational migrant networks and to trade agreements as separate but overlapping and either harmonious or conflicting forces promoting international migration by shaping both migrant motivations and border/migrant-control policies. These approaches allow for diverse outcomes under different historical and geopolitical conditions. They may be found in models that go under different names, such as: *migration systems, globalization and migration, migration under conditions of new community formation, and transnational migration*. The arguments in these different formulations follow a similar logic.

tems) cover the history from early theorizing to the present.

Generation I: Theories of Migrant Motivation

A very early attempt to theorize migration by Ravenstein (1885, 1889), based on trends observed in England during the Industrial Revolution, led him to put forward "laws" on who moved and where they moved. While these so-called "laws" were largely descriptive, they assumed that people moved to areas with better opportunities in order to improve their circumstances. Many years later, in the 1940s, Stouffer put forward a similar formulation as a theory of "intervening opportunities." According to Stouffer (1940: 846), "[t]he number of persons going a given distance is directly proportional to the number of opportunities at that distance and inversely proportional to the number of intervening opportunities." In other words, the likelihood that migrants would move between two locations required that the net push-pull balance be strong enough to carry them over or past the attractions offered by other places located en route. For example, migrants leaving Mexico might find Canada to be a relatively attractive destination, but they may never arrive in Canada due to the many job opportunities and the pull of large Spanish-speaking communities in the United States. The first formal statement of push-pull theory was advanced by Lee (1966), who credited the original ideas to Ravenstein. In the 1970s, a logically similar approach was developed by Harris and Todaro (1970) in a model that argued that migration between two places could be predicted by the difference in wages between them, discounting (1) the expected wage gains in the destination area by the amount of time one would have to wait to find employment and (2) the costs of moving. In a model with many places, such as a country with many states and migratory movement among them, this approach effectively covered Stouffer's concern with intervening opportunities. It also advanced the argument that the main driver of migration was the desire to improve wages specifically. In all these formulations, the forces that generate migration are relative differences in opportunity between two places that are not connected with each other in any way specified by the models (see Figure 2.2).

Push-pull and logically similar frameworks are not wrong. In fact, the basic notion of these models—namely, that differences in opportunities between migrant-origin and migrant-destination places fundamentally influence the direction and volume of migration flows—is retained in all frameworks that have been developed subsequently. However, the push-pull model was originally developed for understanding internal migration within countries. Push-pull is very

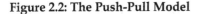

Figure 2.2: The Push-Pull Model

limited in what it can say about the international migration process because it does not address international boundaries, immigration policies, and border controls. Push-pull is also very limited by the fact that it is non-systemic: The push and pull forces are viewed as separate from one another, rather than as being connected to one another as is the case in most real-world instances. For example, if a factory is moved from place A to place B, it will likely lead to a decline in job opportunities in the former and an increase in them in the latter, and this needs to be addressed in any model. Systemic models take into account the fact that when migrants leave their home community, they will have impact on the places they leave and the places they move to, thereby generating systemic outcomes. These impacts, such as taking away talent in the place of departure and adding productive labour and a potential for economic growth in the place of destination, may set in place a dynamic that promotes additional migration.

The household survival strategies model is a more complex and useful approach to the understanding of migrant motivation, although, as we shall see, it covers only migration motivation and does not consider migration controls. Its strength lies in shifting the perspective on migrant motivations from the individual at one point in time to households across time. According to this approach, migration takes place as a result of collective household decisions on how to allocate family labour between two locations (Stark 1991; Stark and Katz 1986; see also Massey et al. 1998: 21–28). One location is where the members currently live. The other location is another town, region, or country where one or more family members could work and live. Having some members working in the home community while others migrate to work in a different location may be understood as a rational choice by the household in order for its members to open new income opportunities while minimizing risk if the migration plan is not successful. If the migration gamble pays off, the migrant sends money home and everyone benefits. At this point the household may decide that other members should move as well. If the migration gamble does not pay off, the migrant can return to an intact, functioning household and community. The home community may be poor, but the household may have some land or access to marginal jobs that permit it to survive when migration ventures fail. In some situations, households can survive only by occasionally sending members elsewhere to engage in seasonal work and return with savings in the off season. This model involves systemic causation with flows influencing outcomes in both sending and receiving areas, and these outcomes in turn leading to future migration patterns (see Figure 2.3). Migrants move back and forth between home and other places and, in the process, generate flows of information and remittances or savings to home communities.

The main limitation of the household decision-making approach is that it does not explicitly address questions of international borders and migration controls, nor does it consider collective outcomes for entire communities. If many households make similar migration decisions, the impacts on sending and receiving communities will be greater. Among other matters, pioneering migrants in destination areas can begin to form institutions that provide support for more recently arrived migrants. In addition, flows of information back and forth between migrant-origin and destination areas will increase as the number of migrants in the destination areas rises. These limitations in Generation I models are addressed in Generation II and III models.

Figure 2.3: Systemic Causation in a Household Survival Model

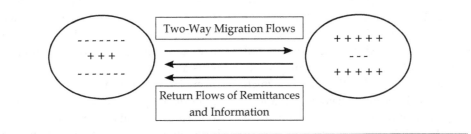

Generation II: Political Economic Models

These models start from the view that international migration is part of larger political and economic systems. The key advantage of starting from a macro-level political-economic framework is that it allows researchers to understand the determinants of migration controls and migrant motivation all within a model. Political-economic systems involving two or more nations include trade, cultural, and political relations among these nations. Such a perspective draws attention to the ways in which migrant motivation, border controls, and migrant-settlement policies fall within a broader historical constellation that helps us understand the overall system. Political-economic approaches also draw attention to issues of who gains the most from political-economic systems, including the migration flows that sustain these systems.

Trade and migration: This political-economic model is based on the principles of neoclassical economic growth and liberal ideals of "voluntary" international movement and "peaceful" settlement involving economic and political co-operation between migrant-origin and migrant-destination nations. Obviously, these assumptions apply only to some historical and contemporary cases and not to others. Studies in the 1960s and 1970s

by Kuznets (1966) and Thomas (1972) drew attention to the key role played by international migration in the economic development of the North Atlantic economy (linking Europe and North America) over the long period from the mid-1850s to the early part of the 20th century. As immigrants moved from land-scarce Europe to land-rich North America, they redistributed their work from smaller, less fertile European farms to larger and more fertile North American farms. The value of what the migrants produced increased dramatically when they moved from Europe to North America. As a key part of this political-economic system, European investors provided financial capital for new enterprises in North America in order to profit from the greater productivity and wealth being generated there. Grain and other farm products produced in North America were then shipped to Europe to satisfy the growing demands of an industrial economy. The transnational flows of migrants, capital, and trade goods led to rapid economic growth in Europe and North America.

The trade and migration approach offers significant macro-level insights, but it also leaves out a great deal. Questions of migrant motivation are not examined; rather, they are simply assumed. The framework contains no details on how immigration policies were formed, nor does it address how well these policies worked. It does not address ethnic relations between immigrants and the host society, social classes, gender roles, or transnational flows of remittances. Nor does it tell us whether a framework that functioned within a quasi-imperial context centred on Great Britain and its former colonies in North America, which then drew in or influenced other nations in Europe and the Americas from 1850 to 1914, might apply to contemporary Canadian immigration. Addressing all these questions cannot readily be done all at once. As a first step, the Innis approach helps to establish Canada's place in the North Atlantic system.

From perspective of the Canadian political-economic framework, the growth of the North Atlantic was yet another stage in Canada's staples economy. As before and as later, Canada was linked politically and economically to other nations through trade, capital flows, and exports. These patterns gave rise to what Innis labelled Canada's outward-looking culture; openness to immigrants from other countries that furnished trade, capital, and export markets; and the basis of ethnocentrism and racism that excluded people from other parts of the world. The cultural and political-economic perspective emerging from the early staples economy and the North Atlantic economic system that was a major factor in Canadian development after Confederation through to the early part of the 20th century were the two main pillars of Canadian immigration up to the 1950s and have a continuing resonance up to the present. Chapter 3 analyzes this history in greater detail.

Labour reserves: The North Atlantic model of trade and migration described above assumes that the migrant-origin and destination nations are exchanging capital, workers, and trade goods relatively freely and equally on the mutual understand-

ing that all will benefit. The first critiques of this approach came from studies in which the countries involved were highly unequal in wealth and political power. Under circumstances of political-economic inequality among nations, migration patterns and outcomes take a very different form. The benefits accrue largely to the more developed country. Workers in or from so-called "labour reservoirs" receive little, often just enough to sustain themselves, feed and clothe their families, and raise children who will become the next generation of workers (Figure 2.4). How such processes work in different settings and historical moments indicates some variation in pattern and outcomes, but many common features as well.

Illustrative cases include the circulation of migrant labour from Mozambique to South Africa during the era of apartheid (Burawoy 1976; Cohen 1987: Chapter 3). South Africa had a dominant political economic position with respect to Mozambique and other neighbouring countries, and used its advantage to obtain co-operation from the government of Mozambique to set up programs to send villagers for periods of up to two years to work in South African mines. The programs were promoted as a way for poor farmers to earn better incomes. The workers could not take their families with them, so they were obliged to send money home over the long periods during which they were away. The wages paid were low, but sufficient to allow families to raise children who would become future mine workers. Over time the process developed a systemic character: The government of Mozambique became dependent on payments it received from South Africa for the arrangement, the villagers entered into repeat cycles of contract work in South Africa, and the male children of the migrant workers grew up to believe that their future lay in taking up the cir-

Figure 2.4: Labour Reservoir Model

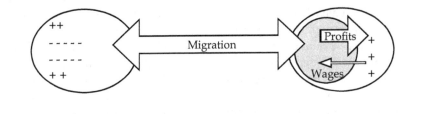

culatory migration patterns established by their fathers.

Other illustrations of the labour reservoirs approach can be found in Piore (1979) and Froebel, Heinrichs, and Kreye (1980) on the new international division of labour (NIDL); Simmons and Guengant (1992) on migration systems in the Caribbean from slavery through abolition to contemporary exodus and international circulation; and Cordell, Gregory, and Piché (1996) on West African colonial and post-colonial migration systems. Each of these cases and the studies on them refer to a different context and variation in how labour reserves are formed and how they operate. The NIDL framework remains particularly relevant to the contemporary world in which many wealthy countries continue to rely on large numbers of migrant workers to fill low-wage gaps in their own labour forces. The model emerged from studies of "guest worker" programs that were set up by northwestern European nations (principally Germany and France) in the 1960s to solve labour shortages that had emerged due to the emigration of many Europeans to North America, Australia, and elsewhere in the 1950s, and labour demand arising from economic growth in Europe. The European nations sought to solve the problem by inviting large numbers of contract workers from Southern Europe, North Africa, Turkey, and other

countries to take on difficult construction and manufacturing jobs at relatively low wages. It was understood that these migrant workers were to return home, but many did not. Those from outside Europe who remained found themselves marginalized and excluded from good jobs. At the same time, the migrant workers sent money home to support family members left behind. For Piore (1979) and Froebel et al. (1980), the continuing poverty of people in the non-European countries of origin and the marginalization of migrant workers from those countries who remained in Europe began to look a lot like the way labour reservoirs had functioned in the colonial era.

The most recent extensions of the labour reservoirs approach are found in models of globalization and migration that address "job exports" (Simmons 2002, 2005). In the emergence of global trade, migrants and immigrants may still be invited to wealthy nations to do difficult work for lower wages than others. At the same time, entrepreneurs in such nations may decide to relocate their manufacturing and income-generating activities (services such as billing and call centres) to developing countries where wages are even lower. If wages rise in one less developed nation, then the productive facilities and related jobs can be exported once again to a still lower-wage nation. The threat of unemployment keeps employees in each place nervous about asking for higher wages, with the result that wages stay lower than would otherwise be the case. If one were to draw a simple diagram of such a system, it might look like a variant of Figure 2.4, with the significant difference being that the low-wage work had been located back to a duty-free production zone in the less developed nation, while the profits and wages circulated between the more and less developed nations to benefit the former. Eventually, according to trade and migration arguments, wages in poor countries should rise, but this does not happen evenly or quickly in all cases (Martin 1993; Martin and Taylor 1991). The result is a situation in which poor countries continue to operate as labour reservoirs for wealthy nations. However, unlike the past, not all workers in the reservoirs need to move for contract jobs; many now find these locally.

Global cities: The global cities model, based on the work of Sassen (1998, 2001, 2006), points to the way that immigrant and migrant labour is organized *within* major Western cities such as London, Paris, New York, and Los Angeles where global international corporations, law firms, and advertizing agencies are located. The key features of Sassen's model overlap with globalization and migration and transnational migration systems arguments examined under Generation III models. The assumptions of the global cities model include the following:

1. The penetration of global trade and capital into less developed nations sparks international migration. Capitalist investments dislocate local workers (e.g., farmers are displaced by tractors or by mining operations) and create communication, cultural, and transportation

bridges over which migrants can cross back to wealthy nations.

2. Migrants are particularly inclined to follow cultural links back to former colonial mother countries. Once established, these flows generate transnational communities that further reinforce the migration streams from former colonies to former mother countries. Large numbers move to global cities such as London, New York, and Los Angeles where global corporations, advertising agencies, banks, and design-engineering firms have their headquarters.

3. Wealth in global cities flows into the hands of a class of owners, managers, and senior professionals who live there. They have a large demand for diverse services—laundry, restaurants, taxis, office cleaning, stores, airports, child care—that draw in migrant workers and immigrants for relatively low-paid work.

4. Immigrants and migrants in global cities experience segmented assimilation into racialized ethnic-class strata. They experience little upward mobility over time. Their children tend to remain in the same strata as their parents.

In Sassen's (1998: 210) analysis, Toronto, Canada's largest city and currently the main headquarters for Canadian banks and other financial institutions, is perhaps a secondary global city. It has some of the features of a global city in terms of being a centre of finance for Canada and attracting immigrants from around the world. But Toronto is not a major centre for global finance or a main location for global corporations, despite some notable exceptions. Whether Toronto or other Canadian cities display outcomes predicted by Sassen's model is a matter that will be examined in subsequent chapters. In general, the findings in Chapters 7, 8, and 9 suggest that Sassen's model fits the Canadian case at best only in part. It is true that immigrants to Canada experience low wages and poverty when they first arrive, and that this pattern often changes slowly. However, most immigrants have earnings fairly close to the level of native-born workers after they have been in the country for many years and some immigrants achieve even higher levels. The greatest departure from Sassen's argument on segmented assimilation is that the children of immigrants in Canada do not seem to suffer from the constraints faced by their parents. They do well in school and find good jobs except for cases of certain specific ethnic communities such as Blacks, Central Americans, and certain other groups that do not fit the general pattern (see Chapter 7).

The various political-economic models described above provide useful perspectives, concepts, and hypotheses for assessing Canadian immigration. However, they also leave out central features of Canadian policies. They do not speak to the emphasis that Canada and a number of other wealthy nations now put on attracting highly skilled immigrants, nor do they attend to debates on the merits of multicultural immigrant-settlement policies that have been taking place within Canada and other countries. In sum, they do not address major developments of concern to many migrant- and immigrant-receiving nations, including Canada. These issues are addressed in the models examined in the next section.

Generation III: Transnational Migration Systems

Generation III approaches extend the insights of the earlier generation models by adding transnational and social and cultural variables, a clearer view of the dynamics of historical change in migration flows, and the role of nation-building ideology in immigration policies and outcomes. The net effect of adding these elements is a combination of greater complexity and a richer set of tolls for analyzing international migration. While one might think of the various new features as separate elements, it is perhaps more useful to think of them as overlapping pieces that together form a single "transnational migration systems" approach. This is the view taken in the book as a whole. The remaining chapters of the book all rely on what I consider a unified transnational migration systems approach. The three key overlapping elements in this approach are as follows:

1. The transnational migration systems approach assists in the mapping of major migration streams over time so that we can understand them in relation to one another and to the transnational and trade-bloc formations that jointly shaped them. The two main pillars on which historical migration systems stand are migrant-formed transnational social-cultural bridges across national boundaries and international trading arrangements among nations related to their resources, including labour supplies.

2. The transnationalism framework points to important inner workings of historical migration systems with respect to social and cultural links among nations and the tendency for international migrants to form "chains" in which flows at a later time follow those that took place earlier, with implications for social-cultural change in both migrant-origin and migrant-destination locations.

3. Globalization as an ideology points to the functioning of the contemporary era and the ideological forces that generate a particular kind of

global political-economic system with its own specific migration and transnational social-cultural dynamics. The ideology is at the core of efforts by Canada and other countries to attract highly skilled immigrants. It is a key element in establishing a demand for both immigrants and, separately, migrant workers. Where the immigrants and migrants come from is heavily determined by transnational migrant family, community, and ethnic connections, in addition to state policies that indirectly affect the process.

The evolution toward a greater understanding of migration systems is recent, but it has early roots. Some years ago, Mabogunje (1970) argued that one could not understand rural-to-urban flows of migrants in a country like Nigeria without understanding the linked changes taking place in rural and urban areas in the overall national system—that is, Nigeria's earlier colonial and current trade relations with other countries—in which these areas were located. By the early 1990s, systemic approaches using Mabogunje's ideas on within-nation migration systems had become incorporated and further developed in studies of international migration patterns. Kritz, Lim, and Zlotnik (1992), in their co-edited book, *International Migration Systems*, noted succinctly that "international migrations do not occur randomly but take place usually between countries that have close historical, cultural or economic ties. Moreover, migrants are increasingly assisted in their moves by networks of earlier migrants, labour recruiters, corporations, travel agents, or even development agencies" (p. 1). They also note that "colonial ties are also an organizing basis for migration systems" (p. 5) and more generally that contemporary migration is shaped by globalization or,

in their words, "rising flows of capital and goods, ... technological advances in communication and transportation" (p. 1). In the same book, Zlotnik (1992) discusses ways of identifying empirical cases of migration systems defined as relatively large flows between at least two countries over a sustained period of time, leaving open for analysis how these systems came into being. Subsequent chapters of the book by invited authors examine in detail migration systems operating in various parts of the world: the South Pacific, West Africa, France in relation to North Africa, the Caribbean, and South America. Additional chapters examine how such systems have been affected by factors such as economic flows and technological transfers among nations, migration networks, migrant remittances, and state policies.

A few years later, in their detailed review of international migration theory and research findings, Massey et al. (1998) adopted the migration systems approach as a framework within which to examine specific patterns of international mobility affecting major regions and countries around the world. They also recognize globalization as a set of forces reshaping migration flows that had their origins in earlier historical periods and in a mix of trade, cultural, and social links among nations in different world regions. They conclude that: "The market economy is expanding to ever farther reaches of the globe, labour markets in the developed countries are growing more rather than less segmented, transnational migration and trade networks are expanding, and the power of the nation state is faltering in the face of this transnational onslaught. The twenty-first century will be one of globalism, and international migration undoubtedly will figure prominently within it" (p. 294). This conclusion confirms the rising awareness that migration systems are complex, involve change, and that change in the contemporary era is linked to globalization and transnational social-cultural bonds. However, they did not offer specific theoretical hypotheses on how globalization was changing international migration patterns, other than the view that it was adding new forces and complexity.

Faist (2000), following on earlier arguments by Kritz and Zlotnik (1992), draws particular attention to the fact that all migration systems are historical systems. They begin at some point in time, develop into a pattern, then eventually, sooner or later, decelerate, accelerate, or change in some other way due to forces they generate or which come from exogenous developments. This insight leads to an understanding of how social networks and migrant transnational practices feed into the development of different phases of specific international migration stream. Some catalyst and set of circumstances lead to the initial establishment of a migration stream. This could be systemic, as when a colonial power sets up an indentured labour or contract labour program, or it could result from contacts between a refugee and a foreigner whom the refugee knows personally that lead to assistance in finding asylum in that foreigner's home country. Once an initial "pioneer" migrant has moved, he or she is in a position to assess the outcomes and either discourage or encourage others in their home community to follow. Encouragement may involve providing help, information, funds to travel, and so on. Insofar as borders are not completely closed, these efforts will lead to more people moving and eventually the formation of transnational networks and institutions that link the countries in question. A migration stream formed in this way will continue to expand until its own dynamics or external forces lead it to stabilize and finally decline. An extreme case of internal dynamics leading to the cessation of migrant flows would be one where all

those who can emigrate from the migrant origin country have done so. More complex internal dynamics were observed in the North Atlantic economy, as described above. In the North Atlantic economy, wages and opportunities increased in the origin countries and eventually people no longer wanted to move. Whatever the reasons, all migration streams tend to die out eventually, although the timing can vary. Such a historical perspective on migration draws attention to the following points:

1. It is important to conceptualize international migration in terms of specific streams that are at one stage or another of initiation, growth, stabilization, and decline. A migrant/immigrant destination country may be more aware of overall numbers of people coming and less aware of the multiple overlapping streams that make up the flows in any given year. These origin-specific flows are always changing.

2. It may be useful at times to understand international migration by examining flows from/to particular large regions. Yet, a greater insight may emerge by also looking at country-to-country specific flows and within these to see who is actually moving in terms of their ethnicity, social class, gender, and other attributes. The shift in viewpoint leads to a deeper appreciation of emerging ethnic diversity in immigrant-receiving nations.

3. Transnational practices, networks, institutions, and flows lie at the core of historical migration systems. This was true in the past and remains true today.

4. Migration systems emerge within particular political economic contexts. In the past colonial and regional forces (proximate nations

linked by trade, travel, and cultural diffusion) generated international migration streams. Today global ideology and global financial institutions (see below) are supplementing and in some cases replacing the systems originally established by colonial and regional forces.

Chapter 1 introduced the concepts of globalization and transnationalism and pointed to some general arguments on how these affect international migration patterns. These same links can be understood more fully within a migration systems framework. The migration systems framework and the related concepts of globalization and transnationalism shift attention from separate *places* of migrant origin and destination to *spaces* of interconnected migrant-generated flows and connections across borders (Levitt and Nyberg-Sorenson 2004; Vertovec 1999). This is compatible with a systems framework that also emphasizes flows and connections. The emphasis shifts from that of looking at *actors* in the places where they are located to *transfers* between actors and places. Put in other terms, international migration and migrant settlement do not operate separately from the flows of capital, trade, and cultural elements in the larger system in which they take place. Rather, they are processes that form part of the overall system of connections and flows.

In a key early study, Basch, Glick Schiller, and Szanton Blanc (1994) examined migrant transnational practices as both social and political in nature. Migrants from the Eastern Caribbean engaged in the negotiation of their identity and political action in their home countries, and at the same time in New York and Miami. Their lives had a strong transnational dimension. They sought to retain their participation in their home communities and, in fact, to participate even more than they had before they left through political action there; at the same time they sought to negotiate a separate Caribbean Black identity in the United States. Studies in Canada reported by various authors in recent edited books (Goldring and Krishnamurti 2007; Satzewich and Wong 2006) on this topic indicate that immigrant transnationalism operates in similar ways in Canada. The studies in these two books report wide variation in practices around a range of matters from political involvement in home countries; dual citizenship; commuting between work and family located in two countries; sending remittances to family in overseas locations; forming dual ethnic identities; and engaging in efforts to expand contacts for work, volunteering, and religious/spiritual engagement within Canada, in home nations, and in transnational spaces connecting these two. The image is one of flows of communication, emotional and financial support, information on jobs and business prospects, and identity-forming contacts, affiliations, and experiences.

Contemporary economic globalization and international migration are also now widely understood to be systemically linked. Globalization ideology and the supporting policies and programs in wealthy nations that are implemented by the international financial institutions that these wealthy nations control, such as the World Bank, the International Monetary Fund (IMF), and the G8 nations, are key actors in promoting free trade. Trade flows respond to and affect the demand for workers with different skills. Through such mechanisms, trade flows influence migrant motivations and wealthy nations' policies with respect to immigration and migrant labour (Castles 2002; Simmons 2002; Stalker 2000). For example, free trade, promoted within a globalization ideology, can have an initial negative impact on employment in less developed nations like Mexico. Corn and wheat produced at low cost on large farms with big machines in the United States and Canada flow into Mexico and erode the profits of poor small farmers, forcing them to seek work and income in other sectors in Mexico or beyond in the United States or Canada (Martin 1993; Simmons 2002, 2005). When migrants do move, they establish social and cultural bridges to the places they move, while retaining those to their home communities. The bridges carry flows of information, emotional support, financial support, and political viewpoint between the places they connect. A brief summary of these and other arguments on the international migration outcomes of globalization and transnationalism can be found near the end of Chapter 1.

Now is perhaps a useful point to summarize the determinants of international migration and its outcomes from the perspective of the flows of capital and goods associated with globalization and the flows of social support, remittances, and ethnic connections associated with migrant transnational social practices and networks. These globalization and transnational influences and outcomes are highly overlapping within a transnational migration systems framework.

With respect to globalization:

1. Globalization ideology and the export-led development strategies that it promotes lead to constant change in the goods and services that nations produce, the kinds of workers required, and the policies they adopt to attract and control migrant and immigrant labour to serve national political-economic interests and cultural goals.

2. Nations vary widely in the extent to which they respond to global opportunities through reliance on immigration. Countries with a his-

tory of successful incorporation of immigrants tend to want to repeat this over time and in planning for the future. Monocultural societies without this earlier successful immigration history tend to rely more on non-immigration approaches to address global opportunities and challenges.

3. Globalization in the contemporary era increases wealthy nations' demand for highly skilled immigrants. They are desired for permanent settlement in the expectation that they will raise their children in the host nation. Less skilled and unskilled migrant workers who are not valued for the long term are admitted only on the condition that they will return to their home country after their contracts have ended. Their children, born abroad, may be the next generation of temporary migrant workers.

4. Immigrants face an uphill battle in finding good jobs in a competitive trading nation undergoing changes in the goods and services it produces to retain a high standard of living. This is because the job market is competitive and young native-born workers with whom they compete for new jobs may have better human capital (such as national education credentials and language skills) and social capital (networks and contacts) relevant to obtaining good jobs.

5. There is a danger that job competition between immigrants and the native-born can reinforce any existing discrimination against minorities and add to anti-immigrant sentiment. Discrimination can hopefully be reduced by strong multicultural and pro-immigration policies, ideologies, and national programs,

but exactly what works in different nations is still a puzzle.

6. Ethnic relations globally and in immigrant-receiving countries are made more difficult when entire ethnic groups are labelled negatively due to the actions, real and at times imagined, of a few of their members. The press, public, and opportunistic political leaders join forces in labelling undocumented migrants from certain countries as threats to the nation. Labelling practices of this kind may be understood as ways of imagining one's own community by rejecting another community.

With respect to transnationalism:

1. Not all immigrants retain strong transnational connections, but insofar as they do, these connections are most intense, frequent, and meaningful at the family level, then at the level of hometown associations, religious organizations, and any equivalent social-organizational grouping involving meaningful direct and trust-building interaction with others. In some cases the meaningful trusting relationships arise through business and professional associations. Having property, holding citizenship, and being involved politically in both nations can also involve meaningful transnational links.

2. Transnationalism at whatever level tends to promote the retention of ethnic identities, cultures, and networks among immigrants within the host society. This supports the cultural incorporation of immigrants into a multicultural society like that found in Canada. It can also tend to slow the development of contacts and relationships of trust outside their ethnic community, which

may be a factor, among others, that reduces their access to good jobs and better incomes.

3. The social bridges that immigrants retain with their home countries are fundamentally important in the development of migration chains in which people from the same family, village, and country tend to follow pioneering immigrants to Canada. This process is reinforced by diverse transnational practices and links. It has profound implications for understanding why many more immigrants come from some countries than from others.

4. Transnationalism adds to the opportunities and complexities of processes of ethnic belonging and identity at both the individual and collective levels. This has been the case for diasporas in the past and may be even more intense within diaspora-like transnational communities and settings.

5. Transnational political ties to other countries and related patterns of dual citizenship create new possibilities for generating peace and democracy in the world, but they also hold the potential to involve the immigrants in home-country ethnic-based civil wars and violent conflicts with ethnically different neighbouring states. This can create violent confrontations among immigrants of different ethnic and or national background in Canada.

The preceding arguments are a partial list of the overlapping dynamics of globalization, transnationalism, and international migration in the contemporary world. They and other related arguments will be examined against empirical evidence, largely with respect to Canada, in the remaining chapters in this book.

Putting the Pieces Together: Round Two

Given that globalization and transnational flows are overlapping and have a joint relationship to international migration, I will refer to the overall system as a global-transnational one. This system reveals a mix of coherence, harmony, incoherence, and conflict. One view is that there are two processes involved. One is "globalization from above" brought about through corporate interest and the influence of powerful capitalist states. The other is "globalization from below" brought about by the efforts of various interest groups to use the Internet, electronic banking, and other globalization technologies to resist or circumvent rules established by dominant interests (Kapoor 2008). Migrant protests and undocumented migration are illustrations of globalization from below. Another illustration of globalization from below is when migrants ignore the national border controls and travel or move to other countries without legal admission or work documents. Undocumented migration is similar to officially approved forms of migration, including immigration, in that

all international movement takes place as part of a global-transnational system of flows of other kinds: financial capital, trade goods, cultural and political influences, and so on.

It is evident that the global-transnational system of which international migration is an important element is loosely, partially, and in varying degrees incoherently integrated. Trade flows can rise and then collapse. International investments can flood into a given country, then fail or change direction. Nations can come together more closely in terms of trade, travel, political, migration, and culture exchanges, or they can drift into hostile interactions. Any attempt to model or theorize the global-transnational system and the place of international migration in it is therefore risky and provisional. At the same time, research on international migration provides ample support for trends and patterns that show coherence within particular historical periods. Some trends and patterns seem to show continuity even as others show more marked changes from one period to another. A flow-oriented chart of the main features of the global-transnational migration system based on observations in this chapter is shown in Figure 2.5.

Figure 2.5: Global-Transnational Flows

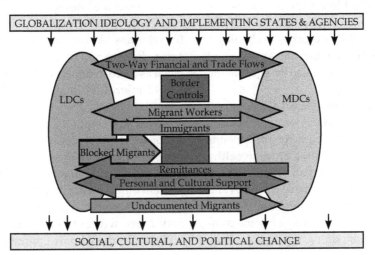

Figure 2.5 draws attention to flows of various kinds that are interdependent in the overall system. Money flows in both directions between less and more developed nations. The wealthier nations invest in less wealthy nations directly through setting up their manufacturing, service, and sales operations abroad. The wealthier nations also transfer money to the less wealthy nations indirectly by investing in firms owned by entrepreneurs in those countries. The return flows of money consist in part of profits earned abroad by firms located in wealthy nations. However, they also consist of profits to owners in the less wealthy nations that are then sent to wealthy nations. Why do wealthy owners in less developed nations send money to more developed nations? They do so because they often feel that their savings will be safer in more developed countries. Their savings can be invested in real estate and relatively secure government treasury bonds in the more developed nation. These funds can then be used at a later time for investments or consumption in their home countries.

Trade goods and services of various kinds also flow in both directions among nations with differing levels of wealth. Less expensive industrial goods are exported from low-wage countries to high-wage countries. The high-wage countries pay for these goods by spending their profits from trade and by exporting technology, sophisticated communication services, and high-end military or security equipment, among other things.

International migration flows correspond variably to the above flows of trade goods and capital. The variation depends on the imagined futures of the wealthy nations. Some, like Japan in the contemporary era, or like Europe in the 1960s and 1970s, do not favour immigration, and as a result these countries rely on some combination of temporary migrant workers,

investments in labour-saving technology, and exporting jobs to low-wage nations. Others, like the United States, rely on a mix of large visa worker programs, substantial inflows of undocumented workers (despite energetic efforts in recent years to control permeable borders with Mexico and the Caribbean), and large inflows of documented immigrants. Canada has for many decades relied heavily on large inflows of immigrants and smaller inflows of temporary migrant workers, but the number of migrant workers has been rising in recent years (see Chapter 11). The inflow of undocumented workers to Canada appears to be modest, although this is difficult to assess (Chapter 5). Whatever the pattern of international migration, the migrants establish social and cultural connections within and across the nations involved, and in this way their practices and the flows of information and support related to them tend to reinforce existing migration patterns and ongoing socio-cultural transformations in their origin and destination nations. From the perspective of the overall system, the coherence comes largely from the globalization ideology and international agencies that promote expanded trade, capital flows, patent regulations, and other mechanisms to orient and lubricate a "machine" designed for increased efficiency, interdependence, and peaceful relations. At the same time, internal contradictions and blocked opportunities (such as those experienced by people who would migrate if they could) also stem from the same system, making it a place of mixed co-operation and conflict.

Border controls play a key role in international migration systems. They allow some individuals to migrate legally, but prevent others from doing the same thing. Some of those not able to migrate legally may move without documents. Others will stay in their home country. Insofar as migrants stay attached to their home families, they will send money and gifts to help those who could not or would not migrate with them. Without borders, remittance flows would be smaller, given that many more family members would likely move to join others who previously migrated elsewhere.

How does Canada fit in the general framework shown in Figure 2.5? Every nation is involved in its own migration subsystem within the larger system of global flows. The remaining chapters examine specific features of Canadian history; the imagined futures of the nation promoted by economic and political leaders to guide trade, immigration, and cultural policies; and the transnational social-cultural links of immigrants. A major dimension of this analysis is to give particular attention to migration systems as a plural concept: Canada has moved from one historical system to another as its relationship with other nations and the global system has evolved. This is consistent with Harold Innis's view that Canada, as an inherently outward-looking nation with a long history of large-scale immigration, would continue to play its "immigration card"; that is, its assumed ability to peacefully absorb productive settlers from other countries as a key element in nation-building. The "immigration card" is a potential advantage over other nations that do not have this ability. This may explain why, in spite of evidence that recently arrived immigrants are not doing well economically in the first years after their arrival, state immigration targets remain high.

Discussion and Conclusions

Theory is to be judged by the extent to which it clarifies and explains empirical patterns and relationships. Understanding international migration and Canadian patterns within global patterns is a very challenging task. The various frameworks or so-called "theories" examined in this chapter do not constitute completely alternative perspectives. Rather, they provide different views that together or in useful combinations illuminate complex, multidimensional processes. From this perspective nearly all the frameworks examined potentially have something to contribute. Specifically:

1. Within the broad range of migration theory, the more recent models concerning migration systems, transnationalism, and globalization are the most relevant for the task in this book. They have the advantage of incorporating useful features of earlier models and examining migration processes and outcomes within a larger framework covering different political-economic formations, trade blocs, and regional clusters of nations.

2. To apply these tools to the Canadian case, it is also helpful to find frameworks—such as the Innis School of Canadian Political Economy—that orient us to the historical evolution of the Canadian case and its contemporary form as an illustration of unique, country-specific, historical processes of transnational migration that fall within the scope of more general theoretical models.

The remaining chapters of the book draw largely on the Innis nation-building framework and migration systems theory to explore Canadian immigration. Each new chapter picks up theoretical arguments reviewed in the present chapter to examine in more detail key issues, such as the historical development of Canadian immigration, changes in imagined futures of the nation associated with shifts in immigration policy, the national and ethnic origins of immigrants, and immigrant settlement in Canada. As a result, the analysis in the remaining chapters moves back and forth between migration theory and an examination of empirical research findings.

The next two chapters clarify the emergence of the historical system that shaped Canadian nation-building and related immigration patterns. The first of these two chapters, Chapter 3, does this by examining key developments in Canadian immigration from early colonization to the 1950s. Chapter 4 addresses global anti-racist movements and the evolution of trade policies that brought to an end White Canada immigration policies and set the stage for further trade negotiations with the United States and a set of redefined Canadian immigration policies in various stages, from 1961 onward, and then from 1989 onward.

CHAPTER 3

Immigration and Nation-Building

Introduction

Given Canada's history of large-scale immigration in the late 1800s and again since the 1950s, the difficulty in encouraging people to settle in Canada in the very early colonizing years may seem paradoxical. However, the puzzle is readily explained. To begin with, Canada was a "wilderness" from the settlers' viewpoint. Farming conditions were bleak, disease and hunger were constant companions, and the Iroquois and other Native peoples were understandably at times very hostile to European settlers. Today, in a different context, there is a large backlog of tens of thousands of people who have applied to come as immigrants and who are wait-

ing in queue for a response from the Canadian government. In a seeming paradox, Canadian news reports draw attention to violence directed toward migrants and immigrants in Canada, even though the country has admitted between 200,000 and 250,000 newcomers each year since the mid-1990s and is generally perceived to be an immigrant-friendly nation. In 1999 the arrival of a few hundred Chinese passengers in dilapidated boats off the British Columbia coast created what Greenberg (2000) viewed as a "moral panic" accompanied by deep hostility to the would-be undocumented migrant workers (see Box 3.1). In January 2007, the mayor of Hérouxville, a small town northeast of Montreal, announced that the town council had passed new rules to warn immigrants and ethnic minorities that people there "consider it completely outside norms to ... kill women by stoning them in public, burning them alive, burning them with acid, [and] circumcising them ... " (BBC 2007). This absurd characterization of immigrants and ethnic minorities set off a storm of controversy that led to a government commission to examine issues of "reasonable accommodation" of cultural diversity (see the final report: Bouchard and Taylor 2008). However, these puzzling hostile reactions to immigrants are also not new. They have earlier historical roots in anti-immigrant and racist sentiment at various points in the past. Recent antagonistic incidents suggest that remnants, and perhaps more, of the attitudes that sparked anti-Chinese riots in Vancouver in the early 1900s and the deportation of thousands of immigrants in the 1930s are still part of Canadian society. What can we learn from the history of Canadian immigration that could help us better understand these current events?

In this chapter I argue that the historical past of Canadian immigration can provide useful perspectives for understanding present-day patterns and developments. In some cases, the present is illuminated by seeing how it emerged from the past; in other cases, the present is made clearer by contrasting it with very different past trends. Perhaps more than anything, the exercise of examining the past reminds us that change is constant and that the present is only the latest instalment in an unfolding story. This is the case even if we don't know when the next wave of change will come or what direction it will take.

This short chapter can only touch upon selected aspects of the long history of Canadian immigration. My objective is to highlight particularly important historical developments and use them to construct a framework for clarifying the major periods

of Canadian immigration and the related imagined futures of the nation in each period. The chapter begins by contrasting main features of present Canadian immigration with very different features found at certain moments in the past. The contrasts raise questions about the possibility that earlier features may not have entirely disappeared and that they could emerge again in the future. The main body of the chapter examines selected episodes or partial histories assembled from longer, much more fleshed out accounts. Unless otherwise noted, what I present is based on Valerie Knowles (1992), *Strangers at Our Gates: Canadian Immigration and Immigration Policy, 1540–1990*, and Ninette Kelley and Michael Trebilcock (2000), *The Making of the Mosaic: A History of Canadian Immigration Policy*. The final section presents a framework of historical periods and imagined futures of immigration and Canadian nation-building.

Past-Present Contrasts

Immigration inflows to Canada have been in the moderate-to-high range since 1945 (see Figure 3.1). Since 1989, there has been little variation in annual immigrant admissions, with inflows being relatively high by Canadian standards and very high by world standards. Throughout this long postwar period, immigration and Canadian nation-building policies have been closely intertwined. Canada actively sought immigrants, first from Europe (up to 1962) then from elsewhere in the world in order to address emerging gaps in the labour market and to help build prosperity and security for the nation over the longer term. In addition, over this period, relatively large numbers of refugees have been admitted to meet international treaty obligations and the humanitarian values of Canadians.

What can the history of Canadian immigration tell us? Among other things, it tells

Box 3.1: Chinese "Boat People" on the B.C. Coast

On July 20, 1999, an unmarked ship transporting 123 passengers from Fujian province in China was tracked and intercepted by Canadian citizenship and immigration authorities off the coast of British Columbia. The conditions aboard the ship ("abysmal" and "horrendous") and the physical state of its passengers ("filthy") became the primary focus of coverage in much of Canada's mainstream daily press. Amid speculation that several other such boats had illegally evaded federal border authorities, three more ships in similar condition arrived at numerous points along the B.C. coastline over the next couple of months (August 12, August 31, and September 9 respectively). In total, 599 migrants arrived without proper legal identification and many subsequently declared refugee status. This was a series of events which precipitated among political elites, media observers, and some Canadian citizens a general consensus that the immigration and refugee systems were in a "state of crisis."

Despite evidence that upwards of 30,000 refugees attempt entry to Canada each year, the general feeling conveyed by news coverage of these events was that the immigration and refugee systems were being flooded by an influx of Asian "gate-crashers," whose presence posed numerous threats to the public. Almost immediately after the arrival of the first boat the Victoria *Times-Colonist*, in a poll of its readership, reported that approximately 97% of respondents felt the migrants should be sent back to China immediately (July 30, 1999). Although claiming to be "sympathetic" to the migrants' life-situations overseas, respondents expressed concern that the new arrivals constituted a threat to law and order and an insult to the integrity of Canadian citizenship.

News coverage assumed an increasingly critical and hyperbolic tone after the arrival of the second boat. With immigration and security officials warning that many more ships were on the way, groups of Canadian citizens began mobilizing at various B.C. ports, some in support of the migrants and many others shouting slurs and waving placards stating unequivocally that the migrants should "GO HOME." The usual slowness of newsworthy events during the summer months, ... a general rightward shift in the national political spectrum, and a highly competitive news media environment thus made the migrants' arrivals especially attractive to news coverage. Indeed, as one reporter put it: "You've got hundreds of people standing on a ship out in the middle of nowhere—on a ship that looks like if you touch it too hard, it's going to sink. For lack of a better way of putting it, it's eye candy."

Source: Extracted from Greenberg, Joshua. 2000. "Opinion Discourse and Canadian Newspapers: The Case of the Chinese 'Boat People.'" *Canadian Journal of Communication* 25, 4:517–538.

us that the postwar immigration patterns described above constitute a unique period in the development of the nation. What we may have come to regard as a normal state of affairs would not have been considered normal in the past. Whether current patterns will continue and for how long is uncertain. By looking backward, we can see that immigration and nation-building were not always joined at the hip in Canada. At times nation-builders in Canada have been hostile to immigrants. In some instances, the hostility escalated due to moral panics of the kind reported above and in Box 3.1. These episodes serve as cautionary tales. Perhaps it is wishful thinking to hope that what took place years ago will not happen again if we understand the past. Whether or not this turns out to be the case, an historical analysis offers several specific lessons that are relevant to the contemporary focus of this book. These include the following:

1. Canada was not always an attractive place for settlers. Early attempts to attract immigrants largely failed. Success came much later.
2. Nation-building in Canada does not necessarily require immigration. Quebec emerged as a nation within Canada with little immigration until recently.
3. Canada has experienced significant fluctuations over time in ethnocentrism, racism, and fear of foreigners.
4. Canadians have not always wanted immigrants or trusted them. At times new immigrants have been excluded and many former immigrants deported.
5. Large numbers of refugees on Canada's doorstep have in the past been refused admission despite their desperate plight and links to communities in Canada.
6. It is well known that the imagined futures that guide Canadian immigration changed dramatically in 1962 with the end of White Canada policies. It is less well known that the global-immigration and multicultural-Canada policies that followed were linked to two different imagined futures, first (from 1962 to 1989) that of an industrial nation in the Americas, and then (from 1989 to the present) that of a global niche player. The two may sound similar, but are quite different.

What accounts for the past circumstances and recent developments? What do they tell us about how Canadian immigration works and its future? The following sections address these questions.

The Fragility of Early Settlement, 1497–1763

Initial European contact with North America did not lead to colonization for a mix of reasons. The economic philosophy of mercantilism at that time did not include settlement. Europeans initially travelled to North America to search for routes to the Orient and to capture resources, particularly fish and furs, which could be obtained readily and transported home on the relatively small ships of the time. Neither exploration nor the exploitation of these particular kinds of natural resources required settlements abroad, with the result that European settlements in Canada were slow to develop.

There is good documentation of Vikings' visits to Labrador and the northeastern tip of Newfoundland at L'anse aux Meadows starting around the year AD 1000. Then there seems to have been a gap of several hundred years before John Cabot, an Italian sailing under the English flag seeking a passage to Asia, caught sight of what is now Newfoundland and reported on the great abundance of codfish in the Grand Banks area. It is possible that Portuguese fishermen were already exploiting the northeastern coast of North America. News of these resources conveyed by Cabot and unknown Portuguese fishermen soon led to the expansion of the European fishery in the region and to the establishment of a Portuguese colony/summer camp on Cape Breton Island around 1520–1524.

Other explorers followed. In July 1534, Jacques Cartier, sailing in the service of France, arrived to the Baie de Chaleur on the Gaspé Peninsula, put up a cross, and claimed the territory for the king of France. Cartier made several more trips that took him to Newfoundland and eventually up the St. Lawrence River as far as Hochelaga (now Montreal). Cartier's initial effort to establish a settlement at Cap-Rouge above Quebec failed. Wars between England, Spain, and France, as well as the long conflict between the Huguenots and Catholics in France in the latter half of the 1500s, led France to ignore New France, leaving it to French fishermen and fur traders who came yearly in a private capacity. The fur traders expanded French contact up the St. Lawrence. Above all else, they sought beaver pelts, which were felted to make gentlemen's hats. The early fur-trade economy did not require European colonial settlements.

The colonization of New France began with a number of failed or, at best, partially successful efforts in the early 1600s. The process was initiated by the king of France when he granted trade monopolies to wealthy merchants or nobles, sometimes as individuals and in other cases as groups, in exchange for their agreement to establish new settlements. Most of these ventures failed. One had, at best, limited success. In 1604, Samuel de Champlain, acting on behalf of his group of fur traders, helped an expedition headed by the Protestant Pierre Dua De Monts to establish a small colony of some 80-odd settlers in Nova Scotia. This colony folded after three years, eroded by disease (about one-third of the colonists died from scurvy in the first year) and terminated because its fur-trading rights were discontinued. However, Champlain had learned that colonization was possible and he and others established new settlements, principally along the St. Lawrence. These remained small and fragile because they had a very restricted economic function; they did not provide an economic base

that would attract and sustain colonists. As Knowles observes:

> Large scale colonization was to remain a dream as long as settlement was tied to the fur trade, for bands of Indians supplied all the labour necessary for its operations and there was no other economic activity in New France to attract immigrants from overseas. The impetus for colonization had to be provided by a change in thinking, and this occurred with the rise of seventeenth-century mercantilism, the theory that called for a state to increase its monetary wealth by severely restricting imports of manufactured goods and obtaining as many of its raw materials from abroad as possible. (Knowles 1992: 4)

Operating under mercantile economic principles, France saw that its future lay in establishing much larger and more vibrant colonies in New France. The colonies would be settled by farmers, loggers, miners, blacksmiths, and other tradesmen who would produce food and other raw materials for France and, as an additional benefit, import some French manufactured goods. Last but not least, they would pay taxes on imported goods. They would be governed as French possessions and served by the Catholic Church, which would attend to the spiritual needs of the colonists and, at the same time, help pacify the Indians (referred to as *les sauvages*) by converting them to Christianity. A powerful commercial company, the Compagnie de la Nouvelle France, was launched under Richelieu in 1627; it was later transformed into the Company of One Hundred Associates, with an infusion of new capital, to administer the seigneurial land grant system that gave wealthy investors tracts of land based on their commitment to clear them and establish farms. The colonists faced hard times due to shortages of funds and supplies and attacks by Iroquois warriors. In 1663, Louis XIV established New France as a province under the Crown. Jean Talon became *Intendant* of New France and set in place plans for major economic expansion to make the colonies self-sufficient and then profitable for France through lumbering, fishing, and trade with the French West Indies.

Immigration and populating the colony became a core preoccupation for Talon, but he faced great difficulties in attracting settlers. He needed soldiers to fight the hostile Iroquois, settlers to clear the land, skilled craftsmen to furnish tools for the farmers, and women to become wives and bear children to ensure an expanding supply of farmers and workers to meet future needs. Between 1663 and 1673, some 2,000 settlers arrived from France. Several hundred colonists of Dutch, Portuguese, and German ethnicity arrived on French ships in 1668. Soldiers who had served in New France were given attractive discharge grants in the hope that they would stay in the colony. In 1666–1667, 192 unmarried young women, known as *filles du roi*, were attracted to New France on the promise that they would receive husbands on arrival. In addition, "steps were taken to encourage natural increase. Fathers, as heads of families, were rewarded with a family allowance if they had at least ten children ... and were fined if their sons and daughters were not married at an early age" (Knowles 1992: 11). The objective was to use high fertility and natural increase to compensate for the difficulty of attracting settlers. Over the following century, New France became open to small numbers of commercial and professional settlers from other parts of Europe. In addition, the settlements expanded to include more distant outposts, such as those in the area

of Detroit and Windsor. Throughout this period France largely ignored its small settlement in Acadia. By the end of the 1700s, over a period of 150 years, only about 12,000 immigrants in total had been attracted to New France despite French efforts. A significant addition to this number came from the incorporation of approximately 4,100 slaves into the colony over this period. Of these, some 1,700 were Indians, mostly Pawnees from Nebraska, while some 2,400 were Blacks, largely from the West Indies.

In sum, initial French settlement in Canada was a struggle. France hoped its settlements would be low cost and would grow and prosper without further investments from France once they were established. Neither France nor its settlers in Canada had a clear image of a future French-speaking nation in the Americas, although such an image was beginning to slowly emerge over time. The number of settlers gradually increased. They fought back the wilderness, established treaties with the Native peoples, and formed the beginning of what was to grow later into a linguistic, ethnic, and political nation within Canada.

It seems unlikely that Canada will face a shortage of immigrants in the near future. As we have noted, large numbers of qualified people from around the world are currently eager to immigrate to Canada. So many have applied to immigrate that there is now a long wait-list—enough to fill immigration targets for three or four years—of people waiting for their applications to be processed. However, this situation may change faster than one might think, and the future could come to resemble the early past when it was difficult to attract settlers. This could happen, for example, if Canada were to experience a serious downturn in economic conditions and rising unemployed with little new investment and few new jobs for skilled workers. Under these conditions, the kinds of skilled immigrants that Canada currently wants might not be interested in coming. They could find better opportunities elsewhere. They might even find that opportunities are better in their home countries. Earlier indications that this is beginning to take place in some cases are already evident. Many computer engineers and software specialists from India who had previously moved to North America have returned home or are thinking of doing so, simply because the growth of high technology production in India has been so rapid in recent years that these individuals have excellent prospects in their home country.

The Rise of Quebec with Modest Immigration, 1763–1947

The British gained control of New France in 1763 and then had to come to terms with what to do next. Britain was preoccupied with its American colonies further south as tensions were building toward the American Revolutionary War, which took place from 1875–1883. In this context, establishing British settlements in Canada became a priority. A related question concerned the future of the 70,000 French-speaking inhabitants of Quebec. What could be done to keep them from joining in revolution with the Americans? The answer was forthcoming in the Quebec Act passed by the British Parliament in 1774. Francophone Quebecers were to become a subordinate partner in the British colonies in America. To put this relationship into effect, the Act recognized the seigneurial system of landholdings, granted the Catholic Church a continuing role as the dominant institution in Quebec by permitting it to collect tithes, and allowed French civil law to prevail. The fact that the Quebec Act still left the French inhab-

itants under British control was a major irritant that enforced their strong ethnic identification as a separate nation. A mix of co-operation and conflict among French Quebec, the British, and (after 1867) the federal government of Canada continued to generate a strong sense of ethnic nationhood in Quebec.

The distinctive feature of French Canada is that it developed as an ethnic nation with relatively limited immigration from the mid-1600s to the late 1800s. During this period its population expanded rapidly through extraordinarily high rates of fertility with women giving birth, on average, to six surviving children. This trend continued until around 1880 when fertility began to gradually decline. Starting from some 70,000 inhabitants in 1763, the population grew to around 1 million by the time of Confederation 100 years later. By the turn of the century in 1900, the population of Quebec was about 1.5 million, and by 1951 it was close to 4 million. Throughout this long period many European immigrants from England, Ireland, and other places settled in Quebec, but the main factor in population increase was high fertility. Rural Quebec received relatively few immigrants, hence it developed into a key component of the French nation in Quebec. The high level of reproduction based on a small population has attracted the attention of genetic researchers. Genizon Biosciences (2009) explains this interest as follows:

> French immigration essentially ceased after [New France was taken over by Britain] and intermarriage with English speaking groups has been minimal because of cultural, linguistic, religious and historical reasons. Early population expansion was rapid as founding couples had an average of 36 children and grandchildren. "Demographic

genetic drift," involving a major over-contribution of some highly prolific families over several early generations, provided increased genetic homogeneity. Emigration to the U.S.A. of over 1 million Quebecers between 1830 and 1930 left a population of only 1 million in 1930 and probably significantly reduced the number of family pedigrees.

Most of the present day French-Canadian population has descended by very rapid natural growth from the original settlers. Over the last 230 years, the Quebec population has grown by 80 times in a time span when the French population in France has grown by a factor of only 6 ... today, the Quebec French-Canadian population represents the largest genetically homogeneous localized founder population worldwide. In addition, there are subpopulations of Quebec, such as the region of Saguenay Lac-St-Jean, that are even more genetically homogeneous. This region was founded by about 600 people from the Charlevoix region of Quebec and has grown in relative isolation to a current population of 300,000.

The fact that the majority French origin population of Quebec can trace their ancestry back to French settlers has been well established. At the same time, immigrants to Quebec from Great Britain, other parts of Europe, the United States, and other places provided a foundation for the intermarriage of people of largely European stock, plus some intermarriage with Native peoples and African-origin peoples, to create a population that has a more mixed and complex genetic heritage that assimilated into the French-majority culture (Brais,

Desjardins, Labuda, St-Hilaire, Tremblay, and Vezina 2007).

The growth of the Quebec population changed dramatically after the end of the Second World War. Montreal became a major destination for postwar immigrants, first from Europe and then, after 1962, from all parts of the world. Fertility rates in Quebec had fallen to high (as opposed to extremely high) levels by the 1950s; they then plummeted to below-replacement levels after 1962. As in other parts of Canada, immigration is the main reason why Quebec's population is continuing to rise at present (see Chapter 10).

The Hérouxville affair of 2007, noted in the introduction to this chapter, can be more easily understood within the historical development of Quebec. French-speaking Quebecers in small towns are less familiar with immigrants in general, particularly those of non-European origin. They live among ethnic kin with whom they are closely linked by intermarriage, have common religious practices, and a long history of living together. Their views percolate through to larger urban centres where immigrants have settled, but in such places they represent a minority view, or at least this is the impression given by the authors of the Bouchard Taylor Commission report (Bouchard and Taylor 2008).

Canada: A European Nation in the Americas, 1867–1960

The early history of English colonization of North America was also based on a mercantile strategy, but with some important differences in specific policies and outcomes. The British established a much larger and more prosperous set of colonies in the northeastern United States. Then, after the American Revolution and loss of British control over these colonies, the British shifted their focus to colonizing Canada. The largest early influx consisted of some 46,000 United Empire Loyalists who left the United States after the revolution to settle in Canada. This was followed by continuing settlement by British colonists in the expanding communities in both Upper and Lower Canada through to Confederation in 1867.

Up until Confederation, it was understood that Canada was a British *colony* in the Americas. After Confederation the image began to shift. Canada was an emerging ethnic European *nation* in the Americas. The first prime minister, Sir John A. Macdonald, dreamed of a unified nation; it would stretch "from sea to sea to sea" across the entire continent from the Atlantic to the Pacific and north to the Northwest Passage and beyond. There were huge gaps between the reality of the time and Macdonald's dream. Prince Edward Island was not yet a part of Canada, but joined soon in 1873. Newfoundland stood on the sidelines, not joining Canada until 1949. However, the biggest challenges concerned the future status of the huge remaining areas of British North America, namely, Rupert's Land, British Columbia, and the North-West Territories. Macdonald and his government put a priority on bringing the West into the Canadian Confederation as quickly as possible in order to counter its possible loss to U.S. imperial ambitions. As a first essential step, in 1868 Canada purchased from the Hudson's Bay Company the huge territory of Rupert's Land, an area that included what later became Manitoba, Saskatchewan, and Alberta. Convincing the West to join Canada politically was yet another task, requiring promises from Canada to develop that region by bringing in settlers, expanding farming, and providing infrastructure, particularly railway lines that would bring in goods for the settlers and provide a way for them to transport their wheat and other products

for domestic consumption and to ports for shipment to foreign markets. Based on these promises and commitments, the Western provinces joined Canada: Manitoba in 1870; British Columbia in 1871; and Alberta and Saskatchewan in 1905.

The immigration programs established after Confederation up to the First World War included various components. A key step was organizing immigration agents to attract new immigrants from Great Britain, the United States, and northern Europe. These were in effect sales agents who were out to market Canada as a place to settle. They targeted particularly desirable kinds of immigrants, principally farmers with resources to invest, but also agricultural labourers. The agents and their supervisors were not above creative advertising: One supervisor proclaimed that Canada wanted "men of good muscle who are willing to hustle" (Skilling 1945: 15; quoted by Knowles 1992: 46). The effort to settle the Prairies was a major element in Canada's strategy to expand farming and grain exports to Europe. European investors supported this through investments in railway and port facilities to move the grain. All this was part of the North Atlantic economy, described in Chapter 2.

The Canadian immigration machine went into high gear after the appointment of Clifford Sifton as minister of the Interior in 1896. Immigration levels shot up year by year to a historical peak of 400,000 in one single year just prior to the collapse in immigration brought about by the onset of the First World War in 1914 (see Figure 3.1). Sifton's dream revealed elements of pragmatic pluralism. He said, "Our desire is to promote the immigration of farmers and farm labourers. We have not been disposed to exclude foreigners of *any nationality* who seemed likely to become successful agriculturalists ... " (Timlin 1960: 518; cited in Knowles 1992: 59; italics added). What Sifton did not say is that

Figure 3.1: Number of Immigrants Landing in Canada by Year

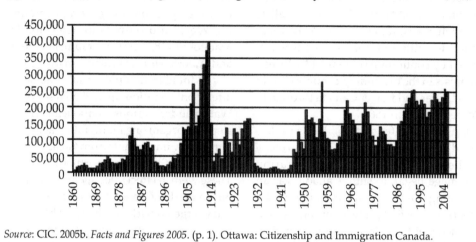

Source: CIC. 2005b. *Facts and Figures 2005*. (p. 1). Ottawa: Citizenship and Immigration Canada.

Canada believed that only Europeans were likely to be successful farmers. At the same time, he was acknowledging that since the 1870s, Canada had been admitting immigrants from diverse countries and ethnic backgrounds who had no familiarity with Canada's official languages. Those admitted included Icelanders, Jews, Hungarians, Mennonites, and Ukrainians. Chinese were also admitted freely between 1870 and 1885, but then increasingly restricted and barred from 1885 onward through a series of head taxes. The image of Canada as a European (not just British) nation in the Americas was firmly established at the core of the national dream, and remained there until the White Canada policies ended in 1962.

Within this long period of national development up to 1962, non-Europeans were largely excluded. In addition to a series of government acts to prohibit Chinese immigration, Canada passed the Act of Direct Passage to cut off immigration from India. Box 3.2 provides a brief summary of the Act and the tragic case of the voyage of the *Komagata Maru* in 1914. In a less known history, various categories of European immigrants also became unwelcome in the 1920s and 1930s for ethnic

and/or political reasons. Like the exclusions of non-Europeans, the exclusions and deportations of Europeans clarify the past and illuminate the present.

The 1919 Immigration Act: New Exclusions, Old Attitudes

After the end of the First World War, Canada brought in a new immigration act and several related Orders in Council to address the aftermath of the war. The main provisions were to exclude the immigration of individuals who were or had been enemy aliens. An additional provision was to exclude Doukhobors, Mennonites, and Hutterites on the grounds that their "peculiar customs, habits, modes of life and methods of holding property" made them unlikely "to become readily assimilated ... Canadian citizens within a reasonable time after their entry" (1919 Immigration Act: Section 38). In the period that followed, politicians and others actively opposed the immigration of Ukrainians and others from Eastern Europe on the grounds that their admission would lead to the "balkanization" of Canada. This was particularly surprising given that by then, there were some 300,000 Ukrainians in Western Canada (Knowles 1992: 101).

Box 3.2: The Frustrated Voyage of the *Komagata Maru*

In the summer of 1914, the Indian community in Canada met their darkest challenge. Kuldeep Singh, a wealthy Indian businessman, had chartered the *Komagata Maru* and sailed the freighter from Hong Kong to Vancouver. On board were 376 Punjabis, mostly Sikhs who had begun their journey in India. They were on their way to Canada where they hoped to immigrate and start a new life. When the *Komagata Maru* arrived at Vancouver, however, most of the passengers were detained on board. They waited for 2 months while immigration officials and the Indian community fought over their admission to the country.

The Canadian authorities had been alerted and were waiting. According to an immigration law called The Act of Direct Passage, these Indians could not land in Canada. The law stated that Indian immigrants had to come to Canada by continuous passage from India. In those days that was impossible. No steamship lines provided direct service from India to Canada.

The *Komagata Maru* was forced to return. The arrival of an armed Royal Canadian Navy cruiser, *Rainbow*, bolstered the Canadian position and on July 23 the *Komagata Maru* was forced to sail for Calcutta. Upon arrival, it was met by police suspicious of the organizers' intentions. Upon disembarking, shooting broke out and 20 passengers were killed. This tragedy strengthened Indian nationalist feeling, but it did not significantly soften Canadian immigration law. From then on, immigration to Canada from India was reduced to a trickle.

Belle Puri, a broadcast journalist for CBC Television in Vancouver, learned to her surprise while filming an educational documentary for the 75th anniversary of the *Komagata Maru*, that her grandfather, Bagga, had played a heroic role in trying to convince Canadian authorities to allow the immigrants to land. It turned out that he had come to Canada earlier and had left his wife and children behind expecting that they would come later. The fate of the *Komagata Maru* and enforcement of Canadian policy led to him having to wait 17 years for this to happen. Belle's mother is one of Bagga's daughters.

Source: Extract from *Scattering Seeds: The Creation of Canada. Passage from India: The* Komagata Maru. [http://www.whitepinepictures.com/seeds/i/10/sidebar.html]

Throughout this period there was renewed interest in "courting British immigrants" with promises of very inexpensive ocean-crossing fares (Knowles 1992: 101).

The 1930s Depression: Deportations and Exclusions

With the onset of the Depression, the rather substantial recovery in Canadian immigration after the First World War was cut short (Figure 3.1). The Depression brought misery, low wages, and high unemployment. Many survived only through odd jobs and charity. Immigrants were feared because they could compete for scarce jobs. In addition to closing down immigration to a mere trickle of special-case agriculturalists with enough capital to start their own farms, the state began to deport large number of unemployed immigrants. Often immigrants were the last hired, hence the first to be laid off. To avoid adding unemployed immigrants to the growing pool of individuals on welfare, they were told to return to their home countries. By 1935 more than 28,000 immigrants had been deported. At the same time, the reasons for deportation expanded to cover political activity that the state viewed as undesirable or dangerous. Immigrants involved in union activity or who belonged to the Communist Party were targeted for deportation.

The Second World War: New Exclusions and Internments

As the war loomed on the horizon, thousands of Jews fleeing Nazi Germany sought refuge in Canada, but only a few, around 5,000 in total, were admitted. In their book *None Is Too Many,* Abella and Troper (1982) indicate that the immigration of Jews to Canada was cut off in the 1920s through to 1945 largely for reasons of anti-Semitism, although this was never stated officially. The official reasons included shortages of jobs and, later, wartime security. Abella and Troper observe that anti-Semitism was widespread in Canada, yet responsibility for its effect on public policy must be placed on leading politicians, teachers, and members of the clergy who supported this direction. When the war itself began, state officials with public support began to "intern" (put in isolated camps) Canadians of Japanese origin on the grounds that they constituted a security threat. By the end of the war, 17,000 Italian Canadians had also been interned. Accounts of the period indicate that these actions were preceded by widespread public fear promoted by political leaders. Many years later, both the ethnic Japanese and Italian Canadians sought apologies from the government.

The exclusions, deportations, and internments that took place over the 1920s to the end of the Second World War reflected the anti-immigrant and ethnic prejudice of the times interacting with the real economic and political threats arising from the Depression and the war. If so, what happened is old history and not relevant

to today, except as a reference to what we want to avoid. However, if some of the same or related prejudices are still present, although more hidden, then the way the world is unfolding provides no lack of stresses that could trigger their reappearance. The problems that Muslims in Canada faced in the post-9/11 era comes to mind as an indication that ethnic prejudice and stressful events can still mobilize hostility toward minorities.

From the End of the Second World War to the Present, 1945 Onward

The postwar period brought an economic boom and the resumption of immigration following the approach in effect prior to the Depression. As before, Canadian immigration policy was constructed around an image of Canada as a European nation in the Americas. However, there had been one important change. When this imagined future first emerged following the first Immigration Act of 1869, it was clear that the state was thinking primarily of an agricultural nation. The focus was on bringing in farmers to settle the West. Then this focus changed dramatically in several steps.

1. By the 1920s, as Canada continued with industrialization policies based on tariffs on industrial imports, it began to see itself increasingly as a manufacturing nation as well as a farming nation.
2. By the 1950s, the imagined future of the nation had moved toward a dominant focus on industrial development. By the end of the 1950s, Canada was particularly concerned about its inability to attract sufficient numbers of more skilled workers suitable for construction, factory

work, and other jobs required for its industrial and urban development.

3. By the early 1960s, the declining number of European immigrants with desired skills was an important factor, along with rising anti-racist sentiment, in the state's decision to change its immigration strategies by abandoning the White Canada policy. Canada was, from 1962 onward, imagined as a multicultural industrial nation in the Americas. Official multicultural policies were adopted later, in 1971 and again in 1988.

4. After 1989, the imagined future changed again. Being a nation in the Americas was still important, but it was increasingly understood that the Americas were part of a global economy and a transnational world. Immigration policies increasingly focused on attracting highly skilled immigrants. Migrant worker programs brought in larger and larger numbers of workers for unskilled work and for short-term skilled work. The new imagined future for Canada, evident in state policy documents, was that of a sophisticated, multicultural niche-player in the global economy.

Discussion and Conclusions

The different imagined futures observed over the period after the Second World War add to those that were observed for earlier periods. Table 3.1 shows the full list of imagined futures that extend from early settlement to the present. Each imagined future is associated with its own cluster of nation-building goals and strategies, including those related to immigration and settlement. Table 3.1 sets forth a conceptual framework for orienting the analysis in this book. In effect, it fleshes out the political economy framework we began with (in Chapter 2) by putting forward observations and hypotheses on how Canada, as an outward-looking nation, has organized its trade, immigration, and cultural strategies as packages intended to address particular challenges and opportunities in different historical periods. The external challenges and opportunities keep changing, as do Canada's internal resources to respond to them. The result is that Canadian immigration policies continue to change over time, even though it is not always clear at each stage what the next step will be or when it will come. The relationship between immigration and other aspects of nation-building is not mechanical and tight; rather, it is flexible and loose, with a tendency for Canada's package of nation-building policies in any given period to become more coherent over time until the package shifts in a different direction and the policy reformulation process begins all over.

Table 3.1 also offers a way of applying and understanding the transnational migration systems approach to Canada specifically. It draws attention to the way that Canada shifts its trade, immigration, and cultural policies in response to shifting external circumstances and opportunities. However, Table 3.1 still leaves many questions unanswered. It does not tell us whether the strategies bring about desired results. Are immigrants offered jobs that increase productivity, exports, and wealth in Canada? Are their earnings good so that they have residential choice and do not all end up in low-rent ethnic ghettoes? What kind of attachments and identities do they form? The model does not answer these questions. It only points to the normative expectations of the state, expressed here in constructs of imagined futures. The remaining chapters examine,

Table 3.1: Canadian Immigration: An Imagined Futures Framework

Period	Imagined Future	Related Nation-Building Policies
Early Settlement: 1497–1763	New France as a French colony; no clear future national image	• Settlement by and from mother country for resource extraction • Mother country imposes tariffs on trade to colonies • Difficult to attract settlers • Some Black and Native slave labour • Settlements grow through high natural reproduction
Quebec: 1763–1947	A French-speaking ethnic nation within Canada	• Trade and commerce dominated by the British • Few immigrants from France • Some immigrants from Britain and elsewhere • High population growth based on natural increase • Church and language promote an inward focus • Francophone majority have a strong collective ethnic-national identity
Canada: 1867–1962	A European nation in the Americas: At first, only an agricultural nation; later one with industrial self-sufficiency as well	• Trade is within the North Atlantic economy (centred on Europe and North America) • Some tariffs to stimulate industrial import substitution • Large-scale settlement by Europeans • Asians admitted as low-wage workers, but discouraged from settling
Sub-period: Canada, 1930s	As above	• Trade shuts down • Immigration shuts down and unemployed immigrants are deported • Tiny flows of immigrants with farm capital • Racialized exclusions of asylum seekers
Sub-period: Canada, 1947–1962	A European industrializing nation in the Americas	• Trade resumes • Import/substitution/industrialization and the expansion of the Canadian branch-plant economy foster an economic boom (up to 1957) • Large inflows of European immigrants resume • Europe begins to dry up as a source of immigration at the end of this period • Anti-racist sentiments gain strength

Sub-period: Canada, 1962–1988	A multicultural industrializing nation in the Americas	• Trade continues with focus on the United States and continental markets • End of White Canada immigration policies • Canada becomes officially multicultural • Focus on selecting immigrants for their job skills • Family-class immigration is a high priority • Refugee policy emerges • Foreign worker programs developed
Sub-period: Canada, 1989 to the present	A sophisticated multicultural global-trading nation	• Trade protections are reduced; Canada becomes a global trader, although most trade is with the U.S. • Policy shift toward highly skilled immigrants • Canadian economy moves toward post-industrial development and knowledge workers • Family class is downscaled • Migrant worker programs expand • State seeks to limit inflows of refugee claimants, and is partially successful • New priority is given to border controls and security issues in a post-9/11 climate
Quebec: 1947 to the present	Follows the stages for Canada as a whole	• Shows much the same nation-building policies as Canada at each stage, with the exception that it is building a French-speaking nation within Canada around "interculturalism," which is arguably somewhat different from "multiculturalism"

where possible, the degree to which the imagined futures correspond to findings from empirical research.

The abridged and stylized history of Canadian immigration from early colonization to the present in this chapter provides a general overview of the historical perspective developed in this book. The next chapter examines in greater detail the period from the end of the Second World War to the present, with particular attention to the emergence of nation-building and immigration strategies that came into effect around or shortly after 1989 and that remain in effect. Other chapters in the book retain a historical perspective as a backdrop to analyses of contemporary issues from the 1990s to the present.

CHAPTER 4

From the End of White Canada to Designer Immigrants

Introduction

The three most fundamental changes in immigration policy between the end of the Second World War and the first years of the current millennium were: (1) the decision to resume large-scale immigration in 1947 and to maintain this pattern to the present; (2) the decision to terminate White Canada immigration rules in 1962 and to later implement anti-racism and multicultural policies to consolidate this move; and (3) the decision to implement skill-selection procedures for immigrants in 1967 and to change admission rules since the early 1990s to emphasize highly skilled immigrant knowledge workers, entrepreneurs, and investors. These three decisions, individually and together, had a profound impact on the kind of nation Canada has become. They are the current bedrock of contemporary immigration policy. This chapter examines these major policy developments to better understand why and how they came about. Particular attention is given to the political process through which the policy decisions were made. The factors that shaped past policy decisions may give us insights into the forces that will shape future immigration strategies.

The analysis of immigration policies in this chapter is based on the imagined futures nation-building perspective developed in the previous chapters. This approach draws attention to the packages of nation-building policies that Canada has put together in the areas of economic development, trade, immigration, and ethnocultural relations. In this chapter we examine the debates among political actors over the kinds of policies that should be adopted and why. The intention is to show that the process is fraught with conflict over differing points of view. The debates take place not only in Canada, but externally with other countries and in international agencies. The exchanges concern matters of tariffs on imports, free trade, anti-racism, the kinds of selection procedures to be used in immigration, and the possibility of multiculturalism. Decisions taken on policies in one area are not always congruent with decisions in other areas. In some cases, pressure from powerful nations pushes Canada in a particular direction and makes it hard to pursue other options. The main argument of this chapter is that the policies in question generally drift toward greater internal coherence over longer time periods of 10–15 years. This is a political-economic approach, but it considers cultural issues as well. The analysis that follows is focused particularly on the centrality of trade and immigration strategies among the various policies that come together to form nation-building packages.

The chapter is organized in four parts. The first part provides an overview of changes in Canada's trade strategies over time. It covers a longer time period, going back to the late 1880s and extending to the present, and examines how immigration policy affected trade options and vice versa. Each of the next three parts examines one of the key contemporary policy decisions of concern: resuming large-scale immigration, ending White Canada policies, and selecting highly skilled knowledge workers. The decisions are examined in terms of how policy-makers understood the challenges requiring such decisions. A final section provides overall conclusions.

Trade and International Migration

Trade policy is a core element in the nation-building framework. It is closely linked to national economic policies with respect to commodity production, transportation systems to move trade goods, and industrial-manufacturing strategies. It is therefore a shorthand way of understanding how many economic policies fit together. Similarly, immigrant workers constitute a major focus in immigration policy, even though they constitute only one class of immigrants. By analyzing the relationship between trade strategy and the demand for immigrant workers, we address a core dimension of Canadian nation-building. This core dimension permits us to first narrow the focus, then add other aspects, such as ethnocultural policies, later.

From 1867 to 1914, Canada moved from being a colonial dependency to becoming recognized as an independent nation. Its main export opportunities were its staples or commodities: grains, meat, fish, lumber, and minerals, all of which were potentially abundant in its resource-rich territory. Over time, with the growth of manufacturing and services in Canada, national export dependency on commodities has declined. However, commodities continue to play a key role in trade. As recently as December 2008, exports of agricultural goods, fish, energy products (coal, petroleum, gas), and forestry products constituted 38 percent of the total value of Canadian export trade that month (Statistics Canada 2008a).

From a very early point in its history, Canada realized that being dependent on commodity exports alone did not generate all the benefits that the nation was seeking. The examples of Europe and the United States made it clear that industrial development was the key to wealth and geopolitical influence. The challenge for

Canada was how to get industrial development underway. Wealthy foreign nations already had a big head start in producing manufactured goods. Manufacturing plants in Europe and the United States were large, their production was headed to big domestic and international markets, and their labour costs were lower per item produced (Hart 2002). Canadian firms, being smaller and serving smaller markets, were less efficient, and produced goods that were more expensive than the equivalent imported items. For these reasons, Canada turned early in its history to mimic what other nations were doing. Specifically, Canada placed tariffs or customs duties on imported manufactured goods. Canadian consumers of imported goods would have to pay whatever the item would cost in the country where it was produced, plus freight, plus the customs duties. With the tariffs in place, Canadian manufacturing plants were more likely to be able to produce and sell their goods in Canada. However, Canadian goods produced under tariff protection would generally be too expensive to be sold through exports to other countries, at least to begin with. The long-term hope was that Canadian manufacturing capability and productivity would eventually build up under tariff protection to the point that custom duties would no longer be required, at which point Canada could export manufactured goods to other countries.

Canada began to place tariffs on most manufactured goods in 1879 as part of the so-called National Policy introduced by John A. Macdonald's Conservative Party at that time (Eden and Molot 1993). The National Policy lowered tariffs on the import of raw materials on the grounds that access to low-cost raw materials that were not available in Canada would benefit Canadian manufacturers. As is the case for most of the policy issues we will be examining, right from the beginning

there was considerable debate in Canada on what would be the best trade policy. Initially, the Liberal Party opposed the National Policy on the grounds that it was inefficient and would lead to high prices for manufactured goods in Canada. The Liberals felt that free trade—that is, trade with very low or no tariffs—with the United States would be a far better option. Continental free trade would create large markets for both Canadian and American manufacturers. This would promote competition, efficiency, and industrial growth in both countries. However, there was a major problem with the Liberal proposal. The United States had erected tariffs to protect its own manufacturing industries, and was not interested in free trade at that time (Hart 2002).

The Liberals realized that free trade with the United States, whatever its assumed advantages, was out of the question. It also became clear to the Liberals that the National Policy was very attractive to manufacturers who were located in the populous provinces of Quebec and Ontario. The National Policy was also popular with workers in the growing manufacturing plants in these locations and, by extension, with a wider range of voters whose incomes and work were tied to the expanding industrial production in their communities. The Liberals dropped their opposition to the National Policy in 1886 and won the federal election that year. They then went back to a free trade platform in 1911, and lost the election at that time. In consequence, the Liberals finally returned to supporting the National Policy originally brought forward by the Conservatives. The National Policy then remained in operation for a long period. It began to be dismantled in steps, first with rising continental trade in the 1950s, then with the Canada–U.S. Auto Pact in 1965, and finally and definitively with the signing of two free trade accords in the late

1980s. The two free trade accords were the Canada–United States Trade Agreement (CUSTA), signed in 1988 and implemented the following year, and the North American Free Trade Agreement (NAFTA), signed in 1992 and implemented in 1994.

The debates over these many years are often framed in terms of choices between two contrasting trade strategies. The first strategy is referred to as "import substitution industrialization" or ISI. The National Policy described above is an ISI approach. The goal of ISI is to protect national industries through a mix of tariffs on imported goods, state subsidies, and price controls. Protected industries are expected to grow, provide employment, and replace the need for foreign imports of manufactured goods. The second strategy is referred to as free trade. It concerns the elimination of tariffs, price controls, and other policies that make imports relatively more costly than they otherwise would be. Both these strategies lead to many questions about the conditions required for them to work and who benefits most from them. They have different implications for immigration policies. A number of important issues in debate and some related challenges for the effectiveness of each of these trade policies are summarized below.

Issues with Respect to Import Substitution Industrialization (ISI)

First, there is the issue of generating sufficient income so that Canadians would be able to pay higher prices for goods produced under ISI and at the same time have funds to pay for imported goods that are not produced in Canada. The National Policy assumed that they could do so by being highly efficient commodity exporters. By producing commodities efficiently at low prices, Canada would be assured of foreign sales of these goods and incomes that would allow them to purchase higher in an ISI framework. Right from the begin-

ning, John A. Macdonald's National Policy was linked to investments in the transnational railway system, from coast to coast, and port facilities to promote the efficiency of commodity exports. Of course, the system did not always work this way, and Canada suffered economically in periods when the demand and prices for its commodity exports fell.

Second, there is the issue of the number and skills of workers. Who is going to produce the commodities, build the transportation systems cheaply and well, and work in the factories producing manufactured good for domestic sale? Canada had a high birth rate and experienced rapid natural population growth from Confederation through to the early 1960s (see Chapter 10). However, it was also clear that immigration could play an important supplementary role in nation-building projects being pursued by economic and political elites. This was particularly true during the late 1800s and early 1900s when Canada wanted to settle the Western provinces and tap their vast potential for producing grains, meat, lumber, and minerals. The main demand in that period was for immigrant farmers and agricultural workers (see Chapter 3). Later, in the immediate post-Second World War period, the demand shifted to skilled construction, industrial, and other immigrant workers suitable for a manufacturing economy. Most recently, since 1989, it has shifted to highly skilled immigrant knowledge workers to promote efficiency in a trade-competitive world. In all cases, governments have concluded that it is attractive to admit relatively large numbers of immigrant workers with the required skills in order to strengthen the national labour force.

Third, there is the issue of ethnocultural policy. Until the 1960s, Canada viewed itself as a European nation located in the Americas. This view was abandoned in 1962 and Canadian immigration became open to individuals from all national and ethnocultural backgrounds for three reasons: (1) rising anti-racism in Canada and in the world at large; (2) shifting Canadian geopolitical aspirations on the world stage that required it to drop racist practices; and (3) a high demand for skilled workers in a context where the kind desired were no longer available in sufficient supply from Europe or nations settled by Europeans. It is difficult to say which of these three reasons was most important as all came together at the same time and all contributed to the decision to abandon White Canada immigration rules. Once the shift took place, it went hand in hand with the recognition that Canada's future was no longer that of a European nation in North America. It was becoming a multicultural nation in North America.

Fourth, there is the issue of who owns the manufacturing plants that develop in the context of tariff protections. This has been, from time to time, an important political issue related to contrasting future images of the nation. Reviews of the impact of the National Policy suggest that it had a mix of impacts. To begin with, the National Policy tended to promote the development of a branch-plant economy in Canada. Large foreign firms saw the Canadian tariff wall as an opportunity to respond by building branch plants within Canada. By setting up a branch plant in Canada, these firms could avoid paying tariffs on goods they produced for the Canadian market. At the same time, they could make good profits from the generally higher prices that Canadian consumers were paying for goods produced in Canada. In addition, the firms could maintain other large plants elsewhere and coordinate technology and management across nations to increase their productivity, markets, and profits. The result was the expansion of international corporations, mostly companies based in the United States, into Canada in various key manufacturing areas: pulp and paper, mining and smelting, automotive production, large appliance manufacturing, chemical and plastics manufacturing, and so on. The names of these international firms haven't changed that much: Ford and General Motors, Dupont, Westinghouse, General Electric, and so on.

By the 1960s, the continuing branch-plant trend sparked a nationalist reaction in Canada. This was evident in policies developed by the Liberal government of Lester Pearson and Pierre Elliott Trudeau. Two policies put into effect by Trudeau's government were particularly controversial. One was the Foreign Investment Review Agency (FIRA), which was created to limit foreign firms' ability to take over control of Canadian firms. The other was the National Energy Program (NEP), which favoured Canadians and Canadian manufacturing firms by keeping the prices of petroleum products (gasoline, heating oil, gas for electricity production transferred via pipelines, etc.) low. The NEP (1980–1985) was met with enormous hostility in Alberta because it meant lower prices for Alberta-produced petroleum products. The NEP and the FIRA (1974–1984) met with strong opposition from the United States: FIRA limited the foreign investment opportunities of U.S. investors, while the NEP disadvantaged U.S. manufacturers wishing to export to Canada. In the end these nationalist economic policies were dropped due to a mix of domestic and international opposition. The signing of the Canada–United States Free Trade Agreement in 1988 and NAFTA in 1989 marked the definitive end of the prior ISI strategies and the beginning of the free trade era in Canada. Debates on the merits of ISI or similar strategies relative to free trade have not disappeared. They continue, for example, in the form of critical reviews of the impact of "deep integration" of the smaller Canadian economy within the much larger U.S. economy and its implications for Canadian sovereignty and the welfare of Canadian workers (Grinspun and Shamsie 2007).

Issues with Respect to Free Trade

Contemporary economic globalization in the form of free trade is associated nearly everywhere with tight rules, controls, and limitations on international migration. This has been and remains the situation in Canada. Free trade, combined with controlled immigration since 1989, raises the following issues among others.

One issue is what to do if the kinds of immigrants desired are not available due to competition for their labour from other countries, including the home countries of potential immigrants. Canada faced such a situation in the late 1950s with respect to European immigrants. Workers in Europe with desired skills were increasingly inclined to remain in Europe due to rising living standards and wages there as the postwar recovery took place. Canada's response to the shortfall in skilled European immigrants was to look for skilled immigrants in other countries. This was not the only reason for the end of White Canada immigration rules, but it was an important one.

Another issue is what to do if native-born residents do not like or accept new immigrants and vice versa. The challenge of ethnocentric and racist hostility between groups is, unfortunately, all too common in the world. However, the extent of it also varies from one nation to another. In the 1960s and since, Canadian policy-makers have assumed that immigration from around the world would be acceptable to Canadians. They believed that this would be the case due to rising anti-racist sentiments in Canada and the possibility that skilled immigrants, whatever their national or ethnic background, would be viewed as making economic and cultural contribu-

tions. This gamble had various components. A selection process would help to make sure that the immigrants entering Canada had job skills that fit with job needs in an industrializing Canada. In addition, multicultural and anti-discrimination policies would help. However, elements of risk remain. What if the immigrants from new origin countries come with training and experience that are so different that they have difficulty finding good jobs? Will the Canadian state embark on a strong program to support retraining and accreditation in Canada? These questions relate to possible future developments, and are considered in the concluding chapter of this book.

Another issue is whether it is more advantageous to export jobs than to attract, select, and admit immigrants. Nations can pursue economic growth either by exporting jobs (that is, sending investments and productive capacity abroad, then importing the goods) or importing workers (immigrants and migrant workers). Economic growth can also come about through investments in labour-saving technology and more skilled workers, so that fewer workers can make more goods. Canada allows firms to export jobs, while at the same time the state selects immigrants to fill jobs that remain or are being created in Canada. It also supports investments in productivity and training. It is widely understood that many wealthy nations have immigration policies, visa worker policies, and strategies for supporting investments in productive machinery and training, yet it is not so well understood that these same nations also have job-export policies. This is because job-export policies are indirect outcomes of free trade policies and are therefore not normally examined within immigration and productivity frameworks. Box 4.1 explains why this is often the case.

Box 4.1: Job Export Policies Are Hidden within Free Trade Policies

North American automotive firms have been struggling over recent years to compete against Japanese and other foreign companies. Periodically their struggle leads to downsizing production in Canada and moving the factories and jobs to other countries where wages are lower. For example, in June 2008, General Motors announced that it would shut down one of its main Canadian factories, lay off more than 1,000 workers, and move the production and jobs to Mexico. The front-page press coverage of this decision mentioned the anger of the workers and the frustration of government officials who had provided tax breaks and other subsidies in an effort to keep the factory open. The press reports did not mention the fact that Canadian state policy contributed to the closing of the factory and the loss of jobs. Without trade rules that Canada had agreed to, the General Motors job exports would not have been as easy.

The rules of the North American Free Trade Agreement (NAFTA), jointly implemented by Canada, Mexico, and the United States in 1994, allow for the free trade of manufactured goods, including automobile parts and vehicles, among these three countries. Firms that want to relocate from Canada to the United States or to Mexico in order to reduce costs can do so without risking access to the Canadian market. While Canadian governments have supported NAFTA for the many benefits it brings, they are unhappy to see well-paid, skilled jobs, such as those in technologically advanced Canadian automotive plants, going south. In other cases, while the government bemoans the loss of jobs when factories close, the state may be secretly happy to see the jobs disappear in some cases, such as when the jobs involve low-wage employment in an inefficient industry. When the low-wage jobs are lost, the state hopes that the unemployed workers will be motivated to upgrade their skills and find work in more productive, higher-wage jobs. The justification for free trade and other forms of trade liberalization is to promote the export of low-wage jobs and the creation of high-wage jobs. These goals are often difficult to realize in practice.

An additional issue is why a nation should pursue immigration at all if other options—such as mechanization, exporting workers, or using migrant workers—can achieve the equivalent economic objectives. Following my previous reflections on this question (Simmons 1999b), I argue that the immigration option is chosen when it is particularly attractive to financial capital and can be pursued at relatively low political-economic costs, including low public opposition. The benefits of immigration are high and the costs of immigration are low under free trade when immigrants:

- are self-financing and pay for their own travel and settlement,
- come with work skills, business experience, and capital that make the host nation's economy more efficient and more competitive with respect to trade,
- fill gaps in the labour force, and sustain profits and new investments,
- are viewed favourably by the host society because the work that immigrants do and the cultures they bring with them are perceived to be positive contributions,

- add to the supply of skilled labour and hence give employers easy access to the skilled or highly skilled workers needed, while reducing upward pressure on wages,
- enter into peaceful relations with others in the host society groups.

The preceding observations can be summarized in the form of a revised and expanded framework covering the recent historical periods of nation-building in Canada. This framework is shown in Table 4.1. It draws attention to the three main decisions that shape current immigration policies. Each decision is understood to be embedded in a policy matrix covering both trade and immigration strategies. The immigration policy decisions are shown as arising in response to shifts in external trade circumstances and/or in responses to external circumstances affecting the supply and national/ethnic origins of immigrants.

Further below in the analysis of the dates and content of specific trade and

Table 4.1: Evolution of Postwar Nation-Building Strategies and Immigration Policies

	1945–1961	1962–1988	1989–
Imagined Future	European industrializing nation in the Americas	Multicultural industrializing nation in the Americas	Multicultural global trader in the international system
Main Transition Decisions	Decision taken in 1945–47 to resume large-scale immigration	Decision taken in 1962–67 to end White Canada policies	Decisions culminating in 1989 to end ISI policies
Nation-Building Policy Package			
1. Trade policies	Classical ISI	ISI plus continentalism	Global trade competition
2. Immigration levels	High/variable	High/variable	High/stable
3. Immigrant skills sought	Industrial workers	Industrial workers Entrepreneurs	Knowledge workers Entrepreneurs Investors
4. Immigrant sources	Europe	Global	Global
5. Ethnocultural policies	Eurocentric and racist	Multicultural and anti-racist	Multicultural and anti-racist
6. Migrant worker policies		Emerging for live-in caregivers and farm workers	Migrant worker programs expand into many other fields
7. Emphasis on productivity	Rising	Rising further	Very high priority

immigration policy initiatives, it will be apparent that trade and immigration policies do not develop in lockstep with each other. Rather, their relationship is loose, spread over time, and in partial adjustment to one another. The Canadian state may plan its imagined futures in complete pictures, but the policies that are to contribute the hoped-for outcomes develop in smaller pieces at different times. The pieces tend to line up with one another within three different historical periods covering about 15 years each within the postwar era.

Various nation-building policies are put in place by political actors who assess circumstances and come to conclusions based on some combination of their ideology and their perception of opportunities and constraints. Insofar as we can understand the viewpoints and perceptions of key political actors, we can better understand the policies they promoted. The points below examine some notable features of the debates that led to the resumption of large-scale immigration after the Second World War, the end of White Canada policies, and the shift to "designer immigrant" policies. These three developments are among the main policies shaping contemporary Canadian immigration.

1. The Resumption of Large-Scale Immigration, 1947

When the war ended in 1945, the national mood was still deeply uncertain about setting off on new immigration ventures. High levels of unemployment and hostility to immigrants during the Depression had shaken the confidence of Canadian leaders and the public regarding the merits of immigration. Public opinion was divided. The Canadian Congress of Labour expressed the view that immigration in the years before 1914 had been poorly planned and should not be used as a model for the future. It argued that: "We cannot afford to expose Canadian workers to the constant threat of having their standards undercut by immigrants who must take any kind of job ... to avoid sheer starvation" (cited by Knowles 1992: 119). Refugee issues were a concern, but even in this area Canada was cautious, with the result that humanitarian steps were modest and sometimes recast in self-serving terms. For example, in 1946 Canada decreed that orphaned nieces and nephews under 16 years of age could be admitted from Europe if their aunts and uncles in Canada were willing to sponsor their entry (Knowles 1992: 122). About the same time, Britain asked for Canada's help in resettling some 3,000 Polish Free Army Veterans who had fought with the British forces and who refused to go home after Poland's occupation by the Soviet Union. Canada initially resisted this proposal, but later Canada agreed to admit approximately 3,000 Polish soldiers. These soldiers were admitted only after Britain agreed to pay for their transport and the Polish soldiers agreed to work as agricultural labourers in Canada for 12 months after arrival in order to help alleviate a postwar labour shortage. Knowles (1992: 123) reports that most of the Polish workers served their one year of farm work and then moved immediately to Canadian cities. These narrow changes to Canadian immigration policy were consistent with the fact that Canada was still in an anti-immigration mindset arising from the high unemployment levels of the 1930s.

While hesitancy about immigration persisted, changes pointing to the opportunities and advantages of renewed mass immigration were building. The Senate Committee on Immigration and Labour, which was established in 1946 and remained in operation until 1953, consulted with the Canadian business community and came to the conclusion early in its deliberations that immigrants should be admitted in large numbers starting immediately in order to rekindle Canadian economic expansion. An unstated but major assumption in this view was that world demand for Canadian commodities was high, and that Canada was well placed to continue its industrialization through ISI policies and growing trade in manufactured goods with the United States.

In May 1947, Prime Minister Mackenzie King declared to the House of Commons that: "The policy of the government is to foster the growth of the population of Canada by the encouragement to immigration." His speech then went on to add a series of qualifications to gain public support and to respond to those who were critical of immigration. He first made clear that the government "will seek by legislation, regulation and vigorous administration, to ensure the careful selection and permanent settlement of such numbers of immigrants as can be advantageously absorbed in our national economy" (Hawkins 1988: 91). This became known as the principle of "absorptive capacity," a concept that has remained embedded in immigration policy to the present time. The concept of "careful selection" was also linked to economic development. Clearly, the goal of immigration was to improve the Canadian standard of living. Mackenzie King made it crystal clear that Canada would remain a White European nation in the Americas. He stated that the government would remain opposed to "large-scale immigration from the Orient." In rejecting the views of the critics of immigration, he set in place a return to large-scale immigration modelled after the period 1885–1914. In seeking public support, he made clear that the goals would be economic, that those admitted would be largely Europeans, and that careful selection and total numbers of immigrants admitted would not exceed absorptive capacity. These principles and various Orders in Council from 1947

to 1952 were incorporated in the 1952 Immigration Act.

With investments flowing into a resource-rich and industrializing Canada, new jobs opening up at a rapid pace, and a large inflow of European immigrants who were happy to leave war-torn and still economically recovering home countries, Canada underwent a postwar economic boom. The boom was centred on resource exports (grains, lumber, and minerals) and growing industrial production (of cars, major appliances, all kinds of consumer goods) for consumption in Canada and for export. Most exports of both commodity and manufactured goods went to the United States due to the increasing interdependence of the economies of these two nations within an emerging North American (U.S. and Canada) continental market.

End of White Canada Policies, 1962–1967

During the boom years there was little questioning of the direction of Canadian trade or immigration policies. However, in 1957 investments began to taper off and unemployment began to rise in what was felt to be a more serious economic dip than had been experienced previously in the boom years. Economic growth and recession cycles have been a standard feature of Canadian economic change. Recessions typically give rise to questions about what can be done to improve the strength of the Canadian economy. Some questions of this kind began to focus directly on Canadian immigration. State officials observed that unemployment was concentrated among less skilled workers. Within this observation, they noted specific concerns, such as the fact that immigration of more skilled workers from the northern parts of Italy was declining. In contrast, immigration of less skilled workers from the southern parts of Italy had remained high. They further noted that the high inflow from southern Italy was maintained through sponsorship of relatives, rather than through screening by immigration officers. This led the government to change the provisions of family sponsorship by tightening who could enter through this channel. Only immediate family members could be sponsored. There was an instant outcry from the Italian community. Policy-makers were in a quandary. They could slow the inflow of less skilled immigrants by changing family sponsorship provisions, but how would they ensure a good supply of better-skilled applicants?

By the late 1950s Europe had recovered from the devastation of the war. Wages were rising and work opportunities were expanding, with the result that Europeans increasingly preferred to remain home. As an indication of the magnitude of the changed circumstances, labour scarcities in Northern Europe were leading to rising demands for immigrants and migrant workers. Workers in Southern Europe were increasingly attracted to Northern Europe rather than to other parts of the world. Canada faced an emerging dilemma. A new supply of skilled workers would have to be found elsewhere. The alternative might lead to a slowdown in its own industrial expansion.

The Canadian state began to think more seriously about the importance of finding skilled immigrant workers for industrial jobs. The 1958–1959 *Annual Report on Immigration* concluded that: "Although total opportunities for foreign labour were down, nevertheless there were still many vacancies for professional, skilled and service workers which could not be filled by Canadians" (cited by Green 1995: 35). The arguments favouring skilled workers and professionals grew stronger over subsequent years and led to various policy measures. Some were to attract "employment-creating" immigration in the form of farmers with capital and other entrepreneurs. Others were to restrict "employment-competing" inflows in the form of unskilled workers who would vie with low-skilled Canadian workers for jobs that were becoming increasingly scarce (Green 1995: 35).

In 1962, Canada abandoned its country-of-origin immigrant selection system that had in the past privileged the entry of British, French, and American citizens and also granted favoured status to other Europeans. By terminating the old policy, Canada opened immigration to individuals with desired work skills from all corners of the world. A few years later, in 1967, Canada adopted a points system to admit economic immigrants on the basis of their job skills, education, and official language abilities (see details in Table 4.2). By adding these new selection procedures, Canada strengthened its ability to attract and select the kinds of immigrants it sought from a very large pool of potential applicants. The 1962 and 1967 policy steps are different, but they can also be viewed as part of a single policy designed to ensure that Canada would have access to large numbers of the kind of skilled immigrants it desired to support industrial expansion.

The new Canadian policies helped to reduce concerns among Canadian leaders and state officials about the nation's potential vulnerability to shortages of professional and skilled workers. Many of these worries focused on the United States as the competitor for skilled immigrants. America, with its larger and wealthier economy, attracted large numbers of skilled European workers and professionals, thereby potentially reducing flows to Canada. In addition, many Canadian skilled workers and professionals had been moving to the United States. Parai (1975) estimated that over the decade beginning in 1953, Canada lost some 41,000 professionals and 38,000 skilled workers to the United States. In the same period Canada gained some 125,000 immigrants, including many professionals, from other countries. These figures made clear to immigration officials that inflows of professionals and skilled workers to Canada had to continue to be large enough to more than cover the losses of similarly skilled Canadians who were emigrating to the United States. However, Canada was not the only nation to wake up to the fact that immigration needed to be changed, both to address anti-racist objectives and labour force demand. In 1965, the United States passed a new Immigration Act that replaced its previous national-origin quotas with a selection system that admitted immigrants with professional and technical skills. Like the Canadian policy, the new U.S. policy was open to individuals from around the world. In 1963, Australia abandoned its Whites-only immigration policy and also began to recruit professional and more skilled immigrants from all world regions. Various nations were facing a widening global competition for skilled and professional immigrants, one that continues to the present. Canada responded to this emerging situation in 1962, somewhat ahead of Australia (1963) and the United States (1965).

The 1962 shift in immigration policy seems to have been part of a set of self-reinforcing changes toward anti-racist practices that were taking place internationally and within Canada at that time. When the end of the White Canada approach was announced, there was no great public outcry or opposition at the time. An inclination to follow the leadership of the state in immigration matters had already developed over many years. Historically, Canadian immigration policy has tended to be top-down, developed by political elites and senior state bureaucrats known as "mandarins" as they seem to have broad authority to propose immigra-

tion solutions, which are then supported by whatever governing party is in power (Hardcastle, Parkin, Simmons, and Suyama 1994). Canadian immigration policy relies on relatively few Acts of Parliament and many Cabinet decisions made behind closed doors on important policy details. This reinforces the public's tendency to often see immigration policy as something that is removed from their influence and put in the hands of state leaders. The fact that neither the public nor Parliament was consulted on the termination of the White Canada policies was consistent with what Canadians had become accustomed to. In her careful history of this transition, Freda Hawkins notes that changes in legislation were merely tabled in the House of Commons by Mrs. Fairclough, the then minister of Immigration, after they had been approved by Cabinet. That is, the House was informed, but had no input into the new policies (Hawkins 1988: 127). After the changes had been introduced, "Mr. Pickersgill, speaking for the Opposition, said that the greatest change in immigration policy since Mackenzie King announced the resumption of immigration in 1947 had gone into effect without approval or even debate in Parliament. He added, "... the real control over immigration has always been at the Cabinet's discretion. The Immigration Act in practice leaves the government free to do almost anything it wants" (House of Commons Debates, cited by Hawkins 1988: 127).

Canadians had been prepared for the end of the White Canada policy by Prime Minister John Diefenbaker's leadership on the Canadian Bill of Rights (Justice Canada 1960). This was Canada's first Bill of Rights, preceding the better known Canadian Human Rights Act of 1977 by nearly 20 years. Diefenbaker (prime minister from 1957 to 1963) had campaigned in 1957 on his support for human rights. Section 1 of the Bill introduced by his government asserts that an impressive list of human rights exists in Canada without "discrimination by reasons of race, national origin, colour, religion or sex." With the passage of this first Bill of Rights, discriminatory features of Canadian immigration policy had immediately become incompatible with non-discriminatory features of Canadian law. While state policies are not always consistent with one another, the Bill of Rights created pressure for a change in immigration policy. The full lead section of the Bill of Rights reads as follows:

> It is hereby recognized and declared that in Canada there have existed and shall continue to exist without discrimination by reason of race, national origin, colour, religion or sex, the following human rights and fundamental freedoms, namely, (a) the right of the individual to life, liberty, security of the person and enjoyment of property, and the right not to be deprived thereof except by due process of law; (b) the right of the individual to equality before the law and the protection of the law; (c) freedom of religion; (d) freedom of speech; (e) freedom of assembly and association; and (f) freedom of the press. (Justice Canada 1960: part 1, p. 1)

The development of anti-racist, anti-sexist policy in Canada took place in an international context that supported these developments. Anti-racist sentiments were gaining strength within the United States. The African-American civil rights movement (1955–1968) was well underway by 1960, and its efforts to overcome racism and expand voting rights among U.S. Blacks had widespread impact in Canada through daily news reports coming across the border. More broadly in the international system, many former British and French colonial states (created in a racist past in Africa, Asia, and the Caribbean) had become independent in the post-Second World War period and had become co-members with Canada in the United Nations and the British Commonwealth. Racism in Canadian immigration policy was increasingly out of place in the emerging world in which Canada aspired to play a more important role. The Canadian International Development Agency (CIDA) was formed in 1968. Canada had been involved in United Nations peacekeeping missions in earlier years (in Israel in 1948 and in the Suez Crisis in Egypt in 1956), and was preparing for a major long-term role in Cyprus (1965–1998). Racism anywhere in Canadian policy was incompatible with Canada's rising aspirations to become a leading nation in international affairs through diplomacy, international development efforts, and peacekeeping.

In sum, the termination of the White Canada immigration policy addressed both domestic economic objectives and international policy goals. In the end the decision was in the hands of a few individuals: Minister of Immigration Mrs. Fairclough, her senior advisers, and the Cabinet. The decision they came to fundamentally altered Canadian immigration and Canada itself. It did more to end racism associated with the old view of Canada as a European nation in the Americas than any other decision Canada has taken, yet, somewhat paradoxically, anti-racism was only one of its goals. Many senior Canadian officials were more concerned with the new policies as a way of promoting immigration of skilled workers for Canadian industrialization. There is little evidence that those who framed the decision to end the national preference system for immigrants had any idea of how quickly this shift in law would transform ethnocultural and transnational features of Canadian society.

The 1967 Points System

The points system, established in 1967, was the centrepiece of a broader set of tools given to immigration officials to permit them to select immigrants according to criteria consistent with Canada's industrialization strategy and related ISI trade policies. Initially, in 1967, the tools given to officials were very simple. They consisted of: (1) several criteria and associated weights (or points) to select workers; (2) additional criteria and procedures to admit close relatives of Canadian residents, including those who had arrived in Canada as immigrants; and (3) the authority to propose admission targets for the number of immigrants to be admitted each year based on a forecast of unemployment. Over time, the overall tool kit for selecting immigrants was expanded. Other categories of immigrants and related admission criteria were added. Table 4.2 shows some of the main additions. Business and investor immigrants were added in the 1970s. Refugees and claimants were also added then or somewhat later. Changes were made over time to the points system and sponsorship rules to tighten the admission of family-class immigrants and to select highly skilled knowledge workers. And, eventually, after 1989, immigration targets were set to meet longer-term objectives and were no longer adjusted annually to reflect year-to-year changes in employment conditions.

Canadian immigration policy has been established in very few legislative acts passed by Parliament. To date there are only five major acts: 1869, 1919, 1952, 1976, and 2001. These acts are occasionally amended, but, generally speaking, they function for long periods by undergoing frequent revisions in the form of Orders in Council passed by the Cabinet. In this way, the Cabinet is able to modify admission criteria, change the weights in the points

system, add new classes of immigrants, and so on. The result is that immigration policy is constantly under review and change. Documenting immigration policy changes in detail and examining the often important implications of each policy change is a huge task and fills large books on the topic, such as those by Green (1976), Hawkins (1988, 1991), and Kelley and Trebilcock (2000). The summary points in Table 4.2 covering the post-Second World War period only are very broad and general. They serve the purpose of providing an understanding of the main drift in policy from the perspective of the tools available to immigration officers. We may summarize these major policy changes as follows.

Immigration selection from 1967 to 1985 sought to reinforce the industrializing economy of that period. Immigrants were selected as workers with specific occupational skills and vocational training on the understanding that they would go to jobs where they were needed. Relatives of immigrants were welcomed in the form of special points for simply having a member of their family living in Canada. If the family member in Canada promised to provide support for his or her relative, then a large number of entry points could be granted to the applicant. This family-friendly policy was pursued for stated reasons and perhaps for unstated ones as well. Family reunification was expressed as a value in state immigration policies. It was a humanitarian consideration. Unstated is the fact that family reunification, nomination, and sponsorship provisions also made Canada more attractive to the kinds of worker-immigrants it wanted. In addition, the total number of skilled workers admitted annually was subject to a tap-on, tap-off adjustment on the basis of projected unemployment figures. This had a kind of factory logic. Factories may employ their managers and engineers for longer-term contracts and keep them employed during

Table 4.2: Evolution of Canadian Points System and Other Policies for Admitting Immigrants

	Prior to 1985	1985	2004
GOALS OF IMMIGRATION			
1. Economic (workers, business class, etc.)	Yes	Yes	Yes
2. Social (family)	Yes	Yes	Yes
3. Humanitarian (refugees)		Yes	Yes
4. Demographic (to address low fertility/ aging)		Yes	
CLASSES OF IMMIGRANTS			
1. Skilled Workers (Selected by Points System):			
Occupation	15	10	0
Vocational preparation	5	15	0
Education	12	12	25
Language skills in English and/or French	10	15	24
Work experience	8	8	21
Prearranged employment	10	10	10
Location: Bonus for settling in areas with few immigrants	5	0	0
Age (bonus for working-age adults)	10	10	10
Personal suitability (assessment by official)	10	10	0
Adaptability (levels control)	0	10	10
Relative in Canada	5	0	0
TOTAL	100	100	100
Pass mark	50	70	67
Bonus for assistance by relatives in Canada	15–30	10	0
OTHER CLASSES AND SUBCLASSES			
2. Dependants of applicant admitted automatically?	Yes	Yes	Yes
3. Family class: Close relatives can be sponsored?	Yes	Yes	Yes
NEW CLASSES (SINCE 1967)			
4. Business class (added in 1978)		Yes	Yes
5. Refugees (added in 1978)		Yes	Yes
6. Investor class (added in 1986)			Yes

7. Refugee claimants via IRB (added in 1989)			Yes
8. Provincial nominees			Yes
9. Canadian experience class (added in 2007)			Yes
FEES FOR APPLICATION AND LANDING (added in 1992)			Yes
ANNUAL TARGETS (stabilized after 1989)	Variable	Variable	Stable/ High

Notes:
- Skilled workers are selected as permanent residents based on their education, work experience, knowledge of English and/or French, and other criteria that have been shown to help them become economically established in Canada. These criteria are shown in the points system, above. Skilled workers require proof that they have savings that are theirs, not borrowed, of $10,833 for a single applicant, or $20,130 for a family of four. These 2009 figures are subject to change.
- *Family class:* A Canadian citizen or a permanent resident of Canada can sponsor a spouse, common-law partner, conjugal partner, dependent child (including adopted child), or other eligible relative (such as a parent or grandparent) to become a permanent resident. Most often spouses and dependent children are admitted automatically with an applicant in another class if they are travelling together. However, they and other close (but not immediate) family can come later in the family class.
- Entrepreneurs must have at least two years of business experience and a net worth of at least Can. $300,000 that was obtained legally, obtain a minimum of 35 points in a selection grid designed to determine ability to become economically established in Canada, and make a commitment to own and operate a business in Canada that will contribute to the economy and create jobs.
- Investors must show that they have business experience, have a minimum net worth of Can. $800,000 that was obtained legally, and make a Can. $400,000 investment.
- Refugees must meet the Convention Refugee criteria established by the United Nations Convention on the Refugees or Designated Class criteria established by the Canadian government.
- Refugee claimants must meet the "Refugee" criteria described above or meet other criteria that are used by the Immigration and Refugee Board.
- Provincial nominees must be nominated by a Canadian province or territory.
- *Canadian experience class:* This is open to (1) a temporary foreign worker with at least two years of full-time (or equivalent) skilled work experience in Canada, or (2) a foreign graduate from a Canadian post-secondary institution with at least one year of full-time (or equivalent) skilled work experience in Canada. In both cases the applicant must have gained experience in Canada with the proper work or study authorization and apply while working in Canada, or within one year of leaving his or her job in Canada. Skilled work experience means: Skill Type "O" (managerial occupations) or Skill Level "A" (professional occupations) or Skill Level "B" (technical occupations and skilled trades). Applicants are judged on work experience and ability in English or French.
- *Fees:* All immigrants pay a $490 fee on landing after they have been approved and arrive in Canada. When they apply, they pay application fees that vary by class and are different for the principal applicant and dependants. For example, a skilled immigrant pays $475 for his or her own individual application, $550 for a dependent spouse, and $150 for each child. The application fees for a family of four would be $1,325. The total landing fees would be $1,560, for a final total of $2,885. Entrepreneurs and investors pay higher fees. These 2009 figures are subject to change.

Sources: For the points system up to and including 1985: EIC. 1985. *The Revised Selection Criteria for Independent Immigrants.* Ottawa: Employment and Immigration Canada, WH-5-086.
   For the current points system, definitions of different classes of immigrants, and fees: CIC. 2009. *Immigrating to Canada.* [http://www.cic.gc.ca/english/immigrate/index.asp]

downturns, but they lay off the factory-floor workers when they are not required. In this case, immigration officials were trying to anticipate the unemployment levels of Canadian workers on a year-by-year basis, and adjust immigration levels of the upcoming year correspondingly.

From 1989 onward, the selection tools and the logic behind them had changed significantly. The shift was clearly away from the short-term, immediate, specific factory job model. Immigration targets remained at relatively high levels without reference to unemployment levels. Occupation and vocational training had been dropped from the criteria shown. Selection of workers was reoriented to criteria intended to admit individuals with post-secondary schooling, skills to work in knowledge-based services, and strong skills in English and or French. New categories of immigrants were added. Two of these reflected an important shift in the perception of immigrants: They included highly trained and productive workers and, in addition, they included entrepreneurs and investors capable of generating employment for others.

Many of the changes that took place over time were the subject of research and policy debate. For example, Green (1995) examined the relationship between the intended occupations of different cohorts of Canadian immigrants and their actual occupations as reported in the 1986 census. He concluded that, "much larger proportions of immigrants end up in service occupations than state an intention to do so." He further concluded that "many more women end up in clearly service and manufacturing occupations than stated an intention to do so" (p. 361). Eventually, in the 2004 points system, Canada abandoned the use of occupation to select immigrants. However, in 2007, the state partially reintroduced occupational criteria in the newly approved Canadian experience class, which is designed to admit as immigrants those individuals who have had successful prior experiences on temporary work and student visas. The use of occupational criteria is quite different in this case: It uses only very broad categories to select applicants with managerial, technical or professional qualifications. This procedure is in line with others that, since 1994, have emphasized highly skilled immigrants.

Admission criteria for new classes of immigrants clarify the state's shifting views on immigrant economic contributions. For example, in 1986, the government added the investor category, on the grounds that investors with capital could make a substantial contribution to the Canadian economy. Individuals could be admitted as investors if they had a net personal worth of $500,000 or more, were prepared to invest at least $250,000 in a project approved by the province in which they planned to make the investment, and had proven skills in the business of concern. In 1988, these requirements were lowered for investors who committed their investments to ventures in any of the six smaller Canadian provinces. This was a response to complaints from these provinces that nearly all investors were proposing projects in the more prosperous, larger provinces. The business class inflows were relatively small in number to begin with, but grew quickly over time to nearly 4,000 in 1987.

The inclusion of refugees in the 1976 Act was a major step, as previously they had been treated outside the immigration policy framework. Major inflows of refugees from Tibet (1972–1973), Asians from Uganda (1972), American draft dodgers (late 1960s to 1972), Chileans (after 1973), and Vietnamese "boat people" (waiting in refugee camps in Southeast Asia since 1975, but not admitted in large numbers to Canada until 1979–1980) made it clear that this was an important source of immigration and should be formally recognized as such.

The addition of procedures in 1989 to admit refugee claimants in a way consistent with the Canadian Bill of Rights was also a big step. Over the 1980s a very serious problem emerged with respect to refugee claimants. These were individuals who had entered Canada to put forward a claim for refugee status. Various civil wars, ethnic conflicts, and repressive governments in other nations had generated a very large number of refugees worldwide, estimated to be in the range of 20 million individuals, mostly in Asia and Africa, but also in Central America and elsewhere. While nearly all these individuals were displaced to countries within their own regions, a number had found ways to travel to Europe, North America, Australia, and other more developed nations. The number of claimants grew quickly in Canada over this period and exceeded Canadian officials' capacity to process their claims. A backlog of 63,000 claimants had developed by 1985; by late 1988, the backlog exceeded 100,000 even though the government provided an amnesty to those who had entered Canada before 21 May 1986.

Processing the backlog became more time-consuming when the Supreme Court handed down a path-breaking decision with respect to H. Singh, a refugee claimant from India. In 1985 the court determined that refugee claimants in Canada were protected by the Charter of Rights and Freedoms, and hence had to be granted a full oral hearing to decide their claims (see Box 4.2). In 1987 the government fought hard for new legislation that would make it more difficult for refugee claimants to enter Canada, but, in the face of major opposition by church and human rights groups, eventually settled for the passage of Bill C-85 in 1988 (implemented in 1989), which set in place the Immigration and Refugee Board (IRB). The IRB was mandated to provide oral hearings and to process refugee claimants quickly. This turned out not to be as simple or as fast as

first proposed. In addition, the government continued to push for measures to restrict the entry of refugee claimants.

In an analysis of the impact of Canadian refugee policy since the inclusion of a refugee category in the 1976 Act, Basok and Simmons (1993) conclude that the state was using economic-class immigration criteria to a large extent when admitting refugees from refugee camps in other countries. As a result, those admitted as "refugees between 1978 and 1987 tended to be young, relatively well-educated males" (p. 133). Since refugees, including those in camps, were and still are largely composed of women and children, and levels of schooling in many refugee camps around the world are low, this pattern presumably reflected the state's desire to play a humanitarian role while keeping in mind economic considerations. The Singh decision and the IRB decision, which were based on purely humanitarian considerations, have, along with other shifts in Canadian refugee policy, moved the subsequent development of refugee policy toward a greater focus on refugee needs rather than on Canada's economic needs.

In March 1992, the government introduced new fees for immigration services. Individuals applying to immigrate to Canada in the independent class would be charged $350. Spouses and each dependent child accompanying the applicant would be charged $350 and $50 respectively. If the application was approved, additional fees were to be paid at the time of landing in Canada. Under the new rules an immigrant couple with two children paid $3,200 in fees in total. The fees were justified as part of cost recovery on budgetary grounds (EIC 1992b). They were, however, highly controversial and widely opposed by immigrant communities and human rights groups. Refugees were to pay the same fees as others. Few refugees were in a position to do so, with the result that

Box 4.2: *Singh v. Minister of Employment and Immigration*, 1985

The best-laid plans and goals of immigration officials can be overturned when they do not fit with the 1976 Canadian Bill of Rights. The key case demonstrating this involved the case of Harbhajan Singh and six other Sikhs of Indian citizenship who entered Canada and made a claim in 1977 for convention refugee status from within the country on the basis that they feared persecution in India. Immigration officials turned down the request on the grounds that foreign nationals in Canada have no right to the protections of the Canadian Charter of Rights. The Sikhs would have been deported except that in 1985, the Canadian Supreme Court struck down the immigra- tion officials' decision. The Court determined that foreigners in Canada do have the right to protections of the Canadian Charter. This decision had an enormous impact on the number of refugee claims made by foreigners after they have travelled to Canada. A backlog of refugee claimants numbering less than 10,000 in 1985 climbed to nearly 100,000 by 1989, and led the government to establish the Immigration and Refugee Board (IRB) with a large administrative structure to adjudicate refugee claims. Chapter 5 provides information on how many of these claimants are admitted.

Source: The author, adapted from the Supreme Court of Canada ruling, *Singh v. Minister of Employment and Immigration*, [1985] 1 S.C.R. 177.

the government agreed to provide loans to refugees when, as is often the case, they did not have money to pay the fees at the time of arrival.

Free Trade and "Designer Immigrants"

Pomfret (1989) concludes that Canadian ISI policies over the postwar period into the 1970s had generally positive economic results with respect to industrial develop- ment (p. 74). Between the 1970s and the mid-1980s, Canadian industrial produc- tion had matured and become competitive within North America, although much of that mature production was within Canadian branch plants of large U.S. corpo- rations. This happened when many of the branch plants stopped producing goods in smaller quantities for Canadian markets only and became adapted to trade with the United States by providing more limited

lines of production for the North American continent. This maturation came about as U.S. firms and their Canadian branch plants were attempting to cut costs in the face of global competition, mostly from lower-cost producers in Asia.

The U.S.–Canada Auto Pact of 1965 was a major step toward making Canada a partner in an integrated North American continental production system. The pact was not a free trade agreement (although some see it this way) in that it was specific to a particular industry and strengthened that industry against off-shore competition by allowing North American firms located in both Canada and the United States to specialize and orient their production to a continental market (Pomfret 1989: 141). The success of the Auto Pact encouraged other North American manufacturers to do the same thing. They organized their production in Canada to complement pro- duction in the United States so that each plant, whether it was in Canada or the U.S., would be highly efficient and serve North America as a whole.

By the 1980s those Canadian firms that had become continental in their production wanted a free trade pact with the United States. Owners of these firms pushed the government in this direction, but the long-standing reliance of Canadian firms on tariff protections and government supports put them, along with many labour organizations, on the opposite side of the struggle. In the mid-1970s, the government under Prime Minister Trudeau had reacted with alarm to a steep rise in international oil prices. Higher oil costs threatened the profits and survivorship of Canadian industrial producers, located primarily in Eastern Canada. In response, the Trudeau government put in place a National Energy Program (NEP), which used special taxes to freeze domestic oil prices at levels lower than those in international markets. While this clearly benefited consumers and industrial producers in Eastern Canada, it lowered profits for Canadian oil producers located primarily in Alberta. They were infuriated, as were the government of Alberta and workers in that province. The government lost oil-tax revenues. Workers in that province lost jobs due to a slowdown in investment in the petroleum sector. The NEP also enraged the U.S. government and President Ronald Reagan. Many of the oil producers in Canada were American firms whose profits were down due to the NEP. The Americans, having previously threatened Canada by removing certain trade preferences, threatened to retaliate even further if Canada did not change its oil-pricing strategy and related trade and industrial policies. Clarkson (1991) reviews these historical events, noting the American response as follows:

President Ronald Reagan's team of radical rightists came to power with no instinctive sympathy for the Liberal Pierre Trudeau and little basic knowledge of Canadian-American relations. They showed no sensitivity to the special conditions that generated the more state-centered approaches taken by Canadian governments to resolving their problems. So when American oil entrepreneurs, who had helped finance the Republican party campaign, started complaining about the NEP, claiming that the "socialist" government in Ottawa was confiscating the assets of their Canadian operations, the Reaganites got angry.... Suddenly the Canadian government found itself the target of strong American pressure to intervene in its affairs and change its laws.... Threats of retaliation emanated from the White House, from the U.S. Department of Commerce, and from the American embassy while protection bills crowded the congressional order papers. (pp. 110–111)

The NEP remained in place from 1980 until 1986, and was finally brought to an end by continuing opposition in Alberta, U.S. threats, and a return to lower oil prices in international markets. Clarkson (1991: 110) argues that the collapse of the NEP was a significant element in the termination of Canada's previous national industrial policy and its tariff and tax supports. The result was that Canada was "pushed off its national mode" and in the direction of free trade. Actually developing and signing the first Canadian free trade agreement, the Canada–United States Free Trade Agreement (CUSTA), took a few more years. CUSTA was finally signed in 1988. By that time Canada had a Progressive Conservative government under Prime Minister Brian Mulroney that was clearly in favour of free trade. Did Canada have any options other than signing CUSTA in 1988? Clearly it did, but strong domestic pressures from certain sectors that felt they would benefit from free trade and strong international pressures tilted the government's decision. Had Canada not signed CUSTA then, would it have done so later? Not necessarily, but the pressures favourable to CUSTA prior to 1988 were growing. The entire international trading system, including China (and, by 1989, the ex-U.S.S.R. as well), was moving toward free trade under the hegemonic leadership of the United States and the major international financial agencies, such as the International Monetary Fund and the World Bank, which America supported. It would have been virtually impossible for Canada, as a trade-dependent nation, to take a different tack. In the end, the transformation in Canada's self-image toward that of a sophisticated, knowledge worker-based global trader and its desire to select many of its immigrants based on criteria that fit this image turned out to be part of a shift in the overall international political-economic order.

Consistent with the shift toward free trade, over the fall of 1989 and the winter of 1990, the government undertook a major Canada-wide consultation on immigration with business, labour, and civil society leaders in eight Canadian cities, from Halifax to Vancouver, and in 19 regions covering smaller communities. These consultations focused on challenges facing Canadian immigration and what should be done about them over the next five years (EIC 1990). The report brought to light the diversity of views and the generally positive attitudes of Canadians with respect to immigration. It also left considerable room for the state to pursue a specific agenda consistent with the broad support for immigration expressed by those who participated in the consultation.

A review and analysis of the consultation process noted that business leaders did not really participate forcefully in the consultation, quite likely because their views were already well understood and promoted by state officials who led the consultative process (Simmons and Keohane 1992). Union leaders who participated were also generally supportive of immigration, a fact that was noteworthy because this had not always been true in Canada, especially not during the Depression and immediately after the Second World War. Labour leaders at the consultations were fully aware of the state's view that immigrants did not take jobs so much as they helped sustain economic growth and higher employment. Either the union leaders agreed with this view or were not prepared to debate in public. Many of those who attended the meetings were part of the immigrant settlement sector, represented by leaders of organizations that provide settlement services (assistance with language training, housing, etc.); they were open to expanded immigration provided that it was accompanied by better service provision to newcomers. Not surprisingly, the report on the consultations concludes by confirming that immigration planning should not be restricted to setting targets on a year-to-year basis, as had been the practice in the past. Planning should be done within a longer, five-year forward perspective. To quote the report: "Participants across Canada are most aware of the benefits of immigration, and their comments and presentations indicate solid support for some increase in immigration over the next five years" (EIC 1990: 6).

Over the following two years (1990–1991), immigration officials working under Barbara McDougall, then minister for Employment and Immigration, developed a series of measures that confirmed a longer-term planning framework, the maintenance of relatively high levels of immigration independent of annual variation in economic circumstances, cost recoveries by charging applicants fees, and a clearer focus on skilled immigrants. The underlying principles were set forward in a report, *Managing Immigration: A Framework for the 1990s* (EIC 1992a). The report proposed amendments to the Immigration Act in order to better manage the administration of immigration and refugee admission, reinforce prohibition and deportation procedures, and work more closely with the provinces. A broad range of issues were addressed. Notably, the language of the document shifted from the earlier policy focus on *skilled workers* for industrial development to *highly skilled knowledge worker*s for global competition. The new policy made clear that immigrant knowledge workers are needed for the long term, so they should be brought in on a steady basis. The report states:

> With development of sophisticated technologies, a new knowledge-based economy, and increasing global competition, Canada must depend more than ever before on the skills and flexibility of its work force. At the same time, our supply of highly-skilled workers is not keeping up with demand. Even though unemployment is relatively high today, hundreds of thousands of jobs go unfilled because there are no applicants to fill them. (EIC 1992a: 5)

The report moves on to state that Canada is entering a "post-industrial" age requiring a "globalized, highly competitive, knowledge-based economy." It then proposes that immigration levels be increased by nearly 25 percent from the 1991 level of 205,000 to 250,000 per year for each year from 1992 to 1995 (p. 14). In order to increase the average skill level of immi-

grants, targets for the family class were set at lower levels over this period, while targets for independent immigrants, assisted relatives, and business immigrants were set at higher levels. In effect, the family class was to be downsized because it was an entry path that involved no state control over the skill level of the immigrant. Education qualifications for admission in the economic class were adjusted upward (Simmons 1999a).

Within these broad objectives, economic development and trade-competitiveness goals are the highest priority. Citizenship and Immigration's overview of the 2001 Act noted that: "Canada needs young, dynamic, well-educated skilled people. It needs innovation, ideas and talents..... Immigration legislation must be adapted to enhance Canada's advantage in the global competition for skilled workers" (CIC 2001: 1). In 2004, the points system was revised once again to reflect the spirit of the new 2001 Act. It promotes schooling rather than occupation-specific skills. Now the focus is on schooling as a measure of flexible skills that can be developed to respond to changing circumstances and competition.

Discussion and Conclusions

From 1989 to the present, Canada shifted its immigration policy discourse and procedures. The most recent policy language no longer refers to Canada as a nation in need of industrial workers, as it frequently did from 1962 to 1988. Nor do selection procedures assess immigrants' skills in narrow occupational terms that one would use if one thought of an economy as a factory with specific jobs to be filled on a year-to-year basis, depending on production levels. Rather, the new language refers to Canada as a post-industrial society in need of knowledge workers who will be experts and innovators able to help Canada compete in the global economy. Immigration targets have been set relatively high in historical terms and emphasize the need to include strong inflows of highly skilled knowledge workers, even in times of unemployment, to meet these more fundamental long-term goals.

The language of contemporary policy discourse is neo-liberal throughout in its focus on productivity and in requiring that immigrants pay fees to meet the state's own cost-recovery and efficiency goals. In effect, the state has shifted toward the admission of "designer immigrants," consisting of individuals who are selected as if they were custom designed to meet the specific criteria of a neo-liberal nation intent on productivity, cost recovery, and immigrant self-settlement. Immigrants are ideally to have the language and work skills to begin employment soon after arrival. They are to come with savings sufficient to look after their needs until they find employment.

From the above we may conclude that Canadian immigration policies have changed over time primarily in response to major changes in Canada's place in the world. This statement is, of course, a simplification. If Canada had not already established itself as an immigrant-receiving nation with its eye on producing commodities, manufactured goods, and services for export markets, it would not have adapted to changing external trade conditions

as it did. It is also the case that Canada does have choices in immigration policy. However, the choices are constrained. All options carry political and economic costs that are unequally distributed in Canadian society. Options that bring high costs to more powerful political and economic interests are naturally opposed by them, and final decisions on the options will tend to reflect their more powerful position. This is true within Canada as well as when it comes to trade negotiations with powerful nations such as the United States.

The timing of two waves of policy shifts, one starting in the early 1960s and the other starting in the late 1980s, reflect important changes in Canada's trade and political relationships with other countries. These external influences are mediated by related significant changes in Canadian values, culture, world view, institutions, and productive organization. Harold Innis, the founder of the Staples School of Canadian Political Economy, who died in 1952, did not live to know about the immigration, industrial, and post-industrial developments examined in this chapter, but he would not have been surprised by the extent to which they were all shaped by Canada's place in the international trading system. The next chapter, Chapter 5, examines the changing social and economic characteristics of immigrants related to the immigration policies and political economic and cultural forces I have explored so far.

CHAPTER 5
Who Gets In?

Introduction

In a documentary entitled *Who Gets In?* (NFB 1989) made a few years ago at a historic moment when the Canadian government had begun to shift toward selecting very highly skilled immigrants, a senior

Canadian immigration official observed that his job is to admit the good guys and keep out the "rascals." This remarkably candid statement puts the selection role of immigration work in moral terms—making sure no "rascals" are admitted and raising the question of how a rascal is defined.

Such a view adds further complexity to the various discourses and practices that come together in Canadian immigration to determine who will be admitted and who will be excluded.

This chapter is the first of two chapters on the forces that determine who gets in. The present chapter concerns the nature and effectiveness of official immigration targets and criteria in determining the total number of immigrants admitted, the number admitted in each class of immigration, and the levels of education and official language skills of those admitted. Chapter 6 extends the analysis to cover the various migration system factors that determine the national and ethnic origins of immigrants. Both chapters are oriented to questions on the nature and limits of immigration control in a globalized and transnational world. The main argument developed in these two chapters is that the Canadian state develops its immigration policies to address what it hopes it can control, but other forces — global trade, Canadian economic performance, and transnational migrant networks — play a significant role in determining what actually takes place. As a result, actual policy outcomes are often significantly different from those advanced in policy rhetoric.

This chapter focuses on the social and economic characteristics of immigrants and immigration control mechanisms that determine these characteristics. The main argument developed is that *there is a considerable gap between the state's policy discourse emphasizing highly skilled, ready-to-work immigrants and the characteristics of immigrants actually admitted*. While many immigrants with an advanced education are admitted in the economic class, many others without such education are admitted as family members and refugees. In addition, many immigrants in all classes of entry have little or no knowledge of either English or French on arrival, thereby delaying their entry into

jobs for which they are otherwise qualified. The result is a number of gaps between *rhetoric* and *reality* that this chapter seeks to examine and understand.

The chapter begins with a short review of the reasons why policy rhetoric and actual policy outcomes with respect to immigrant numbers and characteristics are often not the same. Subsequent sections cover the outcomes of current policies with respect to: (1) immigrant recruitment, (2) immigrant selection, and (3) exclusions and deportation of inadmissible individuals. Prior to exploring these issues, we first examine more carefully the questions of concern within a perspective that brings together an international migration systems viewpoint and a Canadian nation-building framework.

Issues and Questions

Readers will be familiar with the argument developed in previous chapters that Canadian immigration policy is shaped by dominant values and goals associated with nation-building. This framework argues that dominant values involved in nation-building are greatly affected by contradictory aspects of globalization and transnational society. One powerful set of values in official rhetoric promotes economic growth through competition among nations for export markets and through attracting highly skilled and productive immigrants. An additional important but less salient set of values in official rhetoric concerns the need to recognize and support family reunification and refugee admission in order to create a humanitarian and caring society of the kind that Canadians identify with and desire. Such a society is also one that will attract the kinds of highly skilled immigrants that Canada wants and create the kind of national pride that can sustain social harmony even in the face of ethno-class and other inequalities.

The current very high emphasis on economic values sets the tone of immigration discourse: It emphasizes the need for highly educated workers with official-language skills for building an advanced knowledge economy. The social and humanitarian values that support family reunification and refugee admission are retained in rhetoric, while being squeezed into a less important position than they otherwise would have in the setting of immigration targets. This juggling of policy discourse and practice reflects the way the state accommodates contradictions in Canadian immigration. For example, the Canadian government has at times sought to reduce family-class and refugee immigrant admissions. However, actual inflows through family reunification and refugee admissions remain important due to the following additional forces:

- *Migrant motivation in a globalized world:* Desired economic immigrants with high levels of education are more likely to apply and come to Canada if they know they can bring close family members with them or sponsor their immigration later. Canadian immigration policy is aware of this and includes family reunification as an important feature, one that is important to immigrants and to Canadians more generally.
- *Transnational social links:* Immigrant-based ethnic communities in Canada push for family reunification programs in immigration so that their members can sponsor close relatives. Immigrants who come to Canada are often attracted to this country because key family members immigrated earlier and now live in Canada.
- *Global communications and travel:* Asylum seekers make their way to

Canada and put forward refugee claims from within the country.
- *National and global pressure groups:* Humanitarian organizations in Canada lobby for the rights of refugees. They also lobby for the rights of undocumented migrants and others who face deportation.

Together the above forces tend to keep family reunification and refugee admission programs larger than the state would otherwise be. The result is that the state's dominant interest in highly skilled immigrants is retained as a major element in rhetoric; however, it occupies a still dominant but reduced position within a larger system of entry rules that brings in many family-class and refugee-class immigrants who, in fact, have a broad range of educational levels and official language skills. At this point it is necessary to add an important caveat: Immigrants who do not have the attributes that Canadian policy rhetoric most desires often do equally well or even better in finding jobs and integrating in Canada than those with the most desired attributes. Unfortunately, this is the case in large part because highly skilled immigrants' prior work experience and advanced credentials are discounted by employers in Canada (see Chapter 7).

Previous Research on Immigration Policy Outcomes

Studies of Canadian immigrant selection completed in the early 1990s on the basis of previous trends led the state to conclude that immigration policies in effect at that time were not doing a very good job. For example, research indicated that the tap-on, tap-off approach that had been used to slow overall immigration levels in years when unemployment levels were high had negative long-term impacts. When the tap was turned off in a period of high unemployment, there was a large reduction in independent or worker immigrants who were selected under the points system. Family-class immigration was not reduced because it was controlled by the rights of Canadian residents, including immigrants, to invite specified relatives to move to Canada to join them. With all the reductions taking place among those selected for their language, education, and job skills, observers noted that average educational levels of immigrants declined when the tap was off. Later, when the economy improved, Canada found itself once again short of skilled immigrant workers (DeVoretz 1995; Green 1995). From 1989 onward, Canada began to set immigration targets on the basis of long-term assessments of labour force needs without regard to year-by-year unemployment rates (Simmons 1994; Veugelers and Klassen 1994). The evidence over the 1980s also indicated that the family class had become the largest component of overall immigration (Akbari 1995) and concerns that, for this reason, the mix of immigrants had too many with lower levels of skills that, according to economic-productivity models, did not strongly benefit the Canadian economy (DeVoretz 1995: 4–8). Unfortunately, this analysis tended to blame family-class immigrants for job outcomes that later research suggests had more complex roots in problems immigrants generally faced in getting their credentials and experience recognized. However, this insight did not begin to emerge until some years later (see Chapter 7). Policy-makers at the time accepted the conclusion regarding the weak economic contributions of family-class immigrants. Policies were changed to reduce the proportion of immigrants in the family class and to increase the proportion in the economic class.

Studies done in the early 1990s also concluded that there was little connection between the occupational background of immigrants and the work that they eventually ended up doing in Canada (Green 1995). Some years later, in the 2001 Immigration Act, occupation was dropped from the assessment of workers in the economic class. Selection became heavily based on level of education.

Change has been a constant and continuing feature of Canadian immigration policy. In 2008, the Conservative government under Prime Minister Stephen Harper put in place a new immigration category known as the Canadian experience class (CEC). Admissions in this category are intended to fast-track the entry of highly-skilled temporary foreign workers with work experience relevant to Canadian job needs (CIC 2008a). In effect, this was a partial reversal of earlier policies that had removed assessment of relevant work experience from the admission process. The Organisation for Economic Co-operation and Development (OECD) has suggested additional measures for Canada and other developed countries that would address the growing gap between labour deficits in less-skilled and intermediate-skilled areas through immigration, but Canada has not yet responded to this suggestion (CIC 2008b). The Canadian experience class has been subject to much criticism from opposition parties and immigration critics on the grounds that it leads to a form of "queue jumping" in which individuals fast-tracked by the state are moved ahead of previous applicants who also meet immigration criteria, forcing these earlier applicants to wait even longer, perhaps indefinitely. It is too early to assess this most recent policy development, but there are considerable data to assess the selection outcomes of the broad immigration policy framework that has been in place since the early 1990s. We examine this data in the remainder of this chapter.

Part 1: Recruitment, Targets, and Outcomes

Canada has always promoted itself as an attractive immigrant destination in order to be sure that it will meet its immigration goals. The advertising is now done largely in low-key information programs provided by Citizenship and Immigration offices located in countries around the world. For example, following the pattern for all such offices, the CIC office in Manila, Philippines, supports a website with an upfront link to information "About Canada" in which the country is described as follows:

> In its short history, Canada has grown into a knowledge-based nation with world-class governance, corporations, culture and lifestyle. Canada prides itself on its stunning natural attractions and vast open spaces. Committed to education, the environment and health care for all, Canadians look to the future with confidence and optimism. (http://geo. international.gc.ca/asia/manila/ about_apropos/about_apropos-en.aspx)

Other links for visitors and immigrants on the site lead to Parks Canada and information on the "stunning natural attractions and vast open spaces," supported by pictures of Banff National Park and other attractions.

Visitors to the website are not told about the immigration targets, nor are they guided to state documents, such as the CIC *Annual Report to Parliament on Immigration Levels*, which contain such information. Yet, even if prospective immigrants were to do web searches for official documents on immigration targets, they would discover that these are also upbeat regarding

Canada's desirability as an immigrant destination and CIC's role in meeting immigration targets. For example, the 2006 report states that:

> ... the traditional role that immigration has played in building Canada as a strong, diverse and prosperous country is set to continue in the coming years. Canada continues to enjoy a reputation as a destination of choice for immigrants worldwide and 2005 marked the sixth consecutive year that CIC met or exceeded planned immigration levels. (CIC 2006a: section 1, paragraph 2)

The report then notes that planned targets were achieved in a context in which an abundance of applications were received:

> Despite the success in bringing roughly a quarter of a million new permanent residents to Canada each year, there are still many more individuals who would like to come. This high demand for immigration to Canada has pushed the overall inventory of applications beyond 800,000 individuals. (CIC 2006a: section 1, paragraph 4)

In other words, the backlog of applications is sufficiently large to cover Canada's planned intake at recent levels (around 250,000 per year) for more than three years into the future. While CIC's information programs and online application procedures undoubtedly facilitated the number of applications that led to this situation, it would seem that Canada's attractive reputation and links between former immigrants and prospective new ones (see Chapters 6 and 8) play an equally important or even greater role in this outcome.

Following the above report, new applications continued to flow in at a rate faster than existing ones were being processed, with the result that a year later in 2007, the application backlog had grown to 850,000 (CIC 2007a). By 2008 the backlog had grown further to more than 900,000 (CIC 2008c). Qualified professional applicants now wait up to several years to be approved, due in large part to this backlog. In sum, a new problem had emerged: how to manage a program in which more applicants were applying than were planned for.

Global income inequalities and transnational connections drawing people to Canada have created a context in which it is easy for Canada to meet its immigration targets. Canada is an attractive country in terms of economic, human rights, and political development. It is also a well-known destination due to global connections between previous immigrants and their home communities. In consequence, Canada is in a privileged position in meeting its immigration targets. Historically, Canadian immigration targets and actual inflows tend to differ by only a few percentage points each year and tend to average over time into a near-perfect fit (CIC 2001: 7). From this perspective, the distinctive feature about Canadian immigration since around 1989 is that intake targets and actual inflows have tended to stabilize in the range of between 200,000 and 250,000 per year. This level of inflow is not the highest recorded in history: Still larger numbers arrived for a short period just prior to the First World War. However, the overall annual levels of inflow since 1989 are very high and, moreover, they have been sustained over an extended period of time (see Figure 3.1, Chapter 3). Prior to 1989, there was enormous year-to-year variation. In the era of global trade since 1989, immigration planning has taken on a long-term perspective. It does not matter so much what the unemployment level is

in any given year; immigrants are brought in for anticipated future labour needs and nation-building.

Canadian immigration creates targets not only for overall intake levels but also for each of the major classes of admission: economic, family, and humanitarian/ refugee. In the late 1980s and early 1990s the state felt that economic-class immigration was too low, while family-class and refugee-class admissions were too high (see Chapter 4). This led to setting higher targets for economic immigrants and lower targets for the other two classes. Since 1996 total immigration has been planned to include about 60 percent economic-class immigrants and 40 percent family-class and refugee-class immigrants. Figure 5.1 shows that the state has effectively achieved these broad targets. New immigration targets brought about a sharp increase in the proportion of economic-class immigrants and a corresponding decrease in the proportion of family-class immigrants. Their relative positions in the importance of immigration became the opposite of what they had been. Economic immigrants in the 1980s had occasionally been as low as 30–40 percent of the total inflow. Since 1996, economic immigrants have constituted around 60 percent of the total. The opposite shift took place for family-class immigrants, with this group declining to around a third of the intake. Refugee inflows also declined somewhat, from around 20 percent of the inflow to around 10–15 percent of the total. On the basis of these trends, one might conclude that the state achieved its goal of substantially increasing the proportion of economic migrants in a way that was consistent with its objectives of using immigration to support the high-tech knowledge economy in Canada. Evidence in the next section will show that this conclusion must be qualified by the fact that overall inflows of immigrants in the economic class also include the spouses and children of the

Figure 5.1: Immigrants by Entry Class, 1980–2005

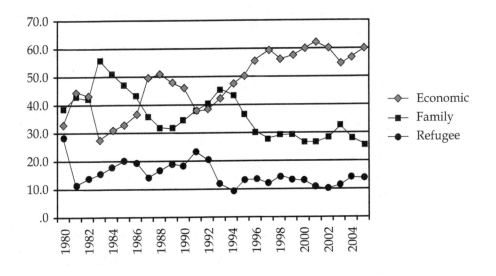

Source: The author, using data from LIDS. 2005. *Landed Immigrant Data System*. Ottawa: Citizenship and Immigration Canada.

principal applicants, and that economic-class immigrants later sponsor other family members who may not be so skilled.

Part 2: Outcomes of Immigrant Selection

Each of the three main Canadian immigration classes is composed of various subclasses or components. For example, the economic class consists largely of skilled workers. However, it also includes business immigrants. In a further step, business immigrants include both entrepreneurs and investors. Live-in caregivers (nannies) are also considered to fall in the economic class when they become landed immigrants. Each of these categories is, in turn, composed of principal applicants, who are subject to selection criteria, and dependent family members (spouse and dependent children) who accompany the

principal applicant. Entry to Canada is therefore best understood as a building with many entry doors for different categories of individuals. Each category is subject to varying entry criteria and procedures. Table 5.1 summarizes the diverse categories of immigrants admitted to Canada in 2005 and the criteria or procedures used to authorize their entry.

Table 5.1 confirms the concern that only a very small proportion of Canadian immigrants are actually selected using education, work experience, and language criteria that correspond to what might be understood as a knowledge worker for a high-tech export economy. Only about one-fifth (19.9 percent in 2005) of all immigrants are directly selected on the basis of the points system. An additional very small proportion (less than 2 percent) of immigrants are selected on the basis of their financial capital and entrepreneurial skills and plans. Live-in caregivers, com-

Table 5.1: Percentage of Immigrants Admitted in 2005 by Entry Class

Class	Category	Selection Criteria and Procedures	
Economic	Skilled workers	Points system	19.9
	Business immigrants	Financial capital and business plans	1.4
	Live-in caregivers	Training as caregivers	1.2
	Dependants of the above	No direct selection*	34.1
	TOTAL ECONOMIC CLASS		56.6
Family	Spouses/children arriving later	No direct selection*	18.6
	Parents and grand-parents	Sponsors must prove they can support	5.6
	TOTAL FAMILY CLASS		24.2
Refugees	Government-assisted	Some selected on skilled-worker criteria	2.8
	Privately sponsored	From "designated" source countries	1.1
	In-land refugee claim-ants	Adjudication by the IRB**	7.6
	Dependants of refu-gees	Proof of dependency status	2.1
	TOTAL REFUGEES		13.6
Others		Humanitarian/compassionate, others	5.7
	TOTAL		100.0

* Since 2004, spouses of skilled workers are indirectly and partially selected on education and work experience. This is because the 2004 revised points system gives principal applicants extra points based on their spouse's education and work experience.
** IRB is the Immigration and Refugee Board (of Canada).

Source: The author, based on data from LIDS. 2005. *Landed Immigrant Data System.* Ottawa: Citizenship and Immigration Canada.

prising slightly more than 1 percent of all immigrants, are selected on the basis of their training. However, they do not contribute directly as high-tech workers, although they presumably make it easier for high income-earning parents in Canada to focus on their occupations by hiring an immigrant live-in caregiver.

The largest component of the economic class is made up of dependants (spouses and children) who accompany principal applicants in this class. Dependants are not selected on any criteria other than their family relationship to the principal applicant. Policy changes introduced in the 2004 points system give the principal applicant up to 10 points (of the 69 required for admission) based on his or her spouse's level of education. This tends to raise the spouse's level of education among highly skilled workers who are admitted. In addition, the foreign-born children of highly educated immigrants may become highly educated themselves due to growing up in a family with highly educated parents. Of course, this possible positive impact on skill levels in Canada will depend on subsequent intergenerational social mobility processes.

Family-class immigrants are not directly selected on the basis of any social-economic criteria, although their admission is dependent on the incomes of the family members in Canada who sponsor them. The sponsoring family must show evidence of ability to support the member whom they are inviting to come to Canada. Refugees are primarily selected on human rights criteria, as one would expect. Together, these two components constitute about 40 percent of total immigration. Past efforts by the state to further reduce these two classes of immigrants have met with considerable resistance in Canadian society.

Could the family class be reduced further? Current regulations limit the family class to a very narrow range of close kin consisting of spouses, fiancés/fiancées, and dependent children. Brothers, sisters, and adult children of immigrants and other Canadian residents are excluded. In effect, the family class is narrow, but covers the closest kin. The question of further reducing the family class is, in part, a political matter. Immigrants comprise close to 20 percent of the Canadian population and are important sources of votes in federal elections. Parties that oppose the core values and interests of immigrants are at risk of losing political support and elections in key urban ridings where immigrants may be 50 percent of the electorate. In addition, Canada competes with other highly developed nations for college- and university-trained immigrants. A dilution of family reunification provisions in Canadian policy could make it more difficult to attract the

highly skilled immigrant workers who stand at the core of immigration policy. Immigrants are less likely to move without their immediate family. Their family, in turn, will not support a key member who moves away unless they can join them. We may conclude that it may be possible for an elected government of Canada to further reduce family-class immigration, but to do so would entail costs to immigration goals and electoral support.

Public opposition to efforts to reduce refugee admission is more narrowly based in smaller human rights organizations, but these are vocal and are at times able to generate wide support from the Canadian public. During the 1980s, Canadian refugee admissions increased and Canada became one of the world's leading nations in refugee settlement (Adelman 1991: 174). This happened in part because of public pressure and rising concern among bureaucrats and politicians for the plight of the Indochinese, Central American, and other refugees (see the analysis of the case of the Guatemalan refugees by Nolin 2006). However, by the late 1980s, the official mood shifted. The state became concerned about the relatively high proportion of refugees with low levels of education entering Canada. They were particularly concerned about a cumulative backlog of more than 100,000 inland refugee claimants (resident in Canada), all waiting for an official response to their asylum requests. The state responded by establishing, in 1989, the Immigration and Refugee Board (IRB) to reduce the backlog and set clearer procedures for adjudicating future claims. It then put forward a series of steps to curtail refugee flows, particularly flows of refugee claimants. For example, Guatemalan claimants had previously been immune from deportation to their home country if their refugee claim was declined, but in the early 1990s this immunity was withdrawn. However, other proposed policy changes were strongly opposed by humanitarian groups and eventually dropped by the government. Bill C-55 (which became law in 1990) originally included "safe third country" provisions that would have given officials tools to radically reduce refugee flows. In these proposed provisions, claimants who had travelled through or sojourned in another country en route to Canada could be sent back to that country, and any claim they had made in Canada would not be processed. A high proportion of refugee claimants come from developing countries in Africa, Asia, and Latin America and travel through other countries before arriving in Canada. Some of the countries they travel through are hostile to their presence and would, in turn, deport the claimants to their home countries, namely, the countries from which they had fled to avoid such horrors as ethnic cleansing, torture, and threats of violence. Opposition from human rights organizations, churches, and other groups in Canada was very strong and led the state to remove the "safe third country" measures from law (Adelman 1991: 200–217), yet the state did not entirely give up the policy. It entered into bilateral discussions with the United States that eventually, some years later in 2002, led to an agreement between these two countries that refugee claimants who had travelled first through either Canada or the United States would be processed only in that country (CIC 2002). In the economic class, where the education selection took place, the impact was necessarily more profound. By 2005, nearly 50 percent of economic-class immigrants had college diplomas or university degrees.

From the above it is clear that immigration is not a one-dimensional field. Canada cannot attract immigrants or retain public support for immigration policy without including family reunification and refugee admission within a broader range of nation-building policies. As a result, the state has less direct control over the education, official-language skills, and work experience of immigrants that it would like when it is focused only on the economic goals of immigration. In the following sections we examine the outcomes of state control and its limits on the education and official-language skills of immigrants.

Outcomes Regarding Education

Education is the most important attribute for the admission of highly skilled workers, particularly since the early 1990s when additional points were given to education. Education became even more important for admission of workers following the 2001 Act and the revised 2004 points system. After these most recent changes, a person with a post-secondary diploma or degree involving two or more years of study automatically receives 20 points or roughly 30 percent of the 67 points required for admission. Anyone with less than high school studies completed would get 0 points on the education criterion (see Table 5.2).

The changes in educational requirements had the desired impact. Levels of education increased significantly among immigrants. Figure 5.2 shows how the new rules affected the percentage of immigrants with a university or college degree involving two or more years of study. For immigrants overall, this percentage had held constant at between 10 and 15 percent over the 1980s. Starting in the early 1990s, the percentage rose steadily. By 2002 it had reached roughly 35 percent, where it seems to have stabilized, at least for now. In other words, for all immigrants, the proportion with significant post-secondary studies more than doubled. Among economic-class immigrants, where the education selection took place, the impact was necessarily more profound. By 2005, nearly 50 percent of economic-class immigrants had college diplomas or university degrees.

Table 5.2: Allocation of Points for Education (2004 Regulations)

Level of Education	Points
Did not complete secondary school (also called high school)	0
Obtained a secondary school credential	5
Obtained a *one-year diploma*, trade certificate or apprenticeship **and** completed at least *12 years* of full-time or full-time equivalent studies	12
Obtained a *one-year diploma*, trade certificate or apprenticeship **and** completed at least *13 years* of full-time or full-time equivalent studies	15
Obtained *a one-year university degree* at the bachelor's level **and** completed at least *13 years* of full-time or full-time equivalent studies	15
Obtained a *two-year diploma*, trade certificate or apprenticeship **and** completed at least *14 years* of full-time or full-time equivalent studies	20
Obtained a *university degree* of two years or more at the bachelor's level **and** completed at least *14 years* of full-time or full-time equivalent studies	20
Obtained a *three-year diploma*, trade certificate, or apprenticeship **and** completed at least *15 years* of full-time or full-time equivalent studies	22
Obtained *two or more university degrees* at the bachelor's level **and** completed at least *15 years* of full-time or full-time equivalent studies	22
Obtained a *Master's or Ph.D.* **and** completed at least *17 years* of full-time education or full-time equivalent studies	25

Source: CIC (2008). *Skilled Workers and Professionals Self-Assessment Test*. Ottawa: Citizenship and Immigration Canada. [http://www.cic.gc.ca/english/immigrate/skilled/assess/index.asp]

Additional analysis not shown in Figure 5.2 indicates that by 2005, nearly all principal applicants in the skilled-worker category had at least one university degree. Specifically, 51 percent had a bachelor's degree, 29 percent had a master's degree, and 5 percent had a doctorate. However, others in the economic class who are not selected on educational criteria have much lower levels of schooling. A third of principal applicants in the business class (investors and entrepreneurs) have high school or less schooling; only about one-quarter have a university degree. Thus, state policy has effectively been able to select very highly skilled immigrant workers, but those selected (principal applicants in the highly skilled worker category of the economic class) constitute only about one-fifth of all immigrants. Other immigrants in the economic class have lower levels of education. Those in the family class and refugee class have still lower levels.

More highly educated economic immigrants later sponsor family members who also have higher levels of schooling. Indirect evidence of this can be seen in Figure 5.2, which shows that as the percentage of economic-class immigrants with a university degree has risen over time, the percentage of family-class immigrants with a university degree also rose, even though the family-class immigrants are not selected directly on the basis of education. The effect among family-class immigrants is somewhat delayed and not as dramatic, yet it contributes to the rise

Figure 5.2: Percentage of Immigrants in Different Entry Classes with University Degree Completed

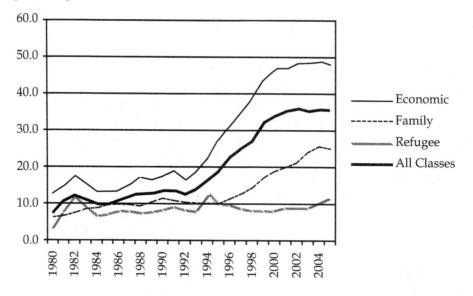

Source: The author, based on data from LIDS. 2005. *Landed Immigrant Data System*. Ottawa: Citizenship and Immigration Canada.

in education levels among all immigrants. There is no such effect for refugees. They are admitted on the basis of criteria that are completely independent of schooling. They tend to have much lower levels of schooling because they come mostly from less developed countries with low levels of education. The net result is that schooling levels among refugees remain low, a situation that creates an ongoing official desire to keep refugee admissions low, while still living up to Canada's international obligations and national policies on refugees.

Does it really matter if two-thirds of immigrants have less than a two-year college diploma or university degree? After all, many jobs in Canada require less demanding credentials. Like others in Canada, adult immigrants can also continue their studies at the college and university level as mature students. In addition, their children growing up in Canada

will have opportunities for post-secondary education and, hopefully, form part of an increasingly skilled national labour force. Yet, it is also the case that nation-building in Canada is outward looking with respect to trade opportunities and strengthening its highly skilled labour force through immigration. From this perspective, high levels of schooling among immigrants matter a lot.

Outcomes Regarding Language

From the first application of the points system in the 1960s, the ability to speak English and/or French has been a criterion in the system, but its importance relative to other criteria has varied. In the current (2004) points system, official-language ability is very important. In fact, it is nearly as important as post-secondary education for admission. As Table 5.3 shows, high proficiency in both English and French would provide the applicant with 24 points out of

Table 5.3: Points for Official Language Skills

First Canadian Official Language (either English or French)

	Read	Write	Speak	Listen
High Proficiency (4 each)				
Moderate Proficiency (2 each)				
Basic Proficiency (1–2 each = Maximum of two (2) points)				
No Proficiency (no points)				

Second Canadian Official Language (either English or French)

	Read	Write	Speak	Listen
High Proficiency (2 each = Maximum of eight (8) points)				
Moderate Proficiency (2 each = Maximum of eight (8) points)				
Basic Proficiency (1–2 each = Maximum of two (2) points)				
No Proficiency (no points)				

Source: CIC. 2008. *Skilled Workers and Professionals Self-Assessment Test*. Ottawa: Citizenship and Immigration Canada. [http://www.cic.gc.ca/english/immigrate/skilled/assess/index.asp]

the 69 needed for entry. High proficiency in one official language alone would yield 16 points. Conversely, those who read, write, speak, or understand neither official language would get 0 points and automatically lose about a third of points they need for admission.

Despite the importance of official-language ability, many immigrants do not speak either English or French at the time of arrival. Roughly two out of five immigrants (more precisely, 43 percent) of those entering Canada between 1980 and 2005 did not speak either of these official languages when they entered the country (Table 5.4). More than half (52 percent) of all immigrants speak English, while only about a tenth (9 percent) speak French. One might expect that ability to speak either English or French would be higher in the

economic class given that it is subject to the points system, while the other classes are not. This turns out to be the case. About 65 percent of economic-class immigrants speak either English and/or French, while the corresponding figures are lower for the family class (51 percent) and the refugee class (43 percent). These patterns have been relatively stable over time, particularly since the early 1990s.

Does it really matter if immigrants do not speak an official Canadian language on arrival? It certainly matters over the short term, given the importance of English and French for employment, access to health care, and many matters of everyday communication. Yet, many immigrants are able to initially find work, health care, and access to other services in their own ethnic communities in

Table 5.4: Percentage of Immigrants Who Speak English and/or French on Landing, 1980–2005

Official Language Spoken	Entry Class	Percent
English	All	47.6
French	All	4.5
Both English and French	All	4.6
Neither	All	43.3
Total	All	100.0
English and/or French	Economic	64.2
English and/or French	Family	51.3
English and/or French	Refugee	43.2
English and/or French	Total	56.7

Source: The author, based on data in LIDS. 2005. *Landed Immigrant Data System*. Ottawa: Citizenship and Immigration Canada.

Canada. Eventually, their children grow up speaking English and/or French and the issue of the parents' official language skills becomes less relevant. However, Canada—a trade-focused society in a globally competitive context—is preoccupied by immediate concerns, such as how to promote monthly and annual trade surpluses, achieve high levels of employment, and encourage economic growth. These goals prompt a desire for more immediate and higher economic returns from immigrants. From this perspective, the fact that 40 percent of immigrants do not speak either of Canada's official languages on arrival is of concern. Limited ability in these languages may limit their immediate job prospects and contributions to the Canadian economy.

Outcomes for Quebec

Quebec was the first province to sign an agreement with the federal government on immigration. This agreement remains the most important one of its kind. The Quebec-Canada accord, known as the Cullen-Couture Agreement, was signed in 1978 and was revised and extended in 1991 to become what is now known as the Canada-Quebec Immigration Accord (CIC 1991). The agreement supports major objectives in Quebec's immigration strategy. These objectives fall in three areas: demographic, linguistic, and economic.

Demographic: Quebec hopes that immigration will increase its population or at least reduce the speed of its population decline. Quebec has been concerned about its very low birth rate and its gradually declining share of the Canadian population. As a result, the Quebec-Canada immigration accord permits Quebec to receive a share of Canadian immigrants that is 5 percent greater than the province's share of the Canadian population.

Linguistic: Quebec is also interested in participating in immigrant selection to increase the number of francophone immigrants settling in the province.

Economic: Like the rest of Canada, Quebec has given increasing priority to attracting highly skilled immigrant workers and business immigrants within an overall program that also admits family-class and refugee immigrants. While this is what Quebec has hoped for, the evidence suggests that it has not been able to achieve all these objectives.

Quebec's share of the Canadian population has fallen very gradually and by only a small amount from 1981 to 2006 (Figure 5.3). In 1981 Quebec's population was 26 percent of the population of Canada. By 2006, its share had fallen to 23 percent. In earlier history, Quebec had closer to one-third of the Canadian population; since around 1991 it has been less than 25 percent. The hope that immigration might help slow this trend has not materialized. Following earlier trends not shown in Figure 5.3, Quebec's share of immigrant landings has remained below its share of the Canadian population since 1981.

Quebec has not been able to achieve its immigrant intake targets. Immigrants destined for Quebec have been fewer in number than Quebec would like to receive. From 1980 to 2005, Quebec received around

17 percent of immigrants arriving in Canada, almost 10 percent less than its share of the Canadian population over this period. It is therefore clear that low immigration intake was an additional factor, beyond its low birth rate, in contributing to Quebec's gradually declining share of the Canadian population. A third factor, not examined here, is net internal migration: Over the same period, Quebec lost more out-migrants to other parts of Canada than it received in the form of in-migrants from these other parts of the nation (Statistics Canada 2004: Table A-1).

Quebec is an officially francophone province and expects immigrants to settle into a French-language society. The more immigrants who speak French on arrival, the better from Quebec's perspective. From 1980 to 1998, the proportion of immigrants destined for Quebec who spoke French on arrival remained low, in the range of 30–40 percent (Figure 5.3). As a result, Quebec intensified its recruitment of francophone immigrants. After 1998, the proportion of immigrants destined for Quebec who spoke

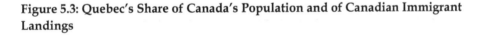

Figure 5.3: Quebec's Share of Canada's Population and of Canadian Immigrant Landings

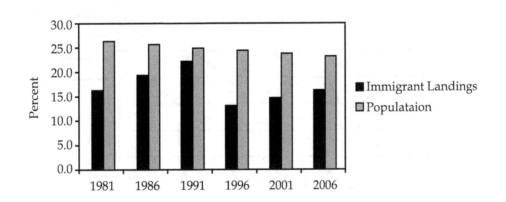

Source: The author, based on population figures from Table 1 and A1 in Statistics Canada. 2007. *Report on the Demographic Situation in Canada, 2007.* Ottawa: Statistics Canada; and data on the intended destination of immigrants at the time of arrival in the LIDS 2005 data set.

French rose steadily to nearly 60 percent. This upward trajectory of Quebec-bound immigrants speaking French through to 2005 suggests that further increases may be possible in the future. The trend should reduce Quebecers' concerns about immigrants' threats to their language.

Anglophone immigrants destined for Quebec are considerably more likely to have a bachelor's degree or more when compared with francophone immigrants destined for that province (Figure 5.4). Immigrants destined for Quebec who speak neither French nor English are least likely to have a B.A. or more education. These differences have persisted over time, even as levels of university education have increased. This suggests that Quebec's difficulty in meeting immigration targets arises at least in part from a worldwide relative shortage of potential immigrants

who have a university degree and who speak French. It is not that the world is short of highly educated francophones, but that they are concentrated in high-income countries such as France, Belgium, and Switzerland where the desire to emigrate is relatively low. Quebec has found it difficult to attract highly qualified francophone immigrants because they appear to be in relatively scarce supply in the world. Francophones potentially interested in moving to Quebec are more likely found in less developed French-speaking countries of North and West Africa where schooling levels are relatively low. While many immigrants to Quebec, including highly skilled immigrants, do come from North and West Africa (see Chapter 6), the numbers are not sufficient to meet Quebec's intake targets. Meanwhile, English is a more dominant global language. It is also

Figure 5.4: Percentage of Immigrant Landings with B.A. or More Education and Official Language Skills, Quebec, 1985–2005

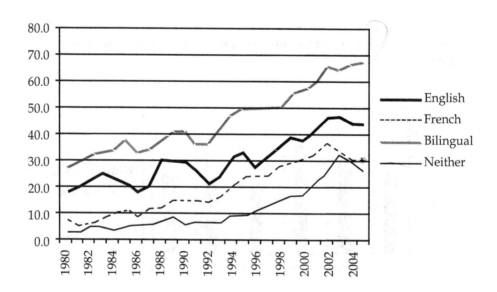

Source: The author, based on data from LIDS. 2005. *Landed Immigrant Data System*. Ottawa: Citizenship and Immigration Canada.

widely spoken in nations with very large populations and significant well-educated urban classes of people, such as India, that have many potential immigrants who meet Quebec's interest in highly skilled immigrants, even though few of them speak French. The result is that Quebec's immigration admission strategy leads to constrained outcomes: Inflows of highly skilled francophone immigrants are rising, but have likely been lower than Quebec would desire; inflows of highly skilled anglophone immigrants are declining, but many are still admitted because their very high levels of education make them attractive; overall immigration targets are not met because not enough very highly skilled francophone immigrants (and family members who would follow them) are available. Despite the constraints imposed by the world supply of highly skilled French-speaking immigrants, Quebec has shown improved ability to attract the kinds of immigrants it wants over time, even if it has not been able to meet its total immigration targets. These findings point to the conclusions that who gets in is not simply a matter of state policy objectives, since global supplies of immigrants, migrant motivation, and other factors determine actual outcomes.

In sum, nation-building in Quebec runs parallel to that in Canada as a whole. Both Quebec and Canada have similar imagined futures. They hope to be prosperous trading economies based on the application of sophisticated technology and inputs from immigrants and native-born in a peaceful multi-ethnic society. The main difference is that Quebec imagines its future as a francophone nation either within Canada (the federalist view) or outside Canada (the sovereignist view). There are, in addition, some differences regarding how the multi-ethnic society is to be formed, with Canada promoting multiculturalism and Quebec promoting the related concept of inter-culturalism. Both these approaches seek to promote inter-ethnic harmony through education, dialogue, and the promotion of citizenship rights for everyone, but, according to Gagnon and Iacovino (2004), interculturalism gives more attention to a possible convergence of viewpoints that will transform society. The language that immigrants speak is more important in Quebec given the minority status of French in Canada and North America generally and the related fear of francophone Quebecers that immigrants will learn and use English to the neglect of French.

Part 3: Prohibitions, Border Controls, and Deportations

In this section we examine the effectiveness of border controls and deportations in controlling who gets in. The analysis is directed at understanding how controls and other factors limit the number of unauthorized migrants living in Canada. Following the definition proposed by Passell (2005: 1), the term "unauthorized migrant" refers to a person who *resides* in Canada but who is *not* a Canadian citizen, has *not* been admitted to Canada for permanent residence, and does *not* have a visa or permit allowing long-term residence and/or work. Sometimes such individuals are referred to in the press as "illegal migrants." In other instances they are described as "undocumented migrants." However, one must take care with such terms. The term "illegal migrant" is particularly problematic because it is ambiguous and suggests that the migrant is a criminal. When the term "illegal migrant" is used, it generally refers to a person who is in Canada after not having followed immigration rules. But not following rules is not a criminal offence. In order to avoid potential confusions and distortions, I and many other writers in this field do not use the term "illegal migrant." The term "undocumented migrant" can also create confusion as it covers diverse circumstances. It can refer to a person who entered Canada without authorizing documents, or to a person who entered on a legal visa but has overstayed the visa. It is also sometimes used to refer to a person who has a visitor's visa to Canada and is working in Canada in violation of the visa. In sum, the advantage of the term "unauthorized migrant" is that it is more general and covers most circumstances that lead to unauthorized presence without implying any criminality.

Passell's useful definition is also a sound base from which to understand unauthorized migration, but it too must be fine-tuned to cover cases this definition does not address. For example, Passell's definition does not cover fraudulent admissions. These are cases in which the person has been admitted legally, but on fraudulent grounds that could lead to his or her subsequent deportation. Fraudulent admission is a serious matter, and immigration officials treat it this way. Sometimes, however, they run into major difficulty in determining whether a fraud has taken place or merely appears to have taken place. This is the case in recent tragic/comic efforts to uncover so-called cases of "bogus marriages" between Canadians and foreigners (see Box 5.1).

It is estimated that the number of unauthorized migrants in Canada is probably in the range of 100,000–200,000 in total. For reasons that will become clear below, this

---

Box 5.1: Marriages of Convenience?

So-called "marriages of convenience," in which Canadians marry foreigners only for the purpose of enabling that foreign person to immigrate to Canada, have received renewed attention recently due to reports that this fraudulent practice is on the increase. While the practice of marrying only to allow a bride or groom to immigrate to Canada is known to have existed for many years, in 2008 the Canadian government decided to adopt a new strategy to control it. The state began "deploying clandestine teams to fan out across foreign countries and gather raw information about elaborately staged phony weddings aimed at duping Canadian immigration officials" (Curry 2008).

Commentators immediately noted the difficulty, perhaps impossibility, of determining which marriages are phony and which are real. Peter Rekai (2008), an immigration lawyer, noted that arranged marriages are common in some ethnic communities in Canada; that other Canadians meet and arrange long-distance marriages by Internet; that financial arrangements are typically part of the discussion between couples before they marry; and that many marriages in Canada break down within months or a year after they were formed. The overlap in practices that the state regards as fraudulent and those that are found more generally in society makes it very difficult to distinguish between the two. The great danger is that state officials will deem legitimate marriages to be contrived ones. Several cases have come to light in which brides or grooms have been refused admission, despite the vocal protests and expressed frustration of the couples concerned (Curry 2008).

Sources: The author, based on or adapted from: Rekai, Peter. 2008. "Whose Marriage? Whose Convenience?" *Globe and Mail* (20 May), A17; Curry, Bill. 2008. "Fraud Squads Chase down Marriages of Convenience." *Globe and Mail* (21 May), A1.

range is only an educated guess. However, there is widespread agreement that the figure is relative low. Figures in the estimated range are less than 1 percent of the total 33 million population of Canada in 2008. Other very wealthy nations and regions, such as the United States and Europe, have significantly higher proportions of unauthorized migrants. For example, Passell (2005: 1) estimates that there were 11.5–12 million unauthorized migrants in the United States in 2006; this number constituted about 4 percent of the 300 million people living in the U.S. at that time. One might therefore conclude that Canadian immigration officials do an outstanding job of making sure that unauthorized migrants do not enter Canada or that they are deported if they do enter. However, the actual reasons for the low number of unauthorized migrants in Canada is more complex and can only be attributed in minor part to the success of immigration officers. Other factors, particularly geography and Canadian humanitarian responses to unauthorized migrants, play an important role, as the following points make clear.

Geography makes unauthorized migrant entry into Canada more difficult, but by no means so difficult as to prevent large numbers from doing so. Europe (with respect to Asia and Africa) and the United States (with respect to Latin America and the Caribbean) have direct land connections or short sea connections to less developed nations. This is one of the main reasons why these destinations experience large inflows of unauthorized migrants. Given that Canada has no direct land connection to less developed nations and that it is separated from them by very wide oceans helps explain why fewer unauthorized migrants enter Canada, but this is only a partial explanation. Global transportation, transnational migrant connections, and migrant smuggling are able to overcome

the barriers of wide oceans and long distances. Every year thousands of unauthorized migrants enter Canada by airplane. Many dozens and perhaps hundreds more enter via ships arriving at Canada's coasts. Still others cross clandestinely from the United States. Large numbers enter legitimately on a visitor's visa, but become unauthorized later when they take jobs and overstay their visas. From this perspective, Canadian officials' efforts to prevent the entry of unauthorized migrants have not been particularly successful.

Those who enter Canada without authorization fall into quite different categories. We know more about the size of some of the flows and very little about the size of other flows. The main paths by which unauthorized migrants enter Canada are as follows:

Asylum seekers: The numbers are known as asylum seekers make a claim that is registered with the IRB. The number of claims varies by year. In the early 2000s, between 25,000 and 30,000 new claims were registered each year. Of these about half were accepted. In 2005, Canada accepted approximately 18,000 claimants, a number that constituted 7.5 percent of all immigrants that year. Claimants who are not accepted sometimes leave Canada, but some remain to put forward appeals and others avoid immigration officials so that they will not be deported.

Workers entering on a visitor's visa: The numbers are estimated from indirect sources. People who work in construction, hotels, and restaurants know that many workers in these fields are unauthorized migrants. They entered Canada mostly legally on a visitor's or a tourist's visa and then remained to work. One of the problems with estimating the numbers is that employment opportunities for such migrant workers vary with economic cycles. In the construction boom in Toronto in 2003, construction union officials and newspaper reporters who talked to them estimated that the construction industry depended on the presence of up to 20,000 unauthorized workers (Jimenez 2003).

Smuggled workers without papers: The difference between migrant smuggling and migrant trafficking is often blurred. Migrant smuggling refers to an organized process to help migrants without authorization to cross borders. Migrant trafficking refers to an organized process of forcing migrants into unlawful employment in a place of destination. Migrants who are trafficked are often smuggled as well. And migrants who are smuggled often pay the smugglers large amounts of money that they borrow and must pay back while working without authorization, leading migrants to accept unsavoury Triple-D jobs (dirty, dangerous, degrading) on the margins of or outside legal employment. The numbers of smuggled migrants are not known, but, based on partial information, are assumed to be small. Box 5.2 summarizes discovery of several landings of unauthorized Chinese migrants off the coast of British Columbia after having been smuggled there on rusty old freighters.

Trafficked workers with papers: From time to time, police raids on massage parlours suspected of operating as businesses to make profits from prostitution lead to the discovery of foreign sex workers who are controlled by migrant traffickers. The number of cases uncovered this way is typically small, at most a few dozen in a given series of police raids, but one does not know if this is because few sex workers are trafficked this way or because few are discovered by the police. Box 5.3 summarizes the circumstances of the workers discovered in a series of police raids in Toronto. This and other such cases raise important questions about the ways in which foreign sex workers are recruited. The literature suggests that recruitment is at times brutal and coercive, with young

poor village girls in poverty-stricken countries being kidnapped or sold by relatives to job brokers who promise that the girl will become a respected household maid in a distant city when, in fact, they plan to turn the girl into a prostitute. The young women are then coerced through beatings and turned into dependent drug addicts before being trafficked to wealthy nations. Other accounts indicate alternative paths. Some foreign sex workers choose their occupation and agree to be smuggled, but only because their other opportunities are so limited. In both cases, the women have little financial, human, or social capital to protect themselves.

While Canadian borders are porous and allow thousands of unauthorized migrants to enter every year, many of these migrants later become authorized to remain in the country, while smaller numbers of others are deported. Of these two mechanisms for resolving the presence of unauthorized migrants, the path involving approval to remain in Canada is by far the most important. This outcome is not due to encouragement by the dominant immigration and nation-building discourse. Rather, the conversion of unauthorized migrants to authorized ones comes from pressures exerted on the state by special interest groups who want access to less-skilled migrant labour, humanitarian groups fighting to protect vulnerable migrants, and transnational networks that support migrant interests. In other words, forces of global competition and transnational humanitarian and ethnic solidarity move the state to approve the admission of more initially unauthorized migrants than would otherwise be the case. Evidence for this argument can be summarized in a few points.

Employers, unions, and other groups all engage from time to time in efforts to convince the state to admit unauthorized workers. In the 2003 construction boom in Toronto referred to earlier, the

Box 5.2: Undocumented Migrants from China

The fourth Chinese among the 590 migrants who arrived on four ships in summer 1999 in British Columbia was recognized as a refugee in January 2000 by the Immigration and Refugee Board. Some 493 of the migrants applied for asylum and 169 cases have been completed, with 92 applications rejected, four accepted, six withdrawn and 67 abandonments, meaning that the migrants who filed applications disappeared. This means that the acceptance rate for Chinese boat people, four percent, is far below the average of other asylum seekers. The Immigration and Refugee Board granted asylum to about 55 percent of applicants in 1998–99, including 44 percent of Chinese applicants.

Immigration Canada announced that it would appeal the IRB's decision to grant asylum to one of the Chinese migrants who claimed persecution as a result of his membership in the Falun Gong religious sect.

Canada detained most of the Chinese who arrived by ship, but not those who arrived by plane. In 1999, some 1,100 foreigners, including 402 Chinese, arrived at Vancouver International Airport and applied for asylum; most were released immediately or within one day.

Most of the migrants are from Fujian, a province of 32 million in southeast China. Fujian has a history of emigration, as summarized by the so-called three eights: eight million Fujianese are abroad, 80 percent of Taiwanese people are of Fujianese descent, and Fujianese are eight percent of Hong Kong's population. One study found that over 80 percent of those leaving Fujian for North America were employed, mostly as store owners, blue-collar workers or farmers, earning 1,000 Yuan a month.

Another Fujian-linked ship with migrants arrived in Vancouver in January. The Canadian government said that "We can expect China will remain the top source country for both improperly documented passengers and refugees" in 2000. The government said that "state-owned enterprises are making drastic reductions in their workforce. Exit controls have been lifted and virtually everyone is entitled to apply and receive a passport." Thus, China "will continue to be the most important, most problematic, source of immigration to Canada for the foreseeable future."

The Chinese government says that it is trying to dissuade its citizens from leaving the country illegally. In January, China brought back 210 stowaways from Japan. They were sentenced to six months in jail instead of the customary two days.

Canadian authorities in early January 2000 found 10 Chinese teenage girls in a van waiting to enter the U.S. via Walpole Island, a Native American reserve on the Ontario–Michigan border along the St. Clair River. After being apprehended without documents, all applied for asylum.

Source: Migration News 6, 4 (February 2000) [http://migration.ucdavis.edu/mn/more.php?id=2024_ 0_2_0].

construction industry was worried that the federal government might start to deport the unauthorized workers who were playing an important role in building projects at that time. Representatives of the industry asked the federal government to give work permits to the unauthorized migrants. Initially, the government

Box 5.3: Migrant Trafficking in Canada

It is known that international crime is significant in Canada (Beare 2007), but how much of this is related to illegal immigration and the trafficking of sex workers, for example, is unknown. Yet many specific instances of sex trafficking have been reported, generally involving a few to several dozen people in each case. In the case of a 1997 Toronto police raid on a "massage parlour" that was really a brothel, information was gathered from those involved to indicate that:

> Agents in Thailand and Malaysia would recruit teen-aged girls and young women, obtain visitors' visas for Canada and put them on a plane to Vancouver. When they arrived in Vancouver they were met at the airport and put on another plane to Toronto, where they were again met and escorted to one of a series of houses or apartments in North York, Scarborough and Markham that were used as brothels.... The women were held as virtual slaves, police said, while they worked as prostitutes to repay the "debt" of $40,000 (U.S.) charged by the people who brought them to Canada and the brothel owners who purchased them. (Hess 1997: A6)

The "madam" or owner of several of the brothels discovered in the raid was identified as a refugee claimant from China whose claim had been turned down and who had been ordered to leave Canada, but had not done so. She was charged with immigration offences and 135 charges related to her role in organizing and profiting from prostitution.

Source: The author, based on: Hess, Harry. 1997. "Toronto Sex Ring Not Alone." *Globe and Mail* (12 September), A6.

responded favourably: The migrants would be offered two-year work permits and later be given the possibility of applying for immigrant status. A caveat was added: In order to qualify for immigration, the workers would have to demonstrate that they had needed skills for the construction industry. However, there was significant opposition to this plan within Parliament on the grounds that accommodating these workers was unfair to individuals who had applied for admission to Canada through legal channels. In effect the "queue jumpers" would be rewarded and those in the official admission stream would be held back. Eventually, the proposed admission scheme was dropped and, in a somewhat surprising move, in 2006 the government began to deport large numbers of unau-

thorized workers (Jimenez 2006). Some of the workers deported had been in Canada for many years, even decades, and were part of established communities, had raised families in Canada, and considered themselves Canadian. The media reported that a "plane load" of unauthorized migrant workers and their family members were deported to Portugal on Sunday, 26 March 2006 (CTV 2006). Some had purchased housing in Toronto; many claimed that they would try to return as immigrants. Members of the Portuguese community in Toronto were very upset. They reacted with deep anger to the deportations. Mr. Manahan, a spokesperson for a union representing construction workers, said, "We need these people and they cannot qualify under the current immigration system, which favours white-collar workers. The best solution would be if the government reformed the points system to encourage skilled trades people to apply" (quote from Jimenez 2006: 1). Auciello (2006: 1) reported: "It is ironic that as Portuguese construction workers are being deported, others are arriving each month thanks to the temporary foreign worker program, known as CREWS. In fact, in the past four months, more than 50 Portuguese foreign workers have been offered jobs in construction through a program called Construction Recruitment External Workers Services (CREWS)." Then the issue dropped from sight as the wave of deportations came to an end.

This specific historical account leads to the following hypotheses consistent with broader patterns. The state often turns a blind eye to unauthorized migrant workers in times when they are in great need. However, the subject is sensitive and the state may, from time to time, deport large numbers of such workers. Opposition to its actions leads to alternative policies, in this case toward increasing reliance on employers to search for foreign workers who meet their short-term needs. When such workers are found, they offer them work contracts that the state then approves. This pattern is discussed in greater detail in Chapter 11, which briefly examines the rapidly rising number of temporary foreign workers entering Canada over the decade up to 2008.

Immigrant and ethnic communities often join with human rights groups to push for the admission of individuals and groups whose lack of authorization to remain in Canada seems deeply unfair. Some of these cases are very specific to unusual individual circumstances. Consider the case of Juana Tejada, a Filipina who had lived and worked in Canada for three years before applying for immigrant status, only to be turned down on grounds of her ill-

ness (see Box 5.4). The case sparked media interest and considerable public support for her. The Philippines, after China and India, has been the third largest source of immigrants to Canada in recent years (see Chapter 6). Petitions from 300 Filipino community organizations across Canada were mobilized on Juana's behalf. Several Canadian unions and public organizations joined the cause. A June 2008 update report stated that: "Because of the dramatic nature of her story public interest has been raised enough to force the government into paying for her OHIP expenses since her OHIP expired last year, approximately $15,000" (Felipe 2008: 1). Then, "[a]t a press conference held July 18, 2008, Juana's lawyer, Rafael Fabregas, announced that CIC has found Juana eligible for permanent residency status and will grant her visa application once all landing requirements have been met" (Tejada 2008: 1). As in other aspects of Canadian immigrant admission policy, the state has great power to make decisions, but when these decisions depart from public values concerning fairness, the state may shift its views to make exceptions.

Pressure from immigrant-based ethnic communities and human rights organizations has led Canada to implement a series of programs to regularize (provide legal immigrant status) specified groups of unauthorized migrants. Since 1960 there have been eight major programs leading to the admission of some 90,000 "non-status" individuals, a term used by the Ontario Council of Agencies Serving Immigrants (OCASI) to cover what we have referred to as unauthorized migrants (see Table 5.5). The most recent program, "Humanitarian and Compassionate Applications," put in place in 2004, has been admitting about 7,500 unauthorized migrants a year. About 30,000 individuals were admitted in the four years from January 2004 to December 2007.

Box 5.4: The Juana Tejada Story

Juana Tejada, a Filipina caregiver stricken with stage 4 cancer, may pay the ultimate price to keep Canada's government-sponsored medical system out of the reach of foreign workers, if the recent *Toronto Star* poll taken June 9 is any indication.

Of 4,459 respondents, 61% said that foreign workers like Tejada should be denied permanent residence if they are sick. Only 30% voted against denying foreign workers permanent status due to sickness. Without permanent residency status, foreign workers like Juana cannot avail of OHIP or similar government health plans.

Tejada served as a nanny in Alberta after her arrival in Canada in 2003. Her application for an open work permit and permanent residency status in 2006 was denied by an Alberta immigration officer after medical tests indicated she had metastatic colon cancer. According to the ruling, her health condition "might reasonably be expected to cause excessive demand on health and social services."

But for her medical condition, Juana would have received permanent residency status, having completed the 3 years required service as a caregiver under the Federal Live-in Caregiver Program. She has been twice denied permanent immigrant status, however, and was recently ordered by immigration officials to leave the country by August 8, a decision that some say is inhumane and tantamount to a death sentence.

Tejada is currently receiving disability pay but she and her visiting husband do not have OHIP coverage. She has been denied OHIP coverage due to her medical condition. Juana pays for her own prescription drugs with the financial support of friends and members of her church. Out of compassion, doctors at Princess Margaret are providing medical services to Juana for free.

Source: The Philippine Reporter (June 16, 2008) [http://www.philippinereporter.com/2008/06/16/no-compassion-for-dying-filipina-caregiver/].

Many of the Canadian regularization programs are not true amnesties for unauthorized individuals. A true amnesty would grant admission based on having established residence in Canada alone. A few of the programs shown in Table 5.5 are of this kind; for example, those in place between 1967 and 1973. In contrast, the other Canadian programs all involve additional criteria, such as being of a particular national group (Chinese, Algerians, Haitians), having spent enough time in Canada to have become integrated, or facing undue hardship if deported to their home country. In addition, nearly all programs involve normal immigration criteria, such as absence of a criminal record and the

need to pay application fees (see OCASI 2005 for details).

Canadian regularization programs have developed in response to particular historical circumstances and efforts by Canadians concerned with the situation of non-status immigrants. The Chinese adjustment program in the 1960s was part of Canada's recognition that past racist exclusions of the Chinese had forced many individuals of Chinese origin in Canada to hide their identities and falsify their names. Regularization was in response to pressures from the Chinese community in Canada and from others keen to make amends for past policies. The regularization programs for Haitians and Algerians

Table 5.5: Programs to Regularize Non-status Individuals

Program and Date	Who	Number
Chinese Adjustment Program, 1960–1972	Chinese people who came to Canada before 1960 who had no papers or who were pretending to be somebody else	About 12,000
Immigration Appeal Board Act, 1967–1973	Anyone living in Canada without legal immigration status	About 13,000
Adjustment of Status Program, 1973	Anyone living in Canada without legal immigration status	About 39,000
Special Program for Haitians in Quebec, 1981	Haitians without full legal status in Canada	More than 4,000
Minister's Review Committee, 1983–1985	Any non-status person in Canada for five years or more who had become "successfully ... integrated"	About 1,000
Deferred Removal Orders Class, 1994–1998	Failed refugee claimants who had not been deported for three years	About 3,000
Special Procedure for Algerians in Quebec, 2002	Failed refugee claimants from Algeria	Over 900
Humanitarian and Compassionate Applications, 2004–2008*	Anyone living in Canada without status who was able to show "undue hardship" if deported	About 30,000 to date over four years**

* This program will continue into 2009, according to CIC plans
** Updated figures based on actual admissions 2004, 2005, and 2006 and targeted inflows for 2007

Sources: OCASI. 2005. *The Regularization of Non-status Immigrants in Canada 1960–2004: Past Policies, Current Perspectives, Active Campaigns.* Toronto: Ontario Council of Agencies Serving Immigrants [http://www.ocasi.org/STATUS/index.asp]; CIC. (yearly, 2004–2007). *Annual Report to Parliament.* Ottawa: Citizenship and Immigration Canada.

in Quebec reflect the special French-language ties of these communities to Quebec and the large numbers of officially admitted immigrants already in Quebec from both countries. Many of those who were regularized had friends, family, and employers in Quebec who supported these special programs. As of 2004, there were in Canada many non-governmental organizations and committees involved in mobilizing support for the admission of particular groups of non-status migrants. These included the Action Committee of Non-status Algerians, the Action Committee of Pakistani Refugees, the Coalition against the Deportation of Palestinian Refugees, the Congolese Catholic Community of Montreal, the Vancouver Association of Chinese Canadians, and many others (see OCASI 2005). Support for specific programs of regularization such as those reviewed above are also promoted by other organizations, such as Don't Ask Don't Tell, Justice for Migrant Workers, and No One Is Illegal, which see their role as serving unauthorized migrants who live and work in Canada in the same way that they serve all others living and working in this country (Justicia 2008; Lowry and Nyers 2003). A report by the Ontario Council of Agencies Serving Immigrants (OCASI 2005) argues that unauthorized migrants (or non-status migrants, in their terms) are a diverse category of people who are largely law-abiding, hard-working taxpayers. Some have lived for several years in Canada and contributed to the nation's development, much like documented immigrants. What distinguishes them from others in Canada is that they face many hardships and uncertainties because they do not have legal papers to reside in Canada.

Discussion and Conclusions

If one begins the analysis of Canadian immigration controls from the perspective of the rhetoric on selecting immigrants who will be very high-level knowledge workers and entrepreneurs, then the conclusion would be that the current system needs to be radically reshaped. Only about a fifth of immigrants are directly selected by the kind of economic-class criteria intended to bring in such immigrants. Even among this category, there are many individuals with less schooling than the concept of knowledge worker would suggest. In addition, many immigrants in the economic class arrive without official-language skills. Family-class and refugee immigrants add significantly to the diversity of cultural, social, and economic characteristics found among Canadian immigrants due to strong pressures arising from Canadian values,

Canada's international obligations, and the internal logic of promoting immigration around principles of pluralism and fairness that are appealing to the economic immigrants that Canada wants to attract.

If one begins the analysis from the perspective of nation-building in a globally competitive and transnational world, then results of Canadian immigration controls make sense, even if the mix of outcomes may be viewed as unsatisfactory both by the state and various critics of state policy. The state does not necessarily get as many "ideal immigrants" as suggested by its policy discourse. This is also true for Quebec with respect to its desire to promote francophone immigrants. Due to various pressures on Canadian immigration policies arising from migrant motivation, transnational linkages, global communications and travel, and humanitarian lobby groups, Canada is able to retain, perhaps at a higher level than would otherwise be the case, flows of family- and refugee-class immigrants with rather diverse levels of education and knowledge of official languages.

The next chapter extends the analysis on the goals and limits of state immigration policy by examining the national origins of immigrants. The subsequent chapters turn to patterns of immigrant economic incorporation and belonging. As we shall see, getting jobs and how immigrants belong in Canada are significantly influenced by their social and economic characteristics and national origins. How this works out is not entirely under the state's control. Global economic, trade, and transnational practices greatly influence immigrant settlement outcomes.

CHAPTER 6
National and Ethnic Origins

Introduction

The national and ethnic origins of immigrants are constantly changing. New national and ethnic origins are continually rising to the list of top new immigrant sources, while old national and ethnic origins are continually slipping from view. If you are of recent immigrant background and know whether new inflows from your country or ethnic origin are rising or declining, you may have insight into what this means for your national-ethnic community's identity, connections to your home country, and its size and strength to provide connections for jobs and business in Canada.

Consider briefly some recent changes. Only a few decades ago, between 1980 and 1990, Vietnam was the most important country of origin for Canadian immigrants. Poland and Italy were other important source countries. Over the more recent period between 2000 and 2005, Poland and Italy have disappeared from the list of the top 36 source countries, and Vietnam is near the bottom of this list and on a downward trajectory. By 2000–2005, Pakistan, the Philippines, and South Korea had moved up from lower positions in the ordering of top source countries to become situated near the top of this list. What accounts for such dramatic short-term fluctuations in the source countries of tens of thousands of immigrants entering Canada? What are the implications of such shifts for multiculturalism and the social-economic incorporation of immigrants?

This chapter continues the examination of who gets in by looking at the national and ethnic origins of immigrants. Understanding where immigrants originate is an important topic in research on immigrant incorporation and social change in Canada for the following three reasons.

First, the changing national-cultural background of immigrants is a main force driving Canadian multicultural transformation. Immigrants from Africa, Asia, the Caribbean, and Latin America have brought and continue to bring new nationalities, languages, and cultures to Canada.

Second, the countries that immigrants come from affect the challenges they face with respect to social, economic, and cultural incorporation in Canada. Over the past five decades, Canadian immigrants have come increasingly from less developed regions where educational institutions are often poorly funded and underdeveloped, with the result that many immigrants from these regions need to upgrade their schooling and credentials after they arrive in Canada (see Chapters 7 and 8). This can be particularly challenging in cases when they also come from countries where English or French are not widely spoken. It means that, after arrival, while they upgrade their work credentials, they are also struggling to improve their skills in English or French.

Third, the continuing inflow of immigrants from new nations and cultures affects the knowledge of Canadians about people from these new places of origin. This, in turn, has an impact on the extent to which immigrants feel that they belong in Canada (see Chapter 9). Canadian society has come a long way in learning to understand and accept people from different parts of the world, but this is an ongoing process, one continually challenged by shifts taking place in the specific countries from which immigrants come and the arrival of new ethnocultural groups.

In previous chapters we have noted that there is a gap between a dominant policy *discourse* emphasizing highly educated "designer" immigrants and a *reality* in which immigrants come with diverse levels of education, knowledge of official languages, and related work skills. This gap reflects the complexity of Canadian immigration policy due to its multiple goals, the motives of migrants, and international opportunities for migrants. In this chapter, we will attempt to extend these conclusions. The argument is as follows: *While Canada does not officially select immigrants on the basis of country of origin, Canadian policy nevertheless uses socio-economic selection criteria that play an important role in determining the countries from which immigrants come. In addition, immigrant social networks and social capital, operating outside the control of Canadian immigration policy, generate country-of-origin and ethnic streams of immigrants. Finally, shifts in immigrant origins over time create challenges for immigrants and for Canadian society that the state cannot avoid but does not always effectively address.* Canada claims to welcome ethnic diversity, but, as will be argued further in subsequent chapters, it has not yet found strategies to ensure that immigrants from all backgrounds are successful in Canada and feel that they belong.

The chapter begins by outlining a framework for understanding why immigrants come in greater numbers and proportions from some countries than from others. It then examines empirical patterns of international migration flows for the world as a whole and for Canada to assess this framework. Subsequently, I examine a question about fairness. Do some people remain "fixed" or immobile in their home country due to racist, ethnocentric, or other unstated bias in Canadian immigrant admission policies? The chapter concludes with a summary of major findings and their implications for the analysis of immigrant jobs, identity, and belonging that is presented in subsequent chapters.

Framework

To be in a position to immigrate to Canada requires three attributes: motivation, resources, and admissibility under Canadian regulations. *Motivation* is essential. Individuals will not apply unless they are motivated to do so. *Resources* are also required. Among those who are motivated, not all will have the resources to travel to Canada and sustain themselves through initial months while they are looking for employment and housing. However, some immigrants without funds of their own can borrow money or receive support from family members to undertake the move. *Admissibility* – the ability to meet the rules of entry – is absolutely necessary for legal admission. Immigrants must meet criteria related to the entry class specified in their application.

Since all three attributes for admission to Canada must cluster in a favourable way, it is clear that successfully immigrating to Canada involves a complex mix of determinants, some affecting motivation, others affecting resources, and still others affecting admissibility. However, in real cases, the process is often not so complex. This is because the three attributes are not independent of each other. For example, immigrants with high levels of education in relatively less developed countries may be more motivated to move to a country like Canada where their education will bring

greater income. At the same time, such individuals are likely to have the resources to move and are likely to meet Canadian admission criteria. Subsequently, some close kin are more likely to be motivated to move in order to stay close to the person who has previously immigrated to Canada. These individuals are likely to have the resources to move because the family members who are already in Canada are able to provide help and are very motivated to do whatever they can to assist those who want to join them. Close family members are also likely to meet family-class entry criteria. Once in Canada, refugees also often seek to sponsor close relatives to follow them.

Social networks and social capital more broadly are central to the processes that bring together motivation, admissibility, and resources for international migration. Consider the case of a non-Canadian who has friends and relatives who are Canadian residents. This person's motivation to move will be greater because he or she will be joining others who are known and liked. These people may also be encouraging the application, thereby increasing the migrant's motivation. Family or friends in Canada may provide advice to the prospective immigrant on how to present an immigration application. Friends and family may also help in paying fees or arranging loans for travel costs. Even admissibility to Canada can be influenced by links between Canadian residents and their kin and friends abroad. If existing entry rules prevent someone from immigrating, friends and relatives in Canada often lobby to try to change the rules. Members of Parliament receive constant requests from members of immigrant and ethnic communities in their ridings to remove visa requirements for people from certain countries and take an interest in "special cases." Thus, the existence of social, cultural, and institutional links between previous immigrants and kin, friends, and members of their home community will tend to promote the future immigration of others with whom they have such links. However, the opposite is also true. If a potential applicant has no friends or family in Canada, they are less likely to be interested in applying, less likely to receive encouragement and offers of support to apply, and less likely to be admitted if they do apply. Thus, non-Canadians in the world as a whole tend to be divided into two camps: (1) a tiny minority with a favourable combination of eligibility, motivation, and resources, and (2) an enormous majority with an unfavourable combination.

The support given to migrants from family, friends, social networks, and other organizations in their decisions to move and efforts to settle in a foreign country is widely conceptualized in the literature as "social capital." The concept of social capital is important for understanding the international migration flows examined in this chapter. It is also a key concept for understanding immigrant incorporation in Canada. Box 6.1 provides a brief summary of the origins and meaning of the term "social capital."

If we classify admissibility, motivation, and resources in terms of each being either *yes* or *no*, then there are eight possible ways in which the three determinants of immigration to Canada can be combined. These are shown in Table 6.1. However, when the eight different patterns are examined, it becomes clear that many of these can be lumped together, while others can be excluded because they are unlikely combinations. Patterns 1, 2, and 3 can be considered together. While different, together they cover most of the population in the world who do not immigrate to Canada because they: (1) do not meet official criteria for admission; (2) do not have the resources; and/or (3) are not motivated. Pattern 7 is an important combination because it defines the pool of individuals who are motivated

and who have or can arrange the resources to move, even if they are not legally admissible. This pool is the main recruiting ground for unauthorized migration. Pattern 8 is the pool from which economic and family immigrants are drawn. It consists of people who are admissible, motivated, and resourced. Individuals in pattern 8 are a small proportion of the world's population, but nevertheless constitute a very large absolute number of people. For this reason, applications to immigrate have tended to exceed Canada's capacity to process those who apply. In 2008, for example, a waiting list of more than 1 million immigration applications had accumulated over time. All these individuals had paid application fees. If all turn out to be admissible, the total number of people waiting for admission will be large enough to fill Canadian immigration targets for the subsequent four years.

Let us now turn to examine how immigration flows generated by the clustering of favourable individual entry attributes can also be understood from a macro-social migration systems perspective. Immigration streams typically begin with a smaller flow of individuals whom we may label "pioneers" in the international migration process. This small flow will typically expand over time as other migrants follow the pioneers to form a chain of linked immigrants. Such a flow may stabilize at a higher level for a period, then eventually, either sooner or later, it will tend to decline due to shifts brought about by the migration process itself or due to other new circumstances. It is useful to think of the typical process in terms of five stages: initiation, acceleration, plateau, deceleration, and termination. Each stage has a logic within a larger historical migration system and the regional or global political economic dynamics of which it is part. The stages are shown graphically in Figure 6.1.

Box 6.1: Social Capital: A Key Concept in Analyzing Migration Systems

Immigrants, like all other individuals, possess various kinds of resources or "capital." They may need *financial capital* to help with their move and settlement. Their ability to meet immigration criteria and find good jobs will depend on their *human capital*, namely, their education, job skills, work experience, and their state of health. The migration and settlement process will be easier if, in addition, they have *social capital* in the form of trusting relations with others who have information and contacts or can provide emotional or other support that will promote good outcomes.

Social capital is a broad concept subject to various definitions. For the purposes of this book, social capital may be defined as the connections among people, including trust, mutual understanding, reciprocity, and shared values that bind them together informally in social networks, more formally as voluntary members of organizations such as churches or ethnic associations, and broadly within organized communities, making co-operation possible. The concept of social capital has wide applicability to the understanding of trust, reciprocity, and solidarity in society across many spheres. It has also become a major concept in studies of international migration for several reasons.

As noted in this chapter, migrant social networks and related information flows and contacts — namely, relationships involving social capital — are fundamentally important determinants of the size and direction of international migration flows.

In addition, the success that immigrants have in finding good jobs, housing, and relationships with others after they have moved is also understood to be influenced by their social capital. This is because various forms of "capital" can replace one another to a certain degree. An individual who lacks the financial capital to migrate may be able to borrow it if he or she has a trusting relationship with others who, individually or collectively, can lend the necessary money. A young immigrant with limited work experience may be able to get a good entry-level job with promotion possibilities if he or she has good contacts through others to employers.

Finally, transnational social spaces are understood to be a manifestation of social capital. Migrants and their families help one another. Some immigrants belong to churches and hometown associations that generate trusting relationships and exchanges within host societies and across nations to their home communities. Social capital is therefore fundamental to the operation of transnational migration systems.

While social capital is a central concept in migration studies, exactly how it operates is a matter of debate. Many studies suggest that the amounts of social capital available to immigrants and migrants should not be exaggerated. Some migrants, such as refugees and women or minority groups within immigrant communities, have so little social capital that they are doubly marginalized in that they have few (if any) trusting relationships to draw on either in their own communities or in the host society (Menjivar 2000: 237). Immigrants' social capital may have little effect on their settlement outcomes if other institutional forces, such as state policies or pre-existing patterns of ethnic racialization, in society provide little opportunity for its expression (Portes 1995: 14–19; Portes and Landolt 1996). Bourdieu's (1977) pioneering work on social capital shows that it can reproduce social inequality over time. Findings from

Kazemipur's (2006b) study shows that the social capital of Canadian immigrants is less than that of native-born individuals, with the result that immigrants have a hard time finding good jobs in a competitive job market.

The concept of social capital is credited to overlapping developments by various contemporary authors, including Bourdieu (1977), Coleman (1988), and Putnam (1995, 2000), building on concepts of community in classical works in the social sciences. Portes (1998) provides a useful review of the origins and applications of the concept. Helliwell (1996) provides evidence that findings from U.S. studies on the relationship of organizational memberships to social capital do not apply well in Canada, indicating that social capital is formed in different ways in different nations.

Table 6.1: Combinations of Determinants of Immigration

Pattern	Admissible?	Motivated?	Resourced?	Comment
1	No	No	No	Covers a large portion of worldwide populations in LDCs*
2	No	No	Yes	Covers many individuals in LDCs who could move, but are not motivated or admissible
3	No	Yes	No	Covers many individuals in LDCs who would move if they could
4	Yes	No	No	Probably a null category: Those who are admissible generally have resources, regardless of motivation
5	Yes	Yes	No	Probably a null category: Those who are admissible generally have resources
6	Yes	No	Yes	Well-to-do professionals and business families in LDCs and MDCs* who are not motivated
7	No	Yes	Yes	This is the pool that generates undocumented migrants; they are motivated and resourced, but officially inadmissible
8	Yes	Yes	Yes	A small portion of the world's LDC population who compete with one another for entry to MDCs; while a small proportion of the total LDC population, the number is, in fact, large

*LDCs and MDCs refer respectively to "less developed countries" and "more developed countries."

Figure 6.1: Migration Streams from Initiation to Termination

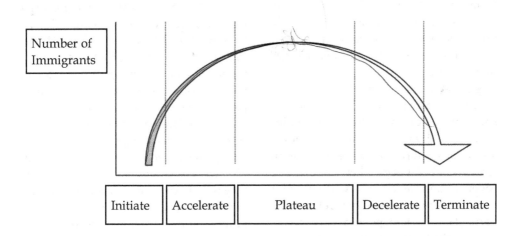

Initiation: Flows are initiated historically by the way in which nations are linked to one another within the larger international system. Historically, the links were often established by colonial labour and settlement practices that moved people from one nation to another, as described in previous chapters. However, flows can also begin due to a refugee crisis, which then leads to at least a short period of follow-on immigration for the purposes of family reunification, as has been noted for refugee-led immigration from Latin America (Goldring 2006; Mata 1985; Simmons 1993a, 1993b). Flows can also emerge from other new historical circumstances that create the necessary conditions for some people to undertake a pioneering movement that can lead to a follow-on flow. Small flows of live-in caregivers (nannies and others) from the Commonwealth Caribbean to Canada in the 1950s and early 1960s, supported by a shared colonial heritage, gave rise to very large immigration flows from this region over the period from the mid-1960s through to the 1990s after Canadian immigration policies shifted to make this possible.

Acceleration: Once underway, flows of migrants tend to accelerate due to the expansion of social, economic, and political transnational links between the migrant-origin nations and Canada. Put in other words, a flow once underway generates momentum by putting in place new and stronger transnational connections. After arrival, new migrants establish transnational communication links with their families and friends in their home country. They also establish stores specializing in home-country foods and churches, mosques, or temples that respond to immigrants' spiritual needs. In this process, transnational communities gradually form. Such communities may include ethnic newspapers, visiting artists, performers, political leaders, and others from home countries, and various professional services provided in the home languages of the immigrants. While these communities may be considered ethnic enclaves within Canada, they are also transnational entities because they are nourished and sustained by back-and-forth flow of information, support, and resources between the home country and Canada. Ethnic newspapers advertise airline ticket sales for travel to home countries, real estate investments in home countries, visitors from home countries, and so on, in addition to providing the latest information on home-country sports teams and other news. The net effect is that transnational communities provide important cultural and social supports for new immigrants and tend to encourage more people to move.

Plateau: Specific immigration streams tend to reach a plateau or high point after some period of time. Flows may maintain themselves at the plateau level for a long or a short period, depending on circumstances. Cases where the plateau covers a short period arise when migrant motivation or admissibility is related to a particular short-term political or economic crisis in the home country. In the case of refugee-led flows, for example, the home country conditions may improve.

Deceleration: Migration streams from particular source countries tend to diminish at some point sooner or later. Deceleration comes about through some change in the relationship between countries in the international system. This may include improved job opportunities in source countries, the emergence of alternative destinations for migrants leaving source countries, or the emergence of new, more restrictive immigrant entry criteria. Racism and ethnic conflict in immigrant destination nations can slow flows of new immigrants. Deceleration can be very quick or very drawn out. Generally streams that involve the development of powerful transnational social and institutional links die out more slowly. Thus, for example, European immigration to Canada began to decelerate in the late 1950s. However, European social, cultural, economic, and political links to Canada were so strongly and deeply established in earlier history that European immigrant flows to Canada continued at moderate levels through to the 1990s and are still important, although at reduced levels, as we will document later in this chapter.

Global Immobility

The view from the wealthiest nations and regions is that the world is being reshaped by very large flows of international migrants. Looking at the transforming Canadian social landscape brought about by immigrants from all parts of the world provides everyday confirmation that large numbers of foreign-born individuals have settled in Canada. Eighteen percent, or nearly one in five residents in Canada, in 2005 were international migrants; that is, they were born in another country and are now living in Canada. High proportions of international migrants are also found in other nations that, like Canada, are considered to be countries of immigration because historically they have officially welcomed international migrants as settlers. These countries include Australia (20.3 percent foreign-born), New Zealand (15.9 percent foreign-born), and the United States (12.9 percent foreign-born). Other prosperous, politically stable nations, such as France, Germany, and the United Kingdom, do *not* consider themselves to be countries of immigration because the planned settlement of foreigners has not been part of their national policy. In fact, historically, these countries have viewed themselves as countries of emigration because they either accepted or encouraged many of their own citizens to resettle overseas. Nevertheless, these wealthy European nations are now *de facto* migrant-destination countries; around 10 percent of their population in 2005 was foreign-born. Among wealthy nations, only Japan has a very low proportion of international migrants. Less than 2 percent of Japan's population is foreign-born. With few exceptions, then, the foreign-born constitute important segments of the populations of the world's wealthiest nations. They constitute a particularly large share of certain wealthy nations, such as Australia and Canada, which have a long history of admitting large numbers of immigrants.

Examining international migration from the perspective of people in sending countries leads to a very different picture. Despite the large number of international migrants in some countries, only a tiny proportion of the world's population is mobile across international borders. It is estimated that about 97 percent of the world's population are living in the country in which they were born (Table 6.2). If one considers only the population of less developed regions, the home of 5.2 billion of the world's 6.4 billion people, then immobility is even more extreme. More than 98 percent of the people in less developed countries were born in the country where they reside. Put in numerical terms, there are about 190 million international migrants in the world. However, this large number is only 2.9 percent of the 6.4 billion people on earth.

From the above, we may conclude that the large numbers of international migrants worldwide are but a small fraction of the world's inhabitants. In addition, international migrants have a major impact on receiving countries because these migrant-destination nations are relatively few in number and have small populations in relation to the total population of the world.

Faist (2000: 124) has argued that immobility (staying home) is the normal case for the vast majority of the world population. Most live in less developed countries and find that other less developed countries in their own region of the world typically do not welcome immigrants. The majority of the world's population are poor and have little schooling, hence members of this majority are unwelcome in those few wealthy nations that do admit immigrants. Given their lack of welcome elsewhere, most of the world's population stay home,

close to relatives and in the supportive confines of their own cultures. Those who would like to move elsewhere, despite the unwelcoming attitudes, often do not have the money to undertake a long-distance move without assistance. The risks of incarceration and deportation and the additional life-threatening dangers of crossing open waters or inhospitable landscapes make undocumented migration hazardous and an option that only a few will seek except when home conditions become intolerable, or in cases where migrant networks supporting undocumented migration have become particularly strong, as noted in Chapter 5.

Wealthy nations attract migrants because they have better economic opportunities and also because they have better civil rights (freedom of religious activities, legal protections), social rights (permanent residents often have a status with access to schooling and other social programs similar to that of citizens), political rights (resident migrants can join unions and, after a period of time, can become citizens). However, not all wealthy states are equal with respect to their civil rights codes. In a notorious exception to the general rule, the oil-rich Arab Gulf states have many employment opportunities for international migrants, but the migrants have few rights: Religious activities of non-Muslims are forbidden or restricted; the migrants have very limited social or political rights and may be expelled at any time; they are not permitted to remain permanently and become citizens; and often they are very poorly paid. Migrant workers rioted in several Gulf states in 2007 to protest their conditions, with the result that some governments of the region have begun to move gradually to address some of the migrants' grievances (Andoni 2007). Many migrant workers are drawn to the Gulf states for work, but these states remain relatively unattractive destinations for

Table 6.2: Foreign-Born by Region and Country, 2005

	Year	Foreign-Born	Population	% Foreign-Born
		(in thousands)	(in thousands)	
WORLD	2005	190,633,565	6,464,749,000	2.9
Highly Developed Countries	2005	115,397	1,211,265	9.5
Less Developed Countries	2005	75,237,044	5,253,484,000	1.4
REGIONS				
Europe	2005	64,116	728,389	8.8
North America	2005	44,493	330,608	13.5
Oceania	2005	5,034	33,056	15.2
Africa	2005	17,069	905,936	1.9
Asia	2005	53,291	3,905,415	1.4
Latin America and the Caribbean	2005	6,631	561,346	1.2
SELECTED COUNTRIES				
Australia	2005	4,097	20,155	20.3
Canada	2005	6,106	32,268	18.9
New Zealand	2005	642	4,028	15.9
U.S.	2005	38,355	298,213	12.9
France	2005	6,471	60,496	10.7
Germany	2005	10,144	82,689	12.3
U.K.	2005	5,408	59,668	9.1
Italy	2005	2,519	58,093	4.3
Spain	2005	4,790	43,064	11.1
Japan	2005	2,048	128,085	1.6

International migrants: They are estimated largely from census data on the number of foreign-born residents. In some cases, citizenship rather than foreign-born status is used.

More developed regions: They comprise all regions of Europe, plus North America, Australia/New Zealand, and Japan. The totals for Europe do not include the successor states of the former U.S.S.R. for the periods before 1990 because it was not possible to derive estimates for these states before their independence. Instead, the former U.S.S.R., as a single unit, is included in the more developed countries between 1960 and 1985 (see composition of major areas and regions, below).

Less developed regions: They comprise all regions of Africa, Asia (excluding Japan), Latin America and the Caribbean, plus Melanesia, Micronesia, and Polynesia. The totals for Asia do not include the successor states of the former U.S.S.R. before 1990 because it was not possible to derive estimates for these states before their independence.

Source: United Nations Population Division. *World Migrant Stock: The 2005 Revision* [http://esa.un.org/migration/index.asp?panel=1].

those migrants who have a choice and can move to a wealthy nation in North America, Europe, or Oceania.

Is globalization leading to higher levels of international migration? From the perspective of the small number of important migrant-destination countries, the answer is *yes*. From the perspective of the many countries that are principally migrant-origin places, the answer is *no*. Table 6.3 shows estimates for international migration from 1960 to 2005 for selected regions and countries. From the perspective of highly developed countries, international mobility has increased over this period. In 1960, only 3.4 percent of the population of highly developed countries was foreign-born. By 2005, the foreign-born had risen to 9.5 percent, close to a threefold increase. Moreover, the trend over time is continu-

ously upward. In other words, despite tight immigrant entry controls, the number and proportion of international migrants in developed countries is increasing. When the world is examined from the view of less developed nations, then the picture is quite different. In 1960 only 2.1 percent of the population of less developed nations were foreign-born (Table 6.2). As low as this percentage was in 1960, over subsequent decades it declined further. By 2005, only 1.4 percent of the population of less developed countries were foreign-born.

Immigrant Links to Canada

Since the 1970s more than three-quarters of all Canadian immigrants have come

Table 6.3: Percentage Foreign-Born by Region and Selected Countries

	1960	1970	1980	1990	2000	2005
Highly Developed Regions	3.4	3.6	4.2	7.2	8.8	9.5
Less Developed Regions	2.1	1.6	1.6	1.8	1.5	1.4
Europe	3.4	4.1	4.5	6.8	8.0	8.8
North America	6.1	5.6	7.1	9.7	12.8	13.5
Oceania	13.4	15.4	16.4	17.8	16.3	15.2
Australia	16.6	19.5	21.1	23.6	21.4	20.3
Canada	15.4	15.0	15.5	15.6	18.1	18.9
New Zealand	14.1	14.5	15.1	15.5	18.5	15.9
U.S.	5.2	4.6	6.2	9.1	12.2	12.9
France	7.7	10.3	10.9	10.4	10.6	10.7
Germany				7.5	11.9	12.3
U.K.	3.2	5.4	6.3	6.6	8.1	9.1
Italy	3.2	5.4	6.3	6.6	8.1	9.1
Spain	0.8	1.1	0.6	1.9	4.0	11.1
Japan	0.6	0.6	0.6	0.7	1.3	1.6

Source: United Nations Population Division. *World Migrant Stock: The 2005 Revision* [http://esa.un.org/migration/index.asp?panel=1]

Figure 6.2: Percentage of Total Immigrants from Each World Region, Canada, 1980–2005

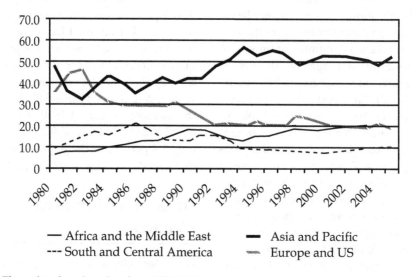

— Africa and the Middle East   ▬ Asia and Pacific
--- South and Central America   ⁓ Europe and US

Source: The author, based on data from LIDS. 2005. *Landed Immigrant Data System*. Ottawa: Citizenship and Immigration Canada.

from non-European regions, a fact that adds substance to the claim that Canada is an increasingly diverse multicultural nation. However, immigrants do not come equally from different regions of the world. Figure 6.2 shows that since 1994, somewhat more than half of immigrants have come from Asia. Over this same period, flows from Africa and the Middle East have grown to about 20 percent of the total, while flows from South and Central America have stabilized around 10 percent of the total. Notably, the numbers of immigrants from Europe and the United States (a country in which European-origin people have formed the majority) declined somewhat and then held constant at around 20 percent of the total inflow. This is almost two times greater than the proportion of Europeans in the world (11 percent, see Table 6.4 ahead). The fact that flows from wealthy nations remain relatively high is likely due in part to the Canadian points system and the way that it favours highly skilled workers

with advanced post-secondary schooling and skills in English or French, and is likely due in part to long established social and cultural ties between these immigrant source countries and Canada.

Those immigrants who do come to Canada from each region come predominantly from a few countries in these regions. Table 6.4 shows the most important Canadian immigrant-origin countries from 1980 to 2005. Consistent with the model of historical migration streams, in the period examined one can distinguish the main origin countries, minor origin countries, and nations from which few immigrants came.

Main origin countries: Between the 1980s and 2005, 10.4 percent of Canadian immigrants came from one country alone: China. Another 8.9 percent came from India. These two countries together contributed nearly a fifth of all immigrants. Four countries (China, India, Hong Kong, and the Philippines) contributed 30 percent of all immigrants. The top 10 sources, consisting of the aforementioned countries, plus the U.K., Vietnam, Pakistan, the U.S., Poland, and Iran, contributed nearly half (48.1 percent) of all immigrants.

Minor origin countries: An additional 25 percent of all immigrants to Canada between 1980 and 2005 came from 23 minor origin countries, including Sri Lanka, Taiwan, South Korea, Jamaica, Lebanon, and many others, through to Colombia. Immigrants from each of these countries contributed on average a little more than 1 percent to total Canadian immigration. The remaining 25 percent of all immigrants came in very small numbers from each of another 218 countries.

From 1980 to 2005, the top 10 countries of immigrant origin changed considerably. Table 6.4 shows the top immigrant-origin countries for each of three periods: the 1980s, the 1990s, and 2000–2005. In each period the countries listed are different. Many are listed in all three periods, but their rank order of importance is different from one time period to another. A number of different patterns can be observed, including the following.

1. *Sustaining top 10 origin countries:* China, India, the Philippines, and the U.S. are in the top 10 origin countries for all three time periods, although they do change their rank position over time.

2. *New top 10 origin countries:* Several countries that were not ranked in the top 10 immigrant origin nations in the 1980s moved up to the top 10 by 2000–2005. These countries are: Pakistan, South Korea, Iran, Russia, and Sri Lanka.

3. *Fading top 10 origin countries:* Six of the top 10 immigrant origin countries in the 1980s were no longer among the top 10 in the 2000–2005 period. Vietnam, the U.K., Hong Kong, and Poland all fell from the top 10 to lower levels. These and all other cases of quickly shifting positions have their own explanations. In the case of Hong Kong, the crisis associated with China's 1997 repossession of this former British colony created a huge exodus prior to the takeover and a return to lower levels of outflow following the takeover. In the case of Poland, a very high demand for foreign workers in the United Kingdom in the 1990s led to a shift in Polish immigration to Britain; the Polish immigrants were able to maintain much closer ties to their families and visit them often due to low-cost airfare and the short travel distance. Over this period, economic growth and political developments continued to make Poland a more desirable place to live, yet wages were still low.

4. *Wealthy European nations gradually decline in importance:* While flows from Europe continued after the earlier declines through the 1980s, these flows subsequently tended to stabilize at smaller but still significant levels. In addition, the United States has been and continues to be one of the top origin nations for Canadian immigrants. The result of these trends is that roughly 20 percent of all immigrants to Canada come from other very wealthy nations. Europe and the United States together hold roughly 11 percent of the world's population (see Table 6.5). Therefore Canadian immigration from these wealthy locations is almost twice what one would expect on the basis of world population distribution. Borjas (1993) argued that relatively high inflows of immigrants to Canada from wealthy nations is a result of the Canadian points system for selecting highly educated workers who are found in greater numbers in wealthy nations. Borjas notes that the United States does not use any similar mechanism to select highly educated workers, with the result that only about 10 percent of U.S. immigrants come from other wealthy nations, a proportion about half of that for Canada.

Table 6.4: Most Important Immigrant Origin Countries, 1980s, 1990s, and 2000–2005, Canada

		1980s					1990s					2000–2005		
		Number	%	Cumulative %			Number	%	Cumulative %			Number	%	Cumulative %
1	Vietnam	92,077	7.3	7.3	1	China	225,555	10.0	10.0	1	China	233,905	16.1	16.1
2	U.K.	91,024	7.2	14.6	2	Hong Kong	203,715	9.0	19.0	2	India	182,185	12.5	28.6
3	India	86,835	6.9	21.5	3	India	180,668	8.0	27.1	3	Pakistan	85,134	5.9	34.5
4	Hong Kong	77,720	6.2	27.6	4	Philippines	138,188	6.1	33.2	4	Philippines	80,339	5.5	40.0
5	China	68,890	5.5	33.1	5	Taiwan	76,621	3.4	36.6	5	South Korea	42,638	2.9	42.9
6	U.S.	66,149	5.3	38.4	6	Sri Lanka	69,739	3.1	39.7	6	Iran	38,787	2.7	45.6
7	Poland	66,102	5.3	43.6	7	Poland	64,356	2.9	42.5	7	U.S.	34,572	2.4	48.0
8	Philippines	61,158	4.9	48.5	8	Pakistan	61,085	2.7	45.2	8	Romania	32,642	2.2	50.2
9	Jamaica	34,760	2.8	51.3	9	Iran	56,378	2.5	47.7	9	Sri Lanka	31,142	2.1	52.4
10	Guyana	32,664	2.6	53.9	10	Vietnam	53,301	2.4	50.1	10	Russia	27,805	1.9	54.3
11	Portugal	25,332	2.0	55.9	11	U.S.	50,936	2.3	52.4	11	U.K.	27,090	1.9	56.2
12	Iran	23,814	1.9	57.8	12	U.K.	50,114	2.2	54.6	12	Colombia	23,832	1.6	57.8
13	Lebanon	23,582	1.9	59.7	13	Lebanon	47,833	2.1	56.7	13	France	21,753	1.5	59.3
14	Haiti	22,519	1.8	61.4	14	Jamaica	40,756	1.8	58.5	14	Morocco	21,054	1.4	60.7
15	El Salvador	21,370	1.7	63.1	15	Yugoslavia	38,624	1.7	60.2	15	Ukraine	20,669	1.4	62.2
16	Germany (FRG)	19,122	1.5	64.7	16	South Korea	38,337	1.7	61.9	16	Algeria	20,000	1.4	63.5
17	Cambodia	16,863	1.3	66.0	17	Romania	35,297	1.6	63.5	17	Afghanistan	19,460	1.3	64.9
18	South Korea	16,381	1.3	67.3	18	Guyana	28,021	1.2	64.7	18	Bangladesh	18,561	1.3	66.1
19	France	14,710	1.2	68.5	19	France	27,606	1.2	66.0	19	Taiwan	16,465	1.1	67.3
20	Sri Lanka	14,615	1.2	69.6	20	Trinidad	25,658	1.1	67.1	20	Lebanon	16,342	1.1	68.4
21	Trinidad	12,665	1.0	70.6	21	El Salvador	24,420	1.1	68.2	21	Jamaica	13,809	0.9	69.4

#					#					#				
22	Romania	12,628	1.0	71.6	22	Somalia	23,015	1.0	69.2	22	Yugoslavia	12,965	0.9	70.2
23	Azores	12,067	1.0	72.6	23	Haiti	21,911	1.0	70.2	23	Iraq	12,590	0.9	71.1
24	Italy	11,995	1.0	73.6	24	Russia	21,704	1.0	71.1	24	Vietnam	12,567	0.9	72.0
25	Laos	11,440	0.9	74.5	25	Bosnia	21,664	1.0	72.1	25	Mexico	12,319	0.8	72.8
26	Taiwan	10,631	0.8	75.3	26	U.S.S.R.	21,271	0.9	73.0	26	Haiti	11,590	0.8	73.6
27	Czechoslovakia	10,599	0.8	76.2	27	Iraq	21,236	0.9	74.0	27	Egypt	11,375	0.8	74.4
28	U.S.S.R.	10,277	0.8	77.0	28	Egypt	19,768	0.9	74.9	28	Germany (FRG)	9,494	0.7	75.1
29	Malaysia	9,717	0.8	77.8	29	Portugal	18,750	0.8	75.7	29	Bulgaria	9,372	0.6	75.7
30	South Africa	9,702	0.8	78.5	30	Bangladesh	18,055	0.8	76.5	30	Sudan	9,212	0.6	76.3
31	Chile	9,602	0.8	79.3	31	Germany (FRG)	16,057	0.7	77.2	31	Nigeria	8,743	0.6	76.9
32	Netherlands	9,573	0.8	80.0	32	Afghanistan	15,567	0.7	77.9	32	Guyana	8,667	0.6	77.5
33	Pakistan	9,370	0.7	80.8	33	Ukraine	15,258	0.7	78.6	33	Turkey	8,628	0.6	78.1
34	Yugoslavia	9,157	0.7	81.5	34	South Africa	14,670	0.7	79.2	34	South Africa	8,504	0.6	78.7
35	Ethiopia	8,629	0.7	82.2	35	Ethiopia	14,647	0.6	79.9	35	Albania	8,045	0.6	79.3
36	Egypt	8,576	0.7	82.9	36	Ghana	13,544	0.6	80.5	36	Ethiopia	8,036	0.6	79.8
	Other*	215,177	17.1	100.0		Other*	44,0082	19.5	100.0		Other*	293,361	20.2	100.0
	TOTAL	1,257,492	100.0			TOTAL	2,254,407	100.0			TOTAL	1,453,652	100.0	

* Number of other countries: in the 1980s (210), 1990s (211), and 2000–2005 (211).

Source: The author, based on data from: LIDS. 2005. *Landed Immigrant Data System*. Ottawa: Citizenship and Immigration Canada.

Table 6.5: Differential Odds of Immigrating to Canada by Region of Origin

	Percent of Canadian Immigrants (1)	Percent of World Population (2)	Relative Representation in Canadian Immigration (3) = (1)/(2)
Africa	7.6	14.7	0.5
Asia	56.8	60.4	0.9
Caribbean	4.8	0.6	7.8
Europe and U.S.	20.0	11.2	1.8
South and Central America	6.6	7.9	0.8
Other	4.2	5.0	0.8
Total	100.0	100.0	1.0

Sources: Percent immigrants from different world regions is based on those arriving in Canada 1980–2005, tabulated by the author from: LIDS. 2005. *Landed Immigrant Data System.* Ottawa: Citizenship and Immigration Canada. Percent of world population from: UNPD. (2008). *World Population Prospects: The 2008 Revision Population Data Base.* New York: United Nations Population Division.

Each Stream Is Unique: Selected Case Studies

Migration streams from different countries of origin to Canada each have their own specific histories. To explore variations in pattern and the insights that each pattern leads to, I briefly examine a few contrasting flows. These are: the origins of the sustained high flows from China, India, and the Philippines; the slightly rising flow from France; and the gradually declining flows from the Caribbean. I will also comment briefly on trends with respect to immigration from Africa and Latin America. These cases are selected to provide insight into the various historical forces that generated immigration flows to Canada and the reasons why these flows are either rising or falling at present.

Chinese immigration: From the 1990s to 2005, China was the most important source of immigrants to Canada. Chinese migrants came to Canada first in the 1880s to assist

with railway building. Their labour was wanted, but they were not viewed as desirable settlers within the Canadian national self-image at the time. In 1885, the Parliament of Canada approved a policy to restrict Chinese immigration by imposing a $50 head tax on each Chinese person coming to Canada. This tax was raised to $100 in 1900 and to $500 in 1903 (Li 1998). At that time, $500 was equivalent to roughly two years of salary for a manual worker. The tax did not totally exclude Chinese immigration, but it came close to that. It had the effect of restricting the inflow of Chinese and making them a community of bachelor workers. The men were wanted for railway construction and other manual work, but the taxes discouraged them from bringing wives and children. Their communities remained small, mostly composed of men, and could not reproduce themselves. The head tax was ended in 1923 and replaced with a new Chinese Exclusion Act, which excluded the Chinese from settling in Canada, although some exceptions were made for small numbers of Chinese business immigrants (Morton 1974). Parliament repealed the Chinese Exclusion Act in 1947 and gave Chinese-Canadians full citizenship rights, with one exception: China was not a country of preference for immigrants. As a result, Chinese immigration was limited to only the spouse and dependants of Chinese who had Canadian citizenship (Li 1998), thereby carrying forward the hurtful racist practices of the past. When many more Chinese immigrants began to arrive after 1962, the memory and legacy of past racism persisted and led to continuing pressure from the Chinese-Canadian community for a formal apology and compensation from the Canadian government. The apology finally materialized in 2006. The tiny number of remaining survivors of those who paid the infamous head tax are to receive approximately Can. $20,000 in compensation. There were only an estimated 20 Chinese-Canadians who paid the tax and were still alive in 2006.

Ethnic Chinese immigrants in Canada come from different locations and backgrounds. In the 1980s, more came from Hong Kong, at that time still a British possession where English was the main language of government and where enormous social and economic development had taken place over the post-Second World War period. Inflows of immigrants from Hong Kong were very high over the period up to 1997, the year in which control over that city-state reverted to China. The immigrants were motivated in part by fear about the negative impact that Chinese control would have on economic opportunities and civil liberties. Ethnic Chinese immigration to Canada from Taiwan, a country very closely connected to Western nations through trade and investment, has also been substantial in recent decades, yet flows from China itself have continued to expand, placing that country as the top source country from 1990s to 2005. In sum,

the ethnic Chinese population in Canada is diverse in origin; arrived through different connections and for different motives; and has created in Canada a very large and complex transnational community that continues to draw very large numbers of immigrants from China itself. Given the enormous total population of China (1.2 billion in 2005) and the fact that the number of Chinese people with advanced schooling is rising, China provides a huge pool of potential highly educated immigrants. However, immigration flows from China may decline in the future. If Chinese economic growth continues at high levels and birth rates in that country stay low, at some point China will begin to experience labour shortages. When this happens, wages will rise in China and Chinese workers' motivation to emigrate may decline. As always, the way the future will actually unfold is unknown.

Immigration from India: India in the recent past has been the second most important source of Canadian immigrants. The history of this movement also has deep historical roots. India, like Canada, was part of the British Empire. As a result, Indian nationals were British subjects and some were interested in immigrating to Canada in the early part of the 19th century. Small numbers of East Indians, mostly Sikhs, had settled in Canada between 1897 and 1907. Most were located in British Columbia. The origins of Sikh settlement in Canada are at least partly linked to the end of the Boer War (1899–1902) in South Africa. At that time, East Indians who had served in the British Army were decommissioned in England and sought settlement opportunities in Australia, Canada, and elsewhere (Johnson 1979: Chapter 1). By 1898 it is estimated that there were about 5,000 East Indians in British Columbia. However, the Canadian government supported the widespread public prejudice against the East Indians by adopting measures to discourage immigration from India. The most effective policy was the shameful Continuous Passage Act of 1908, which required all immigrants to arrive on an uninterrupted journey from their country of origin to Canada. Steamships of the time did not make non-stop trips to Canada from India. This created a major block to immigration from that country. All available passenger ships from East Asia involved stops en route, which violated the requirement of a continuous passage. Between 1908 and 1947, immigration from India was essentially closed (see Chapter 3, Box 3.2 on the frustrated voyage of the *Komagata Maru*). The Continuous Passage Act was repealed in 1947. After repeal of the Act, some Indian immigration resumed because close family members of Indian-born residents (later citizens) of Canada were allowed to enter Canada under family reunification provisions. However, India was not a country of preference for Canadian immigration in 1947 and, as a result, the inflow of immigrants from India remained small until 1962, after which it expanded rapidly due to the major shift in Canadian immigration policies that took place then.

Initial Indian settlement in Western Canada consisted largely of Sikhs. As one would anticipate, the flow of Sikh immigrants to Canada resumed after the new immigration policies were implemented in 1962 to end the White Canada era. In addition, however, flows from other ethnic communities in India, particularly of individuals from the Hindu majority, also rose to great numbers. It is often the case that what we see as a nation-to-nation historical migration flow is composed of several sub-currents based on ethnicity, local community, social class, or other bases of social identity and networking. While these can be quite independent of one another, it is also the case that they are often set in motion and sustained by

overlapping conditions and networks. In the case of India, Sikhs had a special role as police and soldiers in the colonial system, but the Hindus and others also had roles in this system. A fuller examination of their shared history would take into account the impact of the colonial system on the Indian economy and the rise of landless workers and indentured labour practices that took Indian workers to the Caribbean and other parts of the world.

The large streams of immigrants from India over recent decades have been sustained by the fact that India is a very large country with many well-educated, English-speaking individuals who have had lower levels of income and economic opportunity than in Canada. Different Indian ethno-religious communities (Hindu, Muslim, Sikh, etc.) in Canada have each developed extensive transnational institutions and networks to support continuing flows from India. Like China, India has also experienced very rapid economic development in recent years. Some of this has been concentrated in high-technology sectors, such as computer software engineering, which are drawing skilled Indian immigrants in Western nations back to India. Is this an early sign that well-educated, English-speaking Indians will soon become less interested in immigrating to Canada? The answer is unknown at present, but worth keeping in mind as economic development patterns in the international system evolve.

Immigration from the Philippines: From 1990 to 2005, the Philippines ranked after China, India, and Hong Kong as the next most important origin nation of Canadian immigrants. However, it stands out from these countries in one important respect. There was no co-ethnic Philippine community in Canada prior to the 1960s. Hence there were no *direct* institutional or social network links for the Philippine immigration stream to build on. However, there were many *indirect* links and additional circumstances that explain the rapid rise in migration flows from the Philippines to Canada. These include:

- Spanish colonization of the Philippines in the 16th and 17th centuries, leading to the establishment of Catholicism and strong contacts with Western culture
- American military and cultural presence, with respect to Christian missions and schools, from the late 19th century onward
- Widespread use of English as the main language of business, high education, science, and law; the main TV cable channels are broadcast in English
- Large flows of Filipinos to the United States after the Second World War
- Philippine state policies promote international labour migration to various parts of the world as a way of generating remittance flows and related income for national welfare and development
- Low incomes and slow economic growth relative to many other countries in Southeast Asia
- The emergence of a migration culture in the Philippines in which families and entire communities become dependent on migrant remittances for their well-being

Migration links between Canada and the Philippines began to develop in the 1970s as Filipina women were invited to work in Canada as live-in caregivers. Over time, this occupational niche expanded to the point where Filipina women now fill some fourth-fifths of all foreign workers in this field (see more details on this in Chapter 10). In effect, by promoting live-in caregiver programs Canada played a role in the development of the migration cul-ture in the Philippines and then benefited from the access to Philippine workers that this culture generated. Starting from this narrow base, migrant flows from the Philippines expanded quickly, remain high, and at present show no signs that they will abate soon. Transnational connections at the household level remain very strong within the Philippine migration culture. In Canada, these extend to various institutional spheres, including activity in Philippine political developments.

Commonwealth Caribbean immigration: Jamaica, Guyana, Trinidad and Tobago, and a number of other smaller nations in the Eastern Caribbean, such as Barbados, were together an important source of immigrants to Canada in the 1970s and 1980s. These nations remain important, but at a declining level. The two most important immigrant-origin nations in the region, Jamaica and Guyana, occupied ranks 21 and 32 respectively from 2000 to 2005. This is still a high rank when one takes into account that these are very small countries: The population of Jamaica is only 2,585,000 and that of Guyana is even less at 744,000 in 2000 (UNPD 2006). Immigration inflows from these two small nations were even higher in previous years. In the 1980s both nations were among the top 10 sources (at ranks 9 and 10 respectively). What explains these large flows from such small countries? Why have they declined over time?

The explanation for the very large migration flows from the Caribbean to Canada has deep historical roots. The Commonwealth Caribbean and Canada were both part of the British Empire and therefore adopted English as a common dominant language, put in place British parliamentary political structures, and modelled their legal systems after British common law. They were also both subject to the influence of Anglican and other Protestant churches, and set up schooling systems on a British model. Haiti was a French colony until 1804, uses

French and Haitian Creole (heavily French influenced) as its official languages, and has links to French-origin culture and social-political institutions that are similar to those in Quebec. Despite these many background similarities and the legacy of them in contemporary culture, the main origin countries for Caribbean immigrants to Canada (namely, the Commonwealth Caribbean and Haiti) occupied very different positions within the international order. The Caribbean was founded on African slave labour and, in parts of the Commonwealth Caribbean, Asian indentured labour to support plantation sugar production and exports. Canada was founded on voluntary European settlement to create a farming and self-sufficient economy modelled on European society. These two worlds were therefore linked through common cultural and political institutions, but separated by racism and economic specialization in the international economic system.

When the racism that prevented immigration from the Caribbean came to an end in 1962, flows from the Commonwealth Caribbean to Canada grew rapidly for three reasons. First, low incomes and poor job opportunities in the Caribbean stood in marked contrast to higher incomes and many jobs in Canada. Second, the Caribbean had developed a strong migration culture that supported emigration. Third, the existence of strong common cultural, political, and social traditions linked the Caribbean to Canada, so that Caribbean immigrants found much in Canada that was familiar to them, while Canadian employers also found much in the culture of Caribbean workers that was familiar to them. Immigration flows from Haiti to Quebec followed a somewhat different pattern as they were initially sparked by political conflict and refugee flight in the 1960s as many Haitian professionals and their families fled the violently repressive regime of President François Duvalier.

The sugar economy began to decline in the Caribbean in the early 1800s and other economic ventures provided only weak supports for economic development in the region. A Caribbean migration culture emerged in stages after emancipation. First, former slaves moved to live in their own communities outside the plantations where they had been forced to live previously. At the same time, they took up seasonal paid jobs on nearby plantations. Later, they began to seek seasonal work further away on other islands. Eventually, their movement for work evolved into migration flows to more distant places and for longer periods, such as to Panama during construction of the canal in the late 19th century. In the 20th century, the migration flows expanded to the United States, the United Kingdom, and Canada. Throughout these stages, Caribbean families and culture increasingly came to view their future as dependent in part on finding work elsewhere. When Britain needed foreign labour to help with post-Second World War reconstruction in the 1950s, Caribbean workers were quick to respond. When Britain found that it no longer needed Caribbean workers (nor those from Asia) and passed the Commonwealth Immigration Act in 1964 to make it more difficult for these workers to move to the United Kingdom, they shifted their attention to other destinations, particularly the United States and Canada. From the 1950s to the 1990s, the Commonwealth Caribbean experienced an enormous exodus of people. In this period, approximately 20 percent of the population born in the region moved to live elsewhere. About two in five of these migrants moved to Canada (Simmons and Guengant 1992).

Several reasons have combined to gradually decrease the flows from the Caribbean to Canada since the early 1990s. First, slower population growth in the Caribbean has been creating a situation in which there are fewer young workers seeking to emigrate. Second, stronger economic opportunity in the United States compared to Canada has drawn more Caribbean emigrants to the United States. Third, changes in Canadian immigration policy have had a negative impact on the number of people in the region who are eligible to move to Canada. As the Caribbean has a small overall population and a modest number of college and university graduates, the number of people in the region who can meet the higher schooling requirements of Canadian policy imposed since the 1990s and particularly after 2002 has diminished. It has become more difficult for many Caribbean people to qualify for entry to Canada in the economic class. Smaller numbers of economic migrants mean that fewer recently arrived immigrants from the region are able to sponsor relatives in the family class. In addition, requirements for immigration in the family class increased in the mid-1990s. Family reunification was a key element of Caribbean immigration. Hence the fall in family-class immigration from the region has played an additional indirect role in slowing flows. Nevertheless, the Caribbean-origin community in Toronto, Montreal, and other large Canadian cities is large, vibrant, and closely connected to the region through transnational family and social ties; hence it continues to attract significant numbers of new immigrants from the region (Simmons and Plaza 2006).

Diverse Other Streams

The preceding cases illustrate the importance of a combination of factors in generating immigration streams. Strong flows develop when admissibility, motivation, and resources are found in a package that emerges from the historically evolving relationship between the origin community and Canada within the international system. Other streams can be analyzed within

this framework to develop further insights, such as the following.

The United States is among the top sources of Canadian immigrants, a finding that makes sense in terms of the framework. However, the economic opportunity in Canada for American workers has not been based on average higher wages in Canada since this has not historically been the case. Rather, it is based on the interdependence of the two economies, the presence of many of the same large international firms in both countries, and a long shared border that has led to strong marriage and family connections between the two countries.

Pakistan, Sri Lanka, and Iran have also been important source countries, particularly since the 1990s. This presumably reflects common roots in the British Empire and Commonwealth, as well as the ongoing economic and political crises in these countries over this period.

Many other countries appeared as important source countries for short periods, then they dropped to lower ranks. These nations included Vietnam, El Salvador, and Cambodia, which were ranked in the top 20 in the 1980s, but which fell to far lower ranks or entirely off the top 36 list by 2000–2005. Similarly, Chile was among the top 36 in the 1980s, but had fallen off the list by the 1990s. These cases all involve refugee-led flows from nations that did not have previously established co-ethnic communities and related historical social, cultural, and political links to Canada.

Overall flows from Latin America remain modest, involving a few notable streams from particular countries in the top 36 and smaller streams from many countries not shown in Table 6.4. It remains unclear whether the fragmented individual streams from different Hispanic countries in the region share enough in common beyond use of the same language to provide social and institutional links to generate a coherent transnational community and to draw ongoing streams of immigrants (Goldring 2006; Mata 1985; Simmons 1993a, 1993b). Most Latin American immigrants in Canada came as refugees or in refugee-like flows from particular countries in particular periods of violent upheaval: Chile in the 1970s; El Salvador, Guatemala, and Nicaragua in the 1980s. These flows showed a typical refugee pattern of explosive growth during the crisis, short-term follow-on flows through family reunification, and a subsequent decline. The rise of Colombia and Mexico as important immigrant streams to Canada in the most recent period analyzed is somewhat ambiguous: Both streams come from countries with considerable economic and political turbulence. Some of the immigrants arrive as refugees, yet most are economic-class immigrants, followed by family reunification, suggesting that they may be in a phase of acceleration.

African nations remain most isolated in Canadian immigration. Ethiopia, Somalia, and the Sudan, all important sources of refugee flows to Canada, all appear as lower-ranked source countries among the top 36 at some point from 1980 to 2005, but usually for only part of the longer period, suggesting that they follow the refugee-led pattern of short spurts that are not supported by favourable conditions for continuation. Nigeria and South Africa also appear at lower ranks, but only in the 2000–2005 period. It is too early to tell if these streams will turn into sustained flows. Both countries are large; use English as the main language of commerce and government; are linked to Canada through the British Commonwealth; and have extensive, well-educated sectors in the context of economies that provide limited opportunities. These nations have clear potential for sustaining longer flows of economic- and family-class immigrants.

Many immigrants to Canada are francophones who settle in Quebec. They come from France and from other countries,

such as Algeria and Haiti, where French is widely used as a language of schooling and widely spoken. However, Quebec has had difficulty achieving its immigration targets. This is due to various reasons, one of which appears to be a global shortage of highly skilled francophone individuals who are interested in moving to Canada. Further support for this interpretation was presented in Chapter 5.

Is Canadian Immigration Admission Racist?

Satzewich (1988) noted that in the years immediately following 1962 when Canada adopted new non-racist immigration procedures, some immigration officers in the Caribbean continued to favour applicants with lighter skins. Evidence of such a practice makes it clear that state policy and the actions of state officials are not always identical. It is therefore possible that other state immigration practices with racist overtones may have carried on after 1962. Jakubowski (1997: 20) observed that in the 1970s, relatively few immigration officers were assigned to certain regions. While Europe seemed to be well served by immigration officers, Africa, Asia, and Latin America were not. In a subsequent analysis, I observed that over the decade following Jakubowski's analysis, the distribution of Canadian immigration officers had improved, but still remained quite unequal by region (Simmons 1998b: 104). By 1980, there were 46 Canadian immigration officers in Europe, of which 13 were in the United Kingdom alone. At the same time, there were only eight officers in Africa and only eight in Latin America, indicating a lack of interest in these two regions. However, Asia was served with 41 officers, nearly as many officers as were located in Europe. Hong Kong alone had 10 officers, while India and Pakistan had another 10.

The Caribbean, a very small region in terms of population, was served by 11 officers, reflecting large-scale immigrant admissions from the region at that time.

If the above distributions of immigration officers up to 1980 had any racist dimension, it was very hidden in the more obvious bias of immigration officers toward locations where one can find large numbers of individuals who are (1) motivated to come to Canada through established ethnic and family links and, (2) meet Canadian immigration criteria. Efforts to carry the analysis of the distribution of immigration officers forward to the present run into a major problem. Citizenship and Immigration currently has more than 4,000 employees in total. The vast majority are in Canada, where they review applications and manage the diverse programs of the ministry. Applications to immigrate, study, or work in Canada are now available online, so individuals can apply from anywhere. Where immigration officers are located was, by 1980, already a problematic uncertain indicator of ethnocentric or racist bias. The way that immigrant applications and selection are currently organized means that other research strategies must be found to study possible racist bias in immigration practices.

An alternative and perhaps better way of assessing possible bias in Canadian immigration recruitment in different countries and regions is to compare Canadian immigration from each world region relative to what one would expect if inflows from each region were proportional to the number of people living in them. This is admittedly a very rough yardstick to measure possible bias, but it will indicate whether the strategy should be refined and pursued further. Figures for such an assessment are shown in Table 6.5. The data cover the more recent period from 1980 to 2005. An index number of 1.00 would indicate that actual immigration is equal to what it should be if population size in the country of origin was the only determining factor. An index number of less than 1.00 indicates a relative under-representation, while numbers greater than 1.00 indicate a relative overrepresentation. Africans constitute between 7 and 8 percent of Canadian immigrants, but nearly 15 percent of the world's population, so their immigration to Canada is only half (0.5) of what one would expect based on the population of Africa. Asian immigrants are more equally represented (0.9), while Europeans are nearly twice as likely (1.8) to immigrate to Canada as one would expect based on the size of the population of Europe. South and Central America are slightly underrepresented (index of 0.8). At the high extreme, Caribbean immigrants are nearly eight times more likely to immigrate to Canada (index of 7.8) than one would expect. These findings point to enormous regional biases, but once again, possible racist bias reflected by them is uncertain. The differences observed may be due to links formed through prior immigration, cultural affinities, and social-economic factors affecting motivation.

The importance of language and historical institutional connections in determining immigrant inflows is illustrated when one looks more closely at proportional flows from sub-regions and specific countries. For example, not shown in Table 6.5 is the finding, based on the same data set, that shows that immigrants from the Hispanic Caribbean (Cuba, the Dominican Republic, and Puerto Rico) come to Canada in roughly equal proportion to the population of their countries of origin. In contrast, French and French-based Creole-speaking Haitians who settle overwhelmingly in Quebec are highly overrepresented: Their immigration numbers are eight times greater than one would expect based on population of that small nation. In an even more exaggerated outcome, immigrants from the Commonwealth or English-speaking Caribbean are 39 times overrepresented compared to what one would expect based on the population of this region! These differences correspond to the historical social, cultural, and institutional links between the origin countries and Canada. The links are weakest for the Spanish-speaking Caribbean, stronger for Haiti (in relation to Quebec), and strongest for the Commonwealth Caribbean. Since a high proportion of those from the Caribbean are of African origin, these figures suggest that the lower-than-expected immigration from Africa itself cannot be attributed entirely (or perhaps not at all) to ethnic or racial biases in Canadian immigrant selection.

The preceding analysis is not sufficient to counter all concerns about current racist outcomes in Canadian immigration. Richmond (1994) has argued that the restrictions that people in Africa, Asia, the Caribbean, and Latin America face in migrating to wealthier countries constitute a "global apartheid" that reinforces international racial divides and inequalities, much as formal apartheid had done in South Africa up to its elimination in 1991. Others have expressed concern that visa worker programs that admit non-White workers into low-paid temporary jobs tend to reinforce racist stereotypes (Bakan and Stasiulis 1997; Calliste 1991; Jakubowski 1997; Simmons 1998b). These issues are not so much to do with racist immigrant *selection* as they are to do with borders and *limited mobility*, which indirectly reinforce existing social-economic disparities and related ethnic differences that emerged in relation to a racist colonial past.

Discussion and Conclusions

The main question of interest in this chapter is the role of state policies in shaping the national and ethnic origins of immigrants. We may note the following.

The population of the globe is largely immobile. Only a very small proportion of the world's population move to live in another country. Those who do leave are mostly headed to a small number of very wealthy nations. Only from the perspective of those in these wealthy nations can one say that the world is on the move. From the perspective of most less developed nations, only a tiny proportion of the population is mobile, and this proportion is declining. Some small nations with very high levels of emigration stand out as exceptions to these general patterns.

International migration flows from one country to another are not random. Neither are they simply proportional to the population sizes of the respective countries. Rather, international migrants flow in historically specific streams from certain origin countries to certain destination countries. These historical streams are generated by the evolution of political-economic forces that create various historical links between the societies, cultures, and economies of migrant-sending and migrant-receiving nations. In the case of Canada, similar to that of other wealthy immigrant-destination countries, contemporary migration-system links were formed within colonial, racist, and exclusionary structures of the past. When these structures weakened and then were officially abandoned, the previously established links were reinvigorated, and the once excluded were not only included but became leaders in further efforts to eradicate reaming informal discrimination.

Canadian policy does not directly select immigrants based on their national origin, but other selection criteria do influence the countries and regions from which immigrants come. The high educational standards set for being admitted as a highly skilled worker, the main category in the economic class, tends to generate proportionally higher than expected flows of immigrants from developed countries and regions such as the United States and Europe. Points given to highly skilled workers for their skills in English and/or French also tend to increase flows from countries in other parts of the world where English and French are widely spoken or where there are large middle-class, well-educated, urban populations containing individuals who have studied English or French. Family reunification policies tend to promote follow-on flows of immigrants once pioneer movers have led the way.

Because immigrants must combine motivation, admissibility, and resources, some 80 percent of immigrants to Canada come from developing regions: Africa, Asia, the Caribbean, and Latin America. The great majority of these immigrants have high levels of education. In addition, the specific countries from which most immigrants come have shown a great deal of change over time. While a few very large countries (China and India, for example) and populous regions (e.g., Europe) and certain other countries with strong historical migration links to Canada (the Philippines, the Caribbean, etc.) have been important sources of Canadian immigrants over past decades, many other countries have been important for shorter periods of time. The result is that Canadian immigration is composed of a constantly changing mix of national and ethnic origins. This turbulence creates a constant challenge for multicultural Canadian society as it seeks to understand and appreciate the national backgrounds and cultural attributes of immigrants.

Current major sources of Canadian immigration, such as China and India, may not be the main sources in the future. Both countries are experiencing a trend to slower population growth, reduced labour force growth, and rising internal demand for highly skilled workers that could lead to lower emigration. Places such as Africa, which have been underrepresented in Canadian immigration flows over the recent past, may become the next main recruiting ground for Canadian immigrants. Current trends and possible future developments suggest that Canada will face continuing challenges to welcome diversity and help new immigrants settle in Canada. The following three chapters indicate that at present these challenges are formidable in the area of jobs and earnings (Chapter 7) and significant in the areas of social-cultural incorporation (Chapter 8) and ethnic identity and relations (Chapter 9).

CHAPTER 7
Jobs and Earnings

Introduction

The *Globe and Mail*, the newspaper with the largest distribution in Canada, nominated Olympic gold-medal winner Carol Huynh as a candidate for its 2008 Nation Builder of the Year Award (see Box 7.1). The story is meaningful to many Canadians because her success is understood to have come about through a combination of the best qualities that immigrants bring and the best welcome that Canada offers. The story involves members of the United Church in Hazelton, a small town in northern British

Columbia, who sponsored her family as refugees; the support of neighbours and community sports programs; the sacrifices of her parents, who began life in Canada very poor and worked their way from manual jobs to become owners of a motel; and Carol Huynh's own remarkable talent and grit in training to become an international champion while completing university studies and serving as a volunteer and motivational speaker for youth sports (Maki 2008). Do such exceptional cases of welcome and success point to a general pattern? How welcomed and successful are Canadian immigrants and their children?

This is the first of three chapters on immigrant incorporation and belonging in Canadian society. This chapter addresses these matters in terms of social-economic outcomes such as jobs, wages, and housing for immigrants, and in terms of schooling and jobs for children born in Canada to immigrant parents. Chapter 8 addresses

immigrant incorporation from an ethnic and transnational perspective. Chapter 9, the final in this sequence, examines belonging in terms of individual and collective ethnic identities. All three chapters build on the nation-building/imagined futures framework to understanding Canadian immigration in a global and transnational world. This framework draws attention to belonging as a multidimensional field in which individuals are motivated by hoped-for futures and where the state also has hopes, based on imagined outcomes at the national level, concerning how immigrants will settle and belong. The main question in this chapter is: How do immigrants' jobs and earnings in Canada fit with the imagined national futures of Canadian political leaders?

Let us first briefly review the state's hopes and how these set the tone for the hopes of various other actors. Canadian immigration policy is officially set forth in a discourse

---

Box 7.1: Carol Huynh Celebrates Olympic Gold

Carol Huynh competed in the 48-kilogram weight-class women's wrestling at the 2008 Summer Olympics. Her gold medal was the first ever for Canada in women's wrestling. Carol was born in Canada to immigrant parents from Vietnam who arrived as refugees in the 1970s. The picture shows her joy at winning and draws attention to a symbolic configuration of the winner holding the Canadian flag, gender relations in sport, visible minority status relations to others, and vice versa, and gold medal success. This configuration expresses well many of the ideals associated with Canadian immigration and multicultural nation-building.

Source: The author, based on the article by: Maki, Allan. 2008. "Nation Builder 2008. The finalists. Wrestler's win stood for something bigger." *Globe and Mail* (24 December), A3. AP Photo/Ed Wray. © Canadian Press Images, 2009.

that emphasizes the *potential* social and economic success and related contributions of immigrants. In this discourse, immigrants are expected to play a key role in Canada's future economic prosperity. Highly skilled workers and business immigrants are specifically selected on criteria to increase the likelihood that they will find jobs quickly and/or use their business skills to make the Canadian economy more profitable. According to this policy narrative, these successful economic-class immigrants will create a happy juncture for the country as a whole. Employers seeking to increase their profits will want to hire the well-educated immigrants. Investors will gain as the profits of Canadian firms rise. Workers of all kinds and levels of skill will be in greater demand. Immigrants will find it easier to get good jobs. The state will win by being able to show that its immigration policy works to meet shared national goals.

The win-win scenario described above is hypothetical. *Real* outcomes are more mixed and, at times, can depart considerably from what is suggested by ideology, policy rhetoric, and the earnest hopes of planners. The analysis in this chapter will review evidence that each successive cohort of new immigrants since 1980 has found it more difficult to earn wages equivalent to comparable Canadian-born workers. Immigrant earnings relative to those of Canadian-born workers are particularly low in their first few years in Canada. Low earnings have direct implications for what they can pay for housing and implications for the neighbourhoods in which they settle. However, the *children* of immigrants are generally achieving high levels of education and doing well in their initial job placements, although there are important exceptions to the general pattern that we also must consider. My objective is to examine these seemingly contradictory social-economic trends for the two generations, to ask why they have come about,

and to reach some initial conclusions on what the findings mean for understanding immigrant belonging in Canada.

The Declining Earnings of Recently Arrived Immigrants

Earnings are the portion of total individual and household income that comes from wages and employment. Other sources of income – such as returns from investments, withdrawals from savings, gifts from family members, unemployment insurance, welfare and social security payments – are not included in earnings. The reason for focusing on earnings is that they address directly the economic hopes of the immigrants and those of the state as well. Earnings give a picture of the market value of immigrant work in the Canadian economy. They therefore reflect employers' judgments – whether based on bias, ignorance, or informed experience – of what immigrants should be paid. If immigrants' credentials are undervalued or if they face discrimination, this should be reflected in their earnings. It would not be reflected in returns from investments, gifts, or welfare payments.

The most studied question in this field is how much immigrants earn *compared to* Canadian-born workers (Picot and Sweetman 2005: 5). Research on immigrants arriving in decades prior to the 1980s showed that they initially had lower earnings than native-born workers with similar training, but that over time the earnings gap between immigrants and native-born workers narrowed fairly quickly (Chiswick 1978; Meng 1987; Hum and Simpson 2003). However, this early positive pattern did not continue. Of greatest concern is evidence that the earnings gap increased for immigrants arriving in the 1980s (Abbott and Beach 1993; Bloom and Gunderson 1991). This gap continued to be evident for immigrants arriving in the 1990s (Frenette and Morissette 2003; Green and Worswick 2002; Reitz 2001). Evidence covering the period up to 2005 shows an increasing earnings gap for immigrants arriving in the late 1990s and early 2000s (Picot, Hou, and Coulombe 2007). Labour market studies in 2006–2007 indicate that immigrants who had arrived in the previous five years were less likely to be actively engaged in the labour force, and that a higher proportion were unemployed; that is, without a job and looking for work (Gilmore and Le Petit 2008: Table 4.1).

Table 7.1 provides a summary of Canadian census estimates of the earnings gap for recently arrived immigrants in 1980, 1990, 2000, and 2005. A recently arrived immigrant is an individual who first settled in Canada between one and five years prior to the year in which his or her income is examined. Annual earnings figures are based on the wages of full-time and part-time workers so that they summarize the combined effects of the amount earned on a weekly basis and the number of weeks worked over the year.

The bottom panel of figures in Table 7.1 shows the relative earnings of recent immigrants compared to Canadian-born workers of the same sex and education level. They confirm the findings of many studies in the field. Recent immigrants have lower earnings than Canadian-born workers of the same sex and level of education. This earnings gap has increased over time from 1980 to 2005. Each more recent cohort of immigrants has experienced a greater earnings disadvantage in the years immediately following their arrival than the cohort that arrived five years earlier. In 1980, the income of recently arrived immigrants ranged from 59–86 percent of that of Canadian-born workers, depending on sex and education. However, in 2005 recently arrived immigrants received only 43–61 percent (the lowest and highest

figures, respectively, for 2005 in the bottom panel of Table 7.1) of those of Canadian-born workers, depending on their sex and educational level. To take one specific example, in 1980 recently arrived women immigrants without university education had earnings that were 86 percent of those of equivalent Canadian-born workers—a 14 percent gap that is appreciable, but not so great that the immigrants could not hope to close it in a few years as they adjusted to the Canadian labour market. By 2005, female immigrants without a university degree earned only 56 percent of the wages of Canadian-born female workers without a university degree. This is a huge gap. The average female immigrant in this cohort would need to nearly double her earnings in order to catch up. The disadvantage of recently arrived female immigrants without university education had grown by one-third over 25 years. Similar growth in the earnings gap can be observed for other sex–education categories of recently arrived immigrants shown in Table 7.1.

The above trends are worrying on two accounts. Firstly, they suggest that when immigrants find themselves in a deeper hole of initial disadvantage, they will have to climb further and for longer to get out of the hole. This raises the question of whether they will be able to do so. Secondly, the *relative* earnings gap is just as great for university-educated immigrants as it is for those without university. If the situation is examined in terms of the *absolute* income figures themselves (comparing figures in the top two panels in Table 7.1), then recently arrived university-educated male immigrants in 2005 should be the most disappointed of all: Their median annual earnings of $30,000 were $32,000 less than those of an equivalent Canadian-born worker. This is the greatest *absolute* earnings gap that can be observed in Table 7.1, although it is not the greatest *relative* gap.

Table 7.1: Median Annual Earnings of Recent Immigrants and Canadian-Born

	With a University Degree		With No University Degree	
	Males	Females	Males	Females
Median earnings of recent immigrant				
1980	48,541	24,317	36,467	18,548
1990	38,351	25,959	27,301	17,931
2000	35,816	22,511	25,951	16,794
2005	30,332	18,969	24,470	14,233
Median earnings of Canadian-born				
1980	63,040	41,241	43,641	21,463
1990	61,332	41,245	40,757	23,267
2000	61,505	43,637	39,902	25,622
2005	62,566	44,545	40,235	25,590
Earnings ratio (1:00 = equal earnings)				
1980	0.77	0.59	0.84	0.86
1990	0.63	0.63	0.67	0.77
2000	0.58	0.52	0.65	0.66
2005	0.48	0.43	0.61	0.56

Notes:
1. Data are from Statistics Canada censuses of population, 1981, 1991, 2001, and 2006. *Source:* Statistics Canada. 2008. *Earnings and Incomes of Canadians over the Past Quarter Century, 2006 Census* (p. 22). Catalogue no. 97-563-22. Ottawa: Statistics Canada. [http://www12.statcan.ca/english/census06/analysis/income/pdf/97-563-XIE2006001.pdf]. Last accessed 4 December 2008.
2. Earnings refer to income from wages and self-employment in 2005 constant dollars. The numbers are based on all earners, both full-time and part-time, with or without a university degree, aged 25–54, over the full year or part of the year. Individuals living in institutions are excluded.
3. Earnings are expressed in 2005 constant dollars and are for the calendar years shown in the table. This year, known as the reference year, is always the one immediately preceding the year of the census in which the data were collected.
4. A "recent immigrant" is a person who arrived in Canada between one and five years before the "reference year" (see note 3). Such individuals will all have been in Canada for at least one year, and hence will have already passed through the first year of settlement in which their wages would have been particularly low.

Sources: Statistics Canada censuses of population, 1981, 1991, 2001, and 2006; Statistics Canada. 2008. *Earnings and Incomes of Canadians over the Past Quarter Century, 2006 Census* (p. 22). Catalogue no. 97-563-22. Ottawa: Statistics Canada. [http://www12.statcan.ca/english/census06/analysis/income/pdf/97-563-XIE2006001.pdf]. Last accessed 4 December 2008.

Trends by Duration of Residence in Canada

An important question is whether the low incomes among recently arrived immigrants are temporary or long-term. If the relative poverty of immigrants continues for a long period, then the problem is more serious for them and for Canada. In such a case, the official discourse of Canadian immigration policy comes increasingly into question. Studies on the earnings trajectories of immigrants lead to two findings; one is more optimistic while the other is less so. The optimistic side is that earnings among new immigrants in recent cohorts increase over time after initial arrival. This was true in the past and continues to be true today (see Figure 7.1 for recent trends, and Frenette and Morissette 2003 for comments on the period before 1980).

On the less optimistic side, immigrants who have particularly low earnings in the years immediately following their arrival may take a very long time to catch up. Some may never catch up. Of course, the future is never known. However, patterns shown in Figure 7.1 suggest a troubling future scenario. No cohort of immigrants arriving since 1980 has caught up to the earnings of the cohorts that preceded it, controlling for length of residence in Canada. More precisely, no cohort has caught up so far. The earnings of more recent cohorts could still catch up and even surpass those of earlier cohorts at some point in an unknown future if the causes of low immigrant wages were to be eliminated. Significant changes in the variables that determine immigrant earnings will need to take place to shift the trends shown in the chart toward more positive outcomes.

Figure 7.1 is based on an analysis that compares immigrant earnings with those of equivalent native-born workers. Equivalency is based on statistical controls for variables such as level of education, work experience, marital status, visible minority status, and region of residence. In this case, the analysis is done separately by sex, so this too is controlled in the comparisons. With all these controls in place, the 1975–1979 immigrant cohort had not quite achieved the earnings of equivalent Canadian-born workers after 21–25 years of living in Canada. By mentally projecting past trends into the future, readers can observe that male workers in the 1975–1979 immigration cohort who arrived as adults (aged 15 or over) should achieve parity

with native-born workers roughly sometime between 26 to 30 years after arrival in Canada; that is, sometime between 2001 and 2009. Female workers who arrived as adults in this cohort should do the same roughly sometime after living 31–35 years in Canada, or between 2006 and 2014. Given that the median age of immigrants who are aged 15 and over on arrival in the periods under consideration falls between 25 and 29 (LIDS 2005), both male and female immigrants in this cohort should therefore just reach earnings parity with other Canadian workers shortly before they reach age 65, on average. By then they will have spent most of their working lives in Canada earning wages less than equivalent to Canadian-born workers.

The earnings trajectory for the 1980–1984 immigrant cohort starts at a lower level than the starting level for the 1975–1979 cohort, then it rises over time in a trajectory just under the earnings path of this earlier cohort. If this trend continues, the 1980–1984 cohort will not achieve earnings parity until after its members have spent on average roughly 40 years in Canada and worked past age 65. It is more risky to project the short earnings trajectory for the remaining two cohorts because they have spent so little time in Canada. Nevertheless, what is shown is of great concern. The 1985–1989 cohort started from a very low earnings level and over the first 11–15 years in Canada, it has followed the same upward trend as observed for earlier cohorts, but on a lower path that will take longer to reach the earnings level of Canadian-born workers. If this pattern continues, this cohort will not likely achieve income parity with Canadian workers before retirement if this takes place at age 65. In fact, this cohort would have to keep working until age 70 or later to achieve parity.

It is particularly risky to project the earnings trajectory of the 1990–1994 cohort.

Individuals in this cohort have been in Canada a relatively short period of time, so the change noted in Figure 7.1 (based on the 2001 census) is limited to the five-year period from 1995 to 2000. In addition, its steep upward growth over the short period raises additional doubts about how to project its future pattern. If the initial fast upward trajectory of earnings for this cohort continues, it will break the pattern of earlier cohorts: Its members will achieve or exceed the earnings of Canadian-born workers by the time they have spent 21–25 years in Canada. Peter Li's (2003c) model of the "earnings catch-up" potentially clarifies the fact that outcomes vary widely

according to the assumptions about the rate at which earnings will grow over time. An earnings catch-up would be faster if the rate of increase of earnings observed in the first 10 years of immigrant residence in Canada could be maintained over a longer period. While one would hope that this will happen, there are reasons for caution. Readers may note that the 1980–1984 cohort of immigrants experienced a rather rapid growth of earnings over the first six to 10 years in Canada, but for subsequent periods of residence in Canada, this rate slowed to follow a path similar to the longer-term rate of earnings growth for the earlier 1975–1979 cohort.

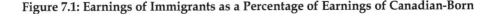

Figure 7.1: Earnings of Immigrants as a Percentage of Earnings of Canadian-Born

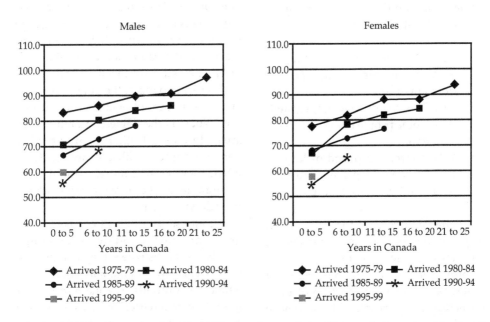

Source: This figure was produced by the author from log earnings differences between immigrants and the Canadian-born published by Frenette, Marc, and Rene Morissette. 2003. *Analytical Studies Research Paper Series. Will They Ever Converge? Earnings of Immigrant and Canadian-Born Workers over the Last Two Decades* (Table 2). Ottawa: Statistics Canada.

Their data are based on the combined censuses of 1981, 1986, 1991, 1996, and 2001. Earnings are the median earnings of individuals between 16 and 64 years old who worked at least 40 weeks in the year immediately preceding each census, and include wages and salaries, net income from self-employment, and other employment income (tips, gratuities, etc.). All earning figures were adjusted through OLS analysis for education, work experience, weeks worked, marital status, visible minority status, and region of Canada. For details on these controls, see Frenette and Morissette (2003).

Earnings, Housing, and Neighbourhoods

Given the earnings levels and trends of immigrants described above, it is not surprising that immigrants, and recently arrived immigrants in particular, are suffering from very high rates of poverty in the major cities where they have settled (Picot 1998). In a significant departure from the past, this poverty is now located in the suburban neighbourhoods. As an indicator of their poverty, immigrants in suburban neighbourhoods spend 50 percent or more of their income on housing payments or rent (Preston 2009). The result has been a gradual but fundamental restructuring of class and ethnic residential clusters. According to Hulchanski (2007), Toronto provides a clear example of this. Toronto is polarizing into three cities in terms of income and cost of housing:

- City One, composed of largely wealthy people living near the downtown core
- City Two, composed of largely middle-income people living somewhat further out
- City Three, composed of largely lower-income people living in more distant suburbs (see Figure 7.2)

Hulchanski observes that since 1981, the proportion of middle-income people in Canadian cities has declined, while the proportion of wealthy has increased somewhat, and the proportion of poor has increased significantly. The poor have been displaced from the centre and near-centre areas, while at the same time large numbers of immigrants with low earnings have found housing in City Three. While people of all ethnic backgrounds can be found in all areas, visible minorities and immigrants are disproportionately located in the fast-growing low-income areas of City Three. Over the period from 1981,

when the income disparities began to grow most quickly and 2001, when the study ended, "the proportion of immigrants in City One remained at about 12%, while the proportion in City Two increased to 25% and that in City Three to 42% (Hulchanski 2007: 7). The results reflect rising housing prices in the core areas, low earnings among immigrants, and more affordable housing in the distant suburbs.

In the past history of Canada, ethnic residential patterns were related to systemic discrimination. From the late 1800s to the 1940s, ethnic Chinese in Canada lived in impoverished Chinatowns because they were excluded from living elsewhere (Li 1998). They engaged in a limited range of jobs — laundry services, restaurants, and grocery stores — because these were the only jobs available to them. They also had high levels of ethnic retention (language use, identity) because they were forced together and because family and ethnic solidarity helped them to survive adversity. In this earlier pattern, the poor immigrant areas were located near the downtown core. Not only the Chinese located in such areas, but so did other newly arriving immigrant groups with low earnings. Only when they became more affluent were immigrants able to move away from the poor downtown areas.

In contrast to the old pattern, new immigrants are now found overwhelmingly in urban suburbs where they live in close proximity to other immigrants from diverse ethnic backgrounds. The main reason for this is that preferences for housing location have shifted. The urban well-to-do now prefer to live closer to downtown. They bid up the prices of housing and rents to live in City One. Former residents of City One, including immigrants, are pushed out by the high real estate and rental costs and move to the more affordable and less-in-demand suburbs. New immigrants then move directly to the suburbs for two reasons: The rents

Figure 7.2: Change in Average Individual Income, City of Toronto, 1970–2005

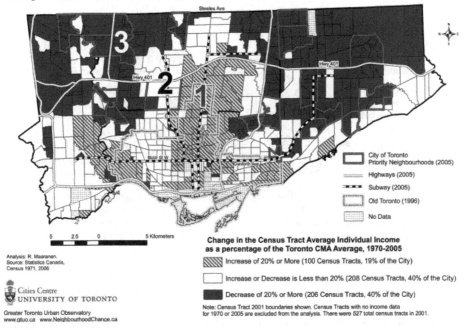

Average Individual Income from all sources, 15 Years and Over, Census Tracts

Legend:

☐ City of Toronto
Priority Neighbourhoods (2005)

‑‑‑‑‑ Highways (2005)

▪▪▪▪ Subway (2005)

☐ Old Toronto (1996)

☐ No Data

Analysis: R. Maaranen.
Source: Statistics Canada,
Census 1971, 2006

Cities Centre
UNIVERSITY OF TORONTO

Greater Toronto Urban Observatory
www.gtuo.ca www.NeighbourhoodChange.ca

**Change in the Census Tract Average Individual Income
as a percentage of the Toronto CMA Average, 1970-2005**

▨ Increase of 20% or More (100 Census Tracts, 19% of the City)

☐ Increase or Decrease is Less than 20% (208 Census Tracts, 40% of the City)

▮ Decrease of 20% or More (206 Census Tracts, 40% of the City)

Note: Census Tract 2001 boundaries shown. Census Tracts with no income data
for 1970 or 2005 are excluded from the analysis. There were 527 total census tracts in 2001.

Source: Hulchanski, David. 2007. *The Three Cities within Toronto: Income Polarization among Toronto's Neighbourhoods, 1970–2000* (p. 1). Research Bulletin 41 (December). Toronto: Centre for Urban and Community Studies, University of Toronto.

are lower and they are more likely to find people of the same ethnicity living there. They tend to locate near others of the same ethnicity and in easy proximity, at least by car or public transport, to ethnic shopping locations and religious institutions (Fong 2006; Hiebert 2005; Kim 2005; Myles and Hou 2004). Unlike the United States, where visible minorities lose their concentrations in the suburbs, Canadian immigrants retain their enclave-like concentrations in suburban areas (Balakrishnan, Maxim, and Jurdi 2005). One of the worrying features of this suburban enclave structure is that it may become an additional reason why immigrant earnings remain low. If immigrants have more limited social contacts outside their neighbourhoods and into mainstream Canadian society, their information about good jobs and their language skills to get good jobs outside their ethnic enclaves may be constrained. This and other possibilities for explaining low and declining incomes among immigrants are examined in the next section.

Explaining the Low Earnings of Recent Immigrants

The imagined future of immigrant integration within Canadian policy documents leaves out a number of factors that may lower the earnings of newly arrived immigrants and keep them from rising quickly. These are shown in Figure 7.3 in the form of an outer circle of causal variables that individually and, in interaction with each other, determine immigrant earnings.

Figure 7.3: Hypotheses Concerning the Declining Earnings of Recently Arrived Immigrants

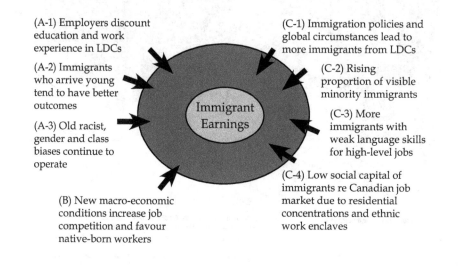

(A-1) Employers discount education and work experience in LDCs

(A-2) Immigrants who arrive young tend to have better outcomes

(A-3) Old racist, gender and class biases continue to operate

(B) New macro-economic conditions increase job competition and favour native-born workers

Immigrant Earnings

(C-1) Immigration policies and global circumstances lead to more immigrants from LDCs

(C-2) Rising proportion of visible minority immigrants

(C-3) More immigrants with weak language skills for high-level jobs

(C-4) Low social capital of immigrants re Canadian job market due to residential concentrations and ethnic work enclaves

I have classified the causal variables into three categories. Category A covers determinants that have been operational in the past and appear to remain in effect. They interact with new circumstances arising from variables in the other two categories to contribute to new outcomes. For example, if employers have always discounted the credentials of immigrants from less developed countries (LDCs), then the rising proportion of immigrants from such countries will lead to more immigrants being subject to having their credentials discounted. Category B refers to new macro-economic conditions arising from global trade and how these affect the job prospects and incomes of immigrants. The hypothesis shown is that a more competitive job market can make it more difficult for immigrants when native-born workers with similar training but more readily recognized credentials are also seeking work. Category C refers to a cluster of outcomes associated with the rising proportion of recently arrived immigrants from less developed countries. These include an

increase in the proportion of immigrants of visible minority status who also have less familiarity with English and French as working languages. The relationships shown in Figure 7.3 can be more clearly stated as hypotheses or tentative generalizations. To emphasize the interactions that lead to deteriorating earnings among recent cohorts of immigrants, I will begin with C-1 (namely, rising numbers of immigrants from LDCs), then clarify how this interacts with other determinants.

1. Canada seeks highly trained immigrants to promote efficiency and exports. Highly trained individuals interested in immigrating to Canada are found in less developed countries primarily. They come with family members and, through network contacts, tend to draw family members and other immigrants from the same countries.

2. The immigrants in question come from countries with educational

systems, professional training standards, and work environments that are unfamiliar to Canadian employers. The credentials, education, and work experience of the immigrants are then very often discounted, which is to say that immigrants are treated as if they have substantially less training and experience than their documents indicate.

3. The immigrants are selected partly on Canadian official language skills, but this is not the only criterion, with the result that many arrive with weak skills in English and/or French. Even if they have good skills in these languages, they may not have the excellent skills that are required for the high-level jobs they hope to obtain with their credentials.

4. Immigrants arriving since 1980 have encountered a more turbulent and competitive job market as Canadian firms have responded to free trade and shifts in the global economy. In this new job market, work experience in Canada became more valued. Immigrants and young workers just entering the labour market have both suffered higher unemployment and lower wages because they lack Canadian work experience. Immigrants may have suffered the most. When employers have had a choice between offering a job to an immigrant or to a young native-born person with similar schooling, they have often shown a preference for the young native-born person because that person was schooled in Canada. Employer biases may be based on ignorance, experience, or some unknown mix of these two.

5. Low immigrant earnings and a desire to live close to others in their own communities leads immigrants to live in low-cost housing and rent areas where other immigrants and those of their own ethnic community have already located. The lower costs, proximity to friends, and access to ethnic stores and institutions help immigrants to find a cultural home in Canada, but the neighbourhoods are not conducive to broader contacts and information about opportunities related to jobs and business possibilities.

6. As a result of the above circumstances, recently arrived immigrants often find themselves accepting jobs far below the level of their training. They hope that these initial jobs will be entry-level positions that will lead to promotion over time, but in fact the jobs often turn out to be dead ends with no prospects. The jobs they get in many cases offer little opportunity for improving their language skills or for practising work and professional skills they had acquired before coming to Canada.

7. Despite these discouraging circumstances, most immigrants continue to improve their earnings the longer they spend in Canada. Even if their earnings never rise to the level of native-born workers, they can anticipate gradual improvements in their situation. In addition, they look hopefully to the future in terms of better prospects for their children growing up in Canada with Canadian schooling and social capital. In effect, their children will become part of the next young generation of native-born workers who will do better than the next cohort of immigrants with respect to jobs and incomes.

8. Last and certainly not least, new immigrants often face cultural and ethnic discrimination. Visible minority immigrants experience racism. How racism and cultural discrimi-

nation affect employment, jobs, and wages is complex and may vary considerably from first to second generation, ethnicity, social class, gender, and other factors. The evidence indicates that some visible minorities, particularly those in the second generation, are able to overcome discrimination, perhaps in part because it is less intense for them. Other visible minority individuals and groups seem less able to overcome the effects of discrimination, perhaps because it is greater for them.

The evidence in support of the above arguments is scattered across diverse studies using different kinds of data and covering various combinations of the variables involved. Illustrative findings are examined below.

Macro-economic Conditions

It is now well established that Canadian workers' purchasing power remained flat or unchanged from 1980 to 2005 (Statistics Canada 2006b). The median annual earnings figure for full-time, full-year workers in 1980 was $41,348. By 2005 this figure was essentially the same, at $41,401. Both these figures are in 2005 constant dollars and therefore they control for inflation. The conclusion we may draw is that workers' pay increases over this 25-year period were entirely consumed by rising prices of goods and services. However, the overall trend must be qualified by wide variation of earnings within the average pattern. Between 1980 and 2005, some earners became wealthier and others poorer. Earnings went up for those at the top of the earnings distribution, stayed the same for those in the middle, and went down for those at the bottom. In other words, the rich got richer and the poor got poorer. To add to the picture, in the period under consideration Canada experienced two major recessions, one in the early 1980s

and another in the early 1990s. Following the 1982 recession, Canada's gross domestic product (GDP) dropped by 6.7 percent over 18 months. Following the 1990 recession, the GDP fell by 3.2 percent over 12 months (Riddell 2009). These economic downturns were accompanied by significant layoffs and rising unemployment. Recently arrived immigrants were among those most affected by these recessions.

There is no simple explanation for the earnings trends described above. Robinson (2007: 265–276) argues that what took place is consistent with three developments. First, the Canadian economy was involved in significant adjustments to trade competition arising initially through CUSTA (Canada–U.S. Trade Agreement), then expanded through NAFTA (North American Free Trade Agreement), and continued to expand with the global trade agreements established by the WTO (World Trade Organization). Canadian firms responded by moving production to other countries and by investing in more sophisticated technology in the hands of fewer but better-trained workers (see the previous analysis of this in Chapter 3). Second, while the above developments were taking place, market forces and changes in state policies tended to erode the power of labour unions, and they, in turn, had a weakened position in pressuring on employers to increase the pay of individuals at the bottom and middle of the earnings distribution. These trends contributed to rising income inequality in Canada. Third, despite Canadian firms' efforts to adjust to the new trade challenges, Canada recorded what might be regarded as a less-than-desired performance in raising economic productivity. It is not that productivity did not rise; rather, it rose more slowly than that of Canada's main trading partner, the United States (Robinson 2007: Figure 10.3). The reasons for this are complex and subject to debate. They include the following claims: that the skills of Canadian workers were inadequate; that Canadian taxes were too high and discouraged investment; that the Canadian dollar was overvalued in comparison with the U.S. dollar; and that high interest rates slowed business investment (Robinson 2007: 265). From this perspective, free trade in itself was not the direct cause of the decline in Canadian productivity relative to that in the United States, but it contributed to this by creating a challenge that the Canadian economy struggled to meet. Robinson (2007: 267) concludes that Canadian monetary and fiscal policies were the main source of this failure. In sum, over the period from 1980 to the present, a combination of macro-economic factors, including slow growth in productivity, stagnant average wages, trade-induced turbulence in the job market, and occasional deep recessions, has contributed to reduced opportunities for recent immigrants. Further details on these points and on other aspects of biases in the job market are provided below.

Turbulence in Sectors Employing Highly Skilled Immigrants

The failures of large firms and declining profits and production from 1980 to 2005 in certain sectors in which highly skilled immigrants were employed is another likely reason for the particularly low incomes of more recently arrived immigrants. Statistics Canada (2008a: 6) notes that the "decline in employment in the information and communication technologies (ICT) sector between 2000 and 2005 had a large impact on the earnings of recent immigrants. The reason is that a disproportionate share of highly trained new immigrants were trained in computer sciences and engineering." Leading Canadian ICT firms — such as Northern Telecom, Bell-Northern Research, Newbridge, and others — had a roller-coaster ride over the 1990s and early in the 2000s. They expanded rapidly in the late 1980s, contracted dramatically in the recession of the early 1990s, recovered in the mid-1990s,

and in the period 2000–2008 had been contracting again, although there was considerable variation from firm to firm and product to product within this sector (Statistics Canada 2008a; Wong 1998). Periods of rapid ICT expansion draw in large numbers of highly trained immigrants to fill shortages in the job market; when the ICT sector goes into a down cycle, it appears to have a major impact on the earnings of recently arrived, highly trained immigrants.

The Impact on New Entrants to the Labour Market

Slower-than-desired growth in productivity in Canada from 1980 to 2005 affected all Canadian workers, but young workers and immigrants were affected more than others. Canadian-born youth completing their studies and entering the job market were deeply affected because they found it more difficult to get well-paying jobs. This was true for young workers regardless of their level of schooling. As a result, the relative earnings of young workers, particularly male workers, declined through the 1980s and 1990s (Beaudry and Green 2000; Picot 1998). While the income gap between younger and older workers did not get worse after 2000, it did not get better either (Statistics Canada 2008a: 15). Even if recently arrived immigrants were older and had previous work experience abroad, their low wages suggest that employers treated them as if they were young workers without prior work experience. Results from the Longitudinal Survey of Immigrants to Canada (Statistics Canada 2005a), covering some 12,000 new immigrants arriving in 2000 and 2001, indicate that "entering the labour market is one of the hardest tasks for *all* immigrants" (p. 721; italics added). The immigrants surveyed reported that the jobs they received were at lower skill levels than they had hoped. This disappointing situation was likely due to a mix of factors including a lack of Canadian job experience, weak official-language knowledge, the fact that employers did not recognize their credentials, and instances of racism and discrimination in hiring and job promotions. Picot and Sweetman (2005) come to a similar conclusion in their examination of various other studies of immigrant earnings. They observe that "there has been a general decline in the labour market outcomes of all new entrants to the Canadian labour market [over the period 1980 to 2005], and when new immigrants arrive in Canada they, regardless of age, face a similar phenomenon" (p. 4).

The Discounting of Foreign Credentials and Experience

Perhaps the highest priority for recently arrived immigrants with professional training is having their credentials re-accredited in Canada. The problem for them is that the process can be complicated, costly, and subject to barriers that they cannot control. The media have given particular attention in recent years to the difficulties faced by foreign-trained medical doctors who simply give up their medical careers and find other work because re-accreditation is so difficult for them. Other health-related professions, such as dentistry, are also affected. Engineers and certified accountants must also be re-accredited to work in Canada. In all these cases, re-accreditation is demanded to protect the public by ensuring that professional workers are competent in their fields in providing safe medical services, building reliable bridges, doing accounting and audits according to Canadian standards, and so on. All professionals affected, including those trained in Canada and those trained abroad, must meet the standards established by their respective professions for practising in Canada.

In the case of foreign-trained physicians, the re-accreditation process is demanding and involves several steps, as shown in Box 7.2. Given the number of difficult steps,

perhaps it is not surprising that only 55 percent of foreign-trained medical doctors are working as physicians; some of the others are working as technicians in the medical field and still others are working in entirely different fields.

Across Canada, particularly in smaller cities, towns, and rural areas, there is a major shortage of physicians. Chan (2002) notes that the number of physicians per capita in Canada peaked in 1993, and then declined for a number of reasons, including the fact that fewer foreign doctors were being re-accredited, while the number of doctors retiring was rising. In 2004 only 9 percent of Canadian doctors worked in rural and small-town Canada, although 21 percent of the country's population live in such areas (Pong and Pitblado 2006). This raises the question of the possibility of fast-tracking the re-accreditation of foreign-trained doctors to make better use of their skills. The 2001 census of Canada reported 5,400 individuals aged 28–54 living in Canada who had medical degrees from foreign institutions, of whom 2,500 (46 percent of the total) were not working as physicians (Boyd and Schellenberg 2008). Given that there were about 60,000 doctors in Canada in 2001, I estimate that about 7,000 new M.D.s in rural areas would bring the proportion of doctors in these areas up to the level of physicians per capita in the overall population. This would potentially solve about 30 percent of the rural shortage. Of course, encouraging these doctors to practise in rural areas might not be easy, since they, like other doctors, would be drawn to cities by the advantages of living and practising in such places.

Concerns have been raised whether fast-tracking is possible for many foreign-trained doctors, given that evidence suggests that many of them may require considerably more training to meet Canadian standards. In February 2005, approximately 1,000 foreign-trained physicians

Box 7.2: Steps in the Re-accreditation of Immigrant Doctors

Only somewhat more than half (54 percent) of foreign-trained doctors living in Canada work as physicians. This contrasts with 90 percent of Canadian-trained doctors who work as physicians. This difference comes about in large part because re-accreditation of a medical degree in Canada requires meeting high standards, completing several difficult steps, and overcoming restrictive barriers.

Step 1: First the applicant must pass the Medical Council of Canada's Evaluating Examination (MCCEE). Individuals who apply to write this exam are only allowed to do so if they have a medical degree from a country or institution that is listed with the World Health Organization or the International Medical Education Directory.

Step 2: Applicants who pass the MCCEE test must then establish accreditation in the province where they wish to set up practice. Most provinces require that graduates of foreign medical schools have two years of postgraduate medical training at a Canadian university to practice family medicine and four to five years of training for other specialities.

Step 3: Applicants must pass the appropriate certification examinations of the College of Family Physicians of Canada or the Royal College of Physicians and Surgeons of Canada.

Step 4: To complete all certification requirements, applicants must undertake a period of "residency" or supervised work in a Canadian hospital. This turns out to be one of the most serious barriers for foreign-trained physicians. The number of residencies is limited by the funds made available by Provincial authorities. In some provinces, Canadian-trained applicants must be given priority.

Source: Boyd, Monica, and Grant Schellenberg. 2007. "Re-accreditation and the Occupations of Immigrant Doctors and Engineers." *Canadian Social Trends* 84: 2–8.

wrote a special International Medical Graduate Exam in Ontario. Of those who wrote the exam, only 54 percent passed and went on to take the clinical tests that provide another hurdle for the applicant. Dr. Henderson Lee, at the University of Toronto Medical School, stated:

> I sit on the post-graduate anesthesia committee at the University of Toronto, which has been assessing foreign-trained "anesthetists" for the past three years. We have assessed 10 so far, and only one was deemed fit to practice in Ontario. The other nine required at least another two years of training in a Canadian anesthesia residency program in order to be up to

our standard of anesthesia care. It might be tempting to "fast track" foreign-trained MDs into clinical service, but at what cost? How much is one life worth when a foreign-trained anesthetist is quickly given a licence to practice and then kills a patient under anesthesia? Is one life worth it to get political brownie points for solving the MD shortage? (Lee 2005)

It has been argued that more foreign doctors can be re-accredited in Canada if special resources and opportunities are put in place for their retraining and certification after arrival. This is the approach adopted by Manitoba (2003) and British Columbia (Health Match B.C. 2009).

Reitz (2001) argues that the most significant immigration issue in the 21st century will be how Canada and other highly advanced economies effectively utilize immigrants' skills. Echoing this concern, Wanner (2001) and Bauder (2003) argue, respectively, that Canada needs to take steps to prevent "brain waste" and "brain abuse" of immigrants. These views arise from many studies over recent decades showing that immigrants receive lower wages than Canadian-born workers with the same level of education (Baker and Benjamin 1994: 104; Li 2003c; Picot, Hou, Coulombe 2007; Reitz 2001). They receive lower wages because they get jobs that require lower levels of skill than one would expect given their level of education. If education is considered an investment that individuals make in order to gain higher earnings, then immigrants get low returns for their educational investment. If the education levels of Canada's labour force are considered an asset, then low returns for immigrants translate into lower returns to the economy as a whole. Reitz (2007a: 19) notes that "lost earnings due to under-utilization of immigrants stills ... amount to the equivalent of approximately $2 billion annually." The Conference Board of Canada estimates that $4.1–$5.9 billion are lost annually to the Canadian economy due to the underutilization of work skills, and that immigrants contribute 74 percent of this total (Bloom and Grant 2001).

Debates on the Reasons for Discounting Immigrant Schooling

What explains low returns from foreign education? Is it due to distrust of the diplomas of people from less developed countries and racist practices in hiring? Or is it because foreign training in less developed countries is of lower quality than equivalent programs of study in Canada? Wanner (1998) and Sweetman (2004) found evidence supporting the latter possibility. Sweetman's study used information from 1986, 1991, and 1996 Canadian censuses to establish the earnings of immigrants. He then added to his data set information based on tests of educational quality in the countries that the immigrants came from. He found that male immigrants from countries that ranked at the top end (70th percentile or better) on educational quality earned about $10,000 per year more than those coming from countries ranked near the bottom (15th percentile or lower) on educational quality. Similar but less dramatic differences appeared for women immigrants. Overall, those immigrants coming from countries with the highest educational quality earned 25–30 percent more than those coming from the countries with the lowest educational quality (Sweetman 2004: 6–7).

However, these findings do not eliminate the possibility that ethnic racial discrimination is one factor among others leading to low scores on the cognitive skills tests. This is because a "conundrum" of multiple overlapping and mutually reinforcing factors may together lead to low test scores. Countries with low educational quality scores are concentrated in less developed regions: Africa, Asia, the Caribbean, and Latin America. Immigrants from these countries may arrive in Canada with multiple challenges: lack of recognition of their skills by employers; accents and other attributes that lead employers to discount their experience and potential; for some, a real need to upgrade their skills to Canadian standards; and ethnic or racial discrimination that pushes them toward jobs where they do not have an opportunity to maintain or improve their problem-solving skills in an official Canadian language. In such a situation, discrimination can be one of several reasons why immigrants from countries in Africa, Asia, the Caribbean, and Latin America have low scores on cognitive skills tests and, at the same time, have poorly paid and less cognitively demanding jobs.

A key question is whether wage returns from foreign education are lower recently than they were some decades ago. It appears that they are not. Aydemir and Skuterud (2005) conclude that returns from schooling for individuals from the same source countries have not changed over time between 1966 and 2000. Immigrants from developed nations in Europe and from the United States receive a higher earnings return from years of schooling than immigrants from Africa, Asia, the Caribbean, and Latin America. This was true in the 1960s and 1970s and remained true in the 1990s. Therefore, the falling earnings of each new immigrant cohort over time are not due to any increase in the degree to which foreign education is discounted in the labour market because no such increase took place. At the same time, the study found that about one-third of the deterioration in earnings is explained by a combination of lower official-language abilities and an increase in the proportion of immigrants coming from less developed regions. The authors note that it is difficult to distinguish whether language ability or various characteristics (such as educational quality or relevance of past work experience to jobs in Canada) associated with country of origin have the greatest impact on earnings because these causal variables are highly associated with one another. "Of particular importance is the shift away from Europeans with an English mother tongue (essentially Great Britain) to immigrants from Asia with a foreign mother tongue" (Aydemir and Skuterud 2005: 656). Waslander (2003) previously came to similar conclusions based on his analysis of census data micro files for the period 1981 and 1996.

Poverty by Immigrant Entry Class

It is useful to examine income at the family level because this allows one to observe how earnings and other sources of income pooled by all members of a family affect their collective economic situation. Low earnings among recently arrived immigrants lead to the expectation that their family incomes will be low. This turns out to be the case. Picot, Hou, and Coulombe (2007) report that roughly two-thirds of immigrant families arriving in the 1990s fell into a low-income category sometime during their first decade in Canada. Low-income families were those whose incomes were half or less of the median income for all Canadian families. The proportion of families experiencing low income over this time period was about 3.5 times higher among immigrants than among the native-born. Most of the immigrants who experienced low income in the first decade after arrival fell into a low-income category in the first year after arrival, as one might expect. However, the surprising finding was that the low-income pattern became chronic for about one-fifth of all the immigrants studied. Chronic low income was defined as being in a low-income situation for four out of the five initial years spent in Canada. Even more surprising was the finding that the chronic low-income pattern was concentrated among immigrants who had arrived in the skilled economic class. By the late 1990s, roughly one half of all chronically low-income immigrant families arriving in that decade had arrived in this class. In fact, the data reveal a startling finding. Picot, Hou, and Coulombe (2007) note the following:

> With respect to immigrant class, immigrants in the skilled economic class were *more* likely to enter low income than their family class counterparts, *possibly because the family class immigrants often entered an already economically established family*. This relative disadvantage observed for the skilled class increased significantly over

the 1992 to 2004 period, when the number of skilled class immigrants rose. (pp. 7–8; italics added)

Source region matters. The prevalence of chronic low income is very low among entering immigrants from North America and Europe; the rate in the 2000 cohort was in the 8% range (controlling for other demographic differences among source regions), whereas immigrants from Africa and East Asia had the highest rates (19% to 24%). (p. 32)

The report makes clear that when immigrants in the skilled economic class did find jobs, their incomes were higher than those of immigrants in the family class, as one would expect based their higher average education. However, once in a chronically low-income category, immigrants in the highly skilled economic class did not exit this category any faster than those in the family class. The authors make clear that these patterns are difficult to explain with certainty based on the data at hand. They note that immigrants in the family class may have been partly protected from chronic low income due to the income and living-arrangement supports provided by relatives who arrived earlier, became established, and then sponsored their relative(s) to come. If true, this would highlight the importance of family networks in immigrant well-being and incorporation. Other hypotheses can also be advanced. The family-class immigrants may have been able to get jobs relatively easily despite their lower levels of schooling due to the contacts provided by their established relatives. These are important possibilities to be addressed in future studies. They raise potentially serious questions regarding the common policy assumption that immigrants in the skilled economic class will necessarily do

better in Canada than immigrants in the family class.

Retraining as a Solution

If low returns from foreign education are a major obstacle to immigrants, one would expect that the immigrants would adapt by engaging in retraining and skill-upgrading in Canada. Contrary to the long-held belief that adult immigrants had largely completed their studies prior to arrival to Canada and did not continue their studies after they arrived, recent studies of the labour force suggest that quite the opposite is true for immigrants arriving from 2002 to 2007 (Gilmore and Le Petit 2008). Nine percent of university-educated immigrants aged 25–54 who arrived in this very recent period had completed their highest level of university studies in Canada. This figure rises to 18 percent among those who had arrived five years earlier and spent longer in Canada (see Gilmore and Le Petit 2008: Chapter 2, Table 2.1).

Declining Returns to Foreign Work Experience

Just as employers tend to discount foreign education, they also tend to discount foreign work experience. Various studies indicate that this pattern can be observed for immigrants arriving from the 1960s onward (Aydemir and Skuterud 2005; Frenette and Morissette 2003; Green and Worswick 2002). An important finding is that the degree to which foreign work experience is discounted has become more pronounced over time. In the 1970s and early 1980s, an older immigrant arriving with more work experience would earn significantly more than younger immigrants with less work experience who arrived at the same time. The earnings advantage of older-at-arrival immigrants has declined over time. Green and Worswick (2002) observe this in two independent data sets. Aydemir and Skuterud (2005: 641) report that there is "a definite deterioration in the returns to foreign labour market experience, most strongly among men from non-traditional source countries." In other words, male immigrants from less developed regions have experienced the greatest declines over time in the recognition of their foreign work experience. Why this is the case is unclear. One hypothesis is that work skills desired by Canadian employers are becoming more specific to Canadian technology and productive organization. If this is the case, then immigrants arriving with more foreign work experience will *not* be regarded as having experience relevant to jobs in Canada. Research findings on discounted foreign experience suggest that this is an important topic for future research. One of the challenges will be to find better measures of foreign work experience. At present, most of the studies discussed above are based on census data that have no direct measure of such experience. Researchers typically estimate foreign work experience in terms of the age of immigrants at the time of their arrival.

Language Skills

Skill in speaking English or French is known to be a major determinant of immigrant earnings. This is hardly surprising. Canada may be a multicultural and multilingual country, but ability to communicate in English or French is nearly always essential for better-paid jobs. Office-cleaning workers and some other low-wage earners may work on crews composed entirely of individuals from a particular ethnic group who speak their home-country language and who are under the supervision of a manager who speaks that language and English or French as well. However, such "ghettoized" work organization patterns, while of deep concern because they trap the workers in low-paid jobs, involve only a minority of immigrant workers. The most pressing research questions have to do

with assessing more precisely the level of skills required for jobs in Canada and how these standards may be changing to affect the earnings of immigrants.

Much of the research on immigrant language skills, such as that by Aydemir and Skuterud (2005) and other studies examined in preceding sections of this chapter, is based on very rough measures. Until very recently, most research in the field has been based on census data that use crude indicators, such as mother tongue and language used at home, to estimate language skills in English and French. The problem is that some individuals who have a foreign mother tongue and use it at home may have excellent skills in English or French, while others may have very poor skills in these official Canadian languages.

Fortunately, new data sets are becoming available that measure language and related cognitive skills directly through individual tests. Green and Riddell (2003) and Bonikowska, Green, and Riddell (2008) have analyzed the International Adult Literacy Skills Survey (IALSS). Ferrer, Green, and Riddell (2006) have done similar analysis of the Ontario Immigrant Literacy Survey (OILS). Both data sets contain survey questions on the characteristics of those surveyed and the results from tests of their literacy and numeracy. The findings of studies based on these data reveal very marked differences between immigrants and Canadian-born in language and numeracy skills; they also find that the lower skills of the immigrants explain a significant part of their earnings disadvantage. However, they also reveal that indicators such as mother tongue and language used at home do not tell us much about cognitive skills in applying these languages in day-to-day problem-solving tasks. It seems that advanced skills in using a language in cognitive-skill tasks is quite different from knowledge of a language that is sufficient for day-to-day communication at home, work, and in the community.

The findings from Bonikowska, Green, and Riddell (2008), shown in Box 7.3, summarize the main points emerging from recent studies using direct measures of *problem-solving skills* on tests written in English or French. To be clear, these are not tests on grammar, vocabulary, reading comprehension, arithmetic skills, or writing ability in English and French, although the tests require a certain basic amount of these skills to understand questions provided in these official Canadian languages. Rather, they require problem solving using an official language. The results shown in Box 7.3 lead to a significant reappraisal of the role of language skills relative to cognitive skills in generating earnings. As the authors of this study point out, "an engineer who is well trained but cannot communicate with his or her employer or fellow employees would be counted as having zero usable engineering skills." On the other hand, the engineer may receive 100 percent credit for these skills if he or she can communicate well enough (perhaps far less than perfectly) to effectively coordinate with others, solve problems, and complete assigned tasks. Correspondingly, mother tongue (the language first spoken) and self-reported measures of knowledge and use of English and French have little or no relationship to cognitive scores on tests conducted in English and French. Perhaps this tentative conclusion helps to explain the puzzle in Grayson's (2008) study showing that the grades of foreign-born university students in Toronto are not related to their self-reported English language skills, nor to whether or not they have taken ESL (English as a second language) courses to upgrade their competency in English. It would seem plausible that high university grades, like higher income jobs, are given to individuals who use certain basic language skills in order to solve problems and demonstrate critical insights into issues.

Various qualitative studies also point to the complexity of the relationship between language skills and job/earnings outcomes. Studies of skilled immigrants reveal the challenge they face to successfully navigate a job interview. McCoy and Masuch (2007) carried out lengthy research interviews with six foreign-educated immigrant women in Calgary who were applying for skilled administrative and management jobs that were not within the category of regulated professional work, such as that of engineers. While these women did not need to pass any tests or certification procedures in order to work in Canada, they found it impossible to find a job in their specialty immediately after arrival. They reported feedback from job interviews that their language skills were not up to the standards required. They also came to realize that their self-presentation in their résumés needed work to fit with Canadian cultural standards and practices. Services to help them develop their skills and presentation were not readily available. The result is that many immigrants must take so-called entry-level jobs, which, in fact, were not designed to give people experience for promotion, with the result that the immigrants remain trapped in positions below their potential. The authors note one very successful program that helped immigrants by giving them on-the-job experience. Similarly, Cardu (2007) observes that highly educated female immigrants living in Quebec City find it initially impossible to get jobs at the level of their foreign training for a variety of reasons: The fact that they are women of colour from non-European backgrounds who are still learning to feel at ease in a new cultural setting and, for many, to learn French all combine to create job barriers. In response, they take lower-level and part-time jobs. They then engage in "career nomadism," involving winding and insecure paths to

Box 7.3: Cognitive Skills and Earnings

The Survey: The International Adult Literacy and Skills Survey (IALSS) survey was carried out in 2003 on some 18,000 individual (of whom approximately 3,700 were immigrants) to understand the cognitive skills of Canadians.

Measures of Cognitive Skills: The survey measured: Prose Literacy, Document Literacy, Numeracy and Problem Solving. The test questions do not attempt to measure *abilities* such as those in mathematics and reading. Rather they try to assess *cognitive skills* such as problem solving in circumstances that arise in everyday life and work settings. Thus, for example, the Document Literacy test asks respondents to identify percentages in categories in a pictorial graph and to assess an average price by combining several pieces of information.

Overall Findings
The various cognitive skill measures are highly correlated with each other. Hence a simple average of the four scores is used as a summary cognitive skill measure.

Canadian-born university graduates have average skill scores that are 22–24 percent higher than individuals who have not completed high school. A similar pattern is found for immigrants.

The cognitive skill distribution of immigrants is much lower on average than that of Canadian-born individuals, as shown in the chart below.

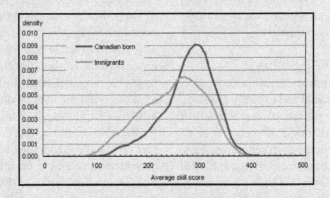

Cognitive skills have a significant impact on earnings. For example, raising the cognitive skill levels of university-educated individuals to those of similarly educated Canadian-born would reduce the male earnings gap by 50 percent and would more than eliminate the female earnings gap.

There is no evidence that immigrants receive a lower earnings return to the types of cognitive skills measured in IALSS than otherwise equivalent Canadian-born workers. Immigrant/Canadian-born earnings differentials cannot be explained by discrimination against immigrants using this assessment.

A foreign mother tongue has practically no relationship to cognitive skills measured on tests written in English or French. Low cognitive scores arising from many cases where respondents did not complete the tests show that these were associated with individuals who reported understanding and using English or French but in fact had lower levels of education and were less likely to use reading and writing skills in these languages in their work.

Forty-two percent of immigrants acquire some education in Canada. The cognitive skills of these immigrants are significantly higher than other immigrants and closer to those of the Canadian-born.

Source: Author's summary of Bonikowska, Aneta, David A. Green, and W.C. Riddell. 2008. *Cognitive Skills and Immigrant Earnings.* Ottawa: Statistics Canada. The figure is Chart 4, page 25, from the report.

try to get a better job. Getting that better job is difficult because the initial jobs they take do not develop their skills or lead to the kinds of experiences that would move them to better positions. Cardu concludes that the process involves the development of a marginalized identity and ghettoization "through atypical employment and professional deskilling, aggravated by systemic discrimination" (p. 437). So while some immigrants may get discouraged by low-wage jobs and unemployment, as Aydemir (2003) suggests, many struggle on despite marginalization.

Visible Minority Status

Many contemporary studies show that certain ethno-racial minorities in Canada continue to experience discrimination and argue that this is a likely cause of their poorer outcomes in schooling, jobs, incomes, and housing (Driedger 2003b; Henry and Tator 2000; Kallen 2003; Pendakur and Pendakur 1998; Satzewich 1998). Nakhaie (2006) concludes that the downward trend in the relative earnings of visible minority immigrants relative to Canadian-born Whites, shown in Figure 7.4, is probably due to racism based on skin colour. The trends shown make clear that visible minority immigrants have been losing ground over time with respect to the earnings of all other categories of individuals, including Canadian-born Whites (whose earnings are shown as the line equal to 100.0 in the figure). However, the

information in Figure 7.4 also highlights the difficulty of attributing the relative decline in earnings of visible minority immigrants entirely to racism based on skin colour. Second-generation visible minority individuals (that is, children born in Canada to previous cohorts of visible minority immigrants) have earnings on average similar to those for White native-born Canadians. Either they are not subject to the same skin-colour-based discrimination, or they have been able to overcome such discrimination in ways that recent immigrants have not been able to do. In sum, the question is not whether visible minority individuals encounter racism because the evidence is overwhelming that many do. However, the earnings outcome may be due to the combined effect of two determining factors: (1) the amount of racism they encounter, and (2) the resources they have available to overcome racism in finding a good job. The issues are complex and are addressed by other authors in works devoted entirely to the subject of racism (see, for example, Satzewich and Liodakis 2007: Chapter 4, and Nakhaie 2006, 2007).

Competition from Immigrant Youth

Several of the studies reviewed above have drawn attention to the fact that young immigrants who arrive in Canada and the second generation of children born in Canada to immigrant parents have far better job and earning prospects than their parents. The often considerable success of

Figure 7.4: Relative Earnings of Visible Minorities and Whites by Place of Birth

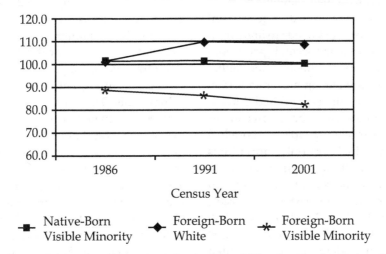

Note: Trend lines over time show the earnings of native-born visible minorities, foreign-born Whites, and foreign-born visible minorities as proportions of the earnings of native-born Whites (native-born White = 100).

Earnings are for individuals 25–64 who are working full-time.

Source: The author, based on data from: Nakhaie, M.R. 2006. "A Comparison of the Earnings of the Canadian Native-Born and Immigrants." *Canadian Ethnic Studies Journal* 38:Table 5.

the children of immigrants, whether born abroad or in Canada, is becoming a major field of study in itself (see, for example, Fernandez-Kelly and Portes 2008). Our objective in this short section on the topic is directed to three linked arguments. First, the children of immigrants are often doing very well in terms of education in Canada for various reasons that are not fully understood, but almost certainly include the very strong support they receive from their parents. Secondly, when the children of immigrants complete schooling and enter the Canadian job market, they, like other well-educated young Canadian workers, may have a competitive edge in the job market over recently arrived immigrants with similar levels of foreign education. This advantage arises through the way the Canadian job market discounts the foreign training and work experience of

adult immigrants, and other factors that we have noted such as the presence of unfamiliar foreign accents, which may reduce their job prospects. In effect, part of the problem faced by newly arrived immigrants in recent cohorts is that they face competition from equally trained youths, including those who are children of an earlier wave of immigrants. The Canadian-trained young workers have similar formal training to that of new immigrants and, as well, have higher levels of job-relevant social capital. Newly arrived immigrants may be unhappy with their own reduced prospective earnings, but may reluctantly accept these as a necessary part of living in Canada, thereby investing in the future success of their own children.

Evidence for the first argument is compelling. Boyd's (2002) analysis of data gathered annually between 1993 and

1996 in the Survey of Labour and Income Dynamics (SLID) showed that immigrants who arrived with their parents and grew up in Canada (the so-called 1.5 generation) and children born in Canada to immigrant parents (the so-called second generation) have more years of schooling and higher percentages completing higher education than other Canadians (so-called third or more generation, since the research in this field tends to exclude people of Aboriginal descent and includes only individuals with foreign ethnic origins). The high educational achievements of the 1.5 and second generation are also found for visible minority individuals. Boyd concludes that: "Contrary to the segmented 'underclass' assimilation model found in the United States, adult visible minority immigrant offspring in Canada exceed the education attainments of other not-visible-minority groups" (Boyd 2002: 1037). Palameta (2007) examined the SLID data through to 2004 and found that the patterns Boyd observed for the earlier period are evident as well in these more recent data.

Findings from the 2000 Statistics Canada Youth in Transition Survey, undertaken in 1,241 Canadian schools, revealed that immigrant youth and visible minority youth were far more likely to aspire to post-graduate or professional university studies leading to a second university degree than were Canadian-born and non-visible minority youth (Krahn and Taylor 2005). The differences are remarkable: For example, 52 percent of visible minority youth, many of whom are children of immigrants, aspire to going beyond a basic university degree, while only 32 percent of non-visible minority students aspired to this. These differences hold for male and female students and for individuals in cities and smaller towns, even though living in a city was associated with higher aspirations. Educational aspirations are higher for youths growing up in larger communities and families with

higher levels of education and income, but even when controlling for these variables, visible minority immigrant status has an upward effect on aspirations (p. 425).

Not only do immigrant youths aspire to more schooling, but the majority of immigrant youths and children born in Canada to immigrant parents go on to achieve this. The 2001 census revealed that second generation individuals (that is, persons who were born in Canada to immigrant parents) had on average 14 years of schooling. This was well above the 11.3 average years of schooling found among individuals whose parents were born in Canada (Aydemir, Chen, and Corak 2005). Individuals born in Canada to immigrant parents also had higher average earnings than other Canadians. In addition, second generation individuals tended to achieve substantially higher average levels of education than their own parents. Corak (2008: 21) notes that the children of recent cohorts of immigrant parents "do well in school and achieve a positive head start in life" despite the fact that their parents have frequently faced difficulties in the labour market. This pattern of upward generation mobility was found among immigrant children from many regions of the world. However, it did not hold for all place-of-origin groups, nor was it equal for sons of immigrants when compared with the daughters of immigrants. Upward intergenerational mobility was almost zero for sons of immigrants from the Caribbean, Central and South America. In contrast, upward intergenerational mobility was particularly high for sons of immigrants from Asia. Upward intergenerational mobility was also generally higher for women in all region-of-origin categories when compared with men from the same regions (Aydemir, Chen, and Corak 2005: Table 6).

Boyd (2008) examined the variation in second-generation achievement by ethnicity rather than region of origin and noted that high school completion rates are particularly elevated for second-generation ethnic Chinese (93 percent graduate), South Asians (90 percent graduate), and Filipinos (88 percent graduate), but much lower for Blacks (81 percent graduate), and lower still for Latin Americans (78 percent graduate). A useful benchmark for assessing this wide variation is the high school completion rate for non-visible minority individuals whose parents were born in Canada (83 percent graduate). We may therefore conclude that high school completion among second generation individuals of different visible minority backgrounds varies widely from well above this benchmark for certain ethnic groups to somewhat below it for others. The rate of high school completion for any ethnic group is a good predictor of the percent who continue their studies to complete a bachelor's degree.

Wilkinson (2008) uses data from the 1998 SLID and a 1998 refugee survey in Alberta to better understand how immigrant youth get their first jobs. Wilkinson's findings point to the importance of first jobs, given that first-time jobs and part-time work while studying are important in financing post-secondary schooling and getting experience for future occupational mobility. The same study also notes the particularly disappointing first job outcomes for 1.5-generation refugees (that is children born outside Canada who arrived young to Canada with parents who immigrated to Canada in the refugee class). In sum, the upward mobility experienced by most children of immigrants does not apply in the case of certain ethnic groups, such as Blacks and Latin Americans, nor does it hold as well for many who arrived as children with their refugee parents. The fact that many children of immigrants from some backgrounds do poorly compared with Canadian born children is a cause for deep public concern. Reasons

for lower than average educational and income outcomes for some second generation individuals are complex and vary from one group to another. Likely explanations of lower outcomes for some groups include racism in the schools and job market, while for other groups the likely explanation may be cultural factors affecting school attainment, or the trauma suffered by refugee families. All these factors may be involved in certain cases.

Reitz (2001) argues that second-generation immigrants have such major advantages with respect to training and background for entering the labour market that they make it even more difficult for recently arrived immigrants to find good jobs. He estimates that from 1981 to 1996, "the earnings of newly arrived immigrant men in Canada declined about 3 percent because native-born education was rising more rapidly than immigrant educational levels, and a further 3 percent because the increases in immigrant education were devalued in the labour market. Together, the two represent about one-third of the overall decline in immigrant earnings" (Reitz 2007a: 50). If we add to these observations the fact that the greatest rise in Canadian educational levels over this period was due to the mobility of the second generation (and also the 1.5 generation, but to a lesser degree), then our argument receives further support: Recent immigrants have trouble getting jobs in part because of several linked factors. The children of earlier cohorts of immigrants have a competitive advantage in the Canadian labour force for the following reasons. They have very high levels of schooling; their schooling is in Canada and hence does not face the same discounting that foreign education is subject to; and being young and well educated without experience does not seem to be a problem when competing with immigrants for jobs since employers heavily discount the greater experience of older age-at-arrival immigrants because it took place outside Canada.

The third argument concerning how recent immigrants achieve through their children's success is supported primarily by qualitative studies that examine immigrant parents' educational aspirations for their children. Suárez-Orozco and Suárez-Orozco (2001) argue that immigrant parents' disappointment in their own economic incorporation may lead them to "will ambition" to their children, and point to evidence for this in their own research on Latin American families in the United States. James (1990) observed that Black parents in his Toronto sample made a particular effort to pass on to their children their belief that individuals are rewarded by hard work. Krahn and Taylor (2005) note that the very high educational aspirations they observed in immigrant and visible minority students across Canada were supported by their parents, and that the parents' aspirations have a "powerful net effect on children's aspirations (partial odds ratio = 3.60)" (p. 23). Lam's (1996) ethnographic study of Vietnamese-Chinese refugees in Montreal notes how blocked and downward mobility among the parents led them to focus on their children's future success. The parents hoped to promote achievement and discourage the gang formation, crime, and violence that some youth in this community were engaged in. Lam quotes one respondent as follows: "We are only the doormats for our children to enter Canada's garden party. We hope that they are going to be the guests and not the jests and they are going to make the honour roll and not the death roll ..." (Lam 1996: 176).

Immigrant Social Capital

If the social capital of immigrants is less than that of non-immigrants, the immigrants will turn out to have a relative disadvantage. While relatively little research has been carried out on this possibility, what is known suggests that "the social networks of immigrants are inferior to those of the native-born in many important aspects; they also yield smaller pay-offs" (Kazemipur 2006b: 47). Compared with native-born individuals, immigrants' network contacts are about a third smaller, tend to be with people who have lower levels of socio-economic status, are less drawn upon for advice and support, and are ethnically less diverse (Kazemipur 2006b: 47). It is also the case that immigrants spend less time volunteering for non-profit organizations in Canada than do native-born individuals (Couton and Gaudet 2008). This may be one of the reasons why their social networks in Canada are smaller. Another reason why immigrants' social capital may be smaller is that they live overwhelmingly in large cities. Large cities have lower levels of social trust than smaller cities and towns (Aizlewood and Pendakur 2005). The lower trust in large cities seems to be a feature of social relations generally. Immigrants may have lower access to job- and business-related social capital in particular. Kazemipur's (2006b) survey reported above showed that immigrants have closer ties to their religious institutions and communities than do native-born individuals. These ties are most likely more related to spiritual, emotional, and ethical matters than they are to matters of jobs and business. In the same vein, Mata and McRae (2000) examined the philanthropy of immigrants. While immigrants generally give less money to philanthropic causes (an outcome that may reflect their lower earnings and assets), what they do contribute is more likely to go to a religious organization rather than a secular institution, in comparison with the native-born.

There is considerable variation in social capital within any given immigrant ethnic community. Men seem to have more social capital than women, and those with more schooling have more social capital than those with less schooling (Kazemipur 2006b: 60). The gender difference is consistent with other findings that immigrant women, particularly those with children, have lower levels of participation than Canadian-born women in activities in the wider Canadian society that are oriented to family, children, and schooling (Couton and Gaudet 2008).

Enclaves: The term "ethnic residential enclave" refers to a residential area within a larger urban settlement that is either exclusive to or made up of a majority of members of a single ethnic group. Ethnic institutions may be prominently visible in such areas. Driving through, one will see store signs in the ethnic language and advertisements for ethnic products. Ethnic churches, mosques, or temples may have locations of privilege. People with ethnic dress may be evident. Such enclaves may also have their own internal economy with employers hiring ethnic workers for jobs to be carried out in their home language within the enclave. The jobs may involve manufacturing of goods, trade, and sales. Such a pattern is referred to as an "ethnic economic enclave."

The vicious cycle outlined in Figure 7.5 may reinforce the poverty of the immigrants living in suburbs. Hou and Picot (2003) find that visible minorities in Canadian cities are more likely to live with or near co-ethnic neighbours due to the rising number of immigrants in cities and the proclivity of immigrants to live within ethnic communities both for reasons of ethnicity and because of a common struggle to find affordable housing. Living in an ethnic residential enclave had a very low (not statistically significant) relationship to low earnings for all immigrant groups together, but this was not the case for certain groups. Black immigrants stood out as exceptions in this regard. Blacks who lived outside their own ethnic enclave had much better labour market outcomes than those who lived within their own ethnic enclaves (p. 567). Kim (2005) found a similar pattern for Canadian cities using more recent 2001 census data. The direction of causality remains murky in these findings: Black immigrants who have more occupational success for whatever reason may use their higher earnings to move out of the enclave, just as enclaves may limit social resources that allow Blacks to move out of these enclaves.

Within a setting tolerant of diversity, ethnic enclaves are generally assumed to provide a cultural buffer zone that helps new immigrants become established. They can initially work and live in their own language and culture within such an enclave. Over time after arriving, immigrants can gradually establish language skills and a broader set of contacts that will permit them to improve their economic situation. From this perspective, ethnic enclaves may be viewed as playing a positive cultural role in a multi-ethnic society such as Canada. Consequently, when immigrants voluntarily choose to live within their own ethnic residential areas, this is not viewed as a problem in itself. However, it is clearly a problem when the immigrants are forced to live with their ethnic kin because of discrimination and poverty. Even in cases in which the choice of living or working begins as a voluntary step, it can become a problem if it leads to low-wage jobs, a slow acquisition of English or French, and reduced access to economic opportunities and full participation in Canadian society. There is a risk that marginalization arising from a voluntary move will then lead to an increase in discrimination by outsiders who begin to label members of the ethnic community as "losers." At this point, immigrants may find themselves repeatedly marginalized in a vicious circle (see Figure 7.5).

Figure 7.5: Ethnic Enclaves: Vicious Circle Model

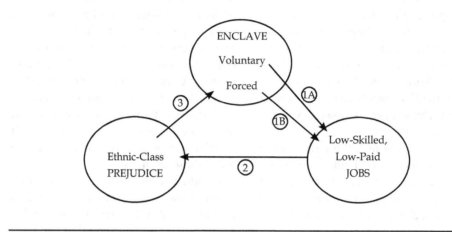

Work enclaves: Immigrants who speak their home language in their jobs in Canada may be assumed to be working in an ethnic enclave work environment. Do such workers have lower or equal incomes compared with those in the same ethnic community who do not speak their home language at work? In the case of Chinese workers in Canada, the answer is that those working within the enclave have lower earnings, controlling for other variables (Li and Dong 2007). The same pattern is found for both male and female workers. Even those who own enclave businesses may find that being confined to an economic enclave leads to reduced opportunities. Immigrant entrepreneurs may at times have difficulty entering into business in the open market in Canada because they lack the social capital (experience, contacts, trust) to do so. When this happens, as it appears to do with some Asian business entrepreneurs, they turn to the closed ethnic market by trading and selling goods to their own ethnic community (Wong and Ng 1998). While this shows flexible economic adaptation, it is also an outcome that is forced on the entrepreneurs by constraining circumstances.

Discussion and Conclusions

The low earnings of recently arrived immigrants, including those with very high levels of education, are a matter of great concern. Even more concerning is the evidence that the causes of their low incomes are deeply rooted in: (1) macro-economic conditions associated with Canada's position in the global economy; (2) the immigrants' countries of origin and associated discounting of their foreign credentials and work experience by Canadian employers; (3) a vicious cycle that keeps immigrants in jobs less skilled than they were trained for; and (4) immigrants' important but relatively weak social capital that serves well for their cultural belonging in multicultural Canada, but apparently less well for obtaining good jobs and finding business opportunities. In addition, for some at least and perhaps for many, racism is an obstacle to their job and earnings success, although exactly how important this may be remains difficult to measure since many immigrants develop resources to overcome discrimination. Possible solutions to these various factors that limit immigrant job and earnings success include major programs to provide immigrants with support and opportunities for on-the-job training and upgrading so that they have the credentials and skills to overcome the many challenges they face to improving their incomes.

The relatively greater schooling and job successes of immigrants who came to Canada as children and the second generation of children born in Canada to immigrant parents provides a bright spot in what otherwise is a sobering picture of the job and earnings outcomes for recently arrived immigrants. However, this bright spot is not found in all immigrant communities: Second-generation Blacks, Latinos,

and those in some recently arrived refugee groups reveal the same disadvantages when it comes to education, jobs, and earnings prospects as their parents. This suggests the need for greater efforts to address a mix of causes, including discrimination, that lead to disadvantages for the immigrants and for their second-generation children born in Canada.

The earnings issues addressed in this chapter have important implications for social and cultural aspects of immigrant incorporation in Canada and in transnational social space extending to their home countries. Chapter 8 examines more fully questions of immigrant belonging from the perspective of their social networks, memberships, and relations.

CHAPTER 8

Being and Belonging in a Transnational World

Introduction

Like many other immigrants in Canada, Jamaican immigrants living in Toronto and Haitian immigrants living in Montreal have intimate and frequent contacts with home. According to Simmons, Plaza, and Piché (2005), most Jamaican and Haitian immigrant families phone home weekly. Some phone daily. The conversations are about everything that one would discuss around the dinner table. They talk about their health and what foods and folk remedies are best for a cold or the flu; who will look after an ailing relative; how the children are doing in school; which local sports team is winning; the weather and threat of storms; jobs, local politics, and much more. When talking by phone, they may express cries of joy about achievements and tears of anguish about losses. Visiting back and forth is fairly common. As the Caribbean is close, a few immigrants visit home once a year, while many others go every few years. When they visit, they take gifts. In between they send gifts and appreciable amounts of money whenever they can. Their world has a "here" and a "there," but they are living a life in both places. This dual way of being and belonging is a common feature in the life of immigrants from other regions of the world, including those from regions suffering ongoing wars and ethnic/religious violence. What does this transnational way of living and being mean for understanding Canadian society and citizenship?

Research on the impacts of immigration has been energized in recent years by newly emerging understandings of immigrant social networks and changing patterns of immigrant belonging in a transnational space covering their home communities and the places to which they have moved. Studies in this field operate on the premise that the flows of people, money, and communication across transnational social spaces are among the most dynamic, transformative developments in recent history. Everyone is affected, not just the migrants and their families. Immigrant-destination nations like Canada are affected, but so too are the home countries of the immigrants. Some of the outcomes are clearly positive, as when immigrants help one another get established, send significant financial support to relatives overseas, and use their networks to enrich the diversity of cultural, economic, and political life in Canada and their home country. Other outcomes create major challenges, such as what to do

when strong transnational ethnic bonds draw immigrants into the opposite sides of foreign and ethnic, religious, and national conflicts.

This chapter concerns the way immigrant transnationalism plays out in Canada. The main focus is on immigrant being and belonging, and the implications of this for immigrants' ethnic retention, identity, and relationships of harmony and conflict with others. The first section clarifies the issues of concern. This is followed by a review of concepts for understanding Canadian official multiculturalism in relation to emerging transnational forms of immigrant and minority being and belonging. The remaining sections examine hypotheses and evidence on immigrant transnationalism in Canada.

Issues: Transnationalism and Canada

Canada currently has an official policy of *multiculturalism* in which immigrants are both allowed and, in some respects, encouraged to retain significant aspects of their cultures and related identities. Multiculturalism includes the hope and expectation that immigrants from different nations and cultures will *integrate* into Canada. Defining "successful integration" is a matter of continuing debate. Basic indicators of it include: *civic integration* (having access to and using basic rights, democratic political means, and the courts to participate as a citizen); *social-economic integration* (often defined in terms of avoiding marginalization with respect to jobs, incomes, and housing); and *multicultural integration* (living peacefully with other cultures by respecting differences in values, religions, and world views).

Transnationalism and multiculturalism are related in three ways. Firstly, the links that immigrants retain with home countries tend to reinforce diversity within a multicultural society and vice versa. This general observation is unlikely to be viewed as controversial, although many details of how transnationalism and multiculturalism relate to one another still require clarification.

Secondly, transnationalism has proven to be such a vibrant force in Canada that the kind of society emerging seems to spill out over the edges of the normative model constituted by official multiculturalism. Immigrants are involved in dual national allegiances and complex identities and senses of belonging involving more than one nation or ethnic affiliation. This contrasts with the official notion of multicultural integration as a Canada-centred process in which what was happening in the wider world was until recently left out of policies and research on immigrant integration. Satzewich and Wong (2006) observe that: "transnational practices ... suggest a sense of belonging and attachment that extends beyond Canadian borders and that poses a challenge to the present form of multicultural policy" (p. 1). Carment and Bercuson (2008) draw attention to the way in which ethnic "diasporas" in Canada affect Canadian foreign policy. Frideres (2008: 83–86) notes the challenge of transnationalism for understanding how immigrants integrate. In this chapter I build on these observations in an effort to extend our understanding of *immigrant integration* in Canada as being shaped within a broader process of *transnational incorporation*.

Thirdly, transnationalism affects how immigrants become incorporated in Canada in specific ways that need to be identified more clearly. Studies carried out so far in Canada suggest several broad patterns, including the following:

1. Transnationalism and multiculturalism together help immigrants to find a cultural home in Canada. Immigrants develop networks and institutions in Canada that are linked to their home countries and create a sense of familiarity and cultural support for other immigrants who arrive later from the same countries and ethnic communities.

2. Later, immigrants develop their social capital by extending their web of friendships, contacts, and memberships within Canada, while at the same time retaining links and participation in their home countries. While these efforts are helpful to them, the social capital they develop may be less than that of native-born Canadians, with the result that many immigrants remain disadvantaged in job searches, employment, and earnings.

3. Over time, more complex individual ethnic identities emerge among immigrants through day-to-day identity politics in which they seek to clarify who they are in a transnational space. The new individual identities may be hyphenated following the established practice in Canada of using terms like Pakistani-Canadian, or they may be hybrid and use new terms like "Latino."

4. In the processes described above, various challenges of ethnic collective representation emerge, with immigrant and ethnic organizations making efforts to develop a more positive image of their collective membership to confront negative stereotyping in the media and by ethnic-nationalist groups in Canada. The stereotyping in a transnational world often draws attention to the foreign links, real or imagined, of a few people and develops these into images that immigrants and foreign-

ers are threats to peace, security, and Canadian values. Out of beliefs that these threats are real or out of a desire to sell sensational news, the media present stories of migrant trafficking and immigrant involvement in foreign wars in a way than can create a moral panic, particularly for members of the Canadian public who are removed from the detailed facts.

Following the main argument of the book, we may say that the imagined futures of the nation and related normative models of immigration and immigrant settlement developed by the Canadian state do not necessarily correspond with what actually takes place. The present chapter follows the same logic. *Multicultural immigrant integration* is a normative model for what the Canadian state hopes — based on its imagined future of the nation — will take place, while what is actually taking place is different due to a multi-layered process of *transnational immigrant incorporation*. The imagined future and associated normative model of immigrant incorporation overlap to some degree with what happens, but the two are definitely not the same.

The Multicultural Normative Model: A Critique

Since Prime Minister Trudeau's proclamation in 1971 that Canada is an officially multicultural nation, ethnic diversity has been promoted and often celebrated by the Canadian state. The Act states that:

> Canada ... recognizes the diversity of Canadians as regards race national or ethnic origin, colour and religion as fundamental char-

acteristics of Canadian society and is committed to a policy of multiculturalism designed to preserve and enhance ... the heritage of Canadians while working to achieve equality of all Canadians in the economic, social, cultural and political life of Canada. (Multiculturalism Act 1988)

From the beginning, it was understood that multiculturalism would operate within a "bilingual framework" to assist cultural groups to retain their identity, overcome barriers to their full participation in Canadian society, engage in creative exchanges with other cultural groups, and acquire at least one of the official languages of Canada. Over time these goals were refined to shape particular strategies of improving "race relations" and to "eliminate discrimination" (Ungerleider 2006: 206–209).

The Standing Committee on Multiculturalism (1987) made clear that the legislation is designed to encourage the integration of immigrants and racial and ethnic minorities, not their assimilation. *Integration* was defined by the committee as a process through which "groups and/or individuals become able to participate fully in the political, economic, social and cultural life of the country" (Standing Committee on Multiculturalism 1987: 87). In other words, in a multicultural Canada, immigrants and minorities could retain their culture while becoming integrated, provided that they had equal access to Canadian economic, social, and political institutions. This would constitute *multicultural integration*, a process that would be very different than *assimilation*, understood then and still today as the coming together or gradual fusing of the cultures and identities of immigrants, ethnic minorities, and mainstream society (Alba and Nee 1997).

Multiculturalism may be viewed as a policy that the Canadian state sought to add as a complement to its immigration policies in order to make Canadian immigration policies and a diverse ethnic labour force and society function more harmoniously for the benefit of dominant economic interests and the Canadian state as a promoter of these interests (Abu-Laban and Gabriel 2002). As it became clear that immigrants with desired skills would be found largely in diverse countries in Africa, Asia, the Caribbean, and Latin America, each with its own distinctive culture, Canada moved to give explicit recognition that people from these and all other regions were welcome. As proof of this welcome, immigrants and their children were permitted (if not encouraged) to keep their own ethnic identities after arrival in Canada. Canada was the first nation to officially develop such a policy. A number of other countries, particularly Australia and Sweden, have adopted similar policies. Several European nations moved in the direction of multicultural policies in the 1980s, but moved away from them in the late 1990s and early 2000s (Castles and Miller 2003: 46). Today, as in the past, multiculturalism is controversial; Canada is exceptional with regard to the explicit way it has adopted and carried forward its multicultural policy (Bloemraad 2006).

The big multiculturalism question is: Does it work in practice? Many nations remain doubtful about official multicultural policies. The murder of filmmaker Théo Van Gogh in the Netherlands by a Muslim extremist and the deeply hostile reaction from fundamentalist Muslims around the world to the Danish cartoons of the prophet Mohammed were key events in shifting public opinion away from embracing cultural diversity in the Netherlands and Denmark. No such traumatic events have taken place in Canada, although there are continual reminders of

threats to multicultural harmony. The daily newspaper and the morning TV provide a constant flow of news items that suggest threats to ethnic relations. Box 8.1 provides a summary of the news on one fairly typical morning. The catch of ethnic-related stories portrays Canada as a hard-to-interpret collage of disparate ethnic identities, transnational communities, inclusions, and violent exclusions. The paradoxes abound in a mix of stories that juxtapose successful immigrants, visible minority individuals, and transnational solidarities with brutal racist acts. In Canada, as in many other immigrant-receiving countries, there is an ongoing fear that sporadic acts of violence against newcomers and minorities reflect deeper underlying tensions that will spark more serious conflict and, in the worst cases, terrorist activities.

Researchers have come to quite different views on the successes and failures of Canadian multiculturalism policies. Biles, Burstein, and Frideres (2008: 3) state that Canada is characterized by "hyper-diversity, prosperity, and a (largely) peaceful co-existence," and that "immigration and diversity are a source of pride for Canadians." Reitz and Lum (2006: 15) give a similarly favourable review of multiculturalism in Toronto. They argue that "although intergroup tensions have surfaced from time to time, the most publicly visible local discourse on race and ethnic relations emphasizes harmony and accommodation. There has even been a tendency to celebrate Toronto as a model for others." Such views suggest that Canadian values of tolerance and openness to diversity, backed by state multicultural policies, have accomplished much, leaving specific gaps, such as the notable marginalization of Blacks and sporadic racist incidents, to be addressed with renewed effort. Kymlicka (1995) has argued that current policies can be expanded through "multicultural citizenship" to provide ethnic minorities

Box 8.1: The Morning News

Canadian news reports on ethnicity and ethnic relations present a collage of stories and images in which items about the successes of ethnic minority members and immigrant transnational progressive solidarities are found side by side with stories and images of violent ethnic and immigrant discrimination. The "catch" of stories I noted on one day only while watching the morning TV news and reading one national newspaper involved the contrasting elements noted below. I don't think that the day in question was particularly unusual in the broader flow of news about ethnicity and ethnic relations in Canada.

The news broke with a story about the early morning savage kicking, beating, and robbery of Feroz (Phil) Khan, a 47-year-old Pakistan-born immigrant newspaper deliveryman in Vancouver. Attacks and robberies are, unfortunately, common enough that they attract the attention of the press only when they are particularly violent, lead to death, or have other attention-grabbing features. In this case, the public was shocked to learn that the alleged attackers were two off-duty police officers. Khan reported that the attackers told him they "did not like brown people."

Senior public officials spoke up immediately to condemn the attack. Reflecting Canadian diversity, the most prominent officials directly responsible for law enforcement in British Columbia and Vancouver were themselves visible minority members. No one commented explicitly on the hidden irony of this, but the news was presented in a way that brought this to the attention of the public.

B.C. Attorney General Wally Oppal, the first Canadian-born of Indian descent to become a Supreme Court judge and who later served as federal minister for Multiculturalism, was among the first to speak out by promising a thorough investigation.

Vancouver Police Chief Jim Chu took immediate action to press charges against the officers involved (Mason 2009). Partially acknowledged in the news and known more widely is that Jim Chu was born in Shanghai, immigrated to Canada with his parents at age three, and became Vancouver's first Asian-origin chief of police in 2007. A popular picture of him shows him being awarded the Order of Merit of the Police Forces by Governor General Michaëlle Jean, Canada's first Black governor general and herself an immigrant from Haiti. This picture had been printed in Vancouver newspapers and was later disseminated more widely by the Chinese community in Vancouver as a point of ethnic pride.

The *Globe and Mail* that same day contained an article on the strong ties that sixth-generation Icelandic settlers in Gimli, Manitoba, have with their home country in the context of the terrible economic crisis unfolding there (White 2009), and an article on the *DiverseCity* [sic] program in Toronto, which taps into the talent pool of immigrants to boost qualified minority members on the boards of public and non-profit agencies (Lewington 2009).

Sources: This box represents the author's summary of news found in the following reports:

Lewington, Jennifer. 2009. "Aggressive Bid to Tackle City's Diversity 'Deficit.'" *Globe and Mail* (27 January), A11. *Photo: Ming Pao.* (21 July 2007). *Vancouver Sun*, the *Province*. Also see: The Chinese in Vancouver website: [http://chineseinvancouver.blogspot.com/2007/06/jim-chu-becomes-vancouvers-first-police.html].

Mason, Gary. 2009. "With Speedy Probe Vancouver's Police Chief Passes First Big Test." *Globe and Mail* (27 January), A8.

White, Patrick. 2009. "In Hard Times, Icelanders Look to Prairie Refuge." *Globe and Mail* (27 January), A9.

with opportunities to engage more fully in Canadian society.

In contrast to the above, a number of critics of official multiculturalism argue that the policy is misleading and ignores underlying unresolved problems. James (1999: 201) has argued that multiculturalism operates as a smokescreen to hide the fact that British and French ethnocultural identities remain dominant. Walcott (1997) argues that multicultural means "foreign," while Canadian is "White." Francophone Canadians and French-speaking Quebec nationalists have long argued that official multiculturalism defines them as yet another ethnic/linguistic minority in a multicultural nation rather than as constitutional partners in a bilingual nation. Cultural critics have complained that official multiculturalism promotes superficial cultural attributes, such as cultural foods and ethnic folk celebrations, thereby hiding the fact that the underlying policy objective is assimilation (Bissoondath 1994). Abu-Laban and Gabriel (2002) argue that Canadian immigration and multiculturalism policies are elements in the establishment of a neo-liberal immigration and labour force agenda in a globalizing world. This agenda favours investors and owners while disadvantaging workers, particularly those who are most vulnerable due to gender bias, racialization, and immigrant status. They conclude that the state, acting on behalf of business interests, supports multiculturalism as an ideology of diversity in order to hide inequalities and make the immigration system work. Aspects of the latter critical perspective can be found in a number of works by other authors, such as Li (2003b) and Arat-Koç (1999), and are reviewed in general texts covering contrasting perspectives (for example, Fleras and Elliott 2002).

All the above criticisms of multiculturalism focus on Canada and do not comment on transnational links. Reading what they say, one might assume that Canadian

multicultural society is being transformed internally by the ethnic diversity of immigrants who are, or soon will be, detached from the ethnic communities in their home countries as they integrate into Canada. When this happens, according to the model, they will "be and belong" only in a multicultural Canada. The elephant in the room is that this detachment from the home country is not the case for many recent immigrants and may not happen in their lifetimes, nor necessarily even in their children's lifetimes. Immigrants are still significantly involved in family, community, and political issues in their home countries. This is not to say that they are not also similarly involved, or even more involved, with these matters in Canada. We need to move from a bifurcated view that immigrants move from being "there" to being "here" to a unified view that they are both "there" and "here." Moreover, following the hypotheses set out earlier, being committed to Canada and having overseas commitments are not incompatible.

Transnational Spheres

A variety of concepts have been developed to address immigrant being and belonging *within* the nations to which they have moved. I want to join with others who have called for the addition of concepts of immigrant belonging in transnational spaces. The most widely used terms for understanding immigrants within a national space are: *assimilation, integration, incorporation*, and *acculturation*. These concepts provide a starting point for developing new concepts, such as *transnational incorporation* and *transnational citizenship*, to address immigrant belonging simultaneously in their home and host countries. These various terms may be clarified briefly as follows:

Assimilation: With the rise of multicultural models, the concept of assimilation came to be viewed as having negative connotations (Gans 1997). The concept was understood to relate to earlier historical moments in which immigrants in North America felt strong normative pressure to discard their home cultures and ethnic identities, while at the same time adopting the dominant culture of the country to which they had moved. Some have argued that this criticism is unfair. They point out that the concept of assimilation has been used over the years to refer simply to a "closing of the gap" between cultures that takes place as a "two-way street," with each culture interacting with others and being changed in the process (Alba and Nee 1997).

Integration: Frideres (2008: 81) states that "integration" involves both the frequency and the intensity of "ties with their surroundings that the individual or group maintains over time." He then hypothesizes that integration is the outcome of two sets of forces: host society institutions and attitudes, and the social and human capital of the immigrants (Frideres 2008: 83). As the ties that define integration are multidimensional and complex, they can be measured in various areas (economic, social, cultural, and political) according to various indicators such as membership in voluntary associations, feelings of belonging, intermarriage rates, residential segregation, and so on in each area (Biles et al. 2008: 275). In Canada, the term "integration" usually means "multicultural integration"; that is, living peacefully with other ethnic groups and engaging in civic citizenship while either retaining one's cultural identity or assimilating.

Incorporation: Isajiw (1997: 82) defines "incorporation" as "a process through which a social unit is included in a larger social unit as an integral part of it." If the larger social unit encompasses cultural diversity, then a new group can be incorporated as a culturally diverse but integral element. Such a process would be one of "multicultural incorporation." In

this framework, adaptation in a pluralist, liberal society such as Canada takes place through interaction among the groups involved, with each social unit adapting to the other. The concept of multicultural incorporation assumes that diversity can be peacefully retained within a multicultural or pluralist ideology, so that assimilation is an option but not a necessity in such settings (see Breton et al. 1990: 10–11). However, even in an officially multicultural nation, it is recognized that incorporation can involve other outcomes, such as hostile relations that can arise depending on external forces (ethnic conflict in the home countries of the immigrants), ethnic leadership (mobilizing the conflict), and ideologies that either promote or reduce tensions (see Bader 1997). The concept of acculturation developed by Berry (2001) has considerable overlap with the concept of incorporation; hence the two can arguably be used as synonyms. Incorporation and acculturation are frameworks. In sum, incorporation does not predict any single specific outcome. Rather, it defines an array of possible outcomes. These range from assimilation to multicultural incorporation to hostile interactions.

The above terms are all concerned with immigrant being and belonging in the national space of the host country. They imply different changing relationships between immigrants and their home countries as incorporation in Canada takes place, but exactly what this changed relationship between nations might be is left unstated and unclear. To take one illustration, "assimilation" suggests moving away from one's original culture and ethnic identity. But does this mean a greater disconnect with home culture? It does only if one assumes that the home culture remained unchanged, yet this may not be the case. Italians who moved to Canada shortly after the Second World War found, when they returned to visit their homeland many years later, that Italy had transformed in ways that made it less different than Canada. Both countries had been developing lifestyles and values more similar to one another over time. Koreans who came to Canada in the 1970s to struggle and establish themselves and who, years later, returned home for visits, discovered to their surprise that the impoverished relatives they had left behind in a struggling developing country had become wealthy and westernized over a period of explosive economic growth in that nation. Of course the opposite has also happened: Professional families that left Iran prior to the return of Ayatollah Khomeini in the 1970s and the subsequent emergence of an Islamic state in that country feel increasingly alienated from the political and cultural developments in their home country. We may conclude that terms such as "assimilation" and "incorporation" are useful, but that we need additional terms to understand dynamic social and ethnic relations across nations in a transnational world.

"Transnational incorporation" and "transnational citizenship" are terms that have been proposed to better understand contemporary immigrant being and belonging. In their groundbreaking study, *Nations Unbound*, Basch, Glick Schiller, and Szanton Blanc (1994) proposed that transnational links in a post-colonial world were leading to de-territorialized nation-states and that the analysis of this trend required new concepts. Vertovec (1999), Castles (2002), and Levitt and Nyberg-Sørenson 2004: 2–4) offer similar views on the need for a new transnational paradigm. My reading of their arguments leads to the following points on why such a development is required.

1. A transnational perspective on international migration is an alternative to "methodological nationalism" in which immigrants are viewed as if they belong only in the country to which they have moved. The receiving-nation standpoint is limited in scope because as a research framework, it poorly reflects the nature of migrant networks, practices, and new community formations.

2. Migrant transnational social and cultural practices constitute a field of action that links migrant origin and destination societies. The links bring about changes within these two societies and also transform the relationship between them.

3. International migrants should be understood in terms of the ways in which they are involved in transnational fields. There is wide variation in practices. The structure of transnational fields needs to be explored more thoroughly.

4. Transnational social and cultural fields involve more than one nation, but are not coterminous with the boundaries of the nations involved. Transnational practices concern relationships among people, institutions, and societies and hence are not limited to relationships among nations, even though nation-states and their relations with one another are also affected by transnational social links and practices.

5. The impact of migration is felt not just because people have changed the places where they reside, but also through the flows of information, personal and business contacts, investment money and remittances that take place when people move and come to belong in more than one place.

6. How immigrants settle is not just a function of the circumstances they find in the countries in which they settle. Settlement is also affected by

immigrants' place in a transnational space and their links to home countries.

7. Last but not least, it is important to add a qualification to the above. Not all immigrants have strong transnational attachments. There is wide variation. For some, the attachments dwindle because all family members have left their home country or passed away. Among these people, attachments may be retained partially by belonging to an ethnic organization in Canada. Yet among those living outside their home country, not all will belong to an ethnic organization. Strong transnational ties are found among those who have close kin still living in home communities and those who belong to ethnic organizations where they have moved. Individuals who own property abroad or work in both countries are likely to have the strongest transnational practices and links. These differences must be kept in mind so as not to inflate the concept of transnational migrant to cover all immigrants (Castles and Miller 2003: 30).

Viewing Transnationalism as a Multi-layered Social Ecology

It is relatively straightforward to understand how individuals are more or less incorporated within a single social space. All social science disciplines have concepts for such incorporation. The concepts variably characterize the single space as an economic market, a geographic location such as a nation, or a culture within or across geographic locations. However, the conceptualization of a transnational social space requires that one go beyond simply imagining markets or cultures spreading across national spaces. This is because in part the concept of transnation bridges *dif-*

ferent markets and cultures. Transnational individuals are not just living in one market or culture spread across nations, they are also living simultaneously in at least two different national economies, political formations, and cultures. Transnational incorporation is inherently a concept that draws attention to duality: transnational actors are both "here" and "there," hence in constant negotiation with others, who are then themselves increasingly transnational, in creating a world in which this is understood and accepted by them as well. Put in other terms, if incorporation into a single space may be understood as an issue of relationships between an individual and a fixed set of others, transnational incorporation may be understood as a dynamic process of flows, communication, and shifting personal relationships and identities and across individuals located in two or more national spaces.

The preceding view of transnational incorporation is broadly consistent with the ways in which cultural scholars have understood globalization and transnationalism. For example, for Nederveen Pieterse (2003), economic globalization is a force operating "from above" to force economic integration and the spread of consumer culture, while "hybridity" is a feature of transnationalism and globalization from below that can provide resources to the less advantaged for mobilizing on their own behalf. Paradoxically, as we have noted, economic globalization creates the conditions of expanding social and cultural transnationalism, hence these dynamics are intertwined in complementary and contradictory ways, as Hall (1992) observed in early observations on the contemporary breakdown of national identities and the emergence of hybrid identities.

Figure 8.1 shows the transnational incorporation as a field involving the overlap of different spheres of life—cutting across two or more nations—involved in "making human beings human" (Bronfenbrenner 2005). One might also think of this diagram as a way of understanding Bourdieu's concept of *habitus* from a transnational perspective. Bourdieu distinguishes the positions and relationships between people from their *habitus*, which he understands as a set of "dispositions" regarding perception, thought, and action that individuals acquire and retain based on their lived experiences in particular contexts (Bourdieu 1998: 5–8). This is a fluid concept, allowing one to perceive *habitus* as having been formed either in a particular nation, place, and culture or in more than one nation, place, and culture.

From the transnational social-ecological framework (shown in Figure 8.1), being and belonging takes place in a series of spheres, from most to least intimate. The most intimate sphere consists of engagements in the family and with friends. Other less intimate spheres are found in the form of meaningful memberships in associations, organizations, residential communities, and nation-states. These various spheres of being and belonging also overlap in large part with global human rights and values, leading to the more distant and less intimate levels of global belonging. Being a resident or citizen in one nation constitutes a sphere, while residence and/or citizenship in two nations involve both nations as spheres that overlap.

Each sphere in the transnational framework has porous boundaries that link it to the others. This is conveyed in Figure 8.1 by the broken lines that surround each sphere. The entire structure forms an ecology of partially interdependent spheres, which is to say that each sphere draws on, gives to, and rubs against other spheres to generate dynamic patterns of change at all levels. The entire structure is crosscut with practices that generate co-operation/harmony and other practices that generate conflict/disharmony.

Our focus in this book has been largely on the presence of transnational practices and identities within Canada, but we need to keep in mind that what takes place in Canada has a counterpart in transnational links and practices in other countries. Insofar as immigrants in Canada interact with people in other countries and/or have memberships, property, and citizenship in other countries, people in these countries have an interaction and relationship with individuals who are also located partially or mostly in Canada. Canada has a presence in immigrant origin countries through embassies, business firms, and Canadian clubs or social associations for Canadians living abroad. Canada also has a presence in these countries through immigrants who may have returned, as Canadian citizens, to their home country to live.

The transnational immigrant incorporation framework shown in Figure 8.1 is not so much a theory as a *habitus* map within which to locate the dispositions that lead to co-operation and immigrant being and belonging across two or more nations. The following sections review hypotheses and findings from studies on immigrant being and belonging in Canada corresponding to a transnational framework that can be mapped in more than one way.

The Upside and the Downside of Transnationalism

Initial formulations of immigrant transnational practices and dispositions tended to draw attention to their positive outcomes. The practices were understood to be immigrants' efforts to mobilize their own resources and access other resources through social networks in order to improve outcomes for themselves, their families, and others within their spheres of belonging. As more research was done, it

Figure 8.1: Immigrant Incorporation in Transnational Spaces

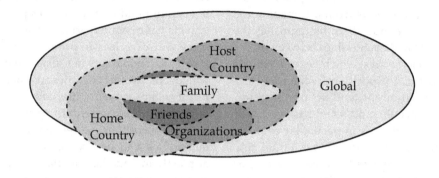

became apparent that transnational practices are a dimension of social practices
more generally. This perspective drew
attention to transnational practices that
reinforced gender inequality, racism, and
hostility to traditional "enemies" within
immigrant communities. The downside
perspective also shed light on problems of
the collective representation of immigrant
and ethnic communities and drew attention to moral panics that arise when immigrants to Canada are *perceived* to be threats
to peace, security, and cherished national
values because they retain transnational
links and affiliations.

Viewing transnationalism as a process
that can lead to diverse outcomes of co-
operation and conflict makes it a more
useful tool for examining normative
frameworks, such as multiculturalism.
Perspectives coming from transnational
research paint a larger picture in which
multicultural policies and outcomes are
affected by host-country conditions and by
immigrant links to their home countries.
The following sections examine the development of the field and its main findings.

Transnationalism as a Progressive Force

Initial studies of transnationalism tended to
focus on evidence that immigrants created

transnational ties and associations that promoted democracy and political reforms in
their home countries and anti-racist efforts
in the host country (Basch et al. 1994).
Immigrant and minority individuals used
their family and ethnic networks, contacts,
and associations with others to promote
their own success and that of their children
through education and business ventures
(Portes 1995; Portes, Haller, and Guarnizo
2002). Various studies pointed to ways that
established immigrants helped newcomers
from their own communities and countries
find jobs and places to live (for example,
see Menjivar 2000: Chapter 1). Immigrants
have historically sent money to support
their family members in home communities. The high total volume of flows associated with contemporary strong transnational family ties generated new attention
regarding the impacts of remittances on
families, communities, and migrant-origin
nations (Durand, Parrado, and Massey
1996; Ratha 2004). Immigrants also form
hometown associations to voluntarily
finance projects that they hope will benefit
their hometowns through projects that
involve repairing local churches, temples,
and mosques; constructing sports fields;
improving parks, water supplies, and
sidewalks; or supporting local schools and
health clinics (Orozco 2005). The overall

picture on the upside is one in which immigrant transnationalism is at the core of a set of actions from below by immigrants and co-ethnic communities in host countries to improve their own lives and those of their families in their home countries. This picture emphasizes immigrants as a source of positive social transformation through action at various levels: within the family, in informal networks, within more formal associations, and at the national political level as well. Such an image contrasts dramatically with the view that immigrants come with little power and then assimilate into a new dominant culture and society by abandoning their roots.

Reality Check: Transnationalism and Complex Interactions

As knowledge on transnational practices and their outcomes developed, it became increasingly clear that immigrants' success in achieving their goals was often less than they had hoped. This is because the outcomes they seek do not rest on immigrants and migrants alone. In fact, many of the outcomes depend more on other economic and political actors and institutions than they do on the immigrants and their institutions (Portes, Guarnizo, and Landolt 1999). Consider the following two examples.

Studies show that immigrant families' welfare abroad depends primarily on political and economic developments and conditions in the countries where these families live. When Haitians in Montreal send money to help their relatives in Haiti to address the seemingly endless stream of crises arising from political conflict, economic collapse, hurricanes, and soil erosion, the funds go entirely for food and emergency help (Simmons, Plaza, and Piché 2005). Little if anything is left over for building a base for improved lives in the future. In contrast, Mexican migrant farm workers in Southern Ontario, who circulate year after year between their home communities and periods of work in Canada, are able to use their earnings to own property, improve their houses, and in some cases establish small businesses, such as a store attached to their home (Binford, Rivas, and Hernandez 2004; Verduzco 1999). The farm worker program has many problems (see Chapter 11), but it also has some positive outcomes because the Mexican towns where the migrants live have, despite their deep poverty, a greater potential for families to improve their living conditions.

Migrants' success in finding good jobs, safety, and belonging in Canada depends, in large part, on the welcome and opportunities provided by Canadian employers and society, but it also depends on migrant networks and resources. It is known that Chinese transnational family and business networks overlap and lead to significant inflows of capital for settlement and entrepreneurial activity in Canada (Wong and Ho 2006). It has also been observed that Chinese immigrants from Hong Kong and Taiwan have more extensive home-country networks related to the kinds of jobs they seek in Canada and in their home country than do immigrants from the People's Republic of China, with the result that the former have more options, including the option of returning home for work when jobs are tight in Canada (Salaff 2006). The way many professional jobs are carried out in Taiwan and Hong Kong is also more similar to the way such jobs are carried out in Canada, with the result that Canadian employers are more likely to hire highly skilled ethnic-Chinese immigrants from Taiwan and Hong Kong than immigrants with similar formal credentials from the People's Republic of China (Salaff 2006). In sum, the outcomes of transnational practices depend on their context and interactions with other actors and circumstances.

When transnationalism intersects with ethnic nationalism, international crime, and terrorism, the outcomes tend to reinforce ethnic conflict and lead to a loss of pluralism. Just as immigrants play only a part in outcomes affecting the economic welfare of their families, so too they play only a part in outcomes concerning ethnic conflict. At times immigrants are the victims of processes that they have nothing to do with. Consider the complexity of how this works in relation to ethnic nationalism. Immigrants are engaged in struggles to overcome discrimination arising from ethnic nationalism, racism, and ethnocentrism in Canada. At the same time, they may be dealing with similar issues in their home countries. Some immigrants carry with them hostilities toward historical ethnic enemies of their people. Others find themselves supporting efforts to purchase weapons in the illegal market and to send them to co-ethnic organizations fighting in civil wars in their home countries. These engagements, even if they are carried out by only a few and even if their goals are to overcome oppression, become the fuel for others who accuse the entire community of being a threat to Canadian peace, security, and well-being. Even if only a few immigrants have strong feelings of ethnic nationalism or engage in illegal or terrorist transnational practices, their activities can be seized on by the press and others to generate a climate of moral panic that portrays *all* immigrants from certain countries as unreliable, untrustworthy, and dangerous to public harmony and security. Arat-Koç (2006b) reports that these kind of interactions have created a situation in which Muslims in Canada feel that they are "under siege" in a post-9/11 world. This is what we may call a conundrum: It is a problem-laden process in which various hostile actors and media practices lead to an exaggerated suspicion and negativity toward large groups of immigrants based on the real or imagined actions of a few individuals who may have no real connection with the larger groups of immigrants who come under suspicion.

It is clear that the most useful transnational framework is one that covers complex processes of co-operation/peace and conflict/hostility in interaction within diverse spheres of social interaction. In the next sections we examine research findings as they relate to the various spheres shown in Figure 8.1.

The Family Sphere

Interactions within families form the core of transnational being and belonging. This is neither a new phenomenon nor a surprising one, but new findings are constantly emerging. A case study of several immigrant households in Vancouver over five years revealed that they extensively used social networks and kin to support a range of re-skilling, job search, and employment strategies (Creese, Dyck, and McLaren 2008). Caribbean immigrants often leave their young children with their grandparents in the home country when they first come to Canada, then bring their children later once they have become established (Simmons and Turner 1993). Grandparents and in-laws may be involved for years in looking after the children of Filipina domestic workers who remain in Canada in order to send remittances home (Arat-Koç 2006b). In the case of Caribbean and Central American immigrants whose home countries are only two to four hours' flying distance from major Canadian cities, sisters and parents may visit for extended periods from abroad in order to engage in family support and child care in Canada (Carranza 2007; Simmons and Turner 1993). Children of immigrants may be sent to stay with relatives in the home country in order to know their families and cultures better or to settle down in a more family-centred environment while their parents often work outside the home, struggling to earn and save for the future benefit of themselves, their children, and other members of the family (Carranza 2007). Brothers and sisters who have emigrated to Canada, the United States, and other wealthy nations may pool funds to support their aging parents in their home country (Simmons, Plaza, and Piché 2005).

The remittances that international migrants send to family members in their home country have attracted a great deal of attention in recent years. While the amounts sent by each migrant may be small, funds are sent frequently and by large numbers of individuals. As a result, total flows of money from migrants are enormous. World Bank statistics show that global remittance flows to developing countries have been rising rapidly since 1990, and that by 2005 they had climbed to a total in the range of U.S. $240 billion a year (see Figure 8.2). The World Bank report from which the figures shown in Figure 8.2 were taken indicates that in 2005 global remittance flows were twice as great as the total amount of official development assistance, more generally known as foreign aid, sent by all wealthy nations to developing nations. By 2004–2005, annual global remittances likely exceeded annual total foreign direct investment by companies in developing countries. Pedro de Vasconcelos (2004) observes that remittances are the single most important source of foreign exchange (hard currencies such as U.S. dollars and euros, which can be used in international trade) in many countries around the world. The Multilateral Investment Fund (MIF) of the Inter-American Development Bank has undertaken a number of studies that lead to the following conclusions (see MIF 2007).

1. Remittances provide shock protection for the poor in developing countries because migrants abroad increase the amounts they send in times of crisis.

2. The funds are often used to support better nutrition, health care, and schooling; hence they can increase human capital in poor countries and resources for future development there.

3. Some recipient families are able to use remittances to save for house improvements and the purchase of land, all of which improves their welfare over the longer term.

4. When remittances are spent on local foods, clothing, construction, or other products and services produced nationally, they can generate a multiplier effect by spreading work and income to other individuals and families in the same community, region, or country.

The extent to which the above and other related conclusions are supported varies from one remittance-receiving household and community to another (Simmons 2008: 72–73). The first two of the four impacts reported above receive the most widespread empirical support (Simmons 2008: 74). It is also known that migrant workers send most of their earnings home because they expect to return home after their contracts are over. Immigrants send less because they have relocated their own nuclear families to the countries where they have resettled, with the result that they must first look after their own immediate family members before they think of sending money to relatives in their home country.

To what extent do immigrants in Canada participate at all in sending household remittances? Do they send money when they first arrive and are struggling with their own needs? Do they continue to send money? How much do they send? Studies in this area are recent and do

Figure 8.2: Global Remittance Flows to Developing Countries, 1990–2005 (in U.S.$ million)

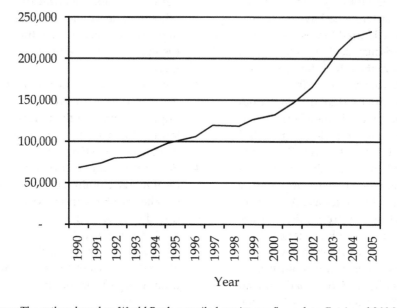

Year

Source: The author, based on World Bank compiled remittance flows data. Retrieved 26 March 2009 from http://siteresources.worldbank.org/EXTGEP2006/Resources/RemittancesDataGEP2006.xls

not cover all the questions. However, what is known leads to the conclusion that Canadian immigrants begin sending remittances soon after arrival, that they continue to do so for many years, and that the amounts sent are appreciable. The Longitudinal Survey of Immigrants to Canada (LSIC) asked all immigrants who arrived in Canada over a 12-month period in 2000–2001 if they had sent money to relatives in the first 24 and 48 months after arrival. Selected results from this study, reported by Houle and Schellenberg (2008), are shown in Table 8.1. While only 23 percent of immigrants had sent money in the first six to 24 months in Canada, this figure varies widely by region of origin. At the high end, roughly half of immigrants from Southeast Asia and the Caribbean reported that they had sent money in this period. The proportion reporting having sent money was higher for those from less

developed countries. Immigrants from developed places such as the United States, Europe, and Australia/New Zealand in Oceania were far less likely to send money home and sent smaller amounts when they did. On average, the amounts sent by those who remitted were appreciable, in the range of $2,500 over the period shown in the table. The authors of the report note that each immigrant was sending about $1,450 per year or around $125 per month. Remittances accounted for about 6 percent of personal income before taxes. These are significant amounts of money for recently arrived immigrants who, as we know from Chapter 7, were facing severe economic hardship and poverty in the years immediately following their move to Canada.

Simmons, Plaza, and Piché (2005) examined the remittance sending of Haitian and Caribbean immigrants who had been in Canada, on average, for more than 10

Table 8.1: Recently Arrived Canadian Immigrants: Remitters and Remittances

	In the Period Six to 24 Months after Arrival	
	Percent Who Remit	*Average Amount Sent ($)*
Total	23	2,500
REGION OF BIRTH		
Southeast Asia	52	2,000
Caribbean, Guyana	47	1,400
Sub-Saharan Africa	37	2,400
Eastern Europe	32	1,800
South Asia	23	3,600
Central, South America	23	2,000
East Asia	13	2,900
West Asia, Middle East, North Africa	13	2,000
North America, Western Europe, Oceania	11	3,200

Sources: This table reproduces selected figures from: Houle, René, and Grant Schellenberg. 2008. *Remittances by Recent Immigrants* (Table 1). Ottawa: Statistics Canada. The data come from the Longitudinal Survey of Immigrants to Canada, 2000/2001 cohort.

years. Eighty-four percent of Jamaicans and 62 percent of Haitians had sent money at least in 2004 to relatives in their home countries (Simmons, Plaza, and Piché 2005: Table 1). The amounts sent were, on average, in the range of $1,000–$1,400 per year in total, or roughly the same range as found in the LSIC study. Funds were usually sent in smaller packets of around $100 spread over the year. Remittance senders talk by phone with remittance receivers very frequently. When money is sent via a money transfer agency, relatives' receipt of the funds is often confirmed by telephone within minutes or, at most, a day. There is also an ongoing communication, usually by telephone, on how the funds are to be spent: for food, house repairs, school uniforms, and so on. If the person receiving remittances to benefit many family members abroad does not spend or distribute the money as agreed, then the sender may look for a more responsible relative to receive remittances in the future. Those who did not send any remittances had different reasons. Some had no relatives left in their home country because all had emigrated. Others reported that their relatives in the home country are well-to-do. The study also noted that remittances are sent in both directions. Some wealthy families in the Caribbean finance the college or university education of their children in Canada; then the children remain in Canada as immigrants. Still others reported that at times they were unable to send money because they were too poor to do so. Nolin (2006) reports a similar situation among Guatemalan refugee families in Canada. Some had been so dislocated and impoverished by their forced migration and problems in finding jobs in Canada that they had no money to send home even though they very much wanted to do so.

Non-family Networks

When immigrants begin to expand their close friendships, associations, and memberships beyond the family, they generally do so through participation in smaller networks within larger communities. Individuals from particular schools or hometowns in the country of origin may use their common background and overlapping friendships to develop a web of trust and information exchange. This has been noted for immigrants who studied in elite schools in the Caribbean (Simmons and Plaza 2006). Many Jamaican immigrants in Toronto belong to churches that put together funds to help churches and church-based social projects in their hometowns in Jamaica. A third of the Jamaicans surveyed by Simmons et al. (2005) had been involved in projects helping churches in Jamaica, while they and others had been involved in projects helping schools in Jamaica. The projects generally involved contact with people in Jamaica whom they had known for years. One pastor reported on the work that her ministry had been doing in Jamaica as follows:

> ... we have been shipping down barrels, many, many barrels [of] new stuff, used stuff, perishable items for the less fortunate. At this time, the ... [church] has taken on a mega, major project, which is also instigated by the Lord. We have now sponsored 75 less fortunate children in Jamaica, five days a week, free lunch, and also in three different parishes.... We have also sponsored eight students, seven from the high school and one from the elementary, regarding their transportation fees to school.... (Simmons et al. 2005: 11)

Transnational networks also function to help immigrants. As noted briefly earlier in this chapter, Salaff (2006) reports that the large body of Chinese immigrants in Canada is composed of distinct national-origin communities: those from Hong Kong, those from Taiwan, and those from the People's Republic of China (PRC). Based on detailed interviews with highly skilled members from each community, she found that the communities differ in the political-economic circumstances of departure and entry to Canada, the ease with which they established networks in Canada, their ability to stay in touch with professional colleagues in home countries, and the resources they could draw upon in transnational ethnic network space. For example, the immigrants from Hong Kong and Taiwan were able to draw on support from colleagues in home countries; one was able to return home for work, leaving his family in Canada. They also found that their work and lives in their home countries were more like those in Canada, allowing them to establish an "astronaut" family and social network pattern of commuting between and living in two places. None of these extensive transnational network elements were available to the immigrants from the PRC. They had arrived more recently, were relative pioneers in establishing the families and community in Canada, had fewer links and fewer resources to share among themselves, and did not have supportive links to their home countries.

In some communities women and men have different family and friendship networks. This is evident in some U.S. research that may also be applicable to Canada. In cultural groups in which women's roles are more restricted, their networks can be too weak to be of much help to their members. Salvadoran women in Los Angeles often found that they could not access the same networks as men in their communities, and that they were largely restricted to drawing on contacts with other women who were similarly disadvantaged (Menjivar 2000). However, gender roles are not fixed. Migrant women working in the janitorial trade in Los Angeles initially found themselves in traditional roles as the main caregivers at home and as invisible members of the janitors' labour union. In the face of these challenges, the women eventually formed a "political motherhood," moved into union leadership positions, and changed their status in their workplaces and community (Cranford 2007a), although their customary child care and domestic responsibilities did not change as much (Cranford 2007b).

Ethnic Communities

The term "community" is ambiguous when referring to immigrants from a particular country. Often what is commonly referred to as an ethnic community is not a community of people who interact with one another or necessarily even like and identify with one another. Immigrants who come from the same country may be highly fragmented and stratified to the point that they do not know one another or feel strong common bonds. The extent to which this is the case varies widely from one situation to another. In consequence, the degree to which broader ethnic communities and associations can be a resource for their members also varies widely.

Some ethnic associations and organizations are loosely organized bodies that function more to celebrate common ethnic roots than to mobilize for the betterment of their members. Kelly (2007: 216) argues that this is the case for Filipinos in Canada who constitute a "multiplicity of voices" and not a coherent community. Members meet around "commonalities of origin rather than common goals" (Kelly 2007: 216). Filipino associations are also divided by political factions arising from affilia-

tion with different political parties in the home country. Yet, as noted in Chapter 5 (Box 5.4), Filipino associations across the Canada are able on occasion to join forces in common causes, such as the observed effort to stop the unfair deportation of a Filipina domestic worker. Salvadoran refugees arriving in Canada in the 1980s were also deeply fractured into a series of political factions in the first years after arrival, even though they shared a common stance against the military government in their home country (Landolt 2007). Ethnic and class differences divide the Caribbean community in Toronto with respect to organization of the annual Caribana Parade: Indo-Caribbean and Afro-Caribbean peoples have their own post-parade parties, and some of these are further divided by class, as when individuals graduated from elite private schools in their home countries get together separately (Simmons and Plaza 2006). Despite these internal differences, Caribbean immigrants do work together around common cultural-political efforts, such as the Caribana Parade and anti-racist mobilization.

Some ethnic and hometown associations in Canada are very well organized around common goals. This is particularly the case for older, larger, well-established ethnic associations whose members include many individuals who have been successful in the professions, business, and government. Organizations such as the Chinese Benevolent Association (CBA) in Vancouver have a long history of lobby activities on behalf of their members. The CBA also organizes the annual Chinese New Year Parade to promote their community. More recently the CBA created "an affiliated non-profit society to provide low cost housing and frequent fund raising campaigns to assist the victims of natural disasters in Canada and China" (CBA 2009: 1). More recently arrived ethnic communities who have not yet developed strong ethnic associations and organizations generally have a greater challenge in setting up programs to benefit themselves and others in their countries of origin, yet some have been remarkably successful, in some cases due to unusual and tragic reasons. The Tamil immigrant community in Canada is large in absolute terms and may be the largest body of Tamils outside of South Asia. Tamil communities in Sri Lanka have been devastated by the civil war there (from the 1970s to the present). Tamil immigrants in Canada have organized in diverse ways to respond to this devastation. The main way has been through many hometown associations that gather money to provide support for health clinics, schools, and housing (Cheran 2007; Wayland 2007).

Nations and belonging: The commitments and attachments that immigrants have to their home nation and to their host nation may be conceptualized and measured in different ways. One method is to sum up the intensity and frequency with which individuals maintain contacts of various kinds with people, organizations, and the state in the nations in question. The indicators might be participating in phoning relatives, visiting, owning property, and paying taxes. Another method is to choose a key indicator, such as identification with the countries in question and citizenship. Both of these methods or variations of them have been adopted in Canadian studies. This said, relatively little research has been done on the topic and, as yet, it is not possible to do more than point to scattered findings.

Using the multi-indicator approach to connection, Hiebert and Ley (2006) found that nearly all (97 percent) of immigrants who arrived in Vancouver during the 10-year period between 1991 and the survey date in 2001 had kept in touch with family in their home country over the previous year; nearly half (45 percent) travelled to

their home country at least once a year; 22 percent had property in their home country; and 14 percent sent money home. Remarkably, there is little variation in these indicators between those who "always" identify as Canadian and those who "seldom" or "never" identify as Canadian. The one exception is property ownership: Those who always identify as Canadian are far less likely to own property in their home country than those who never do (18 versus 45 percent). Similarly, those possessing Canadian citizenship are also less likely to own property abroad. This finding suggests that owning property in one's home country is an indicator of deeper attachment (identity connection) with the home country and a correspondingly reduced attachment with Canada. Overall, the study points to a situation in which many immigrants identify with being Canadian while they continue to have robust communication, travel, and money-sending links with their home countries. Being involved in one place does not preclude involvement in the other.

Citizenship and Belonging

For immigrants, becoming a Canadian citizen is an important legal step. It can also be a significant emotional event insofar as it involves an important development in national identity and belonging in Canada (see Box 8.2). When immigrants do decide to become citizens, this is a fulfillment of what the Canadian multicultural state hopes will happen. It is confirmation that the new citizens have met a number of criteria, including: having lived in Canada for three years, fluency in English and/or French, and sufficient knowledge of Canada and the responsibilities of citizenship to pass a test on these matters. The new Canadian citizens, for their part, acquire a new set of rights and privileges, including:

Box 8.2: Recollections of a Citizenship Ceremony

Having been born in Canada, I first attended a Canadian citizenship ceremony as a friendly observer with some other immigration researchers to learn more about how the formalities were carried out and how people who were becoming citizens felt. I imagined that it might be a stiff and formal process conducted by a citizenship judge, and limited to some official pronouncement and signing of legal papers.

I was surprised to discover that the official steps were folded into a very warm welcome. The event took place in Montreal. The judge, an engaging woman of Asian heritage wearing a beautiful robe of office, addressed those assembled, switching flawlessly between English and French, never exactly repeating what she had just said in the other language, but covering everything that had to be said in both languages. Present were some 20 prospective citizens from all corners of the world. At the end of the formalities, the judge gave a short impromptu talk, expressing her great pleasure in being able to serve in this capacity and the deep personal meaning it had for her to welcome new citizens who wanted to become Canadian and partake of the associated benefits and responsibilities. With a smile, she congratulated all the new Canadians by affirming that they now had this new status.

At the end, the judge came down from her podium and shook hands with the new citizens. It turned out to be a very emotional moment for all present. Friends and observers broke out into spontaneous applause. Some of the new citizens were crying, others were hugging relatives, and then there were many smiles for photos that family members were taking of one another and of them with the judge. People did not just get up and leave when it was over, they lingered to talk to their family and friends, and to say hello and congratulate other new citizens whom they had never before met. I was left with an impression that the critics who claim that immigrants seek citizenship merely for the cold convenience of a Canadian passport may be referring to only a very few people.

Photo source: CIC. 2009. *A Look at Canada.* Ottawa: Citizenship and Immigration. [http://www.cic.gc.ca/english/resources/publications/look/look-02.asp]. Last accessed 14 January 2009.

- the right to vote in political elections in Canada and to stand for political office;
- the right to enter Canada at any time with a Canadian passport;
- access to Canadian embassies and consular services abroad;
- eligibility for resident tuition fees in Canadian colleges and universities;
- transfer to Canada to serve jail time for offences committed in other countries;
- evacuation from foreign countries suffering war or internal strife;
- descendants' eligibility to become Canadian citizens.

When large numbers of immigrants take out Canadian citizenship, the Canadian state views this as a marker of a successful immigration and settlement policy. In fact, more than 73 percent of immigrants living in Canada in 2001 had taken out Canadian citizenship. This is an average for immigrants who have lived longer in Canada (and who are more likely to have become citizens) and immigrants who have arrived more recently, some of whom are not eligible to be citizens because they have not resided in Canada for three years. The proportion of immigrants who have become citizens in Canada is almost twice the level as that found in the United States, a difference that Bloemraad (2006) observes (p. 30) and attributes largely to Canadian multicultural policies (pp. 243–252).

Since 1977, Canadian citizens have had the right to retain or acquire a foreign nationality – provided the foreign country also agrees to this – without losing their Canadian citizenship. A very small proportion (about 1 percent) of Canadian-born individuals take advantage of this provision (Statistics Canada, Citizenship Status, 2006 census). Most likely this is because they have resided abroad for a long period of time. However, about 11

percent of immigrants – or about 700,000 individuals – have citizenship in Canada and one other country. The other immigrants have Canada-only citizenship (62 percent) or other country-only citizenship (27 percent). Not all other countries in the world allow dual citizenship, although legislation permitting this has been growing globally over the past 20 years. In 2005, about 50 countries of 125 for which data were available allowed dual citizenship, whereas in 1999 only about 30 countries did so (Sejersen 2008). As more countries shift their policies to permit dual citizenship, as seems likely by current trends, one may anticipate that the proportion of Canadian immigrants who choose this option will also rise.

Canadian citizens, including those with dual citizenship status, do not necessarily live in Canada. Zhang (2008) has estimated that 8 percent of all Canadian citizens, or 2.7 million people, live outside Canada. These include immigrants with Canadian citizenship who have returned to live in their home country, some of their children born in Canada, and (most of all) Canadian citizens whose parents were not immigrants but who have decided to live elsewhere. Most Canadians residing abroad (44 percent) live in the United States, while the rest live largely in Asia (24 percent) and Europe (18 percent). Zhang also estimates that up to 1.7 million of Canadian citizens living abroad are in countries where violent conflict between or within countries could spark a massive return to Canada. In the worst-case scenario, the situation would be like that in Lebanon in 2006 when thousands of Canadians living there found themselves in the middle of a war and sought emergency help from the Canadian government to be moved to safety and repatriated to Canada. Special aircraft and ships were mobilized and paid for by Canada. A smaller but similar emergency departure of Canadian citizens took place in January 2009 when Israel bombarded Palestine in an effort to stop rockets being launched from Palestine to Israel.

The realization that many Canadians, including those who gained citizenship through immigration, lived in conflict-risk zones in other countries raised three issues. First, this situation drew attention to the fact that these Canadians are in some cases, such as Lebanon and Palestine, associated with one side or the other of violent conflicts that could spill over into ethnic hostilities in Canada. Second, it raised questions about the commitment of some immigrants to Canada. Immigrants who came to Canada for short periods, just sufficient to get citizenship and then returned to work in home countries such as Hong Kong, have been referred to as "sojourners" who have an uncertain future attachment to Canada (Ley and Kobayashi 2005). Third, it raised issues about tax fairness. Chant (2006) has done an analysis of the actual costs to Canada of citizens who live abroad and who do not pay taxes in Canada. He has also examined the potential costs to Canada of repatriating large numbers of citizens in the event of foreign conflicts that would force them to return home. He suggests, among other measures, a special five-year passport renewal fee of about $500 for non-resident citizens in order to cover their real costs to Canada. Meanwhile, the government has proposed controversial changes to the Citizenship Act that will make it possible to remove Canadian citizenship from the children born abroad to parents who became Canadians after having first immigrated to Canada. These proposals respond to pressures within Canadian society to tighten citizenship rules and to require greater commitment from immigrants to retain citizenship and transmit it to their children.

In sum, citizenship status is primarily an indicator of the rights that individuals hold as a result of birth or naturalization. Canadian citizenship is obviously attractive to immigrants because of the protection and access that it provides. This would explain why such a high proportion of immigrants become citizens. Most who become naturalized Canadians drop their original citizenship, perhaps in part because they can return to visit and perhaps even live in their home countries as Canadians with equal or even better rights, plus having a Canadian passport as an insurance policy in case they need to return to Canada. In addition, most appear to be involved in a process of adopting a greater attachment to Canada than to their home country. This corresponds to what Canada wants. Witnesses to the Standing Committee on Citizenship and Immigration in the 1990s encouraged the government to maintain and strengthen provisions requiring that immigrants show a strong commitment to Canada before they be given citizenship (Young 1998). Commitment would be demonstrated by having resided in Canada for three years, speaking one of Canada's official languages, and knowing Canadian geography, culture, and laws. However, given that Canada is a multicultural nation, this does not mean that dual citizenship and transnational social connections to home countries should be discouraged: the Standing Committee retained its support for dual citizenship (Young 1998: Section E). The evidence we have examined suggests that the majority of immigrants are committed to Canada, even when they also retain strong commitments to their home countries.

Global Belonging

Global and international institutions are an important addition to transnational frameworks. Yuval-Davis (1999) argues that claims to international human rights go beyond the protections provided by nation-states and are important for migrants and minorities around the world. Castles and Miller (2003: 46) point to regional agreements, such as the 1991 Maastricht Treaty, which proclaimed the rights of all individuals in the European Union to freedom of movement and residence in the E.U. territory; the right to vote and stand for office in local elections; and the right to petition the European Parliament. The North American Free Trade Agreement provides freedom of mobility rights to professionals, but, unfortunately, does not extend these to other workers (Gabriel and MacDonald 2003; Simmons 1998a). Henders (2007: 43) refers to United Nations and International Labour Organization-supported rights such as the emergence of post-national citizenship. Labelle, Rocher, and Field (2006: 120–125) note that ethnic minorities in Quebec draw on the resources of transnational non-governmental organizations (NGOs) such as the International Federation of Human Rights, B'nai B'rith, the Arab Association for Human Rights, and national NGOs such as the Canadian Council for Refugees. These NGOs, in turn, draw on various international organizations, such as the United Nations and the Pan American Organization, for guiding principles and support.

Global institutions do not just support minority ethnic rights and oppose discrimination. They also support the rights of consumers and investors. These values can be consistent with one another, but at times they come into conflict. Waters (1995) observes that global trade and financial institutions such as the World Bank, the International Monetary Fund, and the World Trade Organization promote the values and rights of individuals, as owners, investors, and consumers. This observation draws attention to the fact that some post-national citizenship rights primarily protect workers, minorities, and those at risk of marginalization. Others protect dominant actors who, as individual share-owners and managers of private corporations, seek to spread the freedoms of capital mobility, trade, patent protection, advertising, and consumer choice, which they see as universal privileges. Tensions between market freedoms and the rights of workers and voters to constrain them are central features of the contemporary global system and spill over into the transnational arena. Some immigrants to Canada are workers, while others are business investors and entrepreneurs. Among the workers there will be many who believe strongly in the right of workers to organize for better pay and employment conditions from business owners. The owners may be more concerned with the right to invest where and how they want, including outside Canada or their home country, if wages are lower there. The views of worker and owner immigrants may coincide around questions of ethnic identity and anti-discrimination. Transnational space is not free of conflict: It is an arena as much structured around tensions and divergent interests as it is around harmony and co-operation. However, the point here is that immigrants who adopt global values, such as those of basic human rights and investor freedoms, perceive that these cut across national boundaries and become part of their identity in whatever country they have a place to be and belong.

Discussion and Conclusions

Immigrants' place in Canada has in the past been largely examined from the normative standpoint of immigrant *integration* into a *multicultural nation*. This chapter argues that the multicultural model is insufficient to fully address the realities of immigrant transnational practices and the outcomes of these arising from interaction with other actors and institutions.

If pluralism is to remain at the core of Canadian nation-building, then it must be increasingly understood as a concept that includes transnational practices and belonging. These practices and places of belonging challenge pluralism and multiculturalism as conventionally understood within a Canada-only focus because they involve "thick" and "hot" communications and affiliations with family and friends in other countries. However, people with strong transnational ties do not necessarily have weak links to Canada and others outside their own ethnic communities. The relationships within a transnational formation can be "both/and" rather than "either/or." Transnational social space is like the social sphere within a nation: It includes wide variations in behaviour and outcomes.

When immigrants seek positive outcomes for themselves, they can potentially help other family members, contribute to prosperity and peace in Canada, assist in the improvement of economic and political conditions in their home countries, and also contribute to understanding and harmony among nations, yet one must be cautious on two accounts. Firstly, these outcomes depend much more on other economic and political actors. Immigrants can play a dynamic and important positive role, but only if the major forces that determine the outcomes in question are supportive. Secondly, the evidence suggests that many of these other forces are only partially supportive, while some block positive developments. Immigrants find that their networks, social capital, and access to resources help them considerably in finding a cultural home in Canada and in supporting the welfare of their families

in home countries. As pointed out earlier in Chapter 7, the same tools and access to resources also help them find jobs and become economically established in Canada, but their success in these areas is reduced because native-born Canadians have even stronger networks, social capital, and access to related resources. In the case of many second-generation visible minority members, their combined resources, including very high levels of human capital (particularly schooling), appear to be sufficient to allow them to overcome discrimination, which might otherwise reduce their job and earnings prospects and their social-cultural incorporation.

In sum, immigrants in Canada engage in a process of transnational incorporation cutting across various spheres of being and belonging. They find ways of belonging in Canada while at the same time they retain ethnic identities and belonging rooted in their home countries. These spheres of belonging tend to become more integrated over time at the family level, among friends in trusted networks, and at the level of their complex personal identities.

Chapter 9 continues the question of belonging to see how it plays out with respect to the processes and outcomes of individual and collective ethnic identity formation. Particular attention will be given to the degree to which immigrants retain home-country ethnic identities, develop hyphenated Canadian-other identities, or form hybrid identities that suggest the quest for a new place of being and belonging. Evidence that points to a prevalence of hyphenated identities or dual affiliations in which the Canadian portion has some significance will be viewed as consistent with the findings in this chapter.

CHAPTER 9
Identity Politics

Introduction

In the documentary *Film Club* (Singh 2001), Cyrus Sundar Singh, the Toronto-based musician and award-winning filmmaker, tells about arriving in Canada as a child with his parents in the 1970s. He recounts his early experiences in school shortly after Prime Minister Trudeau had announced that Canada was a multicultural country; his friendships with other students in a school film club organized by a favourite teacher; and what happened to him and the other students as they grew into adulthood. He recalls his first day at school. Expecting to see all White children, he entered a classroom filled with students from every corner of the world; only a very few were of European background. In the first weeks at school the students did a project on "Indians," which made Cyrus feel centre stage until he discovered that this is really about Native peoples, and that he knows nothing about them except stereotyped images from "western" movies. Soon, however, he gets into the spirit of the project, puts a feather in his hair, and is suddenly transformed into a Native Indian! Apparently the other children and teacher thought this was fine. It is a story of shifting childhood identity and play, and could be dismissed as such, yet the story also provides a glimpse of how Cyrus Sundar Singh's life and career unfolded. He did not fit the stereotype of a Canadian rock or folk singer and was rejected by music managers early in his career. Later, when he visited India, relatives and others there saw him as North American. In time, he became a transnational filmmaker doing projects in India and Canada, and he has become recognized for his original crossover music. He and his career and his identity are unique, yet they bring to light some of the multicultural, hybrid, and transnational aspects of belonging found among immigrants in Canada. What are the diverse forms of ethnic identity commonly created by immigrants and their children? How are these shaped by global and transnational forces? And what are the implications for ethnic relations?

This chapter addresses the preceding questions with a focus on Canada as a particular context for ethnic identity formation among immigrants and their children. The main argument, consistent with the literature, is that ethnic identity is not what it was once understood to be. Or, more precisely, ethnicity is not fixed and immutable as it was once perceived to be.

Physical appearance, cultural background, or country of origin no longer translate directly into ethnic identity. Contemporary ethnic identity in Canada tends to be fluid, changing, often de-linked from geographical location, and frequently re-linked across locations and cultures in transnational and hybrid forms. The chapter begins with a review of concepts and frameworks for understanding ethnicity; I then separately address matters of individual identity formation, collective identity formation, and ethnocultural relations, including racism and discrimination. The chapter ends with several overall conclusions.

Ethnic Identity: What Is It?

The contemporary concept of ethnicity emerged in the context of debates over "race" versus "ethnic group" as ways of understanding increasingly visible divisions within and across societies that were going through the great wave of industrial development, urbanization, and an economic globalization that took place over the late 1800s and early 1900s before the First World War. Winter (2005) examines in careful detail the exchanges that took place from 1910 to 1912 between Max Weber, the German historian and sociologist, and Alfred Poletz, the German biologist, physician, and eugenicist who is credited with inventing the terrifying term "racial hygiene." The context of the debate was a European and North American-dominated world that was still largely racist in orientation, despite important anti-racist developments over the previous century. While engaged in the debate with Poletz, Weber developed a theory of ethnicity that has served as a foundation for understanding historical and contemporary forms. Weber ([1922] 1978: 342) defined ethnicity as *a form of "social closure" in which a group excludes others in order to obtain a status advantage over them.* Weber noted that ethnicities were therefore socially constructed.

Ethnicities tend to develop around "affective criteria," such as religion, language, and culture. Racism, from this perspective, was a manifestation of social closure imposed by a dominant group on the basis of some mix of physical and cultural attributes in order to subjugate, oppress, and exploit others. As such, "race" and "ethnicity" are not biological facts. They are constructs or "social facts" that develop because people believe in them. Weber speculated that ethnic formations (and racism) could weaken or disappear in the future if social class identities, rational-bureaucratic codes of conduct, or other social changes rendered them obsolete. He also noted that this would not happen in cases where ethnicity led to successful and enduring patterns of ethnic dominance and subjugation, or where political opportunists could appeal to ethnic solidarity and promote hostility to others. His speculation has framed a set of questions that remains as relevant today as in the early 1900s. Are ethnic formations changing in form or content, weakening or growing stronger, and how do we explain variability across different nations and places?

Various writers have made important contributions to the study of ethnicity since Weber's early formulation. Fredrik Barth's (1969) work, *Ethnic Groups and Boundaries*, has been particularly influential up to the present. He went further than Weber in examining ethnicity as a constantly renegotiated field of social relationships. The negotiations involved two processes: *ascription* (others' labelling of ethnic groups) and *self-identification* (decisions by those in groups to fix boundaries, labels, and membership criteria). Constant negotiation within groups and among groups regarding ethnic markers and boundaries intended to strengthen the relative positions of the groups leads to a situation in which ethnicity is fluid and constantly changing. This contrasted with other views that saw ethnicity as being more fixed to "tradition," geographical location, and cultural roots. Eriksen (2002) concludes that different approaches to ethnicity form a continuum from those that view ethnicity as relatively fixed and those that see it as relatively fluid. Following his approach and adapting it somewhat, one can distinguish the following four different perspectives.

First are the *primordialists*, such as Geertz (1963), who see ethnicity as deeply grounded in culture, blood bonds, language, speech, custom, and coercive controls over those who challenge the boundaries and identities associated with ethnic group formations. It might be said that Huntington (1993, 1996) adopts a primordialist view of ethnicity when he argues that contemporary globalization has generated a *Clash of Civilizations* (Western, Muslim, Eastern, etc.). The alleged "clash" is between deep historical-cultural formations that are much like "tectonic" cultural plates that move and change slowly. Huntington's deep structures cover great expanses of territory, which he separates into the following "civilizations": Sub-Saharan Africa, North Africa and the Middle East, South Asia, East Asia, Japan, Russia and Central Asia, and the wealthy European nations of the world, including Canada and the United States. His controversial views have been subject to a mix of criticism, particularly on the grounds that they ignore huge communalities and interdependencies across these regions in the contemporary world (see Sacks 2002). On the other side, a number of studies draw attention to places in the world where violent and bloody ethnic conflicts over resources and territory continue and show little sign of coming to an end soon (Toft 2003; Tusicisny 2004).

Second are the *modern-constructivists*, who view ethnicity, ethnic pride, and ethnic nationalism as modern inventions appearing only as the world contracted under expanding shipping, travel, and communications in the 19th century (Wolf 1982: 380–381). According to this view, the emergence of modern nations and the nation-state system brought forth the ideal of ethnic homogeneity within nations, thereby giving rise to efforts to eliminate internal differences based on language, local cultures, and other markers of ethnic heterogeneity. This perspective is consistent with Anderson's (1991) account of nations as "imagined communities," as discussed in Chapter 1. Whereas the primordialists assume that ethnicity is an inherent feature of all societies, the modernist-constructivist view (and the instrumentalist and postmodernist view as well: see below) is that this is not the case.

Third are *instrumentalists*, who treat ethnicities as social formations that can change quickly in response to "political" challenges and opportunities. Canadian multiculturalism may be viewed as an instrumental ethnic-cultural framework within which ethnicities are supposed to be (a normative view) tolerant of one another and at least partially overlapping around a common identification with Canada or aspects of being Canadian. Individuals and groups have earlier ethnic identities that are retained, while they adopt a common nationality (as citizens of Canada) and perhaps a new ethnicity (Canadian) as well.

Fourth are the *postmodern-constructivists*. They substantially extend the modernist and instrumentalist perspective, hence must be addressed as a separate category. From their view, ethnicity in globalized and transnational settings is not singular and fixed, but rather multiple and flexible (Anderson 2001; Appadurai 1996; Basok 2002a; Hall 1992). Generally speaking, the flexibility and multiplicity of identities (the plural form goes well with the postmodern-constructivist framework) is still fundamentally Weberian-Barthian in that individuals and collectivities are

understood to be seeking to protect themselves from unfavourable labelling and promote themselves in a positive light. Hall (1992) was among the pioneers and leaders developing this viewpoint. The main characteristics of ethnocultural formations from a postmodern constructivist perspective include the following:

1. More than one ethnic identity is possible, leading to hyphenated and hybrid forms, such as Vietnamese-Canadian or Afro-Caribbean Canadian (Hall 1992; Howard-Hassman 1999).

2. Fragmented ethnic identities can emerge when the same individual develops several different ethnic identities through travel, dislocation, and settlement in new societies, then finds that these cannot be readily integrated, hence each identity is expressed separately and completely in its own context only (Basok 2002a).

3. Hybrid forms of ethnic identity can emerge through the fusion of elements and the invention of new labels (Bhabha 1994; Nederveen Pieterse 1995). For example, *Latino* has been used to refer to someone of Latin American background raised in North America and seeking recognition of his or her citizenship in these terms (Flores and Benmayor 1997; Simmons and Carrillos 2009).

4. Ethnic identity is subject to constant redefinition through self-presentation and subjective reflexivity in interaction with others in a shifting global landscape of contacts, identity possibilities, and media representations (Featherstone 1990: Chapter 7; Harvey 1992: Part III).

5. Sharp ethnic definitions become blurred as the preceding forms emerge, with the result that people

begin to accept that multiplicity and ambivalence are common when it comes to ethnic identity (Bauman 1991). This creates a new social environment in which everyone understands that ethnicity is not fixed and may be expressed differently in one social context than in another. Examples of identity shifting among Latin American youth in Toronto are provided further ahead in this chapter.

The main difference across the four views outlined above is the extent to which they understand ethnicity as fixed and singular rather than fluid and multiple or hybrid. For the primordialists, ethnicity is fundamentally fixed to geographical locations, cultures, and social institutions that preserve boundaries. For the modernists, instrumentalists, and postmodernists, ethnicity is a cultural artifact, something that emerges only under some circumstances and can take multiple

---

Box 9.1: Hybridity: A Much-Debated Concept

The word "hybrid" refers biologically to an offspring that is mixed, as when two varieties of plants are bred and produce a new hybrid variety. As the colonial world and its racial-ethnic divisions came to a close, and as the emergence of multicultural states and international migration reshaped ethnic categories, the term "hybrid" began to be used in historical, literary, and social-science studies to describe new cultural and identity formations. Someone who is Vietnamese of Chinese ancestry and who is now a Canadian may view himself or herself and/or be viewed by others as a complex ethnic and cultural hybrid: Vietnamese-Chinese-Canadian.

A major debate has been taking place regarding the extent to which hybrid identity and cultural formations challenge all esssentialist thinking about race and ethnicity. Bhabha (1994) claims that hybridity changed colonial power relations, helped bring about the end of colonial rule, and is operating in a similar way to bring about the end of neo-colonialism. Nederveen Pieterse (2004) similarly views hybridity as an emancipatory form of culture, one opposing Westernization and consumer homogenization. Still others, such as Hutynyk (1997), provide a cautionary view by claiming that hybridity does not necessarily have these political consequences because hybrid forms can themselves become dominant and promote homogenization.

A relevant Canadian example of a hybrid ethnic form taking on essentialist qualities would be that of the Métis people. The Métis are culturally a hybrid or "mixed" people descended from the intermarriage of early French fur traders and Native peoples. They have long formed a community of their own and have legal status in Canada, with the result that to be a member and benefit from related government programs, one must be able to show that one's ancestors belonged to this ethnic group.

In this chapter, hybrid ethnic identities are understood to operate in several ways, specifically: (1) new hybrid ethnic identities fracture and disrupt old essentialist versions of "race" and ethnicity; (2) new hybrid identities can, *in specific contexts*, create possibilities of emancipation and anti-racism; and (3) hybrid identities can, *over time in particular settings*, crystallize into more fixed and essentialized forms. This "multiple possible outcomes" approach to hybrid identity and culture is consistent with the logic of postmodern constructivists' views on ethnicity, and also with the earlier writings of Weber and Barth on this subject.

forms. It is also apparent that these different views are based on looking at different historical moments and kinds of overall societies. Ethnicity is viewed as largely fixed in relation to pre-modern social, economic, and cultural contexts. It is viewed as fluid in relation to modern and postmodern contexts. Ethnicity moves from being fixed to fluid when it becomes de-linked from its original geographical location and cultural roots. The fracturing of the triad ethnic label, location, and culture into separate parts allows ethnicity to become fluid, multiple, hyphenated, hybrid, or fractured in contexts where ethnic ambivalence and fluidity are generated and come to be accepted. The fracturing takes place because the world has shifted from being a field of locations to being a field of flows and connections. Globalization and transnational practices are the macro processes that move the world from the former to the latter. Ethnocultural hybridity — one of the key issues in this transformation — is a controversial topic with respect to its role in transforming societies from hierarchical, racist, and colonial to democratic, pluralist, and post-colonial (see Box 9.1).

Table 9.1 draws attention to the way globalization and transnationalism lead to fundamental shifts in ethnicity. For simplicity, only the extremes covering "fixed" and "fluid" identities are presented in this table. One end is what we may call "before." It refers broadly to a pre-modern era in which ethnicities were relatively fixed or slow-changing because each one was linked to its own particular geographical location and culture. The other end is what we may call "now." It refers to an advanced modern era, or globalized and transnational world, in which ethnicities are more fluid and fast-changing because they have become either partially or extensively de-linked from fixed labels, geographical locations, and cultural roots.

In the contemporary period, the labels are fluid, many people are engaged with others in more than one geographical place through travel and telecommunications, and their cultural roots are changing in the process, so that their culture is also no longer fixed.

Table 9.1 is an oversimplification. It does not apply to any particular place. It is simply a tool for understanding general patterns of ethnicity and contextual factors that are associated with them. It tends to suggest that the "fixed" and "fluid" forms of ethnicity are historically separated as the world has moved from "before" to "now." However, this is not entirely true. History and social change are not so linear. The "before" is still present, even if to a lesser extent. The "now" is still emerging, and may experience reversals in its progress at any time. The current mix between fixed and fluid forms of ethnicity will vary from place to place. Canada includes examples that fall across a broad range. The ethnicity of Native peoples is often viewed in primordialist terms. That is, Native peoples are often *viewed* as deeply rooted in their lands, communities, histories, cultures, and customary identities in ways that are relatively fixed and unchanging. The same is often the case for "old French stock" Quebecers, sometimes known by themselves or referred to by others as *pur laine* Québécois who can trace their ancestry back to French colonial roots, although usages of this term vary. Whenever people perceive themselves in such terms or are perceived by others in this way, they are engaged, from an ethnic-social constructivist perspective, in a process of (re)negotiating an ethnic identity.

In the following analysis of ethnic identity in Canada, an ethnic-social constructivist perspective is adopted to examine all ethnic forms, including those that are *seemingly* more fixed as well as others that

Table 9.1: Framework for the Analysis of "Fixed" and "Fluid" Ethnic Formations

	Fixed Formations "Before"	Fluid Formations "Now"
Ethnicity	- Ethnicity tied to a particular geographic and cultural "home" - Ethnic identity is singular - "Hard" ethnic boundaries - Ethnic labelling is powerful - Ethnic nations are idealized - Ethnic nationalism is strong	- Ethnicity is partially de-linked from "home" location and culture - Ethnic identity may be plural - "Blurred" ethnic boundaries - More scope for self-identification - Multi-ethnic nations are an option - Ethnic nationalism is weak
Globalization	- Nations are weakly linked - Time-space is dispersed to create a sense of distance across nations and societies	- Nations are closely linked - Time-space is compressed into "*there* is *here*" close relationships across nations and societies
Transnational communica-tion	- Slow, "thin," and "cool" due to slow communications and travel	- Fast, "thick," and often emotionally intense
Representations	- Maps of places and "races" - Societies and individual identities are reduced to caricatures of their dominant ethnic formations	- Charts of flows and connections - Societies are represented as more internally heterogeneous - Individuals are more often portrayed as hybrids and/or collages of diversity

are more fluid and changing. The ethnic-social constructivist perspective assumes the potential for very fluid, multiple, and hybrid ethnic formations and change related to individual and collective desire to promote the status and security of one's own ethnic group, but it also assumes that this potential is found only in certain kinds of historical moments in which pluralistic values have become more prevalent.

Ethnic Formation Processes in Canada

In multicultural societies such as Canada, the nation itself provides a concept of *multicultural integration* that provides pluralistic normative guidelines for how people are expected to reframe their identities. For example, in a multicultural Canadian setting, people often feel inclined to identify themselves in hyphenated terms, such as Polish-Canadian, Chinese-Canadian, or any other hyphenated form, which suggests duality and a peaceful bridging across a common element, Canadian. At the same time, a label related to home-community identity is retained. Individuals with hyphenated identities can then celebrate both sides of their ethnic affiliations. They can go to a Canada Day parade one week and celebrate a Polish, Chinese, or other home-community ethnic holiday or parade on another. In sum, ethnic identities emerge out of imagined communities and are reshaped within the imagined futures of the nations where they are found.

The preceding arguments and hypothetical examples provide a starting point for examining ethnic identity politics in Canada. They set the stage for a number of questions, including the following. What kinds of ethnic identity transformations are taking place in Canada? Is a Canadian identity emerging? How many immigrants adopt hyphenated or hybrid ethnic identities that include Canadian? How do immigrants form collective identities, and how do immigrants with different ethnic affiliations relate to one another? What role do transnational practices and links play in identity formation? How do immigrant parents seek to influence the ethnic identities of their children? These questions are addressed below.

Canadian Identity

Is there a Canadian identity? It is widely observed that Canada as a whole is a nation in which nationalism and national identity are diffuse and not strong. Such generalizations must be qualified by the fact that there is a very strong Quebec nationalist movement and associated Quebec national identity within Canada, a fact that sets Quebec apart. The question then becomes: Is there an English-Canadian identity? The answer to this question depends in part on who is asked and how English-Canadian identity is defined.

At one extreme, the answer is that there is no such thing as a Canadian identity. All Canadian identities have ethnic roots that specify different ways of belonging. The view that Canada is an ethnic mosaic is expressed in hyphenated identities, such as Scottish-Canadian, Chinese-Canadian, and so on. Hyphenated identities can mean different things, such as "I am really Chinese, but I live in Canada," or it can mean "I have ethnic-Chinese roots, but I identify with Canadian values and Canada." Yet within this range ethnicity is constantly reified. The frequent use of hyphenated identities suggests that Canadian multiculturalism has been successful in "freezing" individuals into old ethnic categories to the point that their sense of belonging in Canada always includes a reference to ethnic roots. Howard-Hassman (1999) argues that such outcomes reflect an "illiberal" version of multiculturalism that is at odds with an alternative "liberal" version that promotes change and, for those who would like it, the adoption of a Canadian identity. She further argues that an English-Canadian identity is well established in multicultural tolerance, pluralist values, democracy, lifestyles (e.g., a one-family house), attachments to the particular Canadian towns and cities where they live, and the sharing of common holidays, some of which have Christian roots (as is the case for Sunday as a day of rest), but are now practised in a non-sectarian, multicultural way (pp. 223–228). Howard-Hassman could have readily added a common identification with iconic symbols and practices, such as the Canadian flag, hockey, and calendar photographs of Lake Louise. She concludes that Canada is composed increasingly of "people who share not only the flat, thin legal state of citizenship, but also the complex, thickening state of fictive kinship that underlies the sense of nationhood" (p. 229).

Support for Howard-Hassman's view can be found in Canadian census data. From 1986 on, the census has allowed individuals to give multiple responses to the question on "ethnic origins" and to include "Canadian" as an ethnic origin. The proportion including Canadian as at least one of their responses has risen to 39 percent and comprises the largest mentioned ethnocultural group in Canada. At the same time, it is difficult to know whether the census data showing identification with Canadian ethnicity means only a superficial attachment or something more profound. We need to look further and dig deeper. As a first step, we need to understand whether the question concerns individual identity, as it would seem to do in the census data, or collective identity, which it may in other contexts.

The Politics of Individual and Collective Identities

Following the previously examined insights of Weber and Barth, the politics of ethnic identity concern individuals' efforts to develop and negotiate ethnic identities and relations with others that protect the interests of their own ethnic group. Identity politics with respect to ethnicity are carried

out at the interpersonal level in face-to-face engagements in all contexts. They are also carried out collectively in cases where ethnic organizations mobilize against negative stereotypes or for the promotion of their well-being as a group. At the individual and the collective level, identity politics involve drawing upon established resources and creating new ones, particularly with respect to the support of family, friends, and others who have similar ethnic identities. Eventually, ethnic identity politics can lead to mutually acceptable and supported identities across ethnic lines, as would be the case if someone says, "Oh, I gather that you are [some ethnic name]. I love the food, culture, and decency of people who have that background." Unfortunately, the process can go the other way and lead to hostile interactions. Hyphenated and hybrid individual identities with a common element, whatever that is, typically build bridges and reduce conflict. Rummens (2003: 17) has referred to the politics of identity as "identity negotiations" with a "political" character.

Efforts to organize collective ethnic identities take a somewhat different process. Being collective, they involve joint action. This can include efforts to mobilize large numbers of people for ethnic festivals, parades, music, and theatre. Collective events build solidarity and a common identity within one's own community, expand contacts and relationships with other groups, and promote the community's positive image. Both individual and collective identity processes can be transnational in nature. At the individual level, personal ties to the home community can affect identity, and vice versa. At the collective level, when ethnic organizations want to sponsor an event, they can invite well-known home-country political figures, musicians, dance groups, and sports teams.

The processes that generate individual identity are different from those that generate collective identity. At the same time, individual and collective identities shape each other. Individual ethnic identity is formed out of one's own personal experiences of being and belonging across various spheres of life. These spheres include interactions with family, friends, acquaintances, others within and outside one's country or countries of citizenship, and so on. Collective ethnic identity arises when individuals recognize one another as belonging to the same ethnic group. Individual and collective ethnic identities overlap insofar as others view individuals who hold a particular ethnic identity as belonging to this same ethnic group. This conventional distinction between individual and collective ethnic identity becomes more complex within a multicultural/ transnational framework in which individual identity is not necessarily contained within a single collective identity category. In a multicultural/transnational setting, an individual may be recognized as belonging to more than one ethnic group, not as a hyphenated person but as a bifurcated person. Take the hypothetical case of a woman whose mother was born in Greece, father was born in France, and she herself was born in Canada. She speaks Greek, French, and English. When with her mother's relatives, she is ethnically Greek; when with her father's relatives, she is French; and when with her work friends, she is Canadian. When asked what her ethnicity is, she could report any one or a combination of these. The woman then has two or more collective identities, and can express her personal identity in a hyphenated form, such as "I am a Canadian of French-Greek background." The complexity of individual ethnic identities tends to push against and transform the simple categories of collective ethnic identity, while at the same time the collective categories provide the root vocabulary for individuals' efforts to describe their collective ethnic identity.

Immigrants and ethnic minorities caught between inadequate collective identity labels to express their individual identities often feel that providing a simple answer to "Where are you from?" is impossible to do in a meaningful shorthand way. We can observe this in findings from studies on individual ethnic identity.

Individual Ethnic Identity

As with all the "upside" features of transnationalism, identity politics are a reaction to "downside" concerns. Immigrants often face negative stereotyping due to various dimensions of social prejudice lingering in Canada. These dimensions of prejudice include: xenophobia (dislike of foreigners), ethnocentrism (discrimination against people of different ethnic backgrounds), and anti-immigrant sentiment (arising from fear that immigrants will "steal" jobs or bring about unwelcome cultural changes). When immigrants react to these sentiments by making it clear that their values are similar to native-born Canadians and that they contribute to economic progress through their work and business skills, they then may face a new problem. Ethnic purists in their own communities may view them as having defected to "the other side." People who have become too assimilated from ethnic traditionalists' point of view are given derogatory names: "banana" (yellow, which is to say Chinese or Japanese, on the outside and White on the inside), "coconut" (brown on the outside and White on the inside), and "Oreo" (Black on the outside and White on the inside). Identity politics is therefore a balancing act in which immigrants and members of ethnic minorities seek to retain varying levels of solidarity with their ethnic roots, while at the same time they attempt to broaden their belonging outside their ethnic community. This leads to rather fluid forms of duality and to new identities that are not a simple blend arising from assimilation. Fluid and dual identities are less evident among adult immigrants, but are often pronounced among their children. Some ethnic identity developments take several generations to unfold.

The complexity and fluidity of identity is most clearly revealed in qualitative interview studies that allow the respondents to speak openly about their experience and cultural allegiance. Carl James (2005) provides details from an extended interview with Mark, a young Trinidadian who grew up in Canada and, at the time of the interview, was making his way in the world as a Canadian-identified athlete. Mark is deeply attached to Trinidad through his family and annual visits to his grandparents, who live there. Mark feels "definitely Trini" and not Canadian because he thinks that "there is no real Canadian identity" (p. 248). This is only one of many different kinds of national or cultural identity expressed by immigrants. Mahtani's (2006) interviews with Canadian women of "mixed race" indicates more complex patterns that include a significant amount of Canadian identity and the use of "I'm Canadian" as a convenient answer to a problem they face in specifying where they are from even when their personal identities are more complex. The mixed race women who participated in Mahtani's study said that they grow weary of trying to explain where they are from. When they tell people they are Canadian, they get the usual response: "But where are you *from*?" One respondent, Emma, reported an instance in which she was visiting Washington, D.C. When asked, "So where are you from?" she answered, "I'm Canadian." This led to the question, "Where are you *really* from?" Emma then added where she was born (England), but she purposefully did not add that her father was half-Chinese. In this way she sought to push the person with whom she was talk-ing to become aware of the implied racist stereotyping involved in the insistence that she clarify where she was from. Emma said that being Canadian has the advantage that there is nothing "identifiable about it" and hence it avoids cultural stereotypes (p. 172). Darius, another participant, said that "being Canadian and being mixed-race ... are not at odds with each other. They are related" (p. 171). Mahtani observes that the views taken by Emma, Darius, and others in her study contrast with Hill's (2001) account in which women of mixed race "find it difficult to identify with being Canadian because of systemic racism and dominant definitions of the national narrative as "white" (p. 174). It seems that self-identification as an ethnic/national "Canadian" provides a zone of protection and comfort for some people who want to avoid racist labelling. However, for others the term "Canadian" will not work because it requires a personal identification with what is perceived as a racially intolerant society.

Interviews with youths and young adults born in Latin America or born in Canada to Latin American immigrant parents revealed that they employ a range of strategies in order to feel they belong and are safe in different contexts (Simmons and Carrillos 2009). Some youth employ identity shifting. They adopt a home-country identity and speak Spanish with their families or when seeking to get a job with a Spanish-speaking employer; in other contexts they find it convenient to "pass" as mainstream Canadians. They and others form Latino friendship groups that bring together youths of Latin American background from different countries, including some who have largely lost their ability to speak Spanish, but who feel that they have a Latin American cultural affinity. These groups occasionally include honorary members from other ethnic minority groups, such as individuals from the

Philippines or the Caribbean, with whom they share friendships based on affinities in music, sports, or other interests. Some of the Latin Americans are also members of sports teams in which they have yet another set of memberships and resources they can call on if faced with verbal or physical violence.

> One youth noted that he was proud to be the sole Latin American on a high school football team where the majority of players were Black. He is occasionally teased by other team members as being a "light-weight" Latino (a joke, since he is a physically big man). This is a kind of banter to confirm team membership and in-group status. He is apparently an excellent player and an esteemed member of the team. Football, moreover, is a very prestigious game in his school. Not surprisingly, the football team has high solidarity. He jokingly noted that he is safe everywhere he goes. If anyone were to start a fight with him, his football teammates and his Latino friends would all come to his rescue. (Simmons and Carrillos 2009: 12)

The core identity of the Latin American youths in this study is that of a Latino, which is to say not Latin American (that is where their parents are from), not Hispanic or Spanish (that is their language, but they are not from Spain), but a new generation with Latin American roots living in North America according to North American lifestyles. Many have lived in the United States or have relatives there; hence they are in contact with U.S. communities where a Latino identity is far more developed. The youths identify with music and dance associated with a broader transnational Latino culture. This hybrid Latino identity

was particularly helpful to one of the participants in this study who said her own mixed-race background (European, Central American Indian, and Black) made it difficult for her to find an identity to express her ethnicity and place in Canada. She was born in El Salvador, but was not accepted in the Salvadoran immigrant community in Toronto because she looked "exotic" (her words) and was subject to racism within that community. Racism and her cultural background also made it difficult for her to feel entirely Canadian. Latin dancing and Latino friends made her feel at home. To be Latino does not conflict with feeling part Canadian. When asked if they feel Canadian, many of the Latino youth said that they did, at least, in part.

The qualitative studies reported above draw attention to the role of transnational connections and contexts for establishing cultural identity. Mark retained a "Trini" identity through close family connections and visits to Trinidad. Emma and others in Mahtani's (2006) study find that they are most clearly Canadian when they are travelling outside Canada. Latin American youth find supports for considering themselves Latino through transnational connections to Latino culture, politics, and dance in the United States and elsewhere. Ethnic identity retention and transformation in Canada are not simply developments within a self-contained multicultural society with its own ethnic and non-ethnic organizations and patterns of social organization; they are developments within a multicultural society within a transnational world.

Compared with the findings of qualitative studies, such as those reported above, questionnaire or survey studies of identity do not provide such rich detail on complex and fluid identity politics and strategies, but they have the advantage of covering larger numbers of people and permit generalization. The results from different surveys vary considerably according to the methodology used (see Table 9.2). Findings from such surveys depend very much on the kinds of questions being asked. Studies that simply ask immigrants to report their "ethnicity" find that most will use their home country or culture to define themselves. For example, the Canadian Ethno-cultural Diversity Survey (EDS) asked respondents to report their ethnicity. Respondents were then told that their ethnicity is "the ethnic or cultural group or groups to which you feel you belong." Using this approach, most immigrants in Canada (61 percent) used their home country or minority status (Chinese, South Asian, Latin American, Black, etc.) to define their identity. Only roughly one in six (15.6 percent) said Canadian. The other quarter (24.5 percent) reported Canadian and one other ethnicity. However, surveys that ask people to express *how much* they identify with "Canadian" and other ethnic categories give quite a different picture. Nearly half of the immigrants surveyed in the Canadian Focus study (48.6 percent) reported that they identify as "mainly Canadian," while another third said that they were "mainly ethnic, then Canadian," with most of the remaining stating that they feel "both equally." Clearly, how one asks people about their ethnic identity makes a very large difference in their responses. If the question is "Please state your ethnicity," the majority of immigrants (60.9 percent) will tend to state their home country or cultural group. However, if the question is "Do you feel mainly ethnic or mainly Canadian?" only one-third (33.3 percent) will say they identify primarily with their home country or cultural group.

Table 9.2: Percentage of Canadian Immigrants Who Report Canadian Ethnicity, Other Ethnicity, or Both by Question Asked

1. To which ethnocultural group do you feel you belong? (Open question; no response categories given; multiple responses were accepted.)		2. I think of myself as …	
Canadian	15.6	Mainly Canadian, then Other	48.6
Canadian plus Other	23.5	Both equally	12.8
Other only	60.9	Mainly Other, then Canadian	33.3
No answer	0.0		5.3
Total	100.0		100.0

Source for question 1: Walters, David, Kelli Phythian, and Paul Anisef. 2007. "The Acculturation of Canadian Immigrants: Determinants of Ethnic Identification with the Host Society." *Canadian Review of Sociology and Anthropology* 44:Table 1. The data come from the 2002 Ethnic Diversity Survey of 42,476 people aged 15 years or over in Canadian provinces.

Source for question 2: Harles, John. 2004. "Immigrant Integration in Canada and the United States." *American Review of Canadian Studies* 34:Table 7. The data come from the Environics, Focus Canada, 1997–1992 survey, "Native and Foreign-Born Attitude toward Issues Relating to Citizenship and Multiculturalism," based on a sample of 2001 individuals over age 18 in Canadian provinces.

While the two surveys cover Canadian and foreign-born respondents, only the responses of the foreign-born (immigrant) respondents are reported above.

Parent-Child Ethnic Identity Formation

From a social constructivist perspective, ethnic formation within groups subject to discrimination should be particularly revealing of the ways in which ethnic pride is used as an antidote to the effects of racism. We have already noted that ethnic identification and pride are important in this respect for biracial individuals and others, such as Latin American youth, seeking to overcome marginalization. Are the same practices of ethnic formation evident in minority immigrant families? Do the parents use ethnic pride as an instrumental tool to strengthen their children and their community to overcome racism and ethnocentrism? If so, is this done in ways that build new essentialized walls of racism and exclusion, or is it done in ways that fit more broadly with pluralist values and the desire to overcome racism?

Lalonde, Jones, and Stroink (2008) address a number of hypotheses relevant to ethnic socialization in Black families in Canada in their study of families in Toronto. They review the U.S. literature and some relevant Canadian studies, noting that the multicultural context in Canada and the lack of the deep history of slavery found in the United States makes the two places very different, hence the need for specific research in Canada. Their pilot study was based on 91 self-identified Black parents recruited via contact with a daycare study centre and through an advertisement in a community newspaper. Of the 91 parents, 75 were born outside the country. Most of the parents identified themselves as of Caribbean background (e.g., 40 were of Jamaican background and 20 of Trinidadian background). While the authors are cautious about the results of findings from a small sample, they note wide variation across those parents

interviewed in their perceptions of racism, personal experiences of racism, concern that their children were or would be facing racism, and their ideology and point of view on what should be done to educate their children about racism. Among other findings, they note that "parents who perceived their children as experiencing more racism were more likely to promote their culture and to talk [to the children] about race" (p. 13). In addition, the researchers report that parents hold off talking about racism with their children until they feel that their children are "cognitively ready" or that "it is necessary to do so" because they are getting older (p. 17). They found that parents were more likely to engage in "cultural socialization" in which children were taught to feel part of their ethnic community, appreciate its clothing, music, and food, and go to community events when they perceive more racism in society and when they have developed a world view or ideology in which race must be taken into account (Lalonde, Jones, and Stroink 2008: Table 3). Parents engage in various degrees, some extensively, in "preparation for bias." This involves teaching their children about the virtues of pluralism and giving them advice: to not tease others about racial features; to argue against all forms of stereotyping; and to not let racial discrimination get in the way of obtaining a good education and succeeding in life. In sum, the study suggests that in a multicultural setting (and likely a transnational one too, although the authors do not discuss transnational family links) visible minority immigrants teach their children ethnic pride as a way of overcoming racism, while at the same time they teach the children pluralist values toward the same objective.

Researchers who have been concerned with "family dynamics" or the relationship between mothers, fathers, and their children within and across generations have suggested that ethnocultural identity is a major issue leading to tension, potential conflict, and negotiation within immigrant families. These identity-related dynamics take place because immigrant parents' experience is often so different from that of their children. Falicov (1998, 2003, 2007) points out that children who immigrate with their parents have little choice in the matter, have not established mature enduring relationships with relatives in the home country before departing, and, upon arrival, are thrust into school and peer environments where there are strong forces for compliance and penalties for not fitting in. Immigrant children often learn the new language and culture more quickly than their parents. Their peers are the active agents of socialization in a process that Berry et al. (2002) have termed "horizontal cultural transmission." Falicov (2003) concludes that there is often signifi-cant conflict between immigrant parents, who are holding onto their mother tongue and home-country values, and their chil-dren, who are learning a new language and adapting to the values and norms of the new culture. However, this conflict is less common than often believed because immigrant parents and their children engage in negotiated solutions. Cultural conflict, including conflict over ethnic identity, is reduced in many immigrant families because the parents and the children undergo a joint, interactive, and transnational family acculturation. Portes and Rumbaut (2001) note that the solutions often come about due to what they refer to as "selective acculturation." This kind of acculturation process involves parents and their children coming to agreement on retaining home-culture values and identi-ties in some areas (such as sexual morality, marriage norms, and so on), while in other areas the children are encouraged to adopt new cultural practices and values regard-less of whether or not the parents also

adopt these new practices (see Box 9.2). Such a solution, if successfully negotiated, reduces ethnic conflict between genera-tions in immigrant households.

Support for the selective acculturation process can be found in Carranza's (2007) interview study of mother-daughter pairs in 16 Salvadoran families living in Canada. While there is variation among families, the dominant pattern was one in which moth-ers had developed an "acculturation plan" to negotiate cultural values and practices with their daughters. In all cases these mothers' acculturation plans included absolute insistence on what they felt to be a core Salvadoran value of family loyalty and connection (*familismo*). Most moth-ers had taken a more flexible position on other traditional values; they made less stringent demands for respect, obedience, and maintaining virginity. However, they still expected their daughters to "be" Salvadoran. One mother comments:

> For example, here [in Canada] the kids grow up with a lot of freedom. I say to [my daughter] many times, "We are in Canada, but our culture is the Salvadorian culture. Our customs and tradi-tions are different. It is not part of our customs that our daughters go to sleep in houses that we don't know and with people we don't know." Yeah, it's hard for the kids, but I tried to maintain our custom of not too much freedom for her. (p. 175)

At the same time as the mothers were promoting retention of certain aspects of ethnic values and identity, they were actively fostering their daughters' social and economic incorporation into Canadian society. Mothers promoted this incorpora-tion by encouraging their daughters to set high achievement goals, work at part-time

---

Box 9.2: The Concept of "Selective Acculturation" Applied to Identity Formation

Portes and Rumbaut (2001) define three different ways that immigrant parents and their children relate to one another in the process of "acculturation." The first is "discordant," involving a situation in which they face different circumstances, such as if the parents work in an ethnic enclave, speak their own language, and do not quickly learn the language of the country to which they have moved, while the children are thrust into school and must learn a new language along with related cultural values. The second is "concordant," as when the parents and children both focus on learning the new language and culture as fast as they can and help one another in the process. The third is "selective," as when the parents and their children agree that the children can move ahead in learning the new language and serve as translators for their parents, as required, while the parents will help the children communicate with others in the home-country language. In their research on these patterns in the United States, Portes and Rumbaut focused primarily, but not exclusively, on language learning issues. Falicov (2003) noted that "selective acculturation" patterns extend very broadly into family dynamics and transnational relations among relatives in the home country, immigrant parents, and the children of immigrants.

These previous works do not specifically discuss "selective acculturation" in terms of the relationship across generations in the socialization of ethnicity and ethnic pride. However, reading the findings of Canadian studies, such as those by Lalonde et al. (2008) and Carranza (2007), leads to the conclusion that immigrant parents play an active role in the selective acculturation of their children. This includes listening to their children report on the children's own context. Carranza (2007) notes that Salvadoran immigrant mothers have "acculturation plans" and negotiate these with their daughters in order that the daughters will retain some deeply cherished aspects of Salvadoran identity and pride, while pursuing successful economic incorporation and gender equality in Canadian society.

---

jobs, attend English-speaking churches, and choose marriage partners who would treat them as equals (Carranza 2007: 171). The mothers talked explicitly about the sacrifices they had made to ensure their daughters' successful acculturation and economic incorporation. Consuelo, a woman who had had a technical job in El Salvador, talks about doing janitorial work in Canada so her two daughters could stay in school:

> We came with our four children. The [immigration] counselor told us that the money we were get-

ting was not going to be enough for our four children and that our oldest child had to work. We said, "No, we will sacrifice ourselves [to work in low-paying jobs] but our children will obtain a career, no matter what." I don't regret anything, but it is hard. (Carranza 2007: 165)

There was little doubt in the minds of either the mothers or their daughters that the families were staying in Canada, even though they had come as refugees and many originally had hopes of returning to El Salvador after the bloody civil war there came to an end (which it did finally in 1992). Nor was there any doubt in the minds of the mothers and daughters that the daughters would become Canadian in terms of their schooling, careers, and future lives. However, the mothers mostly wanted two things for their daughters: Firstly, that the daughters would be Salvadoran in terms of key cultural values and core identities and, secondly, that the daughters would be well educated and successful, socially and economically, in Canada. For the mothers, and eventually for the daughters, this combination was viewed as a "win/win" (my term) situation. One way of reading Carranza's findings is to say that the mothers had an imagined future of their daughters as individuals who would undergo selective acculturation and therefore become hyphenated or hybrid Salvadoran-Canadians. The daughters understood their mothers to be constantly putting forward an acculturation "plan" that they were to fit in with. As adolescents, several of the daughters did some lying and "sneaking out" to get around their mothers' protective vigilance and tight rules, but in most families the mothers talked with their daughters, shifted their own positions, brought in friends and other family members, including those in the United States and El Salvador, to strengthen their own bargaining positions, and were relatively successful in obtaining outcomes that kept the mothers and daughters in close relationship with each other as time went on and the daughters grew up. One of the most successful ways mothers dealt with their daughters' protests was to evoke ethnic pride. An adult daughter recalls:

> Like, some of my friends used to go play billiards, but I couldn't go. I couldn't do that.... My mother did not like that. She said, "You're

Salvadorian, remember that." So I didn't go. She was very strict. She told me why she was doing it. Like she said, "In our culture women don't do those sorts of things because they look bad. People will think that you are an indecent woman and it will be hard for you to find a man that appreciates you and gives you a place as his wife." (Carranza 2007: 188)

Carranza (2007) comments that "When daughters became aware and embraced their ethnic roots they resigned themselves to letting go some aspects of Canadian culture; that is, some of the behaviours that are considered 'normal' and acceptable for women in Canadian society are not necessarily appropriate for 'decent' Salvadorian women" (p. 188). The tensions then dissolved.

Collective Identity as a Labelling Issue

Collective ethnic and national identities — such as being British, Canadian, Chinese, Egyptian, or Latino — involve applying a label to all who are or are assumed to be members of a particular ethnocultural group. Who invents the labels? Some emerge historically through the complex dynamics associated with the emergence of nations, religions, and cultures. Some seem to arise in the present era out of state policies that label people in particular ways. The result is a "stew" of labels that often confuses as much as it clarifies.

In Canada, the stew of official ethnic labels arising from the census includes those of national origin (British, Chinese, Indian, etc.), those reflecting within or across nation ethnic or religious groups (Jewish, Muslim, etc.), and a list of visible minority categories (Black, South Asian,

Chinese). All this leads to a great deal of real and potential confusion on how to understand ethnicity in Canadian. The positive side is that Statistics Canada, the agency responsible for the census and various state-organized economic and social surveys, has allowed respondents to report more than one ethnic origin. However, the multiple responses lead to questions about how to interpret the combinations that individuals put together.

Another important issue is the extent to which the state participates in racist labelling practices, even if this is not its intent. The list of official visible minorities has been particularly controversial because the categories are based on race and thus they run the risk of perpetuating racism. In 1951 Canada stopped measuring race in the census because the concept had become increasingly discredited by the public and the state (Bourhis 2003: 17). However, questions on race were reintroduced in the census in 1996. Why? The answer is that the Canadian state felt that this was necessary to address the provisions of the 1986 Federal Employment Equity Act. This Act requires the state to make an effort in improving the employment opportunities of various disadvantaged groups: women, visible minorities, Aboriginal peoples, and disabled people. The Act was based on the state's desire to help these groups overcome discrimination. The state said that the only way to know if the provisions of the Act were successful was to obtain information over time on the employment conditions of the targeted groups. This led to a controversial census question to identify "visible minorities" defined as "non-White" or "non-Caucasian." Starting in 1996, the census asks Canadian residents, both immigrants and non-immigrants, to indicate whether they are White, Chinese, South Asian, Black, Filipino, Latin American, Southeast Asian, Arab, Western Asian, Japanese, Korean, or other "visible

minority." The criticisms of this question include the following:

1. By measuring visible minorities as "non-White," the state may end up reinforcing the notion of "race" that it wishes to discredit. The measurement of visible minority status itself may reinforce those racist sentiments still operating in society and perpetuate the distinctions that gave rise to the inequalities that the state is trying to eradicate. This is an endless dilemma for social science researchers, historians, and public policy-makers. It enters into this book: In this and other chapters, it is necessary to talk about racism and, in so doing, we end up using ethnic labels, such as Blacks, Chinese, Latin Americans, and others, which are potentially homogenizing and racializing. For this reason, it is important to read any sentence or section in this book from the perspective of the book's arguments as a whole. These arguments emphasize the socially constructed nature of racial-ethnic categories and fluidity, change, and negotiation rather than fixed homogenizing and static labels.

2. Arabs and "West Asians" (the Canadian government's label) and people from South America who are of European background consider themselves to be White and Caucasian, so they may be puzzled by the way they have been labelled. They may critically observe that Canada has officially adopted a highly Eurocentric definition of "White" and "Caucasian."

3. The category "West Asian" is also rather strange. In the detailed official definition of the category, it includes people of Turkey, Iran, and

Armenia. These people do not generally view themselves as Asian.

4. Within the racialized categories, there are individuals and groups who are relatively advantaged as well as those who are relatively disadvantaged. Putting them all in a category of visible minorities who are assumed to be disadvantaged makes no sense to some of those who fall within the official definition of a visible minority.

How Do Immigrants and Ethnic Minorities Want to Be Represented?

In a large diverse country like Canada, immigrants from a given ethnocultural or national background cannot possibly know one another personally. This means that they cannot possibly engage on a personal level with all relevant others in mobilizing around efforts to represent their collective identity. Immigrants therefore turn to developing collective ethnic identities through their home-country and ethnic associations. These, in turn, may make an effort to influence how they are portrayed in the media and by the state. In the process they must imagine themselves and project an image that is attractive to their own members and leaders in their own communities. This is a challenging process, involving at least the following steps:

1. Complex ethnic immigrant identities at the individual level may get lost in the collective identity politics of ethnic associations. Li (2001b) argues that federal immigration policies are also set in a language that has racist undertones.

2. Media representations of immigrants and ethnic minorities are often highly unsatisfactory to those

represented. Some groups feel that they are not even "in the picture" and want to see themselves included in stories, while others note that news about them is often associated with crime or terrorism. Henry and Tator (2002) comment that the public's negative perceptions regarding members of these collectivities are confirmed when the content of newspaper articles is analyzed empirically. Notable examples in their analysis include Blacks who are excessively linked to newspaper crime stories, and Tamils who tend to appear in the stories of certain newspapers, such as the *National Post*, only in association with alleged terrorist organizations. They noted "nothing positive" about Tamils in these stories (p. 123). Abu-Laban and Garber (2005) analyzed news coverage of immigrant settlement policies. They conclude that many stories in this area tend to provide anecdotes about very successful immigrants. They ignore stories in which racism and marginalization have led to failures of settlement policy. Associated with this pattern, the term "racial discrimination" is seldom used (p. 537), and problems associated with marginalization as well as the people affected by it are made invisible.

3. Ethnic associations may join with others to complain about biases and distortions and to ask for more balanced reporting, including better recognition of the contributions of members of their communities. However, media reports and popular entertainment may pay little attention because the agendas of newspapers and television stations are oriented to different goals, particularly making money. Sometimes

the goals nevertheless coincide, as has been the case for the program "Little Mosque on the Prairie," which provides a humorous and pro-pluralism view of Muslims and non-Muslims in a fictitious town in Western Canada. In other cases, the goals do not coincide. Hier and Greenberg (2002) note that news stories about 600 illegal immigrants being discovered off the coast of British Columbia were reported in ways that emphasized threats to national security and that distanced readers from the Chinese migrants by referring to them as "the boat people" and not, for example, as Chinese migrants desperately seeking work. Hier and Greenberg analyze these stories as items seemingly written to create "moral panic." Whether this is how the reporters actually saw the situation or whether this is what they hoped would sell newspapers is unclear. Both possibilities are consistent with the concept of moral panic.

4. Canadian residents who live in large cities side by side with immigrants from all parts of the world and ethnic communities from earlier waves of immigration can check media representations against their daily experiences. This can provide a buffer to moderate biases in the media, at least in some cases. However, those who live in rural areas and smaller communities may not have this opportunity. This gives rise to a greater potential for misinformation and hostility regarding imagined threats from immigrants who bring minority-ethnic cultures and identities to Canada.

5. The future of collective representations of immigrants and ethnic minorities is uncertain, but some positive possibilities are evident. As immigrants become more established in Canada, they are able to play a stronger role in projecting a positive image. This has been the case for large established communities of Ukrainians, Jews, the Chinese, and many others, and could turn out to be the case for more recently arrived immigrants over time. Mahtani's (2008) illuminating examination of how immigrants are seen and want to be seen in Canada points to positive developments on several fronts. These include the role of minority journalists in Canada; courses on critical journalism in Canadian colleges and universities that pay particular attention to issues of minority representation; the popularity of pluralist TV programs such as "Little Mosque on the Prairie," and film studios' decisions to use cities such as Vancouver to portray Canada to itself and to the world as an ethnically diverse and inclusive global country. To this list we may add that Canadians stand out internationally as being relatively favourable to immigrants (see Box 9.3).

Understanding Interethnic Relations in Canada

One can view interethnic relations in Canada as either a glass half-empty or a glass half-full. Cecil Foster (2007), writing as a member of the "Black/African diaspora," points out that there is no single consciousness or meaning of being Black, and that "Canadian multiculturalism is specifically a form of creolization" in which Canadian Blacks become homogenized and essentialized as the Other. He describes the state of being a Black immigrant in Canada as follows:

Box 9.3: Canadian Attitudes to Immigrants and Immigration

Various surveys have been carried out in the past through to the present on how Canadians feel about immigrants and immigration. Similar surveys have been carried out in other countries that receive large numbers of immigrants. These surveys show changes in attitudes over time in each country. However, at two time points, 1995 and 2003, Canada was among the most favourable to immigration of the countries for which comparable data were available. The findings for 2003 are shown below. They show Canadians to be exceptional in terms of their relatively favourable attitudes to immigration. The contrast with all other countries, except Australia, is remarkable.

Percent who say the following with respect to future immigration levels:

	Increase	No change	Decrease	Total
Canada	29	39	32	100
Australia	23	38	39	100
Japan	13	35	52	100
United States	11	32	57	100
France	8	26	66	100
Germany	6	24	70	100
Great Britain	6	16	78	100

Within Canada, views on immigration reflect attitudes regarding the cultural impacts of immigration. Jedwab (2008: 228), using data from a public opinion survey in 2004, finds that "respondents who feel that Canada admits too many immigrants … are far more likely than others to want immigrants to abandon their cultures." However, given that most Canadians favour maintaining or increasing current levels of immigration, it is clear that most are also open to having immigrants retain their cultures.

In an article entitled, "No Thanks, We're Full," Wilkes, Guppy, and Farris (2008) examine 17 national Canadian surveys on attitudes to immigrants and conclude, among other things, that less than half of Canadians in any year for which data were available between 1975 and 2000 wanted less immigration. They also note that individuals who did not speak English or French at home (and hence were more likely to be immigrants) were much more favourable to immigration. People with higher levels of education were also more favourable.

Data source: Simon, Rita J., and Keri W. Sikich. 2007. "Public Attitudes toward Immigrants and Immigration Policies across Seven Nations." *International Migration Review* 41, 4:956–962. The author has recalculated the results to show only three response categories instead of five.

They [Black immigrants from the Caribbean and their descendants] believe cognitively, that even though somatically Black, they are White culturally and in status, and that they are products of a fully formed [Caribbean] culture and civilization. They arrived in

Canada expecting to be treated ethically and idealistically White. Instead, they were homogenized into a Blackness that turned them psychologically into the Other that they had rejected. (p. xxxv)

Foster nevertheless finds a ray of hope in the way that a "somatically Black female" has become a "creation that is idealistically Black and idealistically White at the same time" (p. 480). If this could happen for all Blacks and all racialized minorities in Canada, then perhaps Canada will become the first nation in which "race" and racism disappear and become irrelevant or non-existent for all dimensions of full participation as an equal citizen in a pluralist society. This is an optimistic view of the glass as half-full; some progress has been made, and more can come. Foster had given indications of his guarded but hopeful future views in his earlier book, *Where Race Does Not Matter: The New Spirit of Modernity* (Foster 2005).

Studies of ethnic relations in Canada reveal a very complex, multidimensional, and changing set of patterns, but overall they conform to Foster's appraisal. The evidence points to a more positive outlook for ethnic relations in Canada compared with some other countries and the slow but nevertheless positive changes taking place in Canadian attitudes to diversity. On the other side, they also show that immigrants, visible minority individuals, and the public at large remain concerned about the level of racism in Canada.

Cross-national Comparisons

A social constructivist view of ethnicity would lead one to expect that the way ethnicity and ethnic relations are constructed will vary from one national context to another, depending on the history of the nations, earlier patterns of ethnocultural formation, and current state

policies. Comparative cross-national studies to test this assumption do not cover all nations, but what has been done points to the importance of national context and the cultural values associated with them. Findings from the analysis of the Eurobarometer Opinion Poll on racism and xenophobia showed that differences across and within countries in attitudes toward immigrants and multicultural diversity could be understood in significant part as reflections of cultural values held by individuals in these nations. Specifically negative attitudes toward immigrants and multiculturalism were higher among respondents who valued hierarchy, mastery, and respect for tradition and social order, and who, at the same time, did not value egalitarianism and harmony (Leong and Ward 2006). What evidence for this can be found for Canada?

An experimental study by Esses, Wagner, Wolf, Preiser, and Wilber (2006) examined how social dominance attitudes affect German and Canadian views on immigrants and immigration. Participants were 282 German students and 126 Canadian students. All students completed a social dominance inventory consisting of questions such as: "Please indicate your agreement on a six-point scale from 'do not agree at all' to 'strongly agree,' with regard to the following statement: Some groups of people are just less worthy than others." Then, the students of each nationality were divided into two experimental and one control group. One experimental group—the one the analysis focuses on—was asked to respond to questions designed to increase their perception of common interests between non-immigrants and immigrants, such as the following: "When Canadians/Germans and immigrants are asked about their goals and values in life, how much do you think that the Canadians/Germans and the immigrants will agree with each other?"

Other groups were asked a different set of questions. For example, the control group was asked questions that had nothing to do with nationality or immigration, such as: "What percentage of the population do you think regularly watches the news on T.V.?" As a last step, the students were asked to answer questions on how often they felt sympathy for immigrants (from "never" to "very often") and on their overall attitudes to immigration (from "extremely unfavourable" to "extremely favourable"). The two different sensitizing questions had a significant impact on the attitudes that the students reported toward immigrants, but the nature of this impact was different for the Canadians than for the Germans and varied by social dominance orientation. Among Canadian students, individuals with high social dominance tended to be less favourable to immigrants and immigration. However, this pattern disappeared when the high dominance-orientation students were first reminded of commonalities between immigrants and non-immigrants. For German students, the results were quite different. "[I]t seems that for German participants who are higher in social dominance orientation, there is a negative response to the attempt to suggest commonality with immigrants...." When reminded of possible commonalities, those with high social dominance were angered and became more negative to immigrants. The findings support the view that social dominance orientation is not a necessary predictor of negative attitudes toward immigrants in Canada. This may be because Canada's multicultural policies and pluralist public attitudes provide a favourable context in which it is possible to remind individuals of commonalities between immigrants and native-born people that make the native-born people feel more positive to immigrants. The national context in Germany presumably

does not provide this support. While this is a small experimental study done with a relatively few students, it has both policy and future research implications. The policy implication is that even in multicultural Canada, ongoing reminders of the commonalities between immigrants and the native-born are useful in reducing hostile attitudes to immigrants among people with high social dominance orientations. The research implication is that relatively little is known about why attitudes to immigrants change over time and that more studies are needed.

Changing Attitudes to Immigrants and Minorities over Time

Table 9.3 shows that many Canadians were negative to the immigration of a number of ethnic groups just after the end of the Second World War. The negative attitudes were due partly to immigration from countries with which Canada had been at war (Japan, Germany, and Italy) and also toward non-European origin groups. By 1961, the year before the end of White Canada policies, 53 percent of Canadians were still in favour of restrictions on non-White immigration. By 1991, opinion polls and surveys were no longer interested in public views on the issue of restricting the immigration of visible minorities since this was no longer in question. Rather, the polls focused on attitudes to cultural diversity within Canada. Despite the long development of multiculturalism in Canada (since 1971), not quite half of Canadians supported cultural diversity in 1991 and again in 2003. Perhaps surprisingly, only a similar proportion of visible minority respondents and immigrants feel that cultural diversity is necessarily a good thing. Seventy-four percent of respondents in 2003 agree that there is a lot of racism in Canada, and 30–40 percent say that prejudice is a factor at work/school or that the police treat Blacks and Aboriginals

unfairly. Visible minority respondents perceive more prejudice at work/school and
by the police than does the population as
a whole. This latter finding is supported
by the 2003 Ethnic Diversity Survey,
which also found that visible minority
members and immigrants are more likely
to say that they experience discrimination
"sometimes or often." About 20 percent
of visible minority immigrants say they

Table 9.3: Percentage Who Say "Yes" to Various Measures of Inter-ethnic Relations and Discrimination

Year	Question	All Respondents	Visible Minority Respondents
1946	If Canada does allow more immigra-tion, are there any of these nationalities which you would like to keep out?		
	Japanese	60	
	Jewish	49	
	German	34	
	Russian	33	
	Negro	31	
	Italian	25	
	Chinese	24	
1961	As you know, Canada restricts the admission of non-Whites to this coun-try. Do you think this should continue?	53	
1991	Variety of cultures is good for society?	47	47
2003a	Variety of cultures is good for society?	49	49
2003a	There is a lot of racism in Canada?	74	75
2003a	Prejudice is a factor at work/school?	30	42
2003a	Police treat Blacks, Aboriginals, etc., unfairly?	40	53
2003b	Report personal experiences of discrim-ination sometimes or often		
	- Entire population (Canadian and foreign-born)	7	20
	- First-generation immigrant	13	21
	- Second generation or more	6	18

Sources: The data for 1946 to 2003a is from: CRIC. 2003. *A New Canada? The Evolution of Canadian Identity and Attitudes to Diversity.* Ottawa: Centre for Research and Information on Canada. It contains an analysis of CIPO polls for 1946 and 1961, a 1991 Angus Reid Poll on Multiculturalism and Canadians, and a 2003 survey carried out jointly by CRIC and the *Globe and Mail* using many of the 1991 survey questions, plus others designed by CRIC on racism. The source for 2003b is: Statistics Canada. 2003. *Ethnic Diversity Survey: Portrait of a Multicultural Society.* Catalogue no. 89-593-XIE. Ottawa: Minister of Industry.

experience discrimination sometimes or often. Of particular concern is that the percent reporting such experiences is only somewhat lower (18 percent) among visible minority children of immigrants. This is a "glass half-full" with regard to ethnic prejudice. The White Canada policies are long gone, but there is widespread agreement that racism persists; about a fifth of visible minority individuals in Canada say they experience discrimination sometimes or often.

One of the seeming paradoxes of ethnic discrimination is that immigrants and visible minorities often have prejudices against one another, even though, as we have previously noted, this is not universal and many visible minority group parents teach their children to adopt pluralist and anti-racist views. Figure 9.1 provides a glimpse of the discomfort levels that visible minority people as a whole feel with respect to a sister or daughter deciding to marry someone from various specific minority groups. It is noteworthy that the discomfort levels of visible minority indi-

viduals tend to follow the pattern of those for individuals who are not members of visible minorities. However, in most cases, the visible minority respondents are more uncomfortable with the groups in question than are others. A similar pattern is evident for immigrants.

The above findings may suggest that visible minorities and immigrants are more ethnocentric and more prejudiced that the non-visible minority, non-immigrant majority population in Canada. However, such a conclusion would be premature. At the very least, such a conclusion must be serious qualified because immigrants and visible minority individuals are more likely to believe that marriage should be within their own ethnocultural group, and this appears to be a major reason why they are less favourable to close family members marrying anyone outside their ethnic group. Findings supporting this pattern are shown in Figure 9.2. While immigrants and visible minorities fight against racism, at the same time many within these groups feel

Figure 9.1: Percentage Who Would Be Uncomfortable If a Sister or Daughter Were to Marry Someone Who Is:

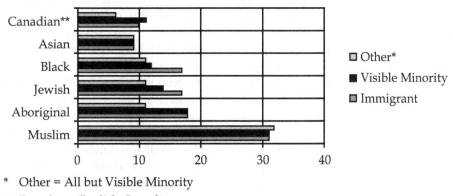

* Other = All but Visible Minority

** French- or English-Canadian

Source: The author, based on data from The Centre for Research and Information on Canada (CRIC).

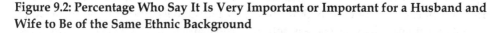

Figure 9.2: Percentage Who Say It Is Very Important or Important for a Husband and Wife to Be of the Same Ethnic Background

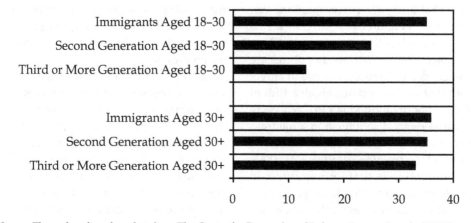

Source: The author, based on data from The Centre for Research and Information on Canada (CRIC).

that it is necessary to retain and build ethnic strength through marriage within the group. This value is clearly age- and generation-related. The value of marrying within one's own ethnic group drops off quickly across generations. It is also far less important to younger people than to older people in any generation. In fact, a fairly high percentage of people over age 30 in all generations seem to have either grown up when marriage within ethnic groups was considered more normative or else growing older has moved them more in this direction. It appears that the younger generation of individuals (those under age 30) is not affected so much by these normative restrictions, particularly once they become second generation or third-plus generation. Insofar that it is the young who marry (or at least, marry for the first time), it is perhaps their attitudes that point to the direction of potential change. Now we are back to the glass half-full, namely, a more optimistic view of how ethnic hybridity and the plural-ist values that go with it can continue to expand over time as the future unfolds.

Discussion and Conclusions

Ethnic identity is an important aspect of immigrant belonging in a transnational space bridging Canada and their home country. It is not surprising to discover that immigrants and immigrant-origin ethnic minorities often have complex hyphenated and hybrid individual ethnic identities; that these identities are expressed with some flexibility in different contexts; and that they are associated with develop-ments and tensions in the construction of collective ethnic identities. These points have been made previously in studies of Canada as a multicultural nation. In this chapter, I sought to show that identity politics among Canadian immigrants at both the individual and collective level are not just matters involving "accommoda-tions" within Canada. Rather, they also involve transnational links and solidarities, as well as negative ethnic stereotyping that emerges when entire immigrant and ethnic-minority communities are portrayed as being associated with terrorists and migrant traffickers. The review of the various studies in this chapter supports the conclusion that identity politics at the individual and collective level are embedded in transnational practices and their complex interactions with other actors and institutions.

The question about whether old racialized ethnic boundaries are breaking down in a multicultural and transnational world remains difficult to answer because of contradictory tendencies. Canada is clearly becoming more multicultural, and Canadians are becoming more hybrid with increasing common ties to an emerging Canadian ethnicity and identity. At the same time, racism and ethnocentrism are still all too common, leading immigrants and ethnic minorities to find support by strengthening their own ethnic communities, in part through transnational ties. However, this does not mean that there is a necessary clash between staying together within ethnic groups and forming bridges across them. It seems that the two processes can take place together through selective acculturation in which minorities and immigrants hold onto certain cultural values that retain a home-country or home-ethnicity identity, while at the same time they selectively adopt new cultural values that allow them to also become Canadian. The evidence in support of these developments is, however, based on relatively few, small qualitative studies. We need to know much more.

This chapter brings to a close the focus on belonging that began with Chapter 7 on social-economic aspects (jobs, earnings, and housing) and included Chapter 8 on transnational aspects (belonging in terms of transnational practices linking home and host countries). The next two chapters give more attention to future issues. Chapter 10 examines Canadian demographic trends and their implications for immigration and migrant labour policies. Chapter 11 concludes the book with an assessment of overall findings and what they suggest for future Canadian policies on immigration and temporary foreign workers.

CHAPTER 10

Immigrants, Migrant Workers, and Babies

Introduction

Currently, Canadians produce few children. Following the baby boom, which took place from the end of the Second World War to the mid-1960s, fertility dropped dramatically in what has been referred to as a baby bust. At current levels of fertility, the average woman in Canada in the early 2000s will give birth to somewhere around 1.5 children over her lifetime. Since fractions of children are hard to imagine, levels of current child-bearing can be stated in more understandable terms as follows: At the end of their child-bearing lives, 100 typical Canadian women will currently produce on average about 150 children. Of these, only about one-half—or 75 children—will be daughters. If the 75 daughters follow the same child-bearing pattern as their mothers, they will produce only about 56 daughters of their own (or granddaughters to the first 100 women). Thus, over three generations, the number of women in this subpopulation will drop from 100 to 56, and the same will happen for the men. If natural increase were the only source of population renewal and all Canadian women followed the pattern of the 100 typical women, the population of the nation would get smaller very quickly. The national population would also be getting older. For example, if the first generation of women is mostly still alive as grandmothers when their grand-daughters are growing up, the grandmoth-ers will substantially outnumber their direct-descendant granddaughters. The result is the opposite of what is found in a population with high levels of fertility in which the generation of granddaughters will be far larger than the generation of their grandmothers.

Population dynamics do not work exactly like the rough scenario outlined above, but the illustration it provides will get us started. One of the main additional factors to take into account in examining population growth is the role of international migra-tion. Immigrants add to children born and growing up within a nation to create a new generation of adults. Several questions arise. To what extent can immigration sustain population growth, slow population aging, and fill in labour force gaps in a Canadian population with below-replacement fertil-ity? If Canada is short of workers due to aging, to what extent can migrant workers fill this gap? What other additional strate-gies need to be considered to address future labour force challenges?

This chapter addresses the preceding questions from the nation-building per-spective set forth earlier in this book. From the perspective of this framework, future visions of the nation and its labour force evolve over time as circumstances change. In the past, the idea of a slow-growing or declining population with many elderly would have been terrifying to national political and economic leaders. However, many new circumstances—such as tech-nological advances, trade developments, the reorganization of production across nations, and migrant worker programs— no longer make the prospects of slower population growth or even of population decline so worrisome. The goal of this chapter is to assess the future implications of current trends in fertility and the role of immigration and migrant labour, along with other possible solutions, in addressing challenges of slower population growth, aging, and labour force gaps.

The chapter is organized in several parts. Part 1 puts Canada in context by examining global patterns of population growth and labour force supply. Part 2 analyzes how the Canadian population grew in the past and the relevance of past growth for Canada's political and economic development. Part 3 examines future challenges arising from the slowing growth of Canada's popula-tion and aging. Part 4 assesses the options for addressing the emerging challenges. The options examined cover a range from encouraging parents to have more babies to expanding migrant worker programs. The chapter ends with a discussion of the main conclusions.

Part 1: The Big Picture: Global Population and Labour Force Trends

Various regions of the world as a whole are moving into an advanced stage of

Box 10.1: Basic Demographic Transition Model

It has been observed that population growth in various nations and regions around the world tends to follow a similar historical pattern, but at different points in time and with many other features that are not entirely comparable. The common logic, despite differences, is often portrayed as a demographic transition model with several stages. The figure below shows this model with three stages.

The first stage is an earlier historical moment when both fertility and mortality are very high. The result is that population growth is slow. This stage covers the human experience from the pre-recorded past to more recent periods when improved sanitation, better food supplies, and medical technology reduced death rates.

The second stage is a period of rapid population growth due to high fertility and low or declining mortality. Why fertility declines typically follow mortality rather than preceding them is not well understood, but assumed to be because parents in earlier historical periods were dependent on having children for their old age security, with the result that they would not consider having fewer children until they were certain that the children they had already would survive.

The third stage is after fertility also declines and population growth rates become very low. A fourth stage in which fertility drops below mortality is not shown, but is often added to cover the situation currently found in Canada, Europe, Japan, and a number of other places.

The demographic transition occurred at a much earlier historical period in industrialized, wealthy nations, all of whom now have low or very low fertility, mortality, and population growth. In contrast, the demographic transition is less advanced in the world's least developed countries, with the result they have young, growing populations with many workers entering labour markets that often provide too few jobs or jobs at very low wages. International migration pressures may be understood to be due to both wealth and income differences and labour force growth differences among nations.

Basic Demographic Transition Model

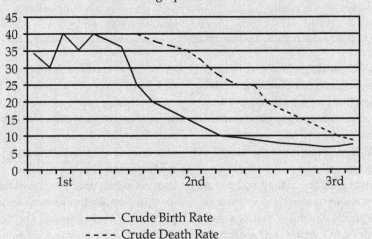

—— Crude Birth Rate

- - - - Crude Death Rate

Each nation undergoes its own specific demographic transition, so the basic model provides at best only an approximation of a general pattern. In the case of Canada, mortality began to decline prior to Confederation. Fertility also began to decline fairly early, but more gradually, with the result that Canada experienced sustained high natural population increase throughout the 1800s and up to the 1960s, as the chart below indicates. Note the baby boom spike from the late 1940s to the mid-1960s. It appears as an unexpected upward "blip" on a birth-rate trend line that is steadily downward from the time of Confederation.

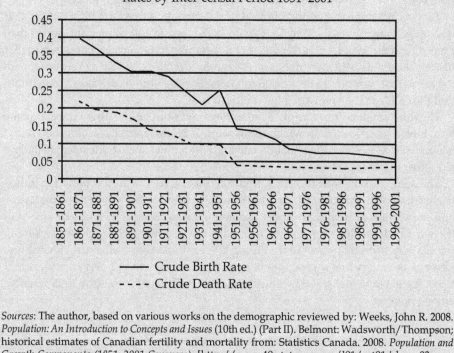

Canadian Crude Birth and Crude Death Rates by Inter-censal Period 1851–2001

— Crude Birth Rate
- - - - Crude Death Rate

Sources: The author, based on various works on the demographic reviewed by: Weeks, John R. 2008. *Population: An Introduction to Concepts and Issues* (10th ed.) (Part II). Belmont: Wadsworth/Thompson; historical estimates of Canadian fertility and mortality from: Statistics Canada. 2008. *Population and Growth Components (1851–2001 Censuses)*. [http://www40.statcan.gc.ca/l01/cst01/demo03-eng.htm]

demographic transition in which human fertility is falling and population growth is slowing. Box 10.1 provides details on three different stages of demographic transition. As explained, stages 1 and 3 are periods of slow population growth, while stage 2 is one of rapid growth.

Canada is merely one of the nations at an advanced stage in its demographic transition. Other highly developed nations, such as most of those in Europe and Japan, have

even lower levels of fertility, in the range of 1.3 children per woman, and are now experiencing rapid aging and declining labour forces. However, there is variation across wealthy nations: The United States and France have fertility levels just above replacement. While less developed countries have had much higher rates of fertility and population growth in the recent past, this is changing quickly. Several less developed countries and regions are also experiencing rapidly declining fertility and will soon begin a process of population aging. This is most clearly the case for China because of its one-child policy since 1979. The Caribbean and Latin America now have moderate fertility, and other countries in Asia, including India, are also moving in this direction, although some still have a long way to go before fertility drops to below-replacement level. Among large regions, only Africa still has high fertility and rapid population growth. Table 10.1 provides some comparative figures on world fertility to draw attention to the very wide differences between more developed and less developed regions. In Africa, for example, women currently bear on average about five children each, a figure that is more than three times greater than the average in Canada and Europe.

Differences in population growth rates contribute to international migration pressures and flows. The low fertility and relative labour force shortages in wealthy nations and high fertility, combined with the relative labour force oversupply in many developing countries, create a buyers' market for the wealthy nations when they seek immigrants and migrant workers to solve their labour supply problems. If wealthy nations need more workers, they can readily find them in less developed nations. If the wealthy countries choose to invite highly skilled foreign professionals to come as immigrants, many individuals with the required

Table 10.1: Total Fertility Rates for World Regions and Selected Nations, 2000–2005

	Total Fertility Rate* (2000–2005)
WORLD	2.65
More developed regions	1.56
Less developed regions	2.90
Least developed regions	4.95
Africa	4.98
Asia	2.47
Europe	1.41
Latin America and the Caribbean	2.52
North America	1.99
Canada	1.52
United States	2.04
Oceania	2.37
Australia and New Zealand	1.79

*Total fertility rate is the average number of children that would be born alive to a woman during her lifetime if she were to pass through her child-bearing years conforming to the age-specific fertility rates of the period of concern, in this case 2000–2005.

Source: UNPD. 2007. *World Population Prospects: The 2006 Revision*. Table 3, p. 11. New York: United Nations Population Division.

qualifications in less wealthy nations will be interested in applying because their salaries are low in their home countries. If wealthy nations decide to invite foreign workers to come as seasonal or temporary migrants for low-wage, difficult, and dirty jobs, they will be flooded with applicants because less skilled workers are so plentiful and even more poorly paid in less developed nations. If neither of the two previous solutions is appealing, wealthy nations can promote free trade arrangements that make it easier for their firms to export production and jobs to low-wage countries, then to import the products for sale to Canadian consumers. As yet another option, wealthy nations and firms can invest in labour-saving technology and highly skilled workers to develop production systems that are automated and require few workers. This does not bring to a close the options. Wealthy nations can also try to encourage women to have more babies so that in the future there will be plenty of workers. As we shall see, some nations seek to do this.

In sum, there is as yet no shortage of workers in the world. However, the workers are not always found where the jobs are located, and this creates opportunities for moving the workers, moving the jobs, or filling labour force gaps through technology and/or adjusting birth rates. The solution adopted makes a big difference for who wins and who loses in relative terms. Table 10.2 outlines several of the main options available for wealthy nations to solve their labour supply problems. Each option is associated with hypothetical outcomes. Some of the hypothetical outcomes correspond to findings in previous chapters. For example, one may compare the hypothetical outcomes for "immigration of highly skilled knowledge workers" with findings in Chapter 7. Outcomes for live-in caregivers will be examined later in this chapter.

Part 2: Growth of the Canadian Population

Canada's political economic history up to the 1960s was deeply dependent on relatively rapid population growth. The population growth came about in part through natural increase over a long stage 2 in its demographic transition: Death rates in Canada fell through the 1900s and particularly in the latter half of the 20th century, while fertility rates declined more slowly and unevenly, with a big drop in the 1930s and early 1940s, and then there was a baby boom from the end of the Second World War to the mid-1960s. Population growth also came about through substantial net gains of international migrants in most years, although in certain periods of early history, such as in the 1870s, more people may have left Canada for the United States than entered Canada as immigrants from all countries combined. From a political-economic perspective, this population growth was very important. It contributed to the settlement of Upper Canada, the historical growth of the francophone population of Quebec (see Chapter 3), and the expansion of farming throughout the Prairie provinces. It also provided ample supplies for workers for the postwar economic boom, which included rising commodity exports and growing industrial production. Since the 1960s, Canadian population growth has begun to slow, but this trend has been dampened by the large number of parents born prior to the mid-1960s (even if they have few children, the large cohorts of parents born earlier produce more children than would otherwise be the case given low fertility) and high levels of immigration. Canada has been adapting to slowing population growth, aging, and labour force gaps for several decades. These trends are discussed below. I begin the analysis with an examination

Table 10.2: Who Wins and Who Loses from Various Strategies Used by Wealthy Nations to Solve Labour Force Shortages

Policy Option	Winners and Losers		
	Winners Include	*Ambiguous Outcomes*	*Losers Include*
Invite highly skilled knowledge workers to settle as immigrants	- Children of immigrants - The receiving nation - MDC firms in need of skilled workers	- The immigrants, particularly in early years after arrival - Immigrants facing discrimination	- Communities in immigrant home countries that have lost highly skilled workers who were trained there
Bring in low-wage migrant workers for seasonal jobs and short-term contracts	- MDC employers in various fields, such as agriculture, child care (via live-in caregivers) and potentially many other areas of work	- Families of migrants in home countries whose welfare is improved via remittances, but who feel the loss of family members who have migrated	- The migrants who trade long periods away from home for low wages and hard work
Export jobs from MDCs to LDCs	- Firms who use this strategy to retain or increase profits - Consumers in MDCs who get access to less-expensive goods	- Workers in LDCs; in some cases they gain from important new opportunities; in other cases, the jobs are low wage and dead end	- Workers in MDCs who lose jobs that were relatively well paid
Use technology to fill gaps and shortages in the labour supply	- MDC firms and their highly skilled workers - Consumers in MDCs may also benefit	- Some MDC workers whose jobs are lost through technological change can retrain for new, better jobs	- Some MDC workers whose jobs are displaced by technological change are too old or too unskilled to retrain for better jobs
Make better use of retired workers and other under-utilized labour pools	- Older workers who like their jobs and wish to continue in them, at least part-time - State and employer pension funds	- Younger workers who find their job mobility blocked by less productive but still employed older workers	- Older workers who would prefer to retire, but find that pension programs have been cut so that they are obliged to continue working

Provide incentives	-	Ethnic nationalists	-	MDC taxpayers	-	Live-in caregivers
and supports so		who prefer pro-		who pay the incen-		who trade long
that women will		creation of their		tives		periods away
have more babies		ethnocultural		-MDC firms seeking		from home for
		community as a		young employees		low wages and
		goal in itself, and		and larger con-		hard work
		as a superior solu-		sumer markets		
		tion to immigra-	-	The parents, mostly		
		tion of ethnically		mothers, who must		
		distinct people		do large amounts of		
				unpaid child care,		
				while cutting back		
				on their careers		
			-	Wealthy parents		
				can reduce their		
				career costs by hir-		
				ing nannies		

of the growth of Canada's population over the past 150 years. Subsequently, the analysis turns to an assessment of different future population growth scenarios.

From 1841 to 1851, the area that now comprises Canada had a population of 2.5 million (Table 10.3). In 2006, Canada had a population of slightly more than 33 million—a more than 10-fold increase. When one examines a graph of population size over this long historical period, the trend had earlier been steadily upward, giving the visual impression that Canada's population growth is on a continuing upward trajectory similar to the historical past (see Figure 10.1). However, the visual impression from this figure is deceptive. The figure does not show clearly that the *rate* of population growth has slowed dramatically. A more careful examination of population growth trends reveals that the percent increase in the Canadian population from one census to another has been extremely variable in the past and has been decreasing steadily since the 1960s (Figure 10.2). Canada's population growth from 1996 to 2001 was less than 1 percent per year, the lowest ever recorded.

Natural increase and international migration have both contributed significantly to Canada's historical pattern of population growth. The contributions of these two over time are shown in Figure 10.3. From this chart, we may conclude the following. Over Canada's history from Confederation to the mid-1960s, natural increase contributed three to four times more to Canadian population growth than net international migration did, although there was a brief period just prior to the Second World War when the two sources of population growth contributed almost equally. However, since the 1960s, net international migration rates have remained steady, while fertility has continued to fall. In 2001 these two sources of population growth made similar contributions. If the trends shown continue, then over time, natural population growth will contribute less and less, while net international migration will contribute about the same amount, hence relatively more.

The contribution of net migration to Canada's population growth has at times been negative, as shown for the periods

Table 10.3: Population Size and Growth in Canada, 1851–2001

Period between Censuses	Population at End of Period	Population Growth over Period
1841–1851	2,437	
1851–1861	3,230	793
1861–1871	3,689	459
1871–1881	4,325	636
1881–1891	4,833	508
1891–1901	5,371	538
1901–1911	7,207	1,836
1911–1921	8,788	1,581
1921–1931	10,377	1,589
1931–1941	11,507	1,130
1941–1951	13,648	2,141
1951–1956	16,081	2,433
1956–1961	18,238	2,157
1961–1966	20,015	1,777
1966–1971	21,568	1,553
1971–1976	23,450	1,488
1976–1981	24,820	1,371
1981–1986	26,101	1,281
1986–1991	28,031	1,930
1991–1996	29,611	1,580
1996–2001	31,021	1,410

Source: Statistics Canada. 2008b. "Estimated Population of Canada, 1605 to Present." Ottawa: Statistics Canada.

from 1861 to 1891 in Figure 10.3. Why? In the late 19th century, large numbers of immigrants came to Canada, but Canada's economic climate and opportunities were not as good as those in the United States over this period. As a result, large numbers of Canadian residents (including Canadian-born residents and those who had recently immigrated to Canada) left Canada for the United States. Emigration exceeded immigration for most years between the 1870s and the 1890s, despite the high levels of immigration. Canada overcame this problem in the early part of the 20th century by admitting larger numbers of new immigrants and developing its economy to the point where fewer Canadians and recent immigrants departed. In sum, the historical lesson is that Canada can either gain population or lose population through international migration. This was very clear in the past. The fact that in recent past decades far more people have entered Canada as immigrants than have left as emigrants is not to say that the reverse might not hap-

Figure 10.1: Canadian Population (in Thousands) by Year

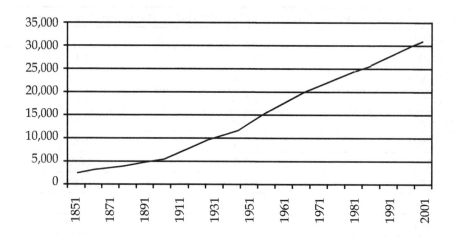

Source: Statistics Canada. 2008b. "Estimated Population of Canada, 1605 to Present." Ottawa: Statistics Canada.

Figure 10.2: Percentage Change in Canadian Population from Start to End of Periods Shown

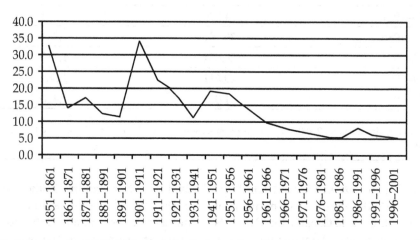

Source: Statistics Canada. 2008b. "Estimated Population of Canada, 1605 to Present." Ottawa: Statistics Canada.

pen in the future. Everything depends on the economic health and labour demand in Canada relative to neighbouring countries, particularly the United States, and other nations in the international system.

Part 3: Future Projections and Challenges

Can future Canadian population growth trends be changed by increasing immi-

Figure 10.3: Natural Increase and Net International Migration Rates, Canada, 1851–2001

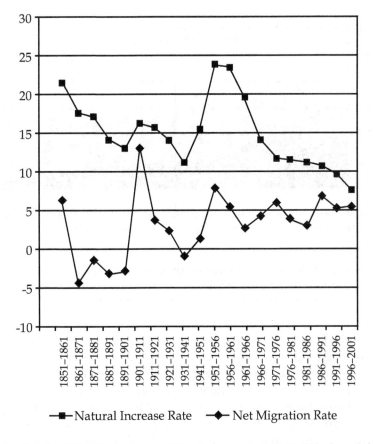

—■—Natural Increase Rate   —◆—Net Migration Rate

Source: Statistics Canada. 2005b. "Population and Growth Components (1851–2001 Censuses)." Ottawa: Statistics Canada.

gration? The answer is a qualified *yes.* Immigration does tend to boost population growth somewhat, but perhaps not by as much as one might think, at least if the inflows of immigrants are similar to what Canada has become accustomed to. One of several plausible future scenarios — namely, low fertility similar to that found currently in Canada and international migration similar to levels in the recent past for Canada — would lead to a Canadian population of about 38 million somewhere around 2030, then continued but slow growth thereafter (see scenario 3 in Figure 10.5).

Of course, the trends in natural increase shown in Figure 10.4 for the period after 2005 are based on assumptions of continuing low fertility in Canada. Specifically, a total fertility rate (TFR) — namely, an estimate of the number of children born per woman over her reproductive years — of 1.6, well below the TFR of 2.1 required for a population to reproduce itself. The future could actually turn out to be quite different, both with respect to fertility and with respect to international migration.

Past trends suggest that the future will be characterized by still slower population

Figure 10.4: Observed (1981–2004) and Projected (2005–2056) Natural and Migratory Increase in Canada According to Scenario 3 (Medium Growth)

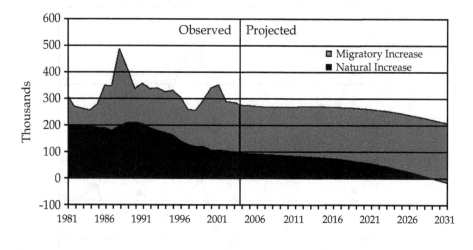

Source: Statistics Canada. 2007c. "Observed (1981–2004) and Projected (2005–2056) Natural and Migratory Increase in Canada According to Scenario 3 (Medium Growth)." Ottawa: Statistics Canada.

growth, despite considerable continuing immigration. Figure 10.4 shows the contributions of natural population increase (births less deaths) and net international migration (in-migrants less out-migrants) to population growth up to 2005 and then, in a medium-growth projection, up to 2031. It also shows how natural increase and international migration are projected to contribute to future population growth under these medium-growth set of assumptions — namely, that fertility, mortality, and net international migration levels remain similar to those found in Canada in the early years of the 21st century. In this scenario, sometime around 2029 deaths are projected to exceed births so that natural increase will be negative. International migration, which is also assumed to remain at levels similar to those in the early 2000s, will maintain positive population growth, but at a declining rate. Overall population growth will continue to be slower and slower as time passes.

It is possible to vary the assumption on immigration levels to produce different future population growth projections. If current levels of Canadian fertility continue, the contribution of natural increase to Canadian population growth will fall over the near future to zero. At that point, international migration will be the sole source of population growth. Models of when this might happen vary according to their assumptions. Three of six different Statistics Canada projections of total population growth in Canada through to the year 2056 are shown in Figure 10.5. The middle assumption, Scenario 3, assumes that levels of fertility and international migration noted for the period 2000–2005 will continue into the future. Under this scenario, the Canadian population will peak at a figure near 42 million around the year 2056. Subsequently, the Canadian population will tend to grow at an increasingly slow rate. This may be contrasted with the low growth projection in Scenario 1: Here, the main change in assumptions is that fertility will decline further toward a Total Fertility Rate of 1.3; this very low fertility has been evident throughout many parts of Europe since the end of the 20th century. Scenario 6, involving contrasting assumptions, shows that with a return to higher fertility, at the level of replacement, and higher levels of net international migration, Canada's population will continue to grow much as it has since 1981.

How many immigrants would have to be admitted to Canada to prevent population decline from setting in due to current below-replacement levels of fertility? Ryder (1997) refers to this number as the "replacement migration" figure: It is the level of immigration required to achieve the same ultimate population size

as would be achieved if fertility were at a replacement level or a zero population growth level. Using 1990s data, Ryder estimated that Canada would need a *net international migration* figure of 167,225 per year to stabilize its population size. The net figure is the total immigration less the total emigration. Given that Canada experiences the loss of about 50,000 individuals a year through emigration of native-born people and previous immigrants, Ryder's estimate suggests that Canada would need an immigration of around 215,000 per year to stabilize its population size. Beaujot (2003: 53–55) has re-estimated this number using more recent data. He concludes that an annual immigration "slightly above 225,000 would prevent population decline in the foreseeable future" (p. 55).

The preceding analysis leads to the following conclusions. First, it is evident

Figure 10.5: Population Observed (1981–2005) and Projected (2006–2056) According to Three Scenarios, Canada

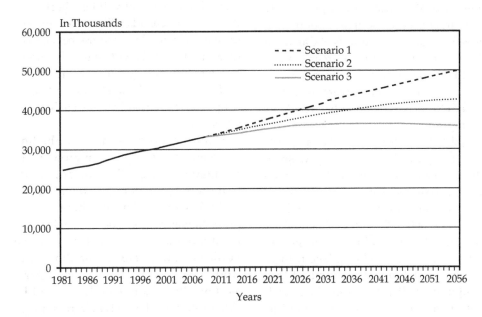

Source: Statistics Canada, 2007b. "Observed (1981–2005) and Projected (2006–2056) Population According to Three Scenarios." Ottawa: Statistics Canada. Retrieved 26 March 2009.

that long-term fertility decline is the key determinant of the trend to slower population growth in Canada. Second, the Canadian state has a long-standing positive attitude to population growth as one of various strategies to solve relative labour shortages and to promote economic development and prosperity. Third, as natural population growth has not recently provided the numbers of workers desired by the state and influential employers, international migration has been the main tool of Canadian population policy. Fourth, immigration has recently provided as much a contribution to population growth as has natural increase. Under current projections, immigration will become more important than natural increase. Yet population growth will gradually slow, perhaps to the level of replacement (no growth or decline) if immigration levels remain somewhat above 225,000 per year, a figure that is within the range of inflows from the early 1990s to the present. Fifth, and finally, international migration is a potentially fickle and uncertain source of population growth as shown by periods of Canadian history when international circumstances closed down immigration flows or when alternative destinations were attractive enough to encourage Canadian residents to emigrate.

Taking these points together suggests that the Canadian state may wish to address labour force gaps and population aging with supplementary policies that go beyond immigration. In fact, as we have previously noted, Canadian state policies have directly and indirectly supported a range of policies to bring labour force supply and labour force demand into configurations that fit within the hoped-for and imagined future of the nation. The next section examines some of the challenges and goals addressed by these state strategies.

Responding to Future Challenges

Concerns about slower and possibly negative future population growth in Canada fall into three areas. One is at the geopolitical level. It is based on the worry that slower population growth and a smaller total population will marginalize Canada in world affairs. The darker view is that Canada, with a smaller population, could become a weak player in global trade, finance, and security or peacekeeping arrangements. It would be more dependent on major powers and less in control of its own destiny.

A second concern is with respect to future labour shortages. The worry is that the economy will suffer if business investors discover that shortages of workers arising from slower population growth make it difficult for them to set up new production facilities and instead decide to invest elsewhere. Under this unhappy scenario, investment will fall short of its potential and Canada will have less income growth than would otherwise be the case. Over time, Canada will tend to become a less wealthy and less important nation, falling in international stature and being dropped from organizations such as the G8 nations.

A third concern is based on the link between slower population growth and population aging. With slower population growth, the population will necessarily become older and there will be proportionally fewer young people. This, in turn, could lead to various unwelcome burdens on the state and on those who work and pay taxes. The negative scenario assumes that many elderly will not be able to support themselves in retirement; that their health care and social support must be paid for in large part by those in the working ages (who will decline as a proportion of the total population as the elderly population grows); and that there may be shortages of health care and social service workers.

The most unwelcome future scenario would combine all of the above worries. In the most dismal case, labour shortages would reduce business investment and the generation of new, better-paid jobs just when a relatively small working-age population will need increased incomes to support the high costs of maintaining an elderly population. Canada would be a less powerful nation and have more difficulty generating made-at-home solutions that would maximize national welfare. Such extremely negative future scenarios have been referred to by Gee (2000) as "Voodoo Demographics": The scenarios are founded on questionable and distorted assumptions, seemingly with the intention of creating great fear of a disastrous future. This is not to say that a slower population growth and possible population decline will not generate a range of significant challenges for social and economic planning. Yet, the assumptions regarding the problems we face and what can be done about them need to be assessed more accurately, then put into more realistic plans to bring about solutions. From this perspective, the future appears uncertain and challenging, but not necessarily gloomy.

The geopolitical concerns in the gloomy scenario above are exaggerated, distorted, and out of context. Canada is a medium nation in terms of population size. As such it has a very small share of the world's population. This share is about one-half of 1 percent, a proportion that has held constant from 1950 to the present and which is projected to hold constant until 2050 (Table 10.4). Without doubt, Canada's current status and autonomy in the international system depends not on its population size, but on the strengths of its social, economic, and political institutions. Like other nations, the main source of international influence and autonomy arises from a skilled workforce; high levels of capitalization for workers; transparent and efficient government; and agreements on trade, security, and human rights negotiated with other like-minded nations, both large and small.

Canada has the smallest population of the current G8 nations, the group of industrially advanced countries that meet to coordinate international economic, security, and other policies (Table 10.4). Very small yet wealthy industrialized nations, such as Sweden and Finland (and many others), have considerable autonomy and world leadership even if they are not part of the G8 association. Sweden and Finland each have only about one-tenth of 1 percent of the world's population. Moreover, the G8 countries taken together are home to an increasingly smaller proportion of the world's population. In 1950 about 22 percent of the world's population lived in these countries, while by 2050 it is projected that approximately 10 percent will live there (less than one-half of the current proportion). In sum, while population size is relevant to national power and autonomy, it is not the only factor nor even the most important factor. The most powerful countries and economic blocs in the world, such as the United States and the European Union, are both populous and wealthy, while very large and poor countries with fast-growing economies, such as China and India, are soon to join the club of dominant geopolitical players. Yet, nations with small populations can garner and retain power and autonomy through advanced social-economic development and participating in international trade and security accords.

Worries about labour shortages and aging in the gloomy scenarios outlined above are also based on poorly calibrated and often erroneous assumptions. Some developed nations with particularly low

Table 10.4: Population of the World and Selected Countries

	Population (in Millions)			% Growth		% Distribution		
	1950	2000	2050	1950–2000	2000–2050	1950	2000	2050
World	2,595	6,124	9,191	136.0	50.1	100.0	100.0	100.0
MDCs	813	1,215	1,245	49.4	2.5	31.3	19.8	13.5
LDCs	1,721	4,929	7,946	186.4	61.2	66.3	80.5	86.5
Two Largest LDCs								
China	554	1,269	1,408	129.1	11.0	21.3	20.7	15.3
India	371	1,046	1,658	181.9	58.5	14.3	17.1	18.0
G8 Countries	561	844	917	50.4	8.6	21.6	13.8	10.0
Canada	13	30	42	130.8	40.0	0.5	0.5	0.5
France	41	59	68	43.9	15.3	1.6	1.0	0.7
Germany	68	82	74	20.6	-9.8	2.6	1.3	0.8
Italy	47	57	54	21.3	-5.3	1.8	0.9	0.6
Japan	83	127	102	53.0	-19.7	3.2	2.1	1.1
Russia	102	147	107	44.1	-27.2	3.9	2.4	1.2
United Kingdom	50	58	68	16.0	17.2	1.9	0.9	0.7
United States	157	284	402	80.9	41.5	6.1	4.6	4.4
Selected Other MDCs								
Sweden	7	9	10	28.6	11.1	0.3	0.1	0.1
Finland	4	5	5	25.0	0.0	0.2	0.1	0.1

Source: UNPD. 2008. *World Population Prospects: The 2008 Revision Population Data Base.* New York: United Nations Population Division. Retrieved 26 March 2009. [http://esa.un.org/unpp/index.asp]

fertility, such as Japan and Italy, are currently moving into a fairly steep trajectory of negative population growth and aging. Others with higher levels of fertility, such as the United States, have relatively high levels of population growth and a slower shift to aging. Canada falls between these extremes.

Corresponding to the anticipated gradual slowing of the Canadian population, future shifts in the age composition are also projected to be relatively moderate. Figure 10.6 shows the proportions (in percent) of the Canadian population in three broad age groups (0–14; 15–64, and 65 plus) from 1950 to 2050, with the projection to the future based on middle-range assumptions about fertility and international migration. The projection also points to the anticipated rise in the proportion aged 65 and over, which is gradual over time, starting around 1980 then accelerating after 2010. Similarly the proportion in the main working ages (15–64 years of age) begins to decline from a high of around 70 percent in 2010–2015 to less than 60 percent of the total in 2050. These are important changes, but they are relatively modest compared to those that will take place in other countries where fertility has fallen to much lower levels and aging is more extreme.

The projected rise in the proportion of Canadian residents who are elderly may also be viewed as a projected fall in the proportion of those in the main working ages. The proportion of a population aged 15–64 (a rough measure of working-age population) is dependent on the proportion of those who are young (under age 15), as well as the proportion of those who are over age 64. In addition, the proportion who are young and the proportion who are older tend to be mirror images of each other (see Figure 10.7). This observation leads to a more complex and interesting set of conclusions. Firstly, a new, serious, and unprecedented challenge of aging is emerging in Canada. According to the projection in Figure 10.7, the proportion over 64 years of age in Canada will roughly double between 2005 and 2050. Secondly, however, the proportion of working-age individuals will remain fairly constant due to the low proportion of children. If one thinks of children and the elderly as together comprising the dependent (largely non-working) population, then the ratio of dependants to workers will not change much over the period in the projection.

The total dependency ratio in Canada was high (about .7 dependants per working-aged person) in the 1960s due to the postwar baby boom (Figure 10.7). It then fell to about .5 around 1980 and is expected to remain at this low level until around 2020. Then it is expected to rise back up to .7 again by 2050. Going back to a dependency ratio that Canada was able to cope with in the 1960s will require effort, but should not be overwhelming. In the 1960s the need was to build more schools, colleges, and universities, while by 2050 there will be a need to build retirement housing, elderly-friendly transport, and care facilities that will respond to more elderly people with specific needs. A very specific and important difference is that the elderly require more health care services than the young, and that this can be particularly expensive for them and for public health care systems. This is a huge issue requiring an examination of diverse complex dimensions. It is addressed in small part in the following section on policy options with regard to the international mobility of medical and health care workers.

Figure 10.6: Percentage of Canadian Population in Selected Age Groups, 1950–2050

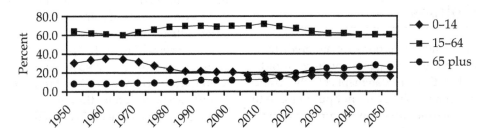

Source: The author, using data from: UNPD. 2007. *World Population Prospects: The 2008 Revision Population Data Base.* New York: United Nations Population Division. Retrieved 26 March 2009 [http://esa.un.org/unpp/index.asp]

Figure 10.7: Elderly Dependency Ratio and Total Dependency Ratio, Canada, 1950–2050

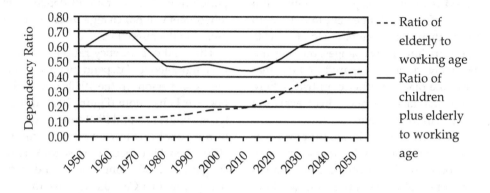

Source: The author, using data from UNPD. 2008. *World Population Prospects: The 2008 Revision Population Data Base.* New York: United Nations Population Division. Retrieved 26 March 2009 [http://esa.un.org/unpp/index.asp]

Many other assumptions need to be questioned in assessing the challenges of slower population growth and aging. As others have argued, it is not correct to assume that the elderly are necessarily poor and dependent. Many individuals over age 65 have accumulated savings, generate revenues from pensions and investments, pay significant taxes (covering their own social service costs), and look after themselves in all respects well into their advanced years (see various papers on this in Gee and Gutman 2000).

Part 4: Future Policy Options

Population projections are not predictions of what will happen as history unfolds; rather, they are statements of what could happen if policies are not put in place to change the direction of current trends. Two population-focused solutions have been proposed to address the challenges of slower population growth and aging. The first is to encourage higher fertility. The sec-

ond is to increase immigration levels in the hope that immigrants will replace or fill in for the shortage of workers brought about by low fertility. The first of these may be difficult to implement, while the second has been shown to have very weak prospects. As a result, a third option may be far more promising: It is to adjust to the population trends in ways that will promote better living conditions for all Canadians in the context of global economic transformations and show future population growth. However, all the adjustment options involve costs and benefits that are unequally distributed. Options will be more palatable if they can be implemented in ways to minimize the often extreme costs of some options compared with others.

More babies? Several countries have adopted policies to increase fertility or keep it from declining further. From 1966 to 1989, Romania, under the authoritarian Ceauscescu government, instituted coercive and punitive policies to restrict contraceptive use and prohibit abortion under all circumstances. These ethically unacceptable policies raised birth rates from 14 to

27 per 1,000, but at a high cost to parents, children, and society, evident, for example, in the high number of maternal deaths resulting from botched illegal abortions (Serbanescu et al. 1995). In 1987 Singapore instituted positive-incentive policies in the form of more subsidized child-care facilities and tax incentives for working mothers to increase fertility from two children or fewer per family to three children per family. These measures improved the well-being of mothers and their children, but the overall impact on fertility was very limited. Some women who had postponed child-bearing had children when the new measures were adopted, leading to an immediate but short-term increase in birth rates. This upward blip in child-bearing soon disappeared and birth rates returned to their previous levels (Saywell 2003). Similar policies have been adopted in Quebec, leading to a similar conclusion there (see Box 10.2). European nations such as France have very strong family-support policies that may play some role in preventing fertility from falling from low to very low levels (Bergman 1996). All mothers in France have access to nursery schools; single mothers get special monthly allowances. While France still has a birth rate slightly below replacement, its fertility level (a total fertility rate around 1.9) is higher than most other countries in Europe. In sum, what works in one country may not work in another. Measures to increase fertility that are ethically acceptable, affordable, and effective, at least to some degree in the Canadian context, are not known, but they could be discovered.

More immigrants? Policies to increase immigration levels above those currently in place in Canada would necessarily have to solve many problems. Would Canada find enough of the skilled or other immigrants to achieve these new immigration levels? After all, the kinds of highly educated immigrants that Canada prefers

are also sought by other countries. Would Canadian immigration policy-makers consider inviting immigrants with lower levels of schooling and work skills? If so, will the immigrants be given schooling and job training in Canada? Will more temporary workers be invited and given the option to become permanent residents? Would the Canadian public be prepared to accept a significant rise in immigration? Answers to these questions require a crystal ball: They cannot be answered until the effects of low fertility and aging on society are more pronounced and Canadians begin to seek ways to address these issues.

Even if all the above questions could be answered positively and immigration levels were to double, for example, Canada would still face a gradual slowing in population growth, eventually a shift to declining population size and aging. The main benefits of the doubling of immigration would be a postponement of the moment when population size will begin to slow or decline. This conclusion may seem counterintuitive, but it is based on clear modelling for Canada (Beaujot 2003) and for other countries (McDonald and Kippen 2001; UNPD 2000). The reasoning is straightforward. Individuals who apply and are accepted as immigrants are mostly well-educated young adults from towns and cities in their countries of origin who, even if they come from countries with higher fertility, have fewer children over their lifetimes. In other words, immigrants to Canada have below-replacement fertility and replicate the existing age structure of Canadian society. Their presence adds temporarily (until they die) to the number of people in Canada, but their reproduction rates are low and will eventually not stop the trend toward population decline due to below-replacement fertility.

We may conclude that the main benefit arising from immigration comes from the skills that immigrants bring to the

Box 10.2: Quebec's Baby Bonus Scheme, 1988–1997

Quebec had higher birth rates than found overall in Canada until 1960. However, when birth rates in Canada overall fell dramatically from 1966 to 1976, those in Quebec fell more quickly and to lower levels than those found across the nation. Between the 1950s and 1988, Quebec's total fertility rate fell from 3.7 lifetime children per woman to 1.4, the lowest rate in Canada. Quebec Finance Minister Gérard-D. Lévesque said, "The fall in birth rates is a sign of a people in decline." In response, Quebec introduced a baby bonus called the Allowance for Newborn Children (ANC). It was explicitly a cash bonus program for having children. From 1988 to 1997, parents received $500 for the birth of a first child, $1,000 for the second, and $8,000 for the third and subsequent children.

Did the ANC increase the number of children born? The answer is both *yes* and *no*. It clearly led to an increase in first births, but then this increase reached a plateau, suggesting that the main effect had been to encourage couples to have their first child sooner than they otherwise might have. The ANC had some short-term impact in increasing very slightly second and third births. Yet, when these changes are viewed as longer term trends, it is harder to determine with any certainty how much impact the ANC had. The main effect seems to have been in the timing of births, with couples having children sooner than they might otherwise have had them, but not having more in total or at least not having many more.

The birth-timing issue may be observed in the figure below. Quebec's birth rate fell very low in the mid-1980s, such that some bounce back later may have been expected in any case. The bounce back was pronounced. How much of this was due to factors other than the ANC and how much due to the ANC? The best guess is that the bounce back was faster because of the ANC, but beyond that it is hard to say.

Total Fertility Rates, Quebec and the Rest of Canada, 1980–1997

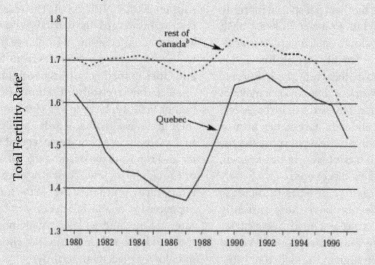

[a] For the definition of total fertility rate, see the text.
[b] The rest of Canada here excludes both Quebec and Newfoundland; the latter is excluded because data are not available for all years.

Milligan (2002) estimates that the ANC may have generated an additional 93,000 births in Quebec during the period 1989–1996. Whether these births would have occurred later is less clear. Milligan also notes that if the ANC did generate these additional births, then each additional child cost the provincial government about $15,000. The Quebec government had already concluded in 1997 that the ANC program was a failure and cancelled the program.

The debate over incentives continues in Quebec and Canada. The 2006 federal budget brought in a child-care allowance of $1,200 per child under age six for daycare whether or not the child is in a formal daycare. Over a period of five years, each child would receive $6,000. Is this a birth incentive program? Or is it, as most observers understood, simply a subsidy for families with one stay-at-home parent? Under Quebec's old ANC plan, a family with three children would receive a total of $9,500 in incentives. Under the new federal incentive, a family with three children could ultimately collect $18,000. It is too early to assess whether that will raise fertility. The experience in various places suggests it could do so, but if so, it might be only a short-term "blip" without longer term impacts, despite its costs.

Sources: Parent, Daniel, and Ling Wang. 2002. *Tax Incentives and Fertility in Canada: Permanent vs. Transitory Effects.* CIRANO Working Papers. Montreal: McGill University; Milligan, Kevin. 2002. *Quebec's Baby Bonus: Can Public Policy Raise Fertility?* Toronto: C.D. Howe Institute.

Canadian economy and their related role in filling gaps in the labour market. Immigration is also valuable for the role it plays in family reunification and refugee asylum. In addition, immigration leads to a postponement of population decline. However, immigration does not reverse the trend toward population aging, although it can postpone population decline.

Adapt to population aging and decline? The challenge of how to solve problems of relative labour force shortages is not new. Nation-states have been working to address these problems over their entire histories. The following four solutions do not require a return to positive population growth.

1. *Exporting jobs:* Instead of importing labour, additional workers can be found by employing them in their home countries. In the past, this mechanism was often applied through force and coercion, as when powerful nations colonized weaker ones and set up plantations or mines that either used slave labour or relied on state-enforced racism to limit local workers to low-paid, dangerous, and dirty jobs. While neo-colonial practices that mimic these old strategies are still, unfortunately, found in very poor countries in the contemporary world, the usual ways of utilizing the labour of foreign workers are now based on incentives and voluntary participation. Typically corporations in a wealthy nation set up a new production facility in a lower-wage nation and invite local workers to take on jobs at wages equal to, and at times higher than, what they would earn in other firms. Unfortunately, local wages are often very poor. In addition, local workplaces are frequently "sweat shops" with bad working conditions that increase risks of injury and illness. However, the goods produced by these workers are then exported throughout the world, with a large proportion going to the wealthy nations, which consume most of the trade goods. The sales contribute to the profits of the international corporation.

Japan was a leading pioneer in the job-export strategy, setting up Japanese-owned manufacturing plants throughout Southeast Asia. Other wealthy nations have followed suit and manufacturing of this kind has spread to China, India, Latin America, the Caribbean, and elsewhere. In the case of Japan, the policy of exporting jobs was linked to a reluctance to bring in large numbers of foreign workers as immigrants to that country (Simmons 1999b: 26). However, countries such as Australia, Canada, and the United States promote a combination of immigration and foreign trade promotion that encourages job exports.

2. *Increase productivity:* Policies that support job training, new technologies, and better economic infrastructure can enable each new worker to produce more than before. Today robots and just-in-time production techniques are more efficient than labour-intensive manufacturing. A highly efficient transportation system (highways, railways, canals, ports, etc.) and other economic infrastructure, such as major hydroelectric and other power plants, will also lower costs. In this way, the "dead hand" of an earlier generation of workers who built the roads and hydroelectric dams continues to assist contemporary workers and make them more productive. All nations around the world, both developed and less developed, are seeking to increase productivity through building their infrastructure, and through increasing the skills of their managers and workers.

3. *Exploit underutilized labour pools:* Certain kinds of work cannot be readily exported. This is particularly the case for service-sector work, such as preparing meals in restaurants, cleaning and maintenance of buildings and streets, sales clerking in stores, providing immediate health care services (nursing, medical treatment), in-class teaching, providing social work services, and so on. When the need for workers in these sectors cannot be met through natural increase, immigration,

or migrant workers, one alternative is to employ underutilized local workers.

Much of the enormous expansion of service-sector employment in Canada and other more developed countries in the second half of the 20th century was met by encouraging more women to enter the workforce (see Li 1996: Chapter 3, for an analysis of the Canadian case). Norms and practices that kept women at home raising children were challenged and overturned. Women became an increasingly large part of the total labour force. They were concentrated particularly in service jobs, but could be found in all sectors. Women no longer constitute an underutilized labour pool in Canada. Retired workers in good health constitute one of the few remaining pools of labour.

Some nations facing population decline are now contemplating legislation to increase the age of retirement in order to resolve three problems. The first problem is a shortage of pension funds to support the large number of baby boomers expected to retire in the near future. The second problem is the rising proportion of retirees to workers as the population gets older due to slowed population growth. The third problem is the fact that training programs for certain professions, such as medical doctors and university professors, have not kept pace with the anticipated shortfall of professionals in these areas if large numbers retire at age 65 or earlier. The logic of addressing pension-fund shortfalls through relaxed retirement rules may become particularly appealing as people continue to live longer after age 65. If workers are employed for a year or two (or more) past age 65, they can accumulate more pension funds; after retirement, they will have a shorter period from retirement to death, hence they will be better off in retirement both because they have saved more and because they will be dependent on these savings for a shorter period. Various forces are pushing more provinces in Canada to abandon compulsory retirement at age 65. In 2006, the Province of Ontario followed the lead of most other provinces (Alberta, British Columbia, Manitoba, Newfoundland and Labrador, Prince Edward Island, and Saskatchewan) in adopting legislation that removed employers' right to require retirement at age 65, except when bona fide reasons required this in certain occupations. The official reason was to promote workers' rights to choose when to retire under the Canadian Human Rights Act (HRSDC 2009). However, this may not have been the only reason. Various sectors, such as universities and colleges, had encouraged this step on the grounds that impending retirements of professional staff were so large in number that the retirees could not be readily replaced in a short time by younger individuals since not enough fully trained younger professionals were available, and professional training takes several years.

4. *Expand migrant worker programs:* Until the post-Second World War period, Canada relied on immigrants for virtually all labour needs that could not be met by native-born workers. Jobs that we now associate with migrant workers, such as live-in caregiver jobs (for nannies, etc.) were done in the early 1900s by immigrant women (Silvera 1989: 8). In 1955 Canada established the Domestic Scheme to recruit live-in caregivers from the Caribbean. These women were given temporary authorizations to work in Canada. They were not eligible for immigration. Each work permit or visa was for a specific job for a specific period. This provided the model for subsequent development of temporary worker programs in Canada. Parliament debated expanding the recruitment of migrant workers between 1969 and 1973, and then subsequently established the Non-Immigrant Employment Authorization

Program (NIEAP) for this purpose and to admit other categories of foreigners, such as entertainers, artists, and professional sports players (Sharma 2006). Major temporary worker programs soon developed. The best-known current programs are the Live-in Caregivers Program, which recruits child-care workers and home helpers, and the Seasonal Agricultural Workers Program (SAWP), which organizes the entry of farm workers from Mexico and the Caribbean for planting, harvesting, and packing Canadian crops. Other programs have been added over time. In the 1990s, the government added provisions to allow the entry of highly skilled computer and software technicians to meet a rocketing demand for such workers at that time. In 2006 immigration officials added a special program to allow firms in Western Canada to recruit migrant workers with various skills to solve acute labour shortages associated with the commodities export boom taking place at the time (CIC 2006b).

Migrant worker programs have been expanding rapidly in Canada over the recent past. The upward trend in the number of foreign workers and their families (who together constitute "temporary residents") entering Canada by year is shown in Figure 10.8. These figures are somewhat less than the total number of foreign workers resident in Canada in a given year because many visa workers stay for longer than one year. However, the entry figures provide a strong measure of change over time. This number increased from around 60,000 in 1983 to around 150,000 in 2007; this is nearly a threefold jump.

Inflows vary with economic conditions, with downturns following the recession of 1989–1992 and again with the short downturn in 2001. The very sharp upward turn between 2003 and 2007 reflects, among other things, the combined booms in commodity-export production and housing construction in that period. If these conditions generated greater inflows of migrant workers, then the sharp downturn in both commodity exports and housing construction starting in 2008 and extending beyond should also lead to a decline in the inflows of migrant workers. In fact, this is the fundamental logic of temporary migrant workers: The migrant workers come to fill labour gaps when required; then they return to their home countries when the jobs end; and finally, their contracts are not renewed in times of economic downturn. In this way, they do not contribute to unemployment in Canada. Their problem of finding a new job is transferred outside Canada to their home country. Migrant labour policies have historically been set up to serve the interests of wealthy nations and firms and to ignore the interests of the migrant workers, their families, and their home communities. Unfortunately, this remains so today, despite the efforts of many developing countries to get wealthy nations to sign the International Convention on Migrant Rights. To date, no wealthy nation has signed this agreement, although 35 developing countries have done so (Simmons 2008: 77; see also Piper 2008).

It is noteworthy that the low point in foreign worker inflows in the most recent recession shown in Figure 10.8 is higher than the low point for the previous recessions. Straight lines drawn to show trends over time in the troughs and high points of the data in Figure 10.8 suggests that Canada is becoming increasingly reliant on migrant workers. The numbers entering are still lower than the number of immigrants entering, but then immigrants include children, so that in fact the differences between the numbers are not that great. That is, the trough for the 2000–2003 recession is higher than the early trough for the recession in 1989–1995. These are only two time points. Conclusions may be premature, yet the data suggest that

Canada is becoming increasingly reliant on migrant workers. Not only are numbers steadily rising, but migrant workers are taking up an ever wider range of jobs in Canada. Table 10.5 shows the jobs taken up in Alberta by foreign workers on temporary work permits in 2005. The data show that live-in caregivers and agricultural workers are the main fields for migrant workers, yet professional business services to management is also a growing field, while foreign worker visas are also extended to teaching and research assistants, professors, truck drivers, and mechanical engineers, among others.

The temporary employment authorization for live-in caregivers and migrant agricultural workers has generated much criticism because the workers employed in these jobs are vulnerable to exploitation, racialization, and forms of exclusion that stand at odds with the rights granted to Canadian citizens. Sharma (2006: 6) says that these forms of contracting fit demands of globalized production very well because they generate "a 'just-in-time,' unfree, migrant workforce that conforms to employers' demands for more flexible cheaper, and more vulnerable workers." Bakan and Stasiulis (1997) argue that Canadian treatment of such workers violates international labour and human rights standards. Basok (2002b) and Binford (2004) are particularly critical of the programs that place Mexican workers in greenhouse tomato-production facilities. The workers are contracted to specific employers and, "if they attempt to quit, abandon the work site without permission, or are dismissed, they are subject to immediate deportation; permanent blacklisting from the program generally follows (Binford 2004: 291). Basok (2002: cover) observes that Mexicans are essential for the survival of many agricultural producers because they "are always available for work, even on holidays and weekends,

Table 10.5: Alberta Foreign Worker Flows, Top Occupations, 2005

Occupation	Number
Live-in caregivers	916
Agricultural workers	563
Professional business services to management	469
Post-secondary teaching and research assistants	263
Labourers in food, processing	236
University professors	168
Truck drivers	137
Insulators	127
Mechanical engineers	125
Computer systems analysts	119
Total—Top 10	3,123
Total—Other and unspecified occupations	6,815
Total	9,938

Source: CIC. 2006. *The Monitor: Foreign Worker Overview.* Ottawa: Citizenship and Immigration Canada.

Figure 10.8: Total Entries of Temporary Residents by Yearly Status, 1983–2007

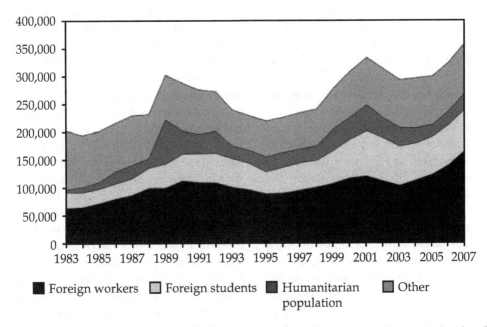

Source: CIC. 2007. "Facts and Figures 2007. Immigration Overview: Permanent and Temporary Residents" (p. 59). Ottawa: Citizenship and Immigration Canada.

or when exhausted, sick or injured." Satzewich (2007: 267) argues that Mexicans were added to the original Caribbean Seasonal Agricultural Workers Program in 1974 in part because the state officials were concerned that employers were becoming reluctant to accept workers from the Eastern Caribbean because these workers were becoming more assertive in claiming rights and resisting the work schedules demanded of them in Canada, while the Mexicans were viewed as more compliant. Similar concerns about racialization and compliance have been raised with respect to the fact that women from the Philippines have become dominant among live-in caregivers. Figures 10.9 and 10.10 show the near total reliance of the live-in-caregiver program on Philippine women and the rising proportion of Mexicans among migrant farm workers.

The problems faced by migrant farm workers in Canada are increasingly subject to public concerns as the workers develop links to Canadian human rights groups, labour organizations, and local community organizations. Raper and Preibisch (2007) highlight this issue. Mr. Raper was previously Canadian coordinator for the United Farm Workers of America. He explains how in the context of this work, he began, with others, to document the conditions of the farm workers and to educate others. Eventually other large unions, such as Auto and Steel, and the Canadian Labour Congress provided small grants for this work, then increasingly greater support over time, leading to the establishment of migrant farm worker support centres in various places across Canada with links to similar support centres in the United States. Barndt (2002: 237–248) and Jeremic (2007) draw attention to broader supports for migrant workers' rights within larger networks of social activists concerned with issues of food quality, environmental protection, pesticide use, and the corporate

agenda of current trade agreements. These efforts point to the constant pressure on the state. The government is pushed to improve the working conditions and labour protections for migrant workers, while at the same time it faces counter-pressures from farmers and agricultural corporations. As previously noted, by 2005 no wealthy nation, Canada included, had yet signed the 2003 International Convention of Migrant Rights, although 35 low- and middle-income nations had done so (Simmons 2008: 77). Kelly (2007: 228–230) notes that the efforts of live-in caregivers in Canada to organize and promote their rights as workers have received mixed support from the Filipino community in Canada because this community views the caregiver workers' issue as a sectorial labour question and not a Filipino issue, even though the vast majority of caregiver workers in Canada are Filipinas. As a result, efforts to support the rights and working conditions of Filipina caregiver workers are undertaken by "a very small group of committed activists, often with support from academics and non-Filipino human rights and church-based groups" (Kelly 2007: 229).

The North-South Institute (2006: 16) recently expressed a concern that the global trend in food production limits "the capacity of Canadian producers to carry higher labour costs" such that it "is likely that real wages paid to CSAWP workers will continue to decline as they have done over the past decade." The institute also notes that over the period 2003–2006, Quebec initiated a program to bring in Guatemalan farm workers while reducing the number of Mexican and Caribbean farm workers. The Guatemalan farm workers have to pay for their own accommodation. They can stay for up to 12 months and are allowed to move from one job to another. There is less government supervision of the workers, hence "fewer safeguards against exploitation" (North-South Institute 2006: 16).

Figure 10.9: Foreign Worker Flows, Live-in Caregiver Program, 1996–2005

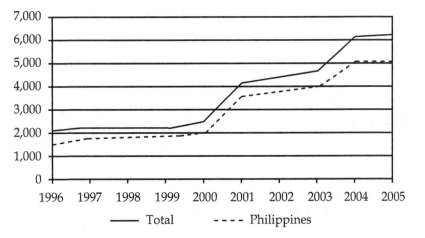

Source: CIC. 2005. "Facts and Figures 2005." Chart 8. Ottawa: Citizenship and Immigration Canada.

Figure 10.10: Foreign Worker Flows, Seasonal Agricultural Workers Program, 1996–2005

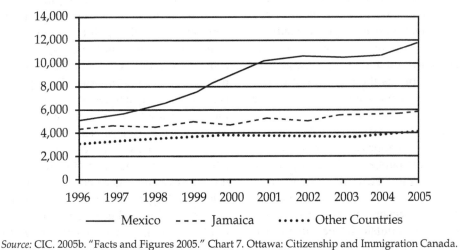

Source: CIC. 2005b. "Facts and Figures 2005." Chart 7. Ottawa: Citizenship and Immigration Canada.

In sum, the Canadian state is already turning more to migrant worker and foreign worker authorizations for addressing a diverse set of labour force issues. Programs for foreign workers are becoming diversified, hence covering more occupations at all levels, including engineers and management consultants, but also truck drivers and food-processing workers in addition to the well-known programs for agricultural labourers and live-in caregivers. Those with high occupational skills are assumed to have more options and to be well treated by their employers. Those in the least-skilled jobs are often locked into contracts under very unfavourable terms. If the state plans to continue to expand the low-skill programs, it will need to pay increasing attention to the rights and wages of the workers, even if this involves opposition from producers.

Discussion and Conclusions

We may conclude that dark scenarios about the impact of slower population growth and even population decline on Canada seem overly pessimistic. They are based on incomplete and narrow assessments of the nature of the challenges and solutions to them. A more careful assessment would lead to the conclusion that the challenges of a slow growing and much older population are indeed serious, but they are amenable to known solutions. In addition, a broader assessment would clarify that the key issue is not population size or aging considered narrowly, but rather how to increase productivity and address specific gaps in labour supply as the population grows more slowly and becomes older. Since various options to achieve these goals are open, the challenges can be met through a combination of approaches. From a political-economic perspective, the key future question is the distribution of costs and benefits of different approaches. From a political-only viewpoint, this boils down to the outcome of public debate and government decision making. Addressing slower population growth and aging will require that new costs be covered by someone, and this will necessarily involve tough decisions.

Future labour force challenges can be through the following mechanisms: raising the birth rate, increasing immigration, exporting jobs, raising productivity, making greater use of underutilized labour

pools, and relying more heavily on temporary migrant labour. These mechanisms are not usually adopted on a one-by-one or either/or basis. Most often states adopt them in some combination. Canada, for example, has policies that involve five of the above six mechanisms (all except raising the birth rate). Quebec has adopted all six.

The strategies do not always reinforce one another. In some cases, one approach may undermine another. For example, the schooling and employment of women solves immediate relative labour shortages, while at the same time it promotes lower fertility, slower natural population growth, and more population aging. Another example is when the use of migrant labour undermines jobs available for immigrants.

Each of the abovementioned strategies generates costs and benefits that are unequally distributed (see Figure 10.1). As a result, many of the options tend to generate conflicting points of view, and political decisions on which options to choose may reflect which point of view has the most powerful supporters. Perhaps the least conflict is generated by the option of increasing productivity since a growing economy tends to benefit large segments of the population. Even those who lose their jobs through technological advances may not lose over a longer period if they are able to undergoing retraining. In Canada, at least until now, keeping immigration relatively high also seems attractive to government, state officials, and a majority of citizens, even though evidence from the recent past suggests that highly skilled immigrants are paying a substantial cost for this in the form of low earnings over many years. Greater use is being made of underutilized labour pools, particularly by policies that eliminate compulsory retirement because this too generates few losers. The most controversial path is that of expanding migrant worker programs, because these programs raise so many troubling questions about migrant rights, social justice, and the values that underlie the nation.

From the above it is clear that international migration is likely to remain one of Canada's key tools in responding to the challenges of slower population growth and aging. This is not because international migration will reverse aging—as we have shown, this is not the case. Rather it is because international migration potentially has other benefits with regard to raising Canadian productivity. Highly skilled immigrants and their children can help Canada develop a more sophisticated and competitive knowledge economy. Immigration as a whole can postpone population decline, perhaps indefinitely, and can reinforce the size and potential efficiency of the Canadian economy. Migrant workers can fill important short-term gaps at various skill levels in the Canadian economy. Each of these hoped-for migration-specific outcomes will depend on the success of many other policies and reforms that are required for an overall package of successful nation building. The next chapter, covering conclusions to the book, examines Canada's current and future international migration policies from the critical perspective and findings of the book as a whole.

CHAPTER 11
Policy Options: Where Are We Headed?

Introduction

Is Canadian immigration about to shift directions? What are the pressures for change, and will these forces be able to overcome others that support the status quo? This chapter examines the preceding questions based on the evidence reviewed in this book and some additional observations on how immigration and migrant worker policies are formed in Canada. Particular attention is given to the pressures that operate to bring about policy change, as well as those that serve to inhibit such change. The main argument is that current gaps between Canada's immigration objectives and outcomes are serious and risk becoming more serious still, given trends in various factors that shape immigration outcomes. The gaps include those related to economic outcomes, such as the low earnings of immigrants, and those related to ethnocultural outcomes, such as the potentially marginalizing residential patterns and weak job-related social capital of immigrant communities.

The chapter begins with a brief review of the contemporary context of Canadian immigration policies and how what Canada seeks through immigration is embedded in the nation's evolving position in the international system. It then proceeds to reflect on how the perspectives and research findings in this book help us to understand whether the state will or will not respond with new strategies to address many of the gaps between policy goals and outcomes that have been observed. The review points to pressures both for and against policy change, and how the relative power of different actors affects the likelihood of policy reforms. The chapter ends by discussing emerging trends, their likely impacts, and the challenges they will create for policy development.

The Current Policy Context

The perspectives and evidence examined in this book support the argument that Canadian immigration policies are best understood as a subset of a wider field of economic and cultural priorities established by political leaders for nation-building. We may summarize the context of Canadian immigration policy in terms of the following arguments.

The goals of nation-building arise in the Canadian case through a process in which economic and political elites play a major role. This is particularly true in the area of immigration and foreign-worker policies where democratic debate and public input have been less present. National elites play a leading role in establishing an imagined future of the nation that then serves as an ideology to garner public support for nation-building policies in diverse interlinked areas, such as trade, economic growth, immigration, and cultural identity.

The nation-building options that Canadian political leaders pursue are established in the context of their perception of two sets of opportunities. One set is oriented outward. It concerns opportunities for attracting financial capital, establishing export markets, and finding sufficient immigrant and migrant labour to promote national economic growth. The other set is oriented inward. It concerns opportunities for using Canadian natural resources, industrial production, and service provision, all in combination with the external opportunities, to promote increased productivity, earnings, and consumption in Canada.

The pursuit of any of the above mentioned opportunities involves costs. As a result, the policy choices of political leaders are significantly shaped by their assessments of the cost-benefit outcomes of particular choices to those constituencies and actors on whose support they and the governments they are part of depend.

Costs and benefits are not measured just in terms of dollars or some other monetary yardstick; rather, they are also assessed politically in terms of who will gain (most) and who will pay (most) of the costs associated with whichever strategy is adopted. All social actors affected by the outcomes will shape the strategies chosen toward their interests, and policy decisions will generally depend on the relative power of the actors. In this context, immigrants have relatively weak power to change policies, but this is not to say that in a country with large numbers of immigrants and children of immigrants that they have no voice whatsoever. They have both a direct political voice, and an indirect voice expressed through the way they impact on Canadian society and its tolerance for diversity.

When the above arguments are put into the context of current globalization and the ideologies that support it, they lead to an examination of particular opportunities, costs, and social relations of power. This approach considers contemporary globalization to be, among other things, a political-economic process based on an ideology that argues for open trade and unrestricted flows of financial capital as the principal means to greater prosperity in the world and as a solution to global conflict and poverty. The most powerful nation-states, and the international financial and global trade institutions supported by these states, strongly encourage nations around the world to engage in neo-liberal policies of various kinds, including cutting costs across all state programs in order to be efficient producers and exporters. At the same time, all nations are encouraged to use whatever resources they have—raw materials, industrial capacity, educational and health institutions, skilled and unskilled workers, immigrants and migrant labour, technology, etc.—to achieve the goals of high productivity, expanding exports, and rising incomes. Whether these strategies and the institutional mechanisms work as well as they should, or even at all with regard to certain goals, such as eliminating global poverty, is widely debated and constitutes a major issue of our times.

International migration—in the form of immigration and migrant labour programs—is among the options that nations will use, if they can, for economic development and nation-building. Some nations, including Japan as an extreme case, do not use immigration very much because the kind of immigrants they seek are in short supply. Japanese society welcomes ethnic Japanese immigrants only. Ethnic Japanese

living outside Japan are relatively few in number and are often well-to-do, such that they have no interest in moving to Japan. Nations like Japan that do not have an immigration option will seek other ways of solving their labour supply problems. They may choose migrant worker programs, for example, yet even this option may be restricted. Western European nations have found that past migrant worker programs tended to generate a permanent population of foreigners that faced ongoing discrimination and marginalization, all associated with ongoing ethnic tensions and inter-ethnic violence.

Canada's Immigration Card

Canada, along with other nations such as Australia, New Zealand, and the United States, is among the countries that can regard large-scale immigration as a strong card in the deck of strategies they can draw on for nation-building. These nations all have a long history of welcoming and settling large numbers of immigrants from diverse backgrounds, with the result that they have a relatively high tolerance for newcomers and for ethnic diversity. In the export-oriented, efficiency-focused framework of contemporary globalization, Canada currently plays this card by admitting as many highly skilled immigrants as it feels it can, given other considerations. The other considerations are important because they expand immigration policy in various directions to cover the values and goals of a liberal state with respect to such matters as family reunification and refugee admissions, and also take into account Canada's ability to absorb immigrants into its economy and multicultural society. The following considerations are particularly important in shaping the overall framework of Canadian immigration policy.

The world is currently structured as a buyer's market for immigrants and migrant workers. Canada, like other countries seeking immigrants, can benefit from its access to: (1) large numbers of well-educated individuals interested in immigrating to Canada with their families; (2) many post-secondary students from well-to-do foreign families who are interested in completing studies in Canada and potentially remaining in Canada as immigrants; and (3) workers across a wide range of skills who are interested in coming to Canada for short-term work, even low-wage, dangerous, dirty work.

Although the potential supply of desired immigrants is large, those immigrants who Canada seeks to attract will not move without their immediate family members. Family-class immigration must necessarily be a major part of Canadian policy and immigrant inflows for two overlapping reasons: it is required to attract highly skilled immigrants, and expresses the humanitarian family reunification concerns of a liberal society. As a result, immigrants actually selected on the basis of their work skills and other nation-building attributes constitute less than a quarter of all those admitted. Immediate family members and other sponsored relatives constitute the majority of all immigrants.

In assessing how many of the most desired immigrants and their family members to admit, Canada has to take into account that it is also committed to humanitarian values and international agreements that permit refugee admission and settlement under specified conditions. The number of refugees will vary over time with changes in international circumstances governing refugee flows and with the arrival of asylum seekers to Canada. In the recent past, refugees have constituted between a fifth and a sixth of all immigrants.

At what point will the total number of immigrants exceed the Canadian economy's capacity to create jobs for them? At what point will the numbers and backgrounds of the immigrants promote cultural changes that exceed what Canadian society can tolerate? Historical and contemporary examples point to the constant risk of anti-immigrant backlash. The very upper ceiling for immigrant targets in contemporary political debates is around 1 percent of the Canadian population per year. This would be around 330,000 immigrants per year. Actual targets have tended to be lower. For example, they are in the range of 240,000–265,000 for 2009. In the future this number could rise or it could fall, depending on public and state perceptions of absorptive capacity.

Another consideration concerns the costs and benefits of alternatives to immigration. These include the greater use of temporary migrant workers, plus a range of other strategies that can be used to address labour shortages, such as the greater use of robots and machines to replace workers, exporting jobs, raising the age of retirement and promoting higher birth rates. In the range of options available, immigration has tended to remain an important nation-building card for Canada because it has been relatively inexpensive and complements other strategies. When immigrants arrive, they are expected to adapt and succeed largely on their own. State supports for adaptation and success are largely limited to language training, orientation and counselling programs covering immigrants in the period immediately after they land. When immigrants succeed, they and everyone else gains. When they do poorly, the immigrants themselves pay the greatest cost in terms of low earnings and marginalization. Not everyone in Canadian society loses when immigrants do poorly: those who are seeking to hire workers or pay for services may be happy to find a large pool of immigrant workers who can be paid relatively little for the work or services they provide.

Eight Main Policy Goals

Canadian immigration is currently shaped by a number of priority goals, beginning with the above noted focus on large numbers of highly skilled immigrants. The other objectives relate to such matters as migrant workers, the decentralization of decisions on the admission of economic immigrants, cost cutting in immigration programs, and efforts to sell state immigration policies to the Canadian public. The eight goals examined below are based on my analysis of both explicit and unstated state objectives. The unstated objectives are evident in trends in state policy even when these trends are not openly rationalized in policy rhetoric. The analysis of unstated goals introduces a critical perspective in which some of the state's goals are understood to be of a "sales" character, as is the case for goal number eight concerning efforts by the state to put forward a policy rhetoric emphasizing hoped for benefits of immigration while downplaying risks and evidence on negative outcomes.

1. To attract large numbers of highly skilled immigrants and their families for a mix of economic and demographic reasons. The highly skilled immigrants are sought for their potential contributions to rising productivity and meeting the needs of Canadian corporations and other employers for knowledge workers. In addition, they and their families are sought to keep the Canadian population from going into decline and that will slow the population aging process. Since 2002, Canada has not explicitly included demographic objectives in its immigration policy. At the same time, immigration targets continue to be set in a manner that suggests that demographic goals are embedded in targets justified on economic goals and filling labour force needs. The costs of admitting large numbers of immigrants are high for the immigrants themselves, because on the average they experience low earnings

on arrival and for many years thereafter. However, this has not led to a decrease in immigration applications. The state seems happy to take advantage of the buyer's market it faces with respect to attracting highly skilled immigrants. The main risk is that over time immigrants with low wages and marginalization will become hostile and increasingly define their situation as one of ethno-racial oppression, with negative consequences for social cohesion and Canadian society.

2. To expand migrant worker programs to cover growing needs in various sectors and across a range of skill levels, from low-wage jobs in agricultural production and food processing to high-wage professional, technical, and administrative fields. The low-wage foreign workers help some firms to survive when they otherwise might have to close shop. They provide an important complement to the national labour force and to the work done by immigrants. The migrants suffer the costs of poor working conditions, but they have little political power. This might change in the future if larger numbers arrive and become better organized in a context where Canadian unions and labour rights activists assist the migrant workers to press their grievances. High-wage professional and technical foreign workers seemingly do not suffer from these disadvantages, although research has not been done on their situation to confirm this fact. The current trajectory of foreign workers' programs indicates that the state is prepared to expand them, particular in times of economic growth. The implications of this new policy direction for Canadian society over the longer term are unknown.

3. To diversify the range of entry doors through which immigrants and migrant workers can enter in order to provide state officials with greater flexibility to meet the flexible production and expansion/contraction cycles of contemporary global trade. The entry doors have been expanded and now place greater emphasis on employers and post-secondary institutions to attract highly skilled potential immigrants by either: (1) first employing them as foreigners on work permits, or (2) advertising for and admitting them first as foreign students to Canadian post-secondary institutions. Under new rules adopted in 2007, skilled foreign workers and foreign students who have successfully completed advanced studies in Canada can apply directly for permanent (immigrant) status in Canada without having to return to their home countries and wait in the queue of people from that country who have already applied to immigrate to Canada. This relieves the state from some responsibilities in selecting future immigrants. It also shifts Canadian training and the acquisition of Canadian work experience to post-secondary institutions, employers, and the migrants/immigrants themselves. These and related options can readily be expanded, but there may be cost constraints on doing so. For example, Canada could expand the number of foreign students at post-secondary institutions by reducing fees for foreign students to the levels paid by Canadian students. However, the public might object given that this would lead to a situation in which foreign students would receive the same public subsidy for their education as national students. If many foreign students apply to stay in Canada after graduation, then the state may be encouraged to invest more in efforts to attract foreign students. If most return to their home countries or move to other wealthy nations, then the state will be less likely to do so. There is uncertainty and a potential for policies regarding foreign students to move in one direction or another.

4. *To cut costs wherever possible in immigrant admission and settlement.* Individuals interested in working as foreigners in Canada or immigrating to Canada can complete application forms and pay application fees through online procedures,

which greatly reduce costs. Independent (skilled worker) applicants are increasingly selected on the basis of their application and supporting documents. Prior to changes to the Immigration Act in 2001, an immigration officer assessed skilled workers for "personal suitability," but since then this has no longer been required, with a result that admission procedures are more efficient. In this respect, admission may also be more objective in that personal suitability was potentially a rather subjective consideration. However, contact between immigrants and the state has become increasingly impersonal, with unknown consequences. In addition, the state has instituted policies to shrink costs by cutting immigrant settlement and related multicultural programs. Several years ago, Richmond (1997) noted pressures across the wealthy nations of the world, including Canada, to cut the funding of multicultural programs for a mix of reasons: ideological dislike of the concept of multiculturalism, a belief that it sets the wrong standards for nation-building, and the view that the integration of immigrants can take place successfully without state support of such programs. Indications that the Canadian state may move in this direction are to be found in proposals put forward in 2007 to reduce funding for multicultural programs to one-half their previous level (Viccari 2007). It is not clear how far such programs can be cut before the reductions will affect Canada's ability to play its immigration card in nation-building. If immigrants feel that their cultural attributes are not valued, they may feel less a part of the Canadian nation in all respects: economically, politically, and culturally. How this might affect immigrant settlement, Canadian society, and the motivation of future highly skilled immigrants is not known.

5. *To find ways to encourage more immigrants to settle in smaller towns and cities.* The great majority of immigrants continue to

settle in Toronto, Montreal, and Vancouver, where they face mixed economic and social-cultural outcomes. As a result, they find themselves in large and often dynamic job markets that provide both low-wage jobs that they can access earlier after arrival and high-wage jobs that they can aspire to later. Unfortunately, they often become trapped in low-wage jobs below the level of their training and experience. Because their earnings after arrival are low, recent immigrants reside largely in low-cost residential districts found in the distant suburban areas of large cities. This places them in close proximity with other recent immigrants from their own and other ethnic backgrounds. Living in such a context provides a welcome cultural cushion for their settlement. However, it also puts them at risk of being socially and residentially cut off from non-immigrant citizens, contributing to worries that new immigrants are being ghettoized. The state has responded in a modest way by opening a new provincial nominee class of immigrant entry to encourage the provinces to engage in programs that would attract prospective immigrants to towns, smaller cities, and regions where they might otherwise not be inclined to go (Carter, Morrish, and Amoyaw 2008). Evidence presented by Derwing and Krahn (2008) suggests that it remains difficult to attract immigrants to such places. On the other hand, the immigrants who do settle in smaller towns and cities have better job and earnings prospects than those who settle in Toronto, Montreal, and Vancouver (Bernard 2008). While the state cannot tell immigrants where in Canada to settle, one may expect that it will continue to search for ways to diversify the locations to which they go to live when they initially arrive. If the programs to this end are successful, immigrants may also benefit.

6. *To tighten border controls and deport undocumented migrants except in extreme humanitarian cases.* The Canadian state has shown a variable interest in apprehending and deporting undocumented migrant workers and others without legal status in Canada. During construction booms when major sectors of the economy have depended on undocumented migrant workers, the state has largely ignored their presence. However, the longer-term trends seems to be moving toward allowing employers more scope to bring in more workers on temporary visas, while at the same time using immigration officers to apprehend and deport migrant workers without visas. The tighter controls reflect the state's desire to exert sovereign control of its territories, heighten the Canadian security environment of the post-9/11 era, and the related desire to keep the border with the United States as open to Canadian business travellers as possible.

As has been the case in the past, the state will likely continue to try to find ways to reduce inflows of refugee claimants. To date, these efforts have focussed on two strategies. One takes the form of the agreement that was signed with the United States in 2002 that allows Canada to deport refugee claimants to the United States for adjudication of their claim if they first landed or passed through the United States on the way to Canada (and conversely the United States can deport to Canada for adjudication refugee claimants in the United States who arrive through Canada). Whether such accords will be signed with other countries remains to be seen. The second is to require travel visas of all travellers coming from countries that produce a large number of refugee claimants. The intent is to screen out potential refugee claimants before they arrive by refusing to grant them a visa. This strategy has a long and controversial history because in protecting Canada from unjustified refugee claims it also runs the risk of excluding legitimate refugees. Countries for whose citizens need a visa to travel to Canada usually then require that Canadians seeking to travel to their country also obtain a visa. The practice becomes a headache for travellers and a burden on state officials who must process visa applications and check visas, but all this continues to be justified in terms of the need for tighter border controls.

7. *To change citizenship rules to reduce the risks of undesired costs and unrealized benefits to the state.* This can be done in various ways. One is to eliminate the ability of Canadians living abroad (including Canadians who acquired their citizenship through immigration) to automatically confer Canadian citizenship on their children who are born abroad. Legal changes that took effect in April 2009 require that children born outside Canada to parents who are non-resident Canadian citizens by virtue of previous immigration will have to demonstrate knowledge of Canada and the ability to speak English or French if they want to receive Canadian citizenship. According to Brender (2009: 19), "The new law stems from the 2006 removal of 15,000 Canadian citizens from war in Lebanon, many of whom subsequently returned there." The costs of evacuating these individuals was never announced by the government, but are assumed to have been in the tens of millions of dollars. Later, those Lebanese-Canadians who returned to Lebanon were criticized by some as "citizens of convenience," a claim that then sparked counterclaims that such individuals play a positive role as informal ambassadors for Canada and for cross-cultural understanding (Brender 2009: 19). However, to a cost-cutting state, the numbers of former Canadian immigrants who have returned to their home countries to live constitute a potential burden that is not sufficiently justified by such benefits. As yet, other steps that would limit the citizenship rights of non-resident Canadians have not been pursued. However, as noted in Chapter 9, proposals have been put forward that would require citizens living abroad to demonstrate civic commitment by, for example, paying taxes or voting in Canada. These steps are promoted for various reasons, including cutting costs to the state and generating needed tax revenues. Opponents of these policy proposals see the world differently and argue that it would be far better to retain current multicultural orientations in immigration, settlement, and society as a way of building a more harmonious nation with constructive links to diverse cultures and nations around the world.

8. *To sell immigration to the Canadian public and to future immigrants through a policy rhetoric that emphasizes the hoped-for benefits of immigration while downplaying risks and disappointing outcomes.* Abu-Laban and Gabriel (2002) argued that the Canadian state proactively sells the image of Canada as a peaceful multicultural nation in order to hide significant racialized ethno-cultural inequalities. The case can be made even more persuasively for the way the state promotes large-scale immigration. While the state spends relatively little on multicultural programs, it spends very large sums on immigrant selection, border controls, refugee admissions, and immigrant settlement. In addition, multiculturalism may be viewed both as a goal in itself for an ethnically diverse Canadian nation, and as an essential support to future immigration. The result is, as the evidence reviewed confirms, a policy rhetoric that points out the many hoped-for positive benefits of immigration for all Canadians. The gaps between this rhetoric and actual outcomes in the recent period are of deep concern to the state, but how the state will respond — or whether it will respond at all — is less clear. Immigrants may bring benefits to powerful Canadian interests even when, or perhaps because, their wages are low and they risk marginalization.

The Gap Between Policy Rhetoric and Outcomes

Canadian immigration policy is such a wide field that it covers many goals, some of which are more precisely stated and others of which are put forward as broad objectives without precise targets. Immigration officials might justifiably claim that they do meet many of their targets, particularly the ones that are more precisely set, such as those concerning the numbers and characteristics of immigrants. The problem for them and for researchers is that the crucial outcomes of what is hoped for from immigration with respect to nation-building goals are not set in ways that can be easily measured. Many measures are possible, which in itself creates a problem. If all were measured, how they should be summed up is hard to determine from the broad way that the social and economic goals of immigration are put forward by the state. Criticism of Canadian immigration successes and failures with regard to nation-building outcomes is currently a more qualitative exercise in which the observer reads across statements of policy goals to capture their essence and then uses scattered and incomplete evidence to assess success and failure. The following points clarify these conclusions.

Immigration targets: There is no doubt that Canada is very successful in meeting its immigration goals, narrowly defined. Immigration targets have been met on a year-by-year basis for a long time. The system largely excludes people who are not admissible though legal channels, although from time to time there are large numbers of undocumented migrant workers in a "grey area" in which they are not officially admitted but not deported. Such space emerges when work done by unauthorized migrants is greatly needed and supported by politically influential

business leaders and labour unions, as may happen in a construction boom. There is also evidence of international sex-trade activities in Canada, although the extent is hard to assess. If anything, immigration officials, aided by other forces, seem to have overshot the mark in advertising Canada as a welcoming place for immigrants. As noted above, the current backlog consisting of tens of thousands of immigrant applicants waiting for their applications to be processed provides evidence of this.

There is also a gap between the rhetoric of immigration policy and its outcomes when it comes to the size of immigrant entry classes. Policy rhetoric implies that the points-selected immigrants reflect what the state is promoting and what Canada is getting, but this is an overstatement. Immigrants selected on points constitute less than one-quarter of all those entering. However, the internal logic of immigration rhetoric tends to play down this fact and to focus on highly skilled immigrants as if they were the largest portion of those admitted. While immigration rhetoric does recognize that family-class admissions are important de facto, the state has tried to reduce family-class admissions, perhaps to the point where it would be difficult to reduce these admissions further without undermining the policy priority for attracting highly skilled points-selected immigrants. Highly skilled immigrants will likely be less inclined to resettle in Canada if the immigration of their immediate family members and other eligible relatives is blocked. The state would also like to keep refugee admissions down to lower numbers than are actually found, but the inflows of refugee claimants who meet Canadian humanitarian entry criteria tend to keep overall refugee admissions higher than they otherwise would be. These developments reflect pressures from immigrants and the humanitarian groups in Canada.

Although the state sells its immigration policy as a largely economic-only enterprise, the policy is in fact somewhat more balanced across economic, family, and humanitarian goals, even if not as balanced across these as some critics would like. The only concern one might raise is that the rhetoric used to sell an immigration program does not achieve its economic goals very well, at least not with respect to the incorporation of immigrants directly in highly productive and well-paying jobs. This problem raises serious questions about the fundamental rationale of current policies. I say more about this point below.

Economic goals and multicultural integration. The state does not set precise indicators of what it hopes for in terms of immigrant economic impacts and ethnocultural integration. Rather, it states broad general visions of what it seeks in terms of national economic productivity and cultural outcomes of immigration. Policy-oriented research on immigration therefore covers many different dimensions of the process and its outcomes. It also tends to focus – as this book does – on immigrant jobs, earnings, residential patterns, and ethnocultural relations with others in Canadian society. In each of these areas, the evidence points to significant gaps and challenges.

With respect to jobs and incomes, it has been well documented that highly skilled immigrants in many fields have major problems in getting their credentials recognized in Canada. The very low earnings of recently arrived immigrants have also been observed for the past two decades. The new observation is that the low-earnings pattern seems to be getting worse. Of even more concern is the finding that estimates of future trajectories based on past trends, while not conclusive, indicate that it will likely take a long time for recently arrived immigrants to reach the earnings levels of similarly educated and experienced Canadian-born workers.

With respect to residential patterns and ethnocultural relations, the evidence reviewed suggests that, now as in the past, new immigrants live near other immigrants from the same national and ethnic backgrounds. However, what has changed is the extent to which the low-earnings dynamics (described above), ethnocultural preferences, and shifting residential desirability and costs are together leading to high concentrations of newly arrived immigrants in the least expensive suburban housing in large cities. These areas are characterized by monocultural blocks of rental and owned housing clustered within ethnically more mixed larger low-cost suburban residential and commercial areas within which visible-minority immigrants predominate. In such settings, multiculturalism takes a distinct and disturbing form: that of an emerging ethnically stratified multicultural visible-minority underclass. One needs to ask whether this reality is consistent with within the broad scope of multicultural policy. Perhaps the time has come to revisit what Canada hopes for in terms of a future multicultural society and to establish new and clearer goals, along with strategies to achieve them.

Low immigrant earnings arise in part due to *declining returns from human capital*, an outcome that must surely distress Canadian policy-makers since this outcome challenges the core logic of selecting economic immigrants through criteria that give a great deal of weight to education. It has been known across the history of immigration to various countries, Canada included, that employers discount immigrants' foreign work experience and foreign educational credentials. However, what is new and surprising is the evidence that this discounting is increasing and that it applied to very highly educated immigrants with college diplomas and university degrees. Why this is the case is unclear. The evidence examined provides support for various hypotheses, including for example that foreign education is not always equivalent to Canadian education and that even when it is, initially poor language skills may channel immigrants into jobs in which they have little opportunity to maintain or improve problem-solving skills in English and French. Of course, the fact that racism and other pre-existing barriers to jobs are still present in Canada does not make matters easier.

The problem of skill discounting could be resolved in part through more careful immigrant selection, but this is not so easy to do. Foreign work experience and education are often discounted for individuals from less developed nations where English and French are secondary languages or ones learned in school and where day-to-day problem-solving is not conducted in them. The large backlog of immigration applications suggests that Canada could be more selective in language and problem-solving skills in English and French and still meet its immigration targets. However, an overemphasis on language and language-based problem-solving skills would run the risk of biasing immigration against applicants from developing countries where Canada's official languages are not widely spoken. The solution that remains most fair to talented immigrant applicants from various parts of the world is for Canada to provide immigrants with far stronger opportunities for skill upgrading, study, and job internships that promote skill development in problem-solving in English and French. While such measures would be expensive in the short term, they could pay for themselves and reap additional benefits over the longer term as immigrants become placed in jobs where their skills contribute more to the profits of employers, Canadian income taxes, and national productivity. A cost-cutting state will be reluctant to spend the extra money required for such programs,

but if such programs are required to make the system work better for immigrants and Canadian society, then the state may accept the necessity of paying the price to get what is wanted and required. In this way, immigrant integration programs would be expanded as part of the cluster of other expensive but necessary social policies with respect to education, health and worker-training that are supported by the Canadian state.

Racism and ethnocentrism are experienced by many immigrants, particularly those of visible minority status. Concern over this, mobilized by anti-racist organizations often led by visible-minority Canadians but involving wider sectors of the population, puts constant pressure on the state to re-assess how official anti-racist goals can be made more specific and achieved. A major goal must be to eliminate racism because its effects are so dreadful with respect to the morale and dignity of those targeted and so negative for social cohesion and harmony. There is also the goal of reducing to zero the impact of racism on the schooling, jobs and earnings of visible-minority individuals. These two goals go together because they reinforce one another.

One of the highest priorities in this area is therefore to better understand why some visible minority immigrants and their children are able to overcome discrimination in schools and when searching for jobs. Positive evidence indicates that many visible-minority immigrants and particularly their born-in-Canada children are able to eventually do well in Canada. These findings draw attention to the importance of understanding how they were able to do so, because such knowledge would assist in developing policies that reinforce the capacity of visible-minority immigrants and citizens to achieve well in school and the job market. Such strategies could benefit all visible-minority individuals insofar as they help to destroy the negative stereotypes underlying racism. New policies need to be particularly oriented to support members of some visible-minority groups — including Blacks, Latin Americans and some refugee-origin communities — who reveal low schooling and job outcomes. In sum, the state puts forward anti-racist objectives and an image of Canada as peaceful multiethnic, immigrant-friendly nation, but there remains a significant gap between this self-image and the experiences of many visible-minority immigrants and their born-in-Canada children.

Immigrant *social capital in the form of networks, contacts, and information sources* has the potential to play an important role in economic and cultural incorporation in Canada, yet the state has not set any particular policy goals or programs to expand immigrant social capital. Evidence reviewed in this book suggests that immigrant social networks play a particularly strong role in developing a sense of cultural belonging in Canada or, more correctly, developing a sense of transnational belonging that includes Canada. Evidence also points to more mixed findings on the potential of immigrant social capital that can be helpful for finding good jobs or business opportunities. Some immigrants were able to use their contacts and networks for this purpose, but others were not. The social capital that many recently arrived immigrants are able to access either has not been relevant for job or business opportunity, or it has only been relevant for such opportunity within their own ethnic community. Jobs and business opportunities within ethnic enclaves seem to lead to lower earnings, although the evidence is based on just a few studies. These are all matters that need to be taken into account in strategies to improve earnings and other settlement outcomes of immigrants.

Transnational incorporation is not explicitly part of the Canadian immigration policy framework at present. This may be changing as it becomes apparent that multicultural integration in Canada cannot be understood well without considering that, for many immigrants, their enduring attachments to and involvements with family and community in their home countries are very meaningful as they establish new lives in Canada. The Canadian state is clearly aware of and responding to such issues in the area of dual citizenship. Canadian citizens living abroad in their home countries are provided safe passage back to Canada if required by adverse circumstances in their home countries. So, bit by bit, the state is becoming more aware of the need to respond to certain specific implications of transnationalism. And yet the state's response is largely with regard to matters of citizenship rights, not with regard to citizenship duties. Perhaps this balance is as it should be in a liberal-democratic society, although there are calls for immigrants (and Canadian-born individuals) who live permanently abroad with citizenship elsewhere to meet certain minimum norms of civic engagement with Canada in order to retain their citizenship rights. How these debates will develop is at present unclear.

From a research perspective, transnationalism remains one of the most interesting and transformative aspects linked to, but not entirely dependent on, international migration. The evidence reviewed pointed repeatedly to the often thick and emotionally rich or "hot" links that many immigrants retain to their home countries. It also pointed to evidence suggesting that these links did not necessarily rule out strong attachments to Canada. Immigrants identify in varying degrees and appear to develop, on average, somewhat stronger attachments to Canada than to their home countries. Such findings should encourage Canadian policy-makers to take advantage of the positive aspects of immigrant social transnationalism. However, the evidence also points to related to entanglements in foreign ethnic and national conflicts, and more research is required to clarify how to avoid these risks while benefitting more generally from positive outcomes for Canada, the immigrant home countries, and peace in the international system.

Pressure for and Resistance to Policy Reforms

There is no shortage criticism of Canadian immigration policy. Some of the criticism makes good sense in terms of the approach and findings in the present book, while others do not. Stoffman (2002) claims that the failures of Canadian immigration stem from poor selection, with the result that too many unskilled family members and "bogus" refugee claimants are admitted. These arguments find little support in the evidence examined: even immigrants who have been selected to meet the high educational and other job-linked criteria in the points system for those entering in the economic class have difficulty finding good jobs; family class immigrants do as well if not better than highly skilled economic immigrants in the job market; and refugee claimants, who come overwhelmingly from countries where civil wars and human rights abuses are widespread, are less than ten percent of total immigration. Many others (such as Nakhaie 2006; Reitz and Banerjee 2007) argue that Canadian society and employers are largely to blame because they do not recognize immigrant skills, or because they feel uncomfortable around unfamiliar accents, or because they are prejudiced. These arguments find strong support in the large number of studies cited in this book on the racism experienced by many visible minority immigrants. This leads to the clear conclusion that the Canadian state must do more to overcome racism. While the findings examined confirm this conclusion, they also point out that racism

is reinforced through its systemic linkages to other features of Canadian immigration policies, practices, and outcomes. As result, the goal should be to eliminate racism by addressing as many as possible of the forces that help generate it.

The evidence in his book supports the view that racism is part of what we have called a conundrum of historically and structurally linked factors that interact with each other to restrict the opportunities for immigrants from less developed countries who form the majority of all immigrants now coming to Canada. The linked factors include: lower or different schooling standards in source countries; the fact that many immigrants come with skills in English and French that are insufficient, in the eyes of employers, to take on the jobs they were trained for; the tendency for immigrants to end up immediately after arrival in dead-end, low-wage jobs that do not provide opportunities to retain or improve job skills or to advance their problem-solving in English or French; the low social capital of immigrants with respect to trusting relations in Canadian society that would increase their job prospects; and residential patterns related to low income. These factors are all linked to visible-minority status among immigrants. They tend to reinforce pre-existing ethnocultural stereotypes and racism.

In sum, the complex interdependencies between the factors described above creates a challenge for devising state policies to improve settlement outcomes for immigrants and Canadian society. At the same time, the mix of entwined factors presents opportunities for strategic action. The state cannot change where immigrants come from, because this is shaped largely by economic trends, demographic transitions, and transcultural linkages in the international arena outside Canadian control. However, the state has many options for providing opportunities for immigrants to improve their language and language-linked cognitive skills in English and French through settlement programs promoting job and cultural mentoring and meaningful internships.

One of the more puzzling questions to emerge from the evidence reviewed in this book is why Canadian policy has been slow to respond with new programs that would reverse the persistent low earnings and related marginalization of recently arrived immigrants. It is not that the state has not responded, but that its responses taken together seem scattered and weak. The following hypotheses, some supported in part by findings in this book, may be helpful to understand why policies that would promote better earnings and settlement outcomes among immigrants have been weak.

Ideology trumps political judgment. We live in a trade-centred world of competition among nations for export markets, competition among firms across borders for profits and survival, and competition among workers for jobs. The ideological and institutional supports for this system are powerful at the international, regional North American, and Canadian levels. The two dominant political parties in Canada, namely the Conservatives and the Liberals, both favour—with some differences and jockeying for political advantage—policy packages regarding trade, improved productivity, multiculturalism, and immigration that are consistent with the position of dominant players in the international economic system. This ideology says that immigration of skilled workers into a multicultural context can be an attractive nation-building option with diverse positive outcomes for nations that can manage high levels of ethnic diversity. In such a situation, the ideology—expressed as a hope for what should take place—leads national leaders to discount evidence of weak policy outcomes as being temporary or exceptional, hence matters that can be ignored.

The state develops immigration policy largely behind closed doors, such that it can remove itself from day-to-day public criticism of its policies and programs. The evidence examined leads to the conclusion that today, as in the past, debates on contemporary immigration policy are largely confined to political elites and senior bureaucrats rather than extended to involve Parliament or the general public (Hardcastle et al. 1994). In addition, Canadian immigration includes a very large state bureaucracy and an extensive body of immigrant-serving agencies that may have a "business as usual" mindset that discourages thinking about major changes. This too is conjectural since the only studies I am aware of that sought to address such matters were done many years ago (see, for example, Simmons and Keohane 1992). It is therefore difficult to know the mindset of Cabinet members of whatever government is in power or the views of senior policy advisers on immigration matters. One can only glean the drift of their thinking from what they have done and what they have not done. To date, the Canadian state continues to insist that it does not need to become signatory to the International Convention on Migrant Rights because, in its view, the issues addressed by the convention are not relevant to Canada. The official position is that, unlike some other countries, all migrant workers in Canada are legal and, as such, they are protected by the rules of the programs that officially admit them to Canada. However, this position has come under increasing criticism due to evidence, noted in Chapter 10, that low-wage migrant workers are vulnerable to significant levels of abuse and exploitation, despite what the state says is (or should be) the case.

Canadian public support for immigration programs is divided. While public opinion in Canada tends to favour immigration, there are also many who doubt the merits of current immigrant admission levels and still others who are opposed to immigration for diverse reasons including a distrust of foreigners, worries about cultural change, and concerns about competition for jobs. In this context, immigrants may be hesitant to speak up about their problems for fear that to do so will provoke a backlash.

Immigrants also have imagined futures, and when they fail to achieve their goals they may blame themselves or at least not want to make their failures public. Immigrants and their families are motivated by goals, possibilities, and their own personal imagined futures that emerge through transnational interactions with previous emigrants. One assumes that the imagined futures of immigrants are "reality based," yet, as noted in our analysis, the normative aspects of the process can create "cultures of migration" in which people hide disappointment and failure relative to expected outcomes, and in so doing they contribute, along with other institutional forces, to the maintenance of a system with weak or mixed outcomes for themselves and other immigrants who follow their lead. This is not to blame the victim: The migrants are often coming from positions with little political power and restricted opportunities. They adopt cultural values and ideologies that help, however imperfectly, some members to improve their opportunities. Keeping up hope despite disappointment can be an important way of coping and "staying in the game" in the hope that circumstances and outcomes will improve in the future. In addition, the success ideology of our times supports the view that people who fail to get good jobs have only themselves to blame. This may be far from the truth, but it reduces the tendency to complain and the energy that will be put into efforts to bring about new policies that could improve outcomes.

Immigrants endure disappointments for themselves by retaining hope for the next generation. Canada has an extended history of multiculturalism, pluralism, and state policies to assist immigrants. These policies may be weaker than required, but are still significant to newcomers materially and symbolically. Canada is also a wealthy nation with strong social programs, such that even an immigrant family with low income will be assured of health care, welfare if required in emergencies, and perhaps, most importantly, fairly good to very good publicly funded education for their children. Immigrants seem to be willing to put up with a great deal in terms of disappointment if they know their children will have better opportunities. The fact that the children of immigrants often do well in Canada when they become adults may be the "deal maker" that keeps their parents working hard despite discouraging job and earnings outcomes, particularly over their first decades in Canada.

Failures in the immigration areas may not be viewed as particularly important by political leaders, leading them to conclude that the failures can be ignored for now and addressed later, which often means that they never get addressed. The big picture of Canadian immigration from the perspective of Canadian nation-building over time leads to the conclusion that immigration policy is fundamentally shaped to fit within national trade, economic growth and cultural goals. Immigration is one of the elements that is to be fitted in with the others but it is not necessarily the most important one at any particular historical juncture. If there is no immigration crisis and mixed or divided pressure from the Canadian public for reforms, then even major gaps between immigration policy goals and outcomes can be tolerated. The risk is that the gaps will be ignored and lead to major breakdowns in social cohesion, thereby eroding the imagined future of Canada as a peaceful, multicultural society.

In sum, combinations of the above factors create a situation in which pressures for policy change are muted. On the one hand it is evident that there are serious gaps between the goals and outcomes of Canadian immigration policy. On the other hand it is evident that pressure for policy-makers to respond to these gaps is reduced by various factors: divided public opinion, concern about the costs of new or expanded programs, and hopes that the system will survive as is and not melt down into explosive conflict.

Will the Future Be Different?

The future is always unknown, but it is useful to examine some trends that are already established on a trajectory that will, if they continue, lead to important developments in Canadian immigration and changes in Canadian society as a whole in relation to these. Among the main trends are the aging of the Canadian population and the demand that it will create for immigrants and foreign workers; important shifts in the source countries of Canadian immigrants with implications for diversity and the successful multicultural integration of newcomers; and the rising proportion of visible minority Canadians and how this will affect cultural identities of Canadians and the kinds of immigration policies they will favour. Each of these are examined briefly below.

Aging and the Demand for Foreign Labour

A combination of low fertility and increased longevity will combine to create a Canadian population with relatively few children growing up to enter the labour force and many older people who will be in need of services. The rising demand for services required by the elderly will place a strain on the private resources of many families. It will also require a reallocation of public funds and potentially rising state costs for old age security and health care. Senior citizens and their families will be looking for trained people to provide the services they need, and will want to keep costs down if they can. States will be looking for talented workers to increase national productivity to pay for new state services for the elderly, and also trying to keep costs down. The state will also face continuing pressure from Canadian employers to admit seasonal and other foreign workers to for jobs in sectors where there is a shortage of national workers. In sum, immigrants will not be sought because they can reverse the aging of the population, for immigration does not have this effect. Rather, immigrants will be sought because they potentially can increase productivity, fill specific job gaps, and help sustain the consumer market in Canada by postponing population decline indefinitely. In addition, migrant workers will be in demand because they come only as working-age adults, hence they add workers in the productive ages and do not contribute to aging. In this way, they too can reinforce the Canadian economy. Thus, both immigrants and migrant workers will be in demand, in large part because they complement each other. These trends do not suggest any major changes in immigration policy, but they do suggest possible major shifts in foreign worker programs.

Pressures for migrant worker programs to expand do not mean necessarily that they will expand. Historical examples point to the fact that migrant worker programs can rise and fall, then perhaps rise again. Migrant worker programs were abandoned in Europe after the 1970s when it became apparent in various studies that nothing is more permanent than a temporary migrant worker (see Castles 1986, 1989). Because migrant workers developed local attachments, many did not want to return home. This defeated the idea of such programs. However, some years have passed, new border control and migrant worker control systems are in place, and it seems that various states around the world are planning a return to migrant worker programs or, as in the case of Canada, to expand existing programs of this kind (Ruhs 2005). The Global Commission on International Migration (GCIM 2005: 16–18, 61–63) concluded that temporary worker programs can be successful only if the host nations provide strong protections for the rights of the workers. This last proviso is important. It is also a major stumbling block. The International Convention on Migrant Rights came into effect in December 2003. By October 2005, the convention had been ratified by 35 countries. However, as noted in Chapter 10, not a single G8 wealthy nation had ratified the convention by that date. Canada is one of the countries that have steadfastly said that they would not sign the convention. The official explanation is that migrant workers already have sufficient protection under Canadian law and the provisions of their contracts. As we have noted, these official views are strongly contested by researchers and activists in the fields of labour and human rights who have observed ongoing vulnerability to workplace danger, abuse, and exploitation among low-wage visa workers.

Would Canada ever replace permanent immigration with larger programs of migrant workers? The idea fits poorly with the history of Canadian immigration practices, yet we need to keep in mind that these practices have on occasion undergone major shifts in direction. Canada shut down immigration in the 1930s when immigrants were perceived as threats to the security of Canadian workers and to Canadian ethnocultural values. In addition,

our imagined futures framework made clear that Canadian policies and outlook are not only toward the external world, but they are often opportunistic. DeVoretz (2008) suggests a particularly opportunistic way that Canadian policy-makers could increase the number of short-term migrant workers and give greater priority to them rather than immigration. He suggests that this could be done in a way that would be perceived as fair to Canadian workers by giving them vouchers that they could auction each year to foreign individuals with relevant qualifications to come to Canada to take up a one-year contract. As Canadian workers start to feel that their own jobs might be affected, they will then bid up the price of their vouchers and fewer foreign visa workers would come.

While the DeVoretz proposal might solve the problem of fairness from the perspective of Canadian workers while meeting the needs of Canadian employers, it would potentially create many additional risks of racialization and exploitation of migrant workers. The workers would be short term, hard to organize or self-organize into labour unions, and potentially at risk to the kinds of problems that have been noted with past and current migrant worker programs. From a Canadian nation-building perspective, moreover, the migrant workers would contribute labour only, not cultural vibrancy and families that raise high-achieving children in Canada. So far, the debate over replacing immigration with more migrant workers does not appear to have gained much momentum in the public domain, but given the history of Canadian immigration policy and its emergence from deliberations by political and state elites, the lack of public debate should not be taken as an indication that the state has no plans.

The easiest trajectory for Canadian policy-makers is to expand foreign worker programs gradually and incrementally in periods of high labour demand. During recessions and periods of high unemployment, foreign worker contracts would not be renewed. Live-in domestic workers have in the past been primarily involved in looking after children in the home of professional Canadian families. They have also been involved in looking after elderly persons, a practice that is likely to increase and become their main focus in the future. However, the pressures to expand foreign worker programs will not be limited to personal care. They will be evident throughout the economy as Canadian firms, the state, and the public debate with one another over the number of foreign workers that should be admitted and the protections to be put in place to guarantee the safety, remuneration and dignity of their work.

From Where Will Future Immigrants Come?

Two deeply structured changes taking place in the world may lead to important impacts on the sources and supplies of Canadian immigrants. One is the rising demand for migrant workers and highly skilled immigrants in other wealthy nations. The other is the rapid fall in birth rates and population growth in countries that have been major sources of Canadian immigrants. China and India have been among Canada's top sources of immigrants for some time (see Chapter 6). China's one-child policy has already brought birth rates down below the replacement level. India's birth rates are declining more slowly, but are now much lower than they were. Both countries have been experiencing very rapid economic growth. They still have many unemployed and underemployed workers, but these workers are those with the least education. Highly skilled workers of the kind sought by Canada and other wealthy nations are in considerable demand in both China and India.

If China and India dry up as sources of highly skilled immigrants, this does not mean that Canada will not find them elsewhere. It does, however, raise the question of where Canada will find them. The Caribbean region and other less developed countries in the Americas have lost so many of their skilled workers to wealthy nations that they now have insufficient numbers for their own needs. Africa remains the least developed region of the world and also has the highest birth rates of any large region. However, levels of education in Africa are generally very low, with the result that highly educated Africans constitute a relatively small proportion of the total workforce in the region.

The above developments in potential supplies of immigrants will unfold slowly and along an uncertain path. However, they suggest that, sooner or later, Canada will find that the kinds of immigrants it most wants will not be available in the numbers that it has become accustomed to from the countries with which it has the strongest transnational social and cultural links. Insofar as the desired immigrants can be found, they will increasingly come from currently poorer countries in Africa and elsewhere where historical formed transnational cultural links are weaker. Large numbers of new immigrants from these countries will have less well-formed co-ethnic communities in Canada to support their arrival. Many will be coming from nations with particularly weak educational systems and with economies that provide different job training and experience than is found or wanted in Canada. These immigrants face the risk of particularly deep discounting of their foreign work experience, problems in having their credentials recognized, and marginalization in jobs that give them few opportunities to improve their official language skills. The fact that these outcomes could feed into ethnocentrism, racism and anti-immigrant sentiment in

Canada is particularly concerning. Once again, we conclude the Canada will face significant future challenges in developing policies to meet its immigration and related nation-building goals.

Expanding Diversity, Hybridity, and Transnationalism

Immigrant-receiving nations are undergoing very significant changes in ethnic composition. A notable case is the United States where projections indicate that the White majority will become a minority sometime around 2042 due to immigration and the higher fertility of the non-White population in that country (Bergman 2004). If trends in Canadian immigration follow the logic anticipated in the analysis in this book, visible minorities will soon become the majority in large Canadian cities. Visible minorities already make up large shares of the populations in Toronto and Vancouver — about 43 per cent and 42 per cent respectively, although the levels are less than half this in smaller cities and rural areas (Statistics Canada 2006a). The same data show that about three in ten visible-minority individuals in Canada are now Canadian born. These trends will generate enormous changes in Canadian society. The overall findings of the present book suggest that the main trends will be toward a rise in hyphenated identities in a national culture where people are increasingly comfortable with hyphenated, fluid and contextually expressed identities. The general thrust of such transformations will be a blurring of single ethnic and racial identification, an increased bridging across ethnic identities, and a mix of old and new transnational links mediated by individuals who maintain a presence both "here" and "there." The evidence reviewed does not suggest that this will be an even or smooth process leading necessarily to a quick end to all racial and ethnic stereotyping, discrimination and conflict, as much as

this might be hoped for. Canada has great potential and has achieved much in becoming a tolerant, multicultural society, but major challenges remain and new issues of a potentially divisive nature keep cropping up in Canada and in nations around the world with which Canada is in contact. In sum, there will be a continuing need for strategies to overcome cultural intolerance and to promote cross-cultural understanding. Fortunately, Canada has developed and hopefully will continue to develop a society that will provide strong support for such measures.

Turning Points?

We seem to be approaching a number of major turning points in Canadian immigration policy and in Canadian society as a result of immigration. Canada's nation-building options continue to favour inflows of immigrants and migrant workers. As a result of recent and past immigration, Canada's nation-building options also include a continuing expansion of ethnic diversity, hybrid identities, and transnationalism. These trends are taking place in the context of continuing debates on how to achieve the goals of immigration policy, improve the earnings and multicultural integration of immigrants and their children, overcome racism and ethnocentrism, and protect the rights of migrant workers. The debates reflect the deeper political struggles between competing images of Canada's national future and related political ideologies favouring different views on what is to be sought and how to get there.

In a larger view, the world as a whole has entered a period of great turbulence, flux, and uncertainty. The global economy is subject to significant instability. Environmental challenges are looming with implications for international population displacements. Fuel prices, transportation costs, and airfares bounce up and down, but the trajectory is for them all to rise, within uncertain impacts on production, trade, and international migration. Whatever happens, we will be required to revise and further elaborate our understanding of the relationship between Canadian immigra-tion and nation-building. The task will require new research efforts, adding to those reviewed in the present book, to refine and build critical perspectives on the processes involved and to contribute to public debate on national imagined futures and how to achieve them.

Appendix: Guide to Further Study

The following guide draws attention to books and websites that supplement what is covered in this volume. Suggested readings are organized by themes that parallel the chapter titles of the book. Useful online sources for data, policy analysis, and recent research findings are at the end of the guide.

Overviews of the Field (Chapter 1)

Stephen Castles and Mark J. Miller's *The Age of Migration* (4th ed.) (2008) provides an up-to-date and wide-ranging book on globalization, transnational community formations, and international migration around the world. Canada is not covered specifically, but Canadian issues and research are frequently cited. Peter Stalker has two short books on globalization and international migration that also provide useful introductions to this topic: *Workers without Frontiers: The Impact of Globalization on International Migration* (2000), and the shorter and more introductory *The No-Nonsense Guide to International Migration* (2002). His website provides highly readable, updated information on many of the topics covered in his books: [http://pstalker.com/migration/mg_about_ps.htm]. Stalker's viewpoint is fairly conventional. For a critical perspective on many of the issues he covers, see Saskia Sassen's *Globalization and Its Discontents: Essays on the New Mobility of People and Money* (1998).

The volume by John Biles, Meyer Burstein, and James Frideres (eds.), *Immigration and Integration in Canada in the Twenty-first Century* (2008), contains eight original papers by researchers on various aspects of immigrant economic, political, and social integration with a particular focus on Canadian state policies, accompanied by substantive introductory and concluding chapters by the editors. Jeffrey Reitz contributes what might otherwise be a short book on Canadian immigrant settlement in the form of two lengthy research reviews published as back-to-back journal articles: see Reitz (2007a, 2007b). Peter Li's *Destination Canada: Debates and Issues* (2003b) covers many of the topics covered in the present book from an "immigration discourse" perspective and includes topics, such as the social construction of immigrants and the impact of immigration on the total economy, which are not covered in this book.

Migration Theory (Chapter 2)

International migration theory underwent major revisions and consolidation in the 1990s and early 2000s. Mary Kritz, Lin Lean Lim, and Hania Zlotnik (1992), *International Migration Systems: A Global Approach*, is an excellent starting point for learning about migration systems approaches. Douglas Massey and J. Edward Taylor's book, *International Migration: Prospects and Policies in a Global Market* (2004) contains 20 chapters (including the substantive introduction and conclusion) on different countries and receiving-country policies. While the book is not about theory, migration systems theory from a globalization perspective is used extensively throughout and summarized nicely in the final chapter by the editors.

Caroline Brettell and James Hollifield's *Migration Theory: Talking across Disciplines* (2000) contains chapters written by specialists on how international migration is approached by different disciplines, including anthropology, demography, economics, law, political science, and sociology. Many of the preceding books cover issues of social networks and social-political transnationalism to some degree. For more on the emergence of this theoretical perspectives in the period since the early 1990s, see the suggestions under the heading "Transnational World" below.

Nation-Building Perspectives (Chapters 2 and 3)

A fundamental source is Benedict Anderson's *Imagined Communities: Reflections on the Origin and Spread of Nationalism* (rev. ed.) (1991). Another basic source is Eric Hobsbawm's (1992) *Nations and Nationalism Since 1780*. Harold Innis's ideas on Canadian national development developed over time and are found in many books that he published. The best coverage of his original works in one volume is the posthumously published book, *Essays in Canadian Economic History*, edited by Mary Q. Innis (1956). C.R. Acland and W.J. Buxton's *Harold Innis in the New Century* (1999) provides more recent perspectives on Innis's work. Harald Bauder's *Labor Movement: How Migration Regulates Labour Markets* (2006) continues the tradition of political-economic research on Canadian immigration, written from a dual labour force market perspective. It brings to light conclusions that could also be interpreted within an Innis staples economy framework. Christina Gabriel and Hélène Pellerin's edited volume, *Governing International Labour Migration: Current issues, Challenges, and Dilemmas* (2008) provides 11 substantive papers on global institutions, labour policies, migrant rights issues, and migration and development debates, plus a substantive introduction by the editors. The book does not focus on Canada, but several of the chapters are on or include Canadian issues.

Historical Perspectives (Chapter 3)

An easy-to-read and informative introduction to Canadian immigration history is provided by Valerie Knowles's *Strangers at Our Gates: Canadian Immigration and Immigration Policy, 1540–1990* (1992). Ninett Kelley and Michael Trebilcock's *The Making of the Mosaic: A History of Canadian Immigration Policy* (2000) provides a longer and more detailed account, with less on the very early period, and more on the period after Confederation. *From Whence They Came: Deportation from Canada 1900–1935* by Barbara Roberts (1988) and *None Is Too Many: Canada and the Jews of Europe, 1933–1948* (1982) by Irving Abella and Harold Troper are key readings for the topics and years indicated. Cecil Foster's *Where Race Does Not Matter: The New Spirit of Modernity* (2005) examines global racist ideologies and the way they affected racism and pluralism in Canada from the time of America's War of Independence through to contemporary multicultural policies. Peter Li's *The Chinese in Canada* (1998) covers the early history of the Chinese exclusion acts through to partial reopening of immigration in the late 1940s and the end of all racist exclusions from 1962 onward.

Contemporary Immigration Policies (Chapter 4)

The most detailed accounts of the policy developments that led Canada to abandon its Eurocentric and racist immigration policies in 1962, adopt a points system for selecting skilled workers in 1967, and adopt multiculturalism from 1971 onward can be found in two books by Freda Hawkins: *Canada and Immigration: Public Policy and Public Concern* (2nd ed.) (1988) and *Critical Years in Immigration: Canada and Australia Compared* (2nd ed.) (1991). The comparison with Australia is extended in Howard Adelman et al.'s *Immigration and Refugee Policy: Australia and Canada Compared* (1994), a two-volume collection of articles compare immigration levels, immigrant characteristics, immigration and refugee policies, and multiculturalism in these two countries during the 1980s and early 1990s. More recent works providing a critical perspective on Canadian immigration policies approach the topic from contrasting viewpoints. Daniel Stoffman's *Who Gets in: What's Wrong with Canada's Immigration Program – and How to Fix It* (2002) blames immigration problems on lax state controls and the admission of too many immigrants who do not contribute to the Canadian economy. Peter Li's *Destination Canada* (2003b) takes an entirely different critical perspective by examining, among other issues, how the state policy discourse contributes to questionable "benchmarking" for immigrant achievement.

Economic Outcomes (Chapters 5, 6, and 7)

Recent books mentioned above, such as those by Beach, Green, and Reitz (2003); Biles, Burstein, and Frideres (2008); and Li (2003b) cover immigrant characteristics and economic outcomes, in addition to other topics. For a historical contextualization covering policy issues up to around 1990, see the volume edited by Don DeVoretz, *Diminishing Returns: The Economics of Canada's Recent Immigration Policy* (1995). Readers interested in economic outcomes for the second generation will find recent research from the United States a useful complement to the pieces examined in Chapter 7 of this book; for an interesting collection of articles with recent findings, see Patricia Fernandez Kelly and Alejandro Portes (eds.), *Exceptional Outcomes: Achievement in Education and Employment among Children of Immigrants* (2008).

Transnational World (Chapter 8)

The theoretical reorientation toward migration systems theory that took place from the early 1990s onward was accompanied by a somewhat overlapping but nevertheless separate shift from national to transnational perspectives on migration and its impacts. A modern classic study in the transnational migration field is Linda Basch, Nina Glick Schiller, and Cristina Szanton Blanc's *Nations Unbound: Transnational Projects, Postcolonial Predicaments, and Deterritorialized Nation-States* (1994). Peggy Levitt's *God Needs No Passport: Immigrants and the Changing American Religious Landscape* (2007) is highly readable and provides an updated bibliography. For a recent overview of the field, see Steven Vertovec's *Transnationalism* (2009). Several excellent books on transnational practices in Canada have been published recently. These include Vic Satzewich and Lloyd Wong's edited volume, *Transnational Identities and Practices in Canada* (2006), containing 15 original papers by researchers in the field, plus substantive introduction and conclusions. Luin Goldring and Sailaja Krishnamurti's edited collection, *Organizing the Transnational: Labour, Politics, and Social Change* (2007) makes available 16 original papers by researchers in the field along with an introduction reviewing the field and conclusions from the book. David Carment and David Bercuson's *The World in Canada: Diaspora, Demography, and Domestic Politics* (2008) offers a collection of 10 articles by expert authors, plus a substantive introduction and conclusion on the implications of a transnational world for Canadian foreign policies. For a review of global issues with respect to citizenship and transnationalism, see Peter Kivisto and Thomas Faist's *Citizenship Discourse, Theory, and Transnational Prospects* (2007).

Belonging, Identity, and Citizenship (Chapter 9)

Identity issues related to transnationalism are covered to some extent in the works on transnationalism, cited above. Canadian works examining immigrant and minority identity issues from a transnational perspective include Carl James's *Seeing Ourselves: Exploring Race, Ethnicity, and Culture* (3rd ed.) (2003). The title does not include identity, but in fact the book is mostly about cultural identity, based on original qualitative interviews, contextualized in a review of the literature. Vijay Agnew's edited volume, *Diaspora, Memory, and Identity* (2005) contains 11 chapters by researchers who provide qualitative analyses of specific cases of diasporas and immigrant communities in Canada and globally. Irene Bloemraad's *Becoming a Citizen: Incorporating Immigrants and Refugees in the United States and Canada* (2006) is an original study, based on secondary data and key-informant interviews, on the role of state multicultural policies and other factors in immigrant citizenship identities and adoption of citizenship in these two countries.

Migrant Workers (Chapter 10)

The analysis of migrant workers in this book is set in the context of issues of labour force reproduction and low fertility. Roderic Beaujot's *Earning and Caring in Canadian Families* (2000) analyzes original and secondary information on the way Canadian parents organize their paid jobs and domestic work, including child care, and the implications of the struggle in balancing all demands on them for their fertility — they have fewer children than they otherwise would like. Migrant worker programs are well covered in several recent works. Nandita Sharma's *Home Economics: Nationalism and the Making of "Migrant Workers" in Canada*, (2006) examines the racializing and marginalizing policy discourse and outcomes for live-in caregivers. Tanya Basok's *Tortillas and Tomatoes: Transmigrant Mexican Harvesters in Canada* (2002b) is an empirical study of the work and social circumstances of low-wage Mexican migrant workers in Canada. Deborah Barndt's *Tangled Routes: Women, Work, and Globalization on the Tomato Trail* (2002) examines the role of Mexican women workers in Mexico, the United States, and Canada in different stages and aspects of seasonal tomato production and year-round merchandising of tomatoes in North America. The Goldring and Krishnamurti (2007) edited volume referred to above under "Transnational World" includes a focus on migrant labour.

Research Journals

The main English-language international journals in the field are the *International Migration Review*, published by the Center for Migration Studies of New York and *International Migration*, published by the International Organization for Migration in Geneva. Both cover studies from nations around the globe, although the first gives somewhat more attention to the Americas while the second somewhat more to Europe. Articles on international migration, immigration, and immigrant settlement issues can be found in nearly all Canadian journals in the humanities, social sciences, and behavioural sciences.

Canadian Ethnic Studies, published for the Canadian Association of Ethnic Studies by the University of Calgary, is interdisciplinary and publishes papers on Canadian immigration and refugee policy, immigrant settlement, and ethnic identity and relations in Canada. The *International Journal of Migration and Integration*, sponsored by the Metropolis Project and various Canadian immigration policy research institutions, covers integration issues in Canada and other wealthy immigrant-receiving nations.

Web-Based Data and Analysis

A number of international institutions provide data on international migration and/or ongoing analysis of these data. In nearly all cases these institutions provide their data and research findings online. The United Nations Population Division provides estimates of population dynamics and the impact of emigration and immigration on population growth in nations around the world [http://esa.un.org/unpp/]. The Global Commission on International Migration completed its work in 2005, but its website continues to make available a wide range of excellent policy studies and other valuable reports on the global patterns of migration of all kinds, including trafficking and irregular or undocumented migration [http://www.gcim.org/en/]. The Centre for Migration Policy in Washington, D.C., offers an online database of information and maps on international migration flows around the world and a separate online database of information on national immigration policies around the world, in addition to links to diverse policy studies [http://www.migrationpolicy.org/]. The main source for current information on global refugee trends and policy issues and trends is the United Nations High Commissioner for Refugees (UNHCR) [http://www.unhcr.org/cgi-bin/texis/vtx/home].

The main Canadian sources for data and/or recent analysis of immigration issues are Citizenship and Immigration Canada (CIC) and Statistics Canada. CIC publishes an *Annual Report to Parliament*, providing an update on immigration objectives, targets, inflows by country of origin, and class of entry [http://www.cic.gc.ca/english/resources/publications/index.asp]. CIC also publishes an annual *Facts and Figures* report with far more detailed tables and charts on immigrant and migrant worker inflows and selected characteristics [http://www.cic.gc.ca/english/resources/statistics/menu-fact.asp]. Statistics Canada provides the results of analyses of census data and large surveys across a wide variety of immigration-related topics, including particularly the education, employment, jobs, earnings, and housing of immigrants. This is an extremely large, constantly updated website supported by an excellent key-word search engine from the main web page [http://www.statcan.gc.ca/]. Metropolis, an international network for comparative research and public policy development on migration, diversity, and immigrant integration, publishes short policy-oriented articles on Canadian immigration policy and integration issues under several series of reports, including *Diversity, Our Diverse Cities*, and *Canadian Issues*, all available in both English and French in hard copy, and online [http://canada.metropolis.net/publications/index_e.htm]. *Metropolis* also makes available online new research reports and information on upcoming conferences involving immigration policy advisers, community agencies serving immigrants, and researchers.

References

Abbott, Michael G. 2003. "The IMDB: A User's Overview of the Immigration Database." In *Canadian Immigration Policy for the 21st Century,* edited by Charles M. Beach, Alan G. Green, and Jeffrey G. Reitz (pp. 315–322). Montreal and Kingston: McGill-Queen's University Press.

Abbott, Michael G., and Charles M. Beach. 1993. "Immigrant Earnings Differentials and Birth-Year-Effects for Men in Canada: Post-war-1972." *Canadian Journal of Economics* 25:505–524.

Abella, Irving, and Harold Troper. 1982. *None Is Too Many: Canada and the Jews of Europe, 1933–1948.* Toronto: Lester & Orpen Dennys.

Abu-Laban, Yasmeen. 1998. "Welcome/STAY OUT: The Contradictions of Canadian Integration and Immigration Policies at the Millennium." *Canadian Ethnic Studies* XXX, 3:190–211.

Abu-Laban, Yasmeen, and Christina Gabriel. 2002. *Selling Diversity: Immigration, Multiculturalism, Employment Equity, and Globalization.* Peterborough: Broadview Press.

Abu-Laban, Yasmeen, and Judith Garber. 2005. "The Construction of the Geography of Immigration as a Policy Problem: The United States and Canada Compared." *Urban Affairs Review* 40(4): 520–561.

Acland, C.R., and W.J. Buxton. 1999. *Harold Innis in the New Century.* Montreal and Kingston: McGill-Queen's University Press.

Adelman, Howard. 1991. "Canadian Refugee Policy in the Postwar Period: An Analysis." In *Refugee Policy: Canada and the United States,* edited by Howard Adelman (pp. 172–223). Toronto: York Lanes Press.

Adelman, Howard, Allan Borowski, Meyer Burstein, and Lois Foster, eds. 1994. *Immigration and Refugee Policy: Australia and Canada Compared.* Melbourne: Melbourne University Press.

Agnew, Vijay, ed. 2005. *Diaspora, Memory, and Identity.* Toronto: University of Toronto Press.

Aizlewood, Amanda, and Ravi Pendakur. 2005. "Ethnicity and Social Capital in Canada." *Canadian Ethnic Studies* 37, 2:77–102.

Akbari, Ather H. 1995. "The Impact of Immigrants on Canada's Treasury, Circa 1990." In *Diminishing Returns: The Economics of Canada's Recent Immigration Policy,* edited by Don DeVoretz (pp. 113–127). Toronto: C.D. Howe Institute.

Alba, Richard, and Victor Nee. 1997. "Rethinking Assimilation Theory for a New Era of Immigration." *International Migration Review* 31, 4:826–874.

Anderson, A.B. 2001. "The Complexity of Ethnic Identities: A Postmodern Reevaluation." *Identity: An International Journal of Theory and Research* 1:209–223.

Anderson, Benedict. 1991. *Imagined Communities: Reflections on the Origin and Spread of Nationalism.* London: Verso.

Anderson, Christopher G., and Jerome H. Black. 2008. "The Political Integration of Newcomers, Minorities, and the Canadian-Born: Perspectives on Naturalization, Participation, and Representation." In *Immigration and Integration in Canada,* edited by John Biles, Meyer Burstein, and James Frideres (pp. 45–76). Montreal and Kingston: McGill-Queen's University Press.

Andoni, Lamis. 2007. "Protect Migrant Labour in Arab Nations." PostGlobal Archives. Retrieved 26 March 2009 [http://newsweek.washingtonpost.com/postglobal/lamis_andoni/2007/03/protect_migrant_labor_in_arab.html].

Appadurai, A. 1996. *Modernity at Large: Cultural Dimensions of Globalization.* Minneapolis: University of Minnesota Press.

Arat-Koç, Sedef. 1997. "From "Mothers of the Nation" to Migrant Workers." In *Not One of the Family: Foreign Domestic Workers in Canada,* edited by Abigail Bakan and Daiva Stasiulis (pp. 53–80). Toronto: University of Toronto Press.

Arat-Koç, Sedef. 1999. "Neo-liberalism, States Restructuring, and Immigration: Changes in Canadian Policies in the 1990s." *Journal of Canadian Studies* 34, 2:31–57.

Arat-Koç, Sedef. 2006a. "Whose Transnationalism? Canada 'Clash of Civilizations' Discourse, and Arab and Muslim Canadians." In *Transnational Identities and Practices in Canada,* edited by Vic Satzewich and Lloyd Wong (pp. 216–240). Vancouver: UBC Press.

Arat-Koç, Sedef. 2006b. "Whose Social Reproduction? Transnational Motherhood and Challenges to Feminist Political Economy." In *Social Reproduction: Feminist Political Economy Challenges Neo-liberalism,* edited by Meg Luxton and Kate Bezanson (pp. 75–92). Montreal and Kingston: McGill-Queen's University Press.

Auciello, Desi. 2006. "Workers Imported, Not Deported." *Toronto Sun,* April 28.

Aydemir, Abdurrahaman. 2003. "Effects of Business Cycles on the Labour Market Participation and Employment Rate Assimilation of Immigrants." In *Canadian Immigration Policy for the 21st Century,* edited by Charles M. Beach, Alan G. Green, and Jeffrey G. Reitz (pp. 373–412). Montreal and Kingston: McGill-Queen's University Press.

Aydemir, Abdurrahaman, Wen-Hao Chen, and Miles Corak. 2005. *Intergenerational Earnings Mobility among the Children of Canadian Immigrants.* Ottawa: Family and Labour Studies, Statistics Canada.

Aydemir, Abdurrahaman, Wen-Hao Chen, and Miles Corak. 2008. "Intergenerational Education Mobility among the Children of Canadian Immigrants." Statistics Canada Research Paper No. 267. Ottawa: Statistics Canada.

Aydemir, Abdurrahaman, and Mikal Skuterud. 2005. "Explaining the Deteriorating Entry Earnings of Canada's Immigrant Cohorts, 1966–2000." *Canadian Journal of Economics* 38:641–672.

Bader, Veit. 1997. "Ethnicity and Class: A Proto-Theoretical 'Mapping' Exercise." In *Multiculturalism in North America and Europe: Comparative Perspectives on Interethnic Relations and Social Incorporation,* edited by Wsevolod W. Isajiw (pp. 103–128). Toronto: Canadian Scholars' Press Inc.

Bakan, Abigail, and Daiva Stasiulis. 1997. *Not One of the Family: Foreign Domestic Workers in Canada.* Toronto: University of Toronto Press.

Baker, Michael, and Dwayne Benjamin. 1994. "The Performance of Immigrants in the Canadian Labour Market." *Journal of Labor Economics* 12:369–405.

Balakrishnan, T.R., Paul Maxim, and Rozzet Jurdi. 2005. "Social Class versus Cultural Identity as Factors in the Residential Segregation of Ethnic Groups in Toronto, Montreal, and Vancouver for 2001." *Canadian Studies in Population* 32:203–227.

Banting, Keith, Thomas J. Courchene, and F.L. Seidle, eds. 2007. *Belonging? Diversity, Recognition, and Shared Citizenship in Canada.* Montreal: Institute for Research on Public Policy.

Banton, Michael. 2007. "Weber on Ethnic Communities: A Critique." *Nations and Nationalism* 13, 1:19–35.

Barber, Benjamin R. 1996. *Jihad vs. McWorld.* New York: Ballantine Books.

Barber, Clarence L. 1955. "Canadian Tariff Policy." *Canadian Journal of Economics and Political Science* 21:513–530.

Barndt, Deborah. 2002. *Tangled Routes: Women, Work, and Globalization on the Tomato Trail.* New York: Rowman & Littlefield Publishers, Inc.

Barth, Fredrik. 1969. *Ethnic Groups and Boundaries: The Social Organization of Culture Difference.* Oslo: Universitetsforlaget.

Basch, Linda, Nina Glick Schiller, and Cristina Szanton Blanc. 1994. *Nations Unbound: Transnational Projects, Postcolonial Predicaments, and Deterritorialized Nation-States.* Amsterdam: Gordon and Breach Publishers.

Basok, Tanya. 2002a. "Fragmented Identities: The Case of Former Soviet Jews." *Identity: An International Journal of Theory and Research* 2:341–360.

Basok, Tanya. 2002b. *Tortillas and Tomatoes: Transmigrant Mexican Harvesters in Canada.* Montreal and Kingston: McGill-Queen's University Press.

Basok, Tanya, and Alan Simmons. 1993. "A Review of the Politics of Canadian Refugee Selection." In *The International Refugee Crisis: British and Canadian Responses,* edited by Vaughan Robinson (pp. 132–157). London: Macmillan.

Basran, Gurcharn S., and Li Zong. 1998. "Devaluation of Foreign Credentials as Perceived by Non-White Professional Immigrants." *Canadian Ethnic Studies* XXX, 3:6–23.

Bauder, Harald. 2003. "'Brain Abuse,' Or the Devaluation of Immigrant Labour in Canada." *Antipode* 35:699–717.

Bauder, Harald. 2006. *Labor Movement: How Migration Regulates Labor Markets.* New York: Oxford University Press.

Bauman, Z. 1991. *Modernity and Ambivalence.* Ithaca: Cornell University Press.

BBC. 2007. "No Stoning, Canada Migrants Told." British Broadcasting Corporation. Retrieved 23 March 2009 [http://news.bbc.co.uk/1/hi/world/americas/6316151.stm].

Beach, Charles M., Alan G. Green, and Jeffrey G. Reitz, eds. 2003. *Canadian Immigration Policy for the 21st Century.* Montreal and Kingston: McGill-Queen's University Press.

Beach, Charles M., and C. Worswick. 1993. "Is There a Double-Negative Effect on the Earnings of Immigrant Women?" *Canadian Public Policy* 19:36–53.

Beare, Margaret. 2007. *Money Laundering in Canada: Chasing Dirty and Dangerous Dollars.* Toronto: University of Toronto Press.

Beaudry, P., and D. Green. 2000. "Cohort Patterns in Canadian Earnings: Assessing the Role of Skill Premia in Inequality Trends." *Canadian Journal of Economics* 33, 4:907–936.

Beaujot, Roderic. 2000. *Earning and Caring in Canadian Families.* Peterborough: Broadview Press.

Beaujot, Roderic. 2003. "Effect of Immigration on Demographic Structure." In *Canadian Immigration Policy for the 21st Century,* edited by Charles M. Beach, Alan G. Green, and Jeffrey G. Reitz (pp. 49–92). Montreal and Kingston: McGill-Queen's University Press.

Becerril, Ofelia. 2007. "Transnational Work and the Gendered Politics of Labour: A Study of Male and Female Mexican Migrant Farm Workers in Canada." In *Organizing the Transnational: Labour, Politics, and Social Change,* edited by Luin Goldring and Sailaja Krishnamurti (pp. 157–172). Vancouver: UBC Press.

Bélanger, Alain and Éric Caron Malenfant. 2005. Ethnocultural diversity in Canada: Prospects for 2017. *Canadian Social Trends* 79 (Winter): 18–21.

Belanger, Claude. 2006. *Why Did Canada Refuse to Admit Jewish Refugees in the 1930's?* Montreal: The Quebec History Encyclopedia.

Belkhodja, Chedley. 2008. "The Discourse of New Individual Responsibility: The Controversy over Reasonable Accommodation in some French-Language Newspapers in Quebec and Canada." In *Immigration and Integration in Canada in the Twenty-first Century,* edited by John Biles, Meyer Burstein, and James Frideres (pp. 253–268). Montreal and Kingston: McGill-Queen's University Press.

Berger, Peter L., and Thomas Luckmann. 1966. *The Social Construction of Reality: A Treatise in the Sociology of Knowledge*. Garden City: Doubleday.

Bergman, Barbara. 1996. *Saving Our Children from Poverty: What the United States Can Learn from France*. New York: Russell Sage Foundation.

Bergman, Mike. 2004. "Census Bureau Projects Tripling of Hispanic and Asian Populations in 50 Years; Non-Hispanic Whites May Drop To Half of Total Population". *U.S. Census Bureau News Release*. Retrieved 16 March 2009. [http://www.census.gov/Press-Release/www/releases/archives/population/001720.html]

Bernard, André. 2008. "Immigrants in the Hinterlands." *Perspectives on Labour and Income* 9:1, 5-14. Ottawa: Statistics Canada.

Berry, John W. 2001. "A Psychology of Immigration." *Journal of Social Issues* 57:615-631.

Berry, John W., Y. Poortiga, M. Segall, and P. Dasen. 2002. *Cross-cultural Psychology: Research and Applications* (2nd ed.). New York: Cambridge University Press.

Bhabha, Homi K. 1994. *The Location of Culture* (1st ed.). London: Routledge.

Biles, John. 2008. "Integration Policies in English-Speaking Canada." In *Immigration and Integration in Canada in the Twenty-first Century*, edited by John Biles, Meyer Burstein, and James Frideres (pp. 139-186). Montreal and Kingston: McGill-Queen's University Press.

Biles, John, Meyer Burstein, and James Frideres, eds. 2008. *Immigration and Integration in Canada in the Twenty-first Century*. Montreal and Kingston: McGill-Queen's University Press.

Binford, Leigh. 2004. "Contract Labor in Canada and the United States: A Critical Appreciation of Tanya Basok's *Tortillas and Tomatoes: Transmigrant Mexican Harvesters in Canada*." *Canadian Journal of Latin American and Caribbean Studies* 29:289-308.

Binford, Leigh, Guillermo C. Rivas, and Socorro A. Hernandez. 2004. *Rumbo a Canada: La Migracion Canadiense De Trabajadores Agricolas Tlaxcaltecos*. Colonia San Rafael: Editiones Taller Abierto.

Bissoondath, Neil. 1994. *Selling Illusions: The Cult of Multiculturalism in Canada*. Toronto: Penguin.

Bloemraad, Irene. 2000. "Citizenship and Immigration: A Current Review." *Journal of International Migration and Integration* 1:9-37.

Bloemraad, Irene. 2006. *Becoming a Citizen: Incorporating Immigrants and Refugees in the United States and Canada*. Berkeley: University of California Press.

Bloom, David E., G. Grenier, and Morley Gunderson. 1995. "The Changing Labour Market Position of Canadian Immigrants." *Canadian Journal of Economics* 28:987-1005.

Bloom, David E., and Morley Gunderson. 1991. "An Analysis of the Earnings of Canadian Immigrants." In *Immigration, Trade, and the Labour Market*, edited by John M. Abowd and Richard B. Freeman (pp. 321-342). Chicago: The University of Chicago Press.

Bloom, Michael, and Michael Grant. 2001. *Brain Gain: The Economic Benefits of Recognizing Learning and Learning Credentials in Canada*. Ottawa: Conference Board of Canada.

Bonikowska, Aneta, David A. Green, and W.C. Riddell. 2008. *Cognitive Skills and Immigrant Earnings*. Ottawa: Statistics Canada.

Borjas, G. 1985. "Assimilation, Change in Cohort Quality, and the Earnings of Immigrants." *Journal of Labor Economics* 3:463-489.

Borjas, G.J. 1993. "Immigration Policy, National Origin, and Immigrant Skills: A Comparison of Canada and the United States." In *Small Differences That Matter: Labor Markets and Income Maintenance in Canada and the United States*, edited by D. Card and R.B. Freeman (pp. 21-43). Chicago: University of Chicago Press.

Bouchard, Gerard, and Charles Taylor. 2008. *Building the Future: A Time for Reconciliation*. Quebec City: Government of Quebec.

Bourdieu, Pierre. 1977. *Outline of a Theory of Practice.* Translated by Richard Nice. Cambridge: Cambridge University Press.

Bourdieu, Pierre. 1998. *Practical Reason.* Stanford: Stanford University Press.

Bourhis, Richard. 2003. "Measuring Ethnocultural Diversity Using the Canadian Census." *Canadian Ethnic Studies* 35, 1:9–32.

Boyd, Monica. 1989. "Family and Personal Networks in International Migration: Recent Developments and New Agendas." *International Migration Review* 23:638–670.

Boyd, Monica. 2002. "Educational Attainments of Immigrant Offspring: Success or Segmented Assimilation?" *International Migration Review* 36:1037–1060.

Boyd, Monica. 2008. "Variations in Socioeconomic Outcomes of Second-Generation Young Adults." *Canadian Diversity* 6:20–24.

Boyd, Monica, Gustave Goldman, and Pamela White. 2000. "Race in the Canadian Census." In *Visible Minorities in Canada,* edited by Leo Driedger and Shiva Halli (pp. 33–54). Montreal and Toronto: McGill-Queen's and Carleton University Press.

Boyd, Monica, and Grant Schellenberg. 2007. "Re-accreditation and the Occupations of Immigrant Doctors and Engineers." *Canadian Social Trends* 84: 2–8

Boyd, Monica, and Grant Schellenberg. 2008. *Re-accreditation and the Occupations of Immigrant Doctors and Engineers.* Ottawa: Statistics Canada.

Brais, B., B. Desjardins, D. Labuda, M. St-Hilaire, M. Tremblay, and H. Vezina. 2007. "The Genetics of French Canadians," In *Human Population Genetics: Evolution and Variation,* edited by L. Cavalli-Sforza, and M. Feldman. London: The Biomedical & Life Sciences Collection, Henry Stewart Talks Ltd. Available online [http://www.hstalks.com/bio]

Brender, Natalie. 2009. "If We're Going to Talk Citizenship, Let's Have a Principled Debate." Toronto: *Globe and Mail* (8 April), A19.

Breton, Raymond. 2005. *Ethnic Relations in Canada: Institutional Dynamics.* Montreal and Kingston: McGill-Queen's University Press.

Breton, Raymond, Wsevolod W. Isajiw, Warren E. Kalbach, and Jeffrey G. Reitz. 1990. *Ethnic Identity and Equality: Varieties of Experience in a Canadian City.* Toronto: University of Toronto Press.

Brettell, Caroline, and James Hollifield, eds. 2000. *Migration Theory: Talking across Disciplines.* New York: Routledge.

Bronfenbrenner, Urie, ed. 2005. *Making Human Beings Human: Bioecological Perspectives on Human Development.* Thousand Oaks: Sage Publications.

Burawoy, M. 1976. "The Functions and Reproduction of Migrant Labor: Comparative Material from South Africa and the United States." *American Journal of Sociology* 81:1050–1087.

Calliste, Agnes. 1991. "Canada's Immigration Policy and Domestics from the Caribbean: The Second Domestic Scheme." In *Race, Class, Gender: Bonds and Barriers,* edited by Jesse Vorst (pp. 136–168). Toronto: Garamond Press.

Canada Gazette. 2008. "Regulations Amending the Immigration and Refugee Protection Regulations (Canadian Experience Class)." *Canada Gazette* 142, no. 10.

Cardu, Helene. 2007. "Career Nomadism and the Building of a Professional Identity in Female Immigrants." *Journal of International Migration and Integration* 8:429–439.

Carment, David, and David Bercuson, eds. 2008. *The World in Geography: Diaspora, Demography, and Domestic Politics.* Montreal and Kingston: McGill-Queen's University Press.

Carranza, Mirna E. 2007. "Salvadorian Mothers and Their Daughters: Navigating the Hazards of Acculturation in the Canadian Context." Ph.D. dissertation, Department of Family Relations, University of Guelph, Guelph.

Carter, Tom, Margot Morrish, and Benjamin Amoyaw. 2008. "Attracting Immigrants to Smaller Urban and Rural Communities: Lessons Learned from the Manitoba Provincial Nominee Program." *International Migration and Integration* 9:161–183.

Castles, Stephen. 1986. "The Guestworker in Western Europe: An Obituary." *International Migration Review* 20, 3:761–778.

Castles, Stephen. 1989. *Migrant Workers and the Transformation of Western Societies*. Ithaca: Cornell University Press.

Castles, Stephen. 2002. "Migration and Community Formation under Conditions of Globalization." *International Migration Review* 36, 4:1143–1169.

Castles, Stephen, and Mark J. Miller. 2003. *The Age of Migration: International Population Movements in the Modern World* (3rd ed.). New York: Guilford Press.

CBA. 2009. "Chinese Benevolent Association of Vancouver." Chinese Benevolent Association. Retrieved 14 January 2009 [http://www.cbavancouver.ca/index.html].

CCA. 2006. "Discussion Paper: Immigration and Foreign Workers." Canadian Construction Association. Retrieved 26 March 2009 [www.cca-acc.com/news/government/immigration/immigrationpaper-june06.pdf].

CCA. 2008. "Accomplishments." Canadian Construction Association. Retrieved 26 March 2009 [http://www.cca-acc.com/overview/accomplishments/accomplishments_e.asp].

Chamie, Joseph. 2008. "12 Million Shadows: America's Immigration Dilemma." *Yale Global Online*, February 4. Retrieved 26 March 2008. [http://yaleglobal.yale.edu/display.article?id=10296]

Chan, Benjamin. 2002. *From Perceived Surplus to Perceived Shortage: What Happened to Canada's Physician Workforce in the 1990s?* Ottawa: Canadian Institute for Health Information.

Chant, John. 2006. *The Passport Package: Rethinking the Citizenship Benefits of Non-resident Canadians*. Toronto: C.D. Howe Institute.

Cheran, R. 2007. "Transnationalism, Development, and Social Capital: Tamil Community Networks in Canada." In *Organizing the Transnational: Labour, Politics, and Social Change*, edited by Luin Goldring and Sailaja Krishnamurti (pp. 129–144). Vancouver: UBC Press.

Chiswick, Barry R. 1978. "The Effect of Americanization on the Earnings of Foreign-Born Men." *Journal of Political Economy* 86:897–921.

CIC. 1991. *Immigration: The Canada–Quebec Accord*. Ottawa: Citizenship and Immigration Canada.

CIC. 2001. *Planning Now for Canada's Future: Introducing a Multi-year Planning Process and Immigration Plan for 2001 and 2002*. Ottawa: Citizenship and Immigration Canada. C&I-421-02-01.

CIC. 2002. *Canada–U.S. Safe Third Country Agreement*. Ottawa: Citizenship and Immigration Canada.

CIC. 2004. *Dual Citizenship*. Ottawa: Minister of Public Works and Government Services Canada.

CIC. 2005a. *Annual Report*. Ottawa: Citizenship and Immigration Canada.

CIC. 2005b. "Facts and Figures 2005." Citizenship and Immigration Canada. Retrieved November 2005 [http://www.cic.gc.ca.ezproxy.library.yorku.ca/english/resources/statistics/menu-fact.asp].

CIC. 2006a. *Annual Report to Parliament on Immigration, 2006*. Ottawa: Citizenship and Immigration Canada.

CIC. 2006b. *The Monitor: Foreign Worker Overview*. Ottawa: Citizenship and Immigration Canada.

CIC. 2007a. *Annual Report to Parliament on Immigration, 2007*. Ottawa: Citizenship and Immigration Canada.

CIC. 2007b. "Facts and Figures 2007. Immigration Overview: Permanent and Temporary Residents." Citizenship and Immigration Canada. Retrieved 26 March 2009 [http://www.cic.gc.ca.ezproxy.library.yorku.ca/english/resources/statistics/menu-fact.asp].

CIC. 2008a. *Canadian Experience Class up and Running.* Ottawa: Citizenship and Immigration Canada.

CIC. 2008b. *OECD Recommends That Lower-Income Workers Be Included in Immigration Policy.* Ottawa: Canadian Immigration Canada.

CIC. 2008c. *Annual Report to Parliament on Immigration, 2008.* Ottawa: Citizenship and Immigration Canada.

Clark, Stephen, and Orly Halpern. 2009. "Canada Lagged in Helping Get Citizens out of Gaza." *Globe and Mail*, January 6, A1.

Clarkson, Stephen. 1991. "Disjunctions: Free Trade and the Paradox of Canadian Development." In *The New Era of Global Competition*, edited by Daniel Drache and Meric S. Gertler (pp. 103–126). Montreal and Kingston: McGill-Queen's University Press.

Clement, Wallace, ed. 1997. *Understanding Canada: Building on the New Canadian Political Economy.* Montreal and Kingston: McGill-Queen's University Press.

Cohen, Robin. 1987. *The New Helots: Migrants in the International Division of Labour.* Aldershot: Gower Publishing.

Coleman, James S. 1988. "Social Capital in the Creation of Human Capital." *American Journal of Sociology* 94:S95–S120.

Coleman, James C. 1990. *Foundations of Social Theory.* Cambridge: Harvard University Press.

Conversi, Daniele, ed. 2002. *Ethnonationalism in the Contemporary World.* New York: Routledge.

Corak, Miles. 2008. "Immigration in the Long Run." *IRRP Choices* 14, no. 13 (October): 4–30.

Cordell, Dennis, Joel Gregory, and Victor Piché. 1996. *Hoe and Wage: A Social History of a Circular Migration System in West Africa.* Boulder: Westview Press.

Couton, Philippe, and Stephanie Gaudet. 2008. "Rethinking Social Participation: The Case of Immigrants in Canada." *Journal of International Migration and Integration* 9:21–44.

Cranford, Cynthia J. 2005. "Networks of Exploitation: Immigrant Labor and the Restructuring of the Los Angeles Janitorial Industry." *Social Problems* 52, 3:379–397.

Cranford, Cynthia J. 2007a. "Constructing Union Motherhood: Gender and Social Reproduction in the Los Angeles 'Justice for Janitors' Movement." *Qualitative Sociology* 30:361–381.

Cranford, Cynthia J. 2007b. "'It's Time to Leave Machismo behind!': Challenging Gender Inequality in an Immigrant Union." *Gender & Society* 21:409–438.

Creese, Gillian, Isabel Dyck, and Arlene T. McLaren. 2008. "The 'Flexible' Immigrant? Human Capital Discourse, the Family Household, and Labour Market Strategies." *Journal of International Migration and Integration* 9:269–288.

Creese, Gillian, and Edith N. Kambere. 2003. "What Colour Is Your English?" *Canadian Review of Sociology and Anthropology* 40:565–573.

CRIC. 2003. *A New Canada? The Evolution of Canadian Identity and Attitudes to Diversity.* Ottawa: Centre for Research and Information on Canada.

CTV. 2006. "Planeload of Deportees Flown to Portugal." Toronto: CTV News.

CTV. 2007. "Federal Court Strikes down Refugee Agreement" (30 November 2007). CTV News. Retrieved 23 November 2008 [http://www.ctv.ca/servlet/ArticleNews/story/CTVNews/20071130/refugees_071130/20071130?hub=TopStories].

Curry, Bill. 2008. "Fraud Squads Chase down Marriages of Convenience." *Globe and Mail*, My 21, A1.

da Silva Santos, Orlando. 2005. *Undocumented Workers – An Issue of Particular Relevance to Canadian Residents of Portuguese Origin.* Toronto: Portuguese Canadian National Congress.

de Vasconcelos, P. 2004. "Sending Money Home: Remittances as a Development Tool in Latin America and the Caribbean." Inter-American Development Bank, Multilateral Investment

Fund. Retrieved 14 August 2007 [http://idbdocs.iadb.org.ezproxy.library.yorku.ca/wsdocs/getdocument.aspx?docnum=547263].

Department of Justice. 1982. "Canadian Charter of Rights and Freedoms." Retrieved 26 March 2009. [http://laws.justice.gc/en/charter]

Derwing, Tracey M., and Harvey Krahn. 2008. "Attracting and Retaining Immigrants Outside the Metropolis: Is the Pie Too Small for Everyone to Have a Piece? The Case of Edmonton, Alberta. *International Migration and Integration* 9:185–202.

DeVoretz, Don, ed. 1995. *Diminishing Returns: The Economics of Canada's Recent Immigration Policy.* Toronto: C.D. Howe Institute.

DeVoretz, Don. 2008. "An Auction Model of Canadian Temporary Immigration for the 21st Century." *International Migration* 46:1, 3–17.

Drache, Daniel, and Wallace Clement, eds. 1985. *The New Practical Guide to Canadian Political Economy.* Toronto: James Lorimer & Company, Publishers.

Driedger, Leo. 2003a. *Race and Ethnicity: Finding Identities and Equalities.* Toronto: Oxford University Press.

Driedger, Leo. 2003b. "Changing Boundaries: Sorting Space, Class, Ethnicity, and Race in Ontario." *Canadian Review of Sociology and Anthropology* 40:593–621.

Driedger, Leo, and Shiva Halli, eds. 2000. *Race and Racism: Canada's Challenge.* Montreal and Kingston: McGill-Queen's University Press.

Dryburgh, Heather, and Jason Hamel. 2004. "Immigrants in Demand: Staying or Leaving?" *Canadian Social Trends* 74:12–17.

Durand, Jorge, Emilio Parrado, and Douglas Massey. 1996. "Migradollars and Development: A Reconsideration of the Mexican Case." *International Migration Review* 30:423–444.

Eden, Lorraine, and Maureen A. Molot. 1993. "Canada's National Policies: Reflections on 125 Years." *Canadian Public Policy* 19:232–251.

EIC. 1985. *The Revised Selection Criteria for Independent Immigrants.* Ottawa: Employment and Immigration Canada. WH-5-086.

EIC. 1990. *Report on the Consultations on Immigration for 1991–95.* Ottawa: Employment and Immigration Canada. IM-093/9/90.

EIC. 1992a. *Managing Immigration: A Framework for the 1990s.* Ottawa: Employment and Immigration Canada. IM 199/6/92.

EIC. 1992b. *Press Release 92-12 (31 March 1992): Amendments to Cost Recovery Program Phase 3B.* Ottawa: Employment and Immigration Canada. IM-07/4/92.

Eriksen, Thomas H. 2002. *Ethnicity and Nationalism: Anthropological Perspectives.* London: Pluto Press.

Esses, Victoria M., John F. Dovidio, L.M. Jackson, and T.L. Armstrong. 2001. "Public Attitudes toward Immigration in the United States and Canada in Response to the September 11, 2001 'Attack on America.'" *Journal of Social Issues* 57:389–412.

Esses, Victoria M., Gordon Hodson, and John F. Dovidio. 2003. "Public Attitudes toward Immigrants and Immigration: Determinants and Policy Implications." In *Canadian Immigration Policy for the 21st Century,* edited by Charles M. Beach, Alan G. Green, and Jeffrey G. Reitz (pp. 507–539). Montreal and Kingston: McGill-Queen's University Press.

Esses, Victoria M., U. Wagner, C. Wolf, M. Preisser, and C.J. Wilbur. 2006. "Perceptions of National Identity and Attitudes toward Immigrants and Immigration in Canada and Germany." *International Journal of Intercultural Relations* 30:653–669.

Faist, Thomas. 2000. *The Volume and Dynamics of International Migration and Transnational Social Spaces.* Oxford: Clarendon Press.

Falicov, Celia J. 1998. *Latino Families in Therapy: A Guide to Multicultural Practice.* New York: The Guilford Press.

Falicov, Celia J. 2003. "Immigrant Family Processes." In *Normal Family Processes: Growing Diversity and Complexity,* edited by Froma Walsh (pp. 280–300). New York and London: The Guilford Press.

Falicov, Celia J. 2005. "Emotional Transnationalism and Family Identities." *Family Process* 44, 4:399–406.

Falicov, Celia J. 2007. "Working with Transnational Immigrants: Expanding Meanings of Family, Community, and Culture." *Family Process* 46, 2:157–171.

Featherstone, M., ed. 1990. *Global Culture: Nationalism, Globalization, and Identity.* London: Sage.

Felipe, Alex. 2008. "Should Canada Deport Juana Tejada?" alex felipe photography [http://alexfelipe.com/2008/06/21/should-canada-deport-jauna-tejada/].

Fernandez Kelly, Patricia, and Alejandro Portes, eds. 2008. *Exceptional Outcomes: Achievement in Education and Employment among Children of Immigrants.* Thousand Oaks: Sage.

Ferrer, Ana, D. Green, and W.C. Riddell. 2006. "The Effect of Literacy on Immigrant Earnings." *The Journal of Human Resources* 41:380.

Ferrer, Ana, and W.C. Riddell. 2008. "Education, Credentials, and Immigrant Earnings." *The Canadian Journal of Economics* 41:186.

Fleras, Augie, and Jean L. Elliott. 2002. *Engaging Diversity: Multiculturalism in Canada.* Toronto: Nelson Thomson Learning.

Flores, William V., and Rina Benmayor, eds. 1997. *Latino Cultural Citizenship: Claiming Identity, Space, and Rights.* Boston: Beacon Press.

Fong, Eric. 2006. "Residential Segregation of Visible Minority Groups in Toronto." In *Inside the Mosaic,* edited by Eric Fong (pp. 51–75). Toronto: University of Toronto Press.

Foster, Cecil. 2005. *Where Race Does Not Matter.* Toronto: Penguin Canada.

Foster, Cecil. 2007. *Blackness and Modernity: The Colour of Humanity and the Quest for Freedom.* Montreal and Kingston: McGill-Queen's University Press.

Frenette, Marc, and Rene Morissette. 2003. *Will They Ever Converge? Earnings of Immigrant and Canadian-Born Workers over the Last Two Decades.* Ottawa: Statistics Canada, Analytical Studies Research Paper Series.

Frideres, James. 1997. "Edging into the Mainstream: A Comparison of Values and Attitudes of Recent Immigrants, Their Children, and Canadian-Born Adults." In *Multiculturalism in North America and Europe: Comparative Perspectives on Interethnic Relations and Social Incorporation,* edited by Wsevolod W. Isajiw (pp. 537–621). Toronto: Canadian Scholars' Press Inc.

Frideres, James. 2008. "Creating an Inclusive Society: Promoting Social Integration in Canada." In *Immigration and Integration in Canada in the Twenty-first Century,* edited by John Biles, Meyer Burstein, and James Frideres (pp. 77–102). Montreal and Kingston: McGill-Queen's University Press.

Froebel, F., J. Heinrichs, and O. Kreye. 1980. *The New International Division of Labour.* Cambridge: Cambridge University Press.

Gabriel, Christina, and Laura MacDonald. 2003. "Beyond the Continentalist/Nationalist Divide: Politics in North America 'Without Borders.'" In *Changing Canada: Political Economy as Transformation,* edited by Wallace Clement and Leah F. Vosko (pp. 213–240). Montreal and Kingston: McGill-Queen's University Press.

Gabriel, Christina, and Hélène Pellerin, eds. 2008. *Governing International Labour Migration: Current Issues, Challenges, and Dilemmas.* London and New York: Routledge.

Gagnon, Alain, and Raffaele Iacovino. 2004. "Interculturalism: Expanding the Boundaries of Citizenship." In *Quebec: State and Society,* edited by Alain Gagnon (pp. 369–388). Peterborough: Broadview Press.

Gans, Herbert J. 1997. "Toward a Reconciliation of 'Assimilation' and 'Pluralism': The Interplay of Acculturation and Ethnic Response." *International Migration Review* 31:875–892.

Garcea, Joseph. 1998. "Bicommunalism and the Bifurcation of the Immigration System." *Canadian Ethnic Studies* XXX, 3:149–172.

GCIM. 2005. *Migration in an Interconnected World: New Directions for Action.* Geneva: Global Commission on International Migration (GCIM). Retrieved 21 August 2008 [http://www.gcim.org/en/].

Gee, Ellen M. 2000. "Voodoo Demography, Population Aging, and Social Policy." In *The Overselling of Population Aging,* edited by Ellen Gee and Gloria Gutman (pp. 5–25). Toronto: Oxford University Press.

Gee, Ellen M., and Gloria Gutman, eds. 2000. *The Overselling of Population Aging: Apocalyptic Demography, Intergenerational Challenges, and Social Policy.* Toronto: Oxford University Press.

Geertz, C., ed. 1963. *Old Societies and New States.* New York: Free Press.

Genizon Biosciences. 2009. "Quebec Founder Population: Its History." Retrieved 23 March 2009 [http://www.genizon.com/english/discovery/quebec_founder_history.html].

Gerber, Linda M. 2006. "The Visible Minority, Immigrant, and Bilingual Composition of Ridings and Party Support in the Canadian Federal Election of 2004." *Canadian Ethnic Studies Journal* 38:65–82.

Giddens, A. 1991. *Modernity and Self-Identity: Self and Society in the Late Modern Age.* Stanford: Stanford University Press.

Gill, S. 2003. *Power and Resistance in the New World Order.* New York: Palgrave Macmillan.

Gilmore, Jason, and Christel Le Petit. 2008. *The Canadian Immigrant Labour Market in 2007: Analysis by Region of Postsecondary Education.* Ottawa: Statistics Canada, Labour Statistics Division.

Globerman, Steven, ed. 1992. *The Immigration Dilemma.* Vancouver: The Fraser Institute.

Gobin, Denise. 1999. "The Differential Incorporation of Racial Minority Youths: Indo-Caribbean, Afro-Caribbean, and Punjabi Sikh Teens in Toronto and Surrounding Areas." Ph.D. dissertation, Department of Sociology, University of Toronto, Toronto.

Goldman, Gustave. 1998. "Shifts in the Ethnic Origins among the Offspring of Immigrants: Is Ethnic Mobility a Measurable Phenomenon?" *Canadian Ethnic Studies* XXX, 3:121–149.

Goldring, Luin. 2006. "Latin American Transnationalism in Canada: Does It Exist, What Forms Does It Take, and Where Is It Going?" In *Transnational Identities and Practices in Canada,* edited by Vic Satzewich and Lloyd Wong (pp. 180–201). Vancouver: UBC Press.

Goldring, Luin, and Sailaja Krishnamurti, eds. 2007. *Organizing the Transnational: Labour, Politics, and Social Change.* Vancouver: UBC Press.

Grant, Hugh, and Ronald Oertel. 1998. "Diminishing Returns to Immigration? Interpreting the Economic Experience of Canadian Immigrants." *Canadian Ethnic Studies* XXX, 3:56–76.

Grant, Hugh, and Arthur Sweetman. 2004. "Introduction to Economic and Urban Issues in Canadian Immigration Policy." *Canadian Journal of Urban Research* 13, 1:1–24.

Grant, M. 1999. "Evidence of New Immigrant Assimilation in Canada." *Canadian Journal of Economics* 32:930–955.

Grant, Peter R. 2007. "Accessing the Higher Echelons of a Host Country's Labour Market: Policy Directions from the Personal Experiences of Skilled Immigrants." *Journal of International Migration and Integration* 8:135–139.

Grant, Peter R., and Shevaun Nadin. 2007. "The Credentialing Problems of Foreign Trained Personnel from Asia and Africa Intending to Make Their Home in Canada: A Social Psychological Perspective." *Journal of International Migration and Integration* 8:141–162.

Grayson, J.P. 2008. "Linguistic Capital and Academic Achievement of Canadian- and Foreign-Born University Students." *Canadian Review of Sociology* 45:127–149.

Green, Alan G. 1976. *Immigration and the Postwar Canadian Economy*. Toronto: Macmillan.

Green, Alan G., and David A. Green. 1999. "The Economic Goals of Canada's Immigration Policy." *Canadian Public Policy* 25:425–451.

Green, David. 1995. "Intended and Actual Occupations of Immigrants." In *Diminishing Returns: The Economics of Canada's Recent Immigration Policy*, edited by Don DeVoretz (pp. 331–378). Toronto: C.D. Howe Institute.

Green, David A., and W.C. Riddell. 2003. "Literacy and Earnings: An Investigation of the Interaction of Cognitive and Unobserved Skills in Earnings Generation." *Labour Economics* 10:165–184.

Green, David A., and Christopher Worswick. 2002. *Earnings of Immigrant Men in Canada: The Roles of Labour Market Entry Effects and Returns to Foreign Experience*. Vancouver: Department of Economics, University of British Columbia.

Greenberg, Joshua. 2000. "Opinion Discourse and Canadian Newspapers: The Case of the Chinese 'Boat People.'" *Canadian Journal of Communication* 25, 4:517–538.

Gregory, Joel W., and Victor Piché. 1985. "Mode de production et régime démographique." *Canadian Journal of African Studies* 19:73–79.

Grinspun, Ricardo, and Yasmine Shamsie, eds. 2007. *Whose Canada? Continental Integration, Fortress North America, and the Corporate Agenda*. Montreal and Kingston: McGill-Queen's University Press.

Grondin, Chantal. 2007. *Knowledge of Official Languages among New Immigrants: How Important Is It in the Labour Market?* Ottawa: Statistics Canada.

Hacking, Ian. 1999. *The Social Construction of What?* Boston: Harvard University Press.

Hall, Stuart. 1992. "The Future of Identity." In *Modernity and Its Futures*, edited by Stuart Hall, David Held, and Tony McGrew (pp. 274–316). Cambridge: Polity Press.

Hardcastle, Leonie, Andrew Parkin, Alan Simmons, and Nobuaki Suyama. 1994. "The Making of Immigration and Refugee Policy: Politicians, Bureaucrats, and Citizens." In *Immigration and Refugee Policy: Australia and Canada Compared*, vol. 1, edited by Howard Adelman, Allan Borowski, Meyer Burstein, and Lois Foster (pp. 95–124). Melbourne: Melbourne University Press.

Harles, John. 2004. "Immigrant Integration in Canada and the United States." *American Review of Canadian Studies* 34, 2:223–258.

Harris, J.R., and Michael P. Todaro. 1970. "Migration, Unemployment, and Development: A Two-Sector Analysis." *American Economic Review* 60:126–142.

Hart, Michael. 2002. *A Trading Nation: Canadian Trade Policy from Colonialism to Globalization*. Vancouver: UBC Press.

Harvey, David. 1992. *The Condition of Postmodernity: An Inquiry into the Origins of Cultural Change*. Oxford: Blackwell Publishing.

Hawkins, Freda. 1988. *Canada and Immigration: Public Policy and Public Concern* (2nd ed.). Montreal and Kingston: McGill-Queen's University Press.

Hawkins, Freda. 1991. *Critical Years in Immigration: Canada and Australia Compared* (2nd ed.). Montreal and Kingston: McGill-Queen's University Press.

Health Match B.C. 2009. "Immigration Information." Health Match B.C. Retrieved 4 January 2009 [www.healthmatch.org/hmbc_physicians.asp?pageid=615].

Helliwell, John F. 1996. *Do Borders Matter for Social Capital: Economic Growth and Civic Culture in U.S. States and Canadian Provinces*. Ottawa: The National Bureau of Economic Research.

Henders, Susan J. 2007. "Emerging Postnational Citizenships in International Law: Implications for Transnational Lives and Organizing." In *Organizing the Transnational: Labour, Politics, and Social Change*, edited by Luin Goldring and Sailaja Krishnamurti (pp. 40–54). Vancouver: UBC Press.

Henry, Frances, and Carol Tator. 2000. *The Colour of Democracy: Racism in Canadian Society.* Toronto: Harcourt Canada.

Henry, Frances, and Carol Tator. 2002. *Discourses of Domination: Racial Bias in the Canadian English-Language Press.* Toronto: University of Toronto Press.

Henry, Frances, and Effie Ginsberg. 1985. *Who Gets to Work? A Test of Racial Discrimination in Employment.* Toronto: The Urban Alliance on Race Relations and the Social Planning Council of Metropolitan Toronto.

Hesse-Biber, Sharlene N., and Michelle L. Yaiser. 2004. *Feminist Perspectives on Social Research.* New York: Oxford University Press.

Hiebert, Daniel. 2003. *Are Immigrants Welcome? Introducing the Vancouver Community Studies Survey.* Vancouver: Vancouver Centre of Excellence: Research on Immigration and Integration in the Metropolis.

Hiebert, Daniel. 2005. *Migration and the Demographic Transformation of Canadian Cities: The Social Geography of Canada's Major Metropolitan Centres in 2017.* Burnaby: Vancouver Centre of Excellence.

Hiebert, Daniel, and David Ley. 2006. "Characteristics of Immigrant Transnationalism in Vancouver." In *Transnational Identities and Practices in Canada,* edited by Vic Satzewich and Lloyd Wong (pp. 71–90). Vancouver: UBC Press.

Hier, Sean, and Joshua Greenberg. 2002. "News Discourse and the Problematization of Chinese Migration to Canada." In *Discourses of Domination: Racial Bias in the Canadian English-Language Press,* by Frances Henry and Carol Tator, with this invited chapter by Hier and Greenberg (pp. 138–162). Toronto: University of Toronto Press.

Hill, Lawrence. 2001. *Black Berry, Sweet Juice: On Being Black and White in Canada.* Toronto: HarperCollins.

Hobsbawm, Eric J. 1992. *Nations and Nationalism since 1780: Programme, Myth, Reality.* New York: Cambridge University Press.

Hotaka Roth, Joshua. 2002. *Brokered Homeland: Japanese Brazilian Migrants in Japan.* Ithaca: Cornell University Press.

Hou, Feng, and Garnett Picot. 2003. "Visible-Minority Neighbourhood Enclaves and Labour Market Outcomes of Immigrants." In *Canadian Immigration Policy for the 21st Century,* edited by Charles M. Beach, Alan G. Green, and Jeffrey G. Reitz (pp. 537–572). Montreal and Kingston: McGill-Queen's University Press.

Houle, Rene, and Grant Schellenberg. 2008. *Remittances by Recent Immigrants.* Ottawa: Statistics Canada.

Howard-Hassman, Rhoda. 1999. "'Canadian' as an Ethnic Category: Implications for Multiculturalism and National Unity." *Canadian Public Policy* 15:523–537.

HRSDC. 2009. "Mandatory Retirement in Canada." Human Resources and Skills Development Canada. Retrieved 20 October 2008 [www.hrsdc.gc.ca/eng/lp/spila/clli/eslc/19Mandatory_Retirement.shtml].

Hulchanski, J.D. 2007. *The Three Cities within Toronto: Income Polarization among Toronto's Neighbourhoods, 1970–2000.* Toronto: Centre for Urban and Community Studies, University of Toronto.

Hum, Derek, and Wayne Simpson. 2003. *Reinterpreting the Performance of Immigrant Wages from Panel Data.* Winnipeg: Department of Economics, University of Manitoba.

Huntington, Samuel P. 1993. "The Clash of Civilizations?" *Foreign Affairs* 72:22–49.

Huntington, Samuel P. 1996. *The Clash of Civilizations and the Remaking of World Order.* New York: Simon & Schuster.

Hutynyk, John. 1997. "Adorno at Womad: South Asian Crossovers and the Limits of Hybridity-Talk." In *Debating Cultural Hybridity,* edited by Tariq Modood and Pnina Werbner (pp. 106–136). London: Zed Books.

Immigration Act. 1919. "An Act to Amend the Immigration Act." Ottawa: Dominion of Canada. Retrieved 23 March 2009 [http://www.canadiana.org.ezproxy.library.yorku.ca/ECO/ItemRecord/9_08048?id=326345caff9f5af6].

Innis, Harold. 1930. *The Fur Trade in Canada: An Introduction to Canadian Economic History.* Toronto: University of Toronto Press.

Innis, Harold. 1940. *The Cod Fisheries: The History of an International Economy.* Toronto: Ryerson Press.

Innis, Harold. 1952. *Changing Concepts of Time.* Toronto: University of Toronto Press.

Innis, Harold. 1956. *Essays in Canadian Economic History,* edited by Mary Innis. Toronto: University of Toronto Press.

IRB. 2009. "About the Immigration and Refugee Board of Canada." Immigration and Refugee Board of Canada. Retrieved 24 February 2009 [http://irb-cisr.gc.ca.ezproxy.library.yorku.ca].

Isajiw, Wsevolod W., ed. 1997. *Multiculturalism in North America and Europe: Comparative Perspectives on Interethnic Relations and Social Incorporation.* Toronto: Canadian Scholars' Press Inc.

Jakubowski, Lisa. 1997. *Immigration and the Legalization of Racism.* Halifax: Fernwood Publishing.

James, Carl E. 1990. *Making It: Black Youth, Racism, and Career Aspirations in a Big City.* Oakville: Mosiac Press.

James, Carl E. 1993. "Getting There and Staying There: Blacks' Employment Experience." In *Transitions: Schooling and Employment in Canada,* edited by P. Anisef and P. Axelrod (pp. 3–20). Toronto: Thompson.

James, Carl E. 1999. *Seeing Ourselves: Exploring Ethnicity, Race, and Culture.* Toronto: Thompson Educational Publishing, Inc.

James, Carl E. 2003. *Seeing Ourselves: Exploring Ethnicity, Race, and Culture,* 3rd ed. Toronto: Thompson Educational Publishing.

James, Carl E. 2005. "'I Feel Like a Trini': Narrative of a Generation-and-a-Half Canadian." In *Diaspora, Memory, and Identity,* edited by Vijay Agnew (pp. 230–254). Toronto: University of Toronto Press.

Jedwab, Jack. 2008. "Receiving and Giving: How Does the Canadian Public Feel about Immigration and Integration?" In *Immigration and Integration in Canada in the Twenty-first Century,* edited by John Biles, Meyer Burstein, and James Frideres (pp. 211–230). Montreal and Kingston: McGill-Queen's University Press.

Jeremic, Rusa. 2007. "Transnational Organizing in the Americas." In *Organizing the Transnational: Labour, Politics, and Social Change,* edited by Luin Goldring and Sailaja Krishnamurti (pp. 232–241). Vancouver: UBC Press.

Jimenez, Marina. 2003a. "200,000 Illegal Immigrants Toiling in Canada's Underground Economy." *Globe and Mail* (15 November), A1.

Jimenez, Marina. 2006. "Ottawa Rules Out Amnesty for 200,000 Illegal Workers." *Globe and Mail* (27 October), A1.

Johnson, Hugh. 1979. *The Voyage of the* Komagata Maru: *The Sikh Challenge to Canada's Colour Bar.* Bombay: Oxford University Press.

Jones Finer, Catherine. 2006. *Migration, Immigration, and Social Policy.* Malden: Blackwell.

Justice Canada. 1960. *Canadian Bill of Rights.* Ottawa: Justice Canada.

Justice Canada. 1982. *Charter of Rights and Freedoms.* Ottawa: Justice Canada.

Justicia. 2008. "Justicia for Migrant Workers." Retrieved 30 September 2008 [http://www.justicia4migrantworkers.org/].

Justus, Martha, and Jessie-Lynn MacDonald. 2003. "Longitudinal Survey of Immigrants to Canada." In *Canadian Immigration Policy for the 21st Century,* edited by Charles M. Beach, Alan G. Green, and Jeffrey G. Reitz (pp. 323–326). Montreal and Kingston: McGill-Queen's University Press.

Kallen, E. 2003. *Ethnicity and Human Rights in Canada.* Toronto: Oxford University Press.

Kapoor, Ilan. 2008. *The Postcolonial Politics of Development.* New York: Routledge.

Kazemipur, Abdolmohommad. 2006a. "A Canadian Exceptionalism? Trust and Diversity in Canadian Cities." *Journal of International Migration and Integration* 7:219–240.

Kazemipur, Abdolmohommad. 2006b. "The Market Value of Friendship: Social Networks of Immigrants." *Canadian Ethnic Studies* 38:47–71.

Kelley, Ninette, and Michael Trebilcock. 2000. *The Making of the Mosaic: A History of Canadian Immigration Policy.* Toronto: University of Toronto Press.

Kelly, Philip F. 2007. "Transnationalism and Political Participation among Filipinos in Canada." In *Organizing the Transnational: Labour, Politics, and Social Change,* edited by Luin Goldring and Sailaja Krishnamurti (pp. 215–231). Vancouver: UBC Press.

Kim, Ann H. 2005. "Panethnicity and Ethnic Resources in Residential Integration: A Comparative Study of Two Host Societies." *Canadian Studies in Population* 32:1–28.

Kivisto, Peter, and Thomas Faist. 2007. *Citizenship: Discourse, Theory, and Transnational Prospects.* Malden: Blackwell Publishing.

Knowles, Valerie. 1992. *Strangers at Our Gates: Canadian Immigration and Immigration Policy, 1540–1990.* Toronto: Dundurn Press.

Krahn, Harvey, and Alison Taylor. 2005. "Resilient Teenagers: Explaining the High Educational Aspirations of Visible-Minority Youth in Canada." *Journal of International Migration and Integration* 6:405–434.

Kritz, Mary M., Lin L. Lim, and Hania Zlotnik, eds. 1992. *International Migration Systems: A Global Approach.* Oxford: Clarendon Press.

Kritz, Mary M., and Hania Zlotnik. 1992. "Global Interactions: Migration Systems, Processes, and Policies." In *International Migration Systems: A Global Approach,* edited by Mary M. Kritz, Lin L. Lim, and Hania Zlotnik (pp. 1–18). Oxford: Clarendon Press.

Kubat, Daniel. 1993. "Canada: Immigration's Humanitarian Challenge." In *The Politics of Migration Policies: Settlement and Integration, the First World into the 1990s* (2nd ed.), edited by Daniel Kubat (pp. 23–44). New York: Center for Migration Studies.

Kuznets, Simon. 1966. *Modern Economic Growth: Rate, Structure, and Spread.* New Haven: Yale University Press.

Kymlicka, Will. 1995. *Multicultural Citizenship: A Liberal Theory of Minority Rights.* Oxford: Clarendon Press.

Labelle, Micheline, François Rocher, and Ann-Marie Field. 2006. "Contentious Politics and Transnationalism from below: The Case of Ethnic and Racialized Minorities in Quebec." In *Transnational Identities and Practices in Canada,* edited by Vic Satzewich and Lloyd Wong (pp. 111–129). Vancouver: UBC Press.

Lalonde, Richard L., Janelle M. Jones, and Mirella L. Stroink. 2008. "Racial Identity, Racial Attitudes, and Race Socialization among Black Canadian Parents." *Canadian Journal of Behavioural Science* 40:129–139.

Lam, Lawrence. 1996. *From Being Uprooted to Surviving.* Toronto: York Lanes Press, Inc.

Landolt, Patricia. 2007. "The Institutional Landscapes of Salvadoran Refugee Migration: Transnational and Local Views from Los Angeles and Toronto." In *Organizing the Transnational: Labour, Politics and Social Change,* edited by Luin Goldring and Sailaja Krishnamurti (pp. 191–205). Vancouver: UBC Press.

Lee, Everett S. 1966. "A Theory of Migration." *Demography* 3:47–57.

Lee, Henderson. 2005. "Foreign Doctors Are Not the Answer." *National Post,* Letter to the Editor (19 February).

Leong, Chan-Hoong, and Colleen Ward. 2006. "The influence of cultural values on attitudes toward immigrants and multiculturalism: The case of the Eurobarometer Survey on Racism and Xenophobia." *International Journal of Intercultural Relations* 30(6): 799–810.

Levitt, Peggy. 2007. *God Needs No Passport: Immigrants and the Changing American Religious Landscape*. New York: The New Press.

Levitt, Peggy, and Ninna Nyberg-Sorenson. 2004. *The Transnational Turn in Migration Studies*. Geneva: Global Commission on International Migration.

Lewington, Jennifer. 2009. "Aggressive Bid to Tackle City's Diversity 'Deficit.'" *Globe and Mail* (27 January), A11.

Ley, David, and Audrey Kobayashi. 2005. "Back to Hong Kong: Return Migration or Transnational Sojourn?" *Global Networks* 5:111–127.

Li, Peter. 1996. *The Making of Post-war Canada*. Toronto: Oxford University Press.

Li, Peter. 1998. *The Chinese in Canada*. Toronto: Oxford University Press.

Li, Peter. 2000. "Earning Disparities between Immigrants and Native-Born Canadians." *Canadian Review of Sociology and Anthropology* 37:289–312.

Li, Peter. 2001a. "The Market Worth of Immigrants' Educational Credentials." *Canadian Public Policy* 27:23–38.

Li, Peter. 2001b. "The Racial Subtext in Canada's Immigration Discourse." *Journal of International Migration and Integration* 2, 1:77–97.

Li, Peter. 2003a. "Deconstructing Canada's Discourse of Immigrant Integration." *Journal of International Migration and Integration* 4:315–33.

Li, Peter. 2003b. *Destination Canada: Immigration Debates and Issues*. Toronto: Oxford University Press.

Li, Peter. 2003c. "Initial Earnings and Catch-up Capacity of Immigrants." *Canadian Public Policy* 29:319–337.

Li, Peter. 2004. "Social Capital and Economic Outcomes for Immigrants and Ethnic Minorities." *Journal of International Migration and Integration* 5:171–190.

Li, Peter, and Chunhong Dong. 2007. "Earnings of Chinese Immigrants in the Enclave and Mainstream Economy." *Canadian Review of Sociology and Anthropology* 44:65–100.

LIDS. 2005. *Landed Immigrant Data System*. Ottawa: Citizenship and Immigration Canada. [The author wishes to thank the Centre of Excellence for Research on Immigrant Settlement, CERIS, Toronto, for access to this data set.]

Lo, Lucia, and Lu Wang. 2004. "A Political Economy Approach to Understanding the Economic Incorporation of Chinese Sub-ethnic Groups." *Journal of International Migration and Integration* 5:107–140.

Lowry, Michelle, and Peter Nyers. 2003. "No One Is Illegal." *Refuge: Canada's Periodical on Refugees* 21:66–72.

Luxton, Meg. 2006. "Feminist Political Economy in Canada and the Politics of Social Reproduction." In *Social Reproduction: Feminist Political Economy Challenges Neo-liberalism*, edited by Kate Bezanson and Meg Luxton (pp. 11–44). Montreal and Kingston: McGill-Queen's University Press.

Mabogunje, A.L. 1970. "Systems Approach to a Theory of Rural-Urban Migration." *Geographical Review* 2, 1:1–18.

Macklin, Audrey. 1994. "On the Inside Looking in: Foreign Domestic Workers in Canada." In *Maid in the Market: Women's Paid Domestic Labour*, edited by Wenona M. Giles and Sedef Arat-Koç (pp. 13–39). Halifax: Fernwood Publishing.

Mahtani, Minelle. 2006. "Interrogating the Hyphen-Nation: Canadian Multicultural Policy and 'Mixed Race' Identities." In *Identity and Belonging: Rethinking Race and Ethnicity in Canadian Society*, edited by Sean P. Hier and B.S. Bolaria (pp. 163–178). Toronto: Canadian Scholars' Press Inc.

Mahtani, Minelle. 2008. "How Are the Immigrants Seen — and What Do They Want to See? Contemporary Research on the Representation of Immigrants in the Canadian English-Language Media." In *Immigration and Integration in Canada in the Twenty-first Century*, edited by John Biles, Meyer Burstein, and James Frideres (pp. 231–252). Montreal and Kingston: McGill-Queen's University Press.

Maki, Allan. 2008. "Wrestler's Win Stood for Something Bigger." *Globe and Mail* (24 December), A3.

Manitoba. 2003. "Recruitment Changes for Foreign-Trained Doctors." Government of Manitoba, news release. Retrieved 15 November 2008 [www.gov.mb.ca/chc/press/top/2003/02/2003-02-06-01.html].

Martin, Philip. 1993. *Trade and Migration: NAFTA and Agriculture.* Washington: Institute for International Economics.

Martin, Philip, and J.E. Taylor. 1991. "Immigration Reform and Farm Labour Contracting in California." In *The Paper Curtain: Employer Sanctions Implementation, Impact, and Reform,* edited by Michael Fix (pp. 239–261). Washington: Urban Institute Press.

Mason, Gary. 2009. "With Speedy Probe Vancouver's Police Chief Passes First Big Test." *Globe and Mail* (27 January), A8.

Massey, Douglas S., Joaquin Arango, Graeme Hugo, Ali Kouaouci, Adela Pellegrino, and J.E. Taylor. 1993. "Theories of International Migration, Review, and Appraisal." *Population and Development Review* 19:431–466.

Massey, Douglas S., Joaquin Arango, Graeme Hugo, Ali Kouaouci, Adela Pellegrino, and J.E. Taylor. 1998. *Worlds in Motion: Understanding International Migration at the End of the Millennium.* Oxford and New York: Clarendon Press.

Massey, Douglas S., Joaquin Arango, Graeme Hugo, Ali Kouaouci, Adela Pellegrino, and J.E. Taylor. 1998. *Worlds in Motion: Understanding International Migration at the End of the Millennium.* New York: Clarendon Press.

Massey, Douglas S., and J.E. Taylor. 2004. *International Migration Prospects and Policies in a Global Market.* New York: Oxford University Press.

Mata, Fernando. 1985. "Latin American Immigration to Canada: Some Reflections on the Immigration Statistics." *Canadian Journal of Latin American and Caribbean Studies* 10, 20:35–40.

Mata, Fernando, and Don McRae. 2000. "Charitable Giving among the Foreign-Born in Canada." *Journal of International Migration and Integration* 1:205–232.

McCoy, Liza, and Cristi Masuch. 2007. "Beyond 'Entry-Level' Jobs: Immigrant Women and Non-regulated Professional Occupations." *Journal of International Migration and Integration* 8:185–206.

McDonald, Peter, and Rebecca Kippen. 2001. "Labor Supply Prospects in 16 Developed Countries, 2000–2050." *Population and Development Review* 27:1–32.

Meng, Ronald. 1987. "The Earnings of Canadian Immigrant and Native-Born Males." *Applied Economics* 19:1107–1119.

Menjivar, Cecilia. 2000. *Fragmented Ties: Salvadoran Immigrant Networks in America.* Los Angeles: University of California Press.

Mercer. 2008. "Mercer's 2008 Quality of Living." Retrieved 30 September 2008 [http://www.mercer.com/qualityofliving].

MIF. 2007. "Remittances: Lessons Learned." Retrieved 12 August 2007 [http://www.iadb.org.ezproxy.library.yorku.ca/mif/remesas.cfm?language=EN&parid=4&item1id=2].

Milligan, Kevin. 2002. *Quebec's Baby Bonus: Can Public Policy Raise Fertility?* Toronto: C.D. Howe Institute.

Morton, James. 1974. *In the Sea of Sterile Mountains: The Chinese in British Columbia.* Vancouver: J.J. Douglas.

Motta, Gaby, Carlos E. Terry, and Luin Goldring. 2007. "The Challenges of Extraterritorial Participation: Advisory Councils for Peruvians Abroad." In *Organizing the Transnational: Labour, Politics, and Social Change,* edited by Luin Goldring and Sailaja Krishnamurti (pp. 242–255). Vancouver: UBC Press.

Muecke, Marjorie M. 1995. "Trust, Abuse of Trust, and Mistrust among Cambodian Refugee Women: A Cultural Interpretation." In *Mistrusting Refugees,* edited by E.V. Daniel and John C. Knudsen (pp. 36–55). Berkeley: University of California Press.

Myles, John, and Feng Hou. 2004. "Changing Colours: Spatial Assimilation and New Racial Minority Immigrants." *Canadian Journal of Sociology* 29:29–58.

Nakamura, Alice, Masao Nakamura, and W.E. Diewert. 2003. "The Potential Impacts of Immigration on Productivity in Canada." In *Canadian Immigration Policy for the 21st Century,* edited by Charles M. Beach, Alan G. Green, and Jeffrey G. Reitz (pp. 255–292). Montreal and Kingston: McGill-Queen's University Press.

Nakhaie, M.R. 2006. "A Comparison of the Earnings of the Canadian Native-Born and Immigrants." *Canadian Ethnic Studies Journal* 38:19–46.

Nakhaie, M. 2007. "Ethnoracial Origins, Social Capital, and Earnings." *Journal of International Migration and Integration* 8:307–325.

Nederveen Peiterse, Jan. 1995. "Globalization as Hybridization." In *Global Modernities,* edited by Mike Featherstone, Scott Lash, and Rolland Robertson (pp. 45–68). London: Sage Publications.

Nederveen Pieterse, Jan. 2003. *Globalization and Culture: Global Melange.* Oxford: Rowman & Littlefield.

NFB. 1989. *Who Gets In?* National Film Board video, 113C 0189 110.

Nolin, Catherine. 2006. *Transnational Ruptures: Gender-Enforced Migration.* Burlington: Ashgate.

Nooneisillegal. 2009. "No One Is Illegal 2." Retrieved 23 March 2009 [http://toronto.nooneisillegal.org/node/253].

Norris, Doug. 2003. "New Household Surveys on Immigration." In *Canadian Immigration Policy for the 21st Century,* edited by Charles M. Beach, Alan G. Green, and Jeffrey G. Reitz (pp. 327–334). Montreal and Kingston: McGill-Queen's University Press.

Norris, Doug, and Monica Boyd. 2001. "Who Are the 'Canadians'? Changing the Census Responses, 1986–1996." *Canadian Ethnic Studies* 33:1–25.

North-South Institute. 2006. *Migrant Workers in Canada: A Review of the Canadian Seasonal Agricultural Workers Program.* Ottawa: North-South Institute.

OCASI. 2005. "The Regularization of Non-status Immigrants in Canada 1960–2004: Past Policies, Current Perspectives, Active Campaigns." Ontario Council of Agencies Serving Immigrants (OCASI). Retrieved 23 March 2009 [http://www.ocasi.org/STATUS/index.asp/].

Orozco, Manuel. 2005. "Hometown Associations and Development: Ownership, Correspondence, Sustainability, and Replicability." In *New Patterns for Mexico: Observations on Remittances, Philanthropic Giving, and Equitable Development,* edited by Barbara J. Merz (pp. 1–38). Cambridge: Global Equity Initiative, Harvard University.

Orozco, Manuel, and Rebecca Rouse. 2007. *Migrant Hometown Associations and Opportunities for Development: A Global Perspective.* Migration Information Source.

Palameta, Boris. 2007. "Economic Integration of Immigrants' Children." *Perspectives on Labour and Income* 8:5–16.

Parai, L. 1975. "Canada's Immigration Policy, 1962–1974." *International Migration Review* 9, 4:449–477.

Parent, Daniel, and Ling Wang. 2002. *Tax Incentives and Fertility in Canada: Permanent vs. Transitory Effects.* CIRANO Working Papers. Montreal: McGill University.

Passell, Geoffrey. 2005. *Unauthorized Migrants: Numbers and Characteristics. Background Briefing Prepared for Task Force on Immigration and America's Future.* Washington: Pew Hispanic Center.

Pendakur, Krishna, and Ravi Pendakur. 1998. "The Colour of Money: Earnings Differentials among Ethnic Groups in Canada." *Canadian Journal of Economics* 31:518–548.

Pendakur, Krishna, and Ravi Pendakur. 2002. "Language as Both Human Capital and Ethnicity." *International Migration Review* 36:147–177.

Perry, Marc D. 2008. "Global Black Self-Fashionings: Hip Hop as Diasporic Space." *Identities* 15:635–664.

Philip, L. Martin, and Andrew Mason, and C.L. Tsay. 1996. "The Anatomy of a Migration Hump." In *Development Strategy, Employment, and Migration: Insights from Models,* edited by J.E. Taylor (pp. 43–62). Paris: OECD Development Center.

Philip, L. Martin, Andrew Mason, Ching-lung Tsay, and Edward Taylor. 1991. "Immigration Reform and Farm Labor Contracting in California." In *The Paper Curtain: Employer Sanctions Implementation, Impact, and Reform,* edited by Michael Fix (pp. 239–261). Washington,: Urban Institute Press.

Picot, Garnett. 1998. *What Is Happening to Earnings Inequality and Youth Wages in the 1990s?* Analytical Studies Research Paper Series. Ottawa: Statistics Canada.

Picot, Garnett, Feng Hou, and Simon Coulombe. 2007. *Chronic Low Income and Low-Income Dynamics among Recent Immigrants.* Analytical Studies Branch Research Paper Series. Ottawa: Statistics Canada

Picot, Garnett, and Arthur Sweetman. 2005. *The Deteriorating Economic Welfare of Immigrants and Possible Causes: Update 2005.* Ottawa: Business and Labour Market Analysis, Statistics Canada.

Piore, Michael J. 1979. *Birds of Passage: Migrant Labor in Industrial Societies.* New York: Cambridge University Press.

Piper, Nicola. 2008. "Governance of Economic Migration and Trasnationalization of Rights." In *Governing International Labour Migration: Current Issues, Challenges and Dilemmas,* edited by Christina Gabriel and Hélène Pellerin (pp. 182–197). London and New York: Routledge.

Plaza, Dwaine. 2000. "Transnational Grannies: The Changing Family Responsibilities of Elderly African Caribbean-Born Women Resident in Britain." *Social Indicators Research 1,* 1:75–105.

Pomfret, Richard. 1989. *The Economic Development of Canada.* Toronto: Nelson Canada.

Pong, Raymond, and Roger Pitblado. 2006. *Geographic Distribution of Physicians in Canada: Beyond How Many and Where.* Ottawa: Canadian Institute for Health Information.

Porter, J. 1965. *The Vertical Mosaic.* Toronto: University of Toronto Press.

Portes, Alejandro, ed. 1995. *The Economic Sociology of Immigration: Essays on Networks, Ethnicity, and Entrepreneurship.* New York: Sage.

Portes, Alejandro. 1998. "Social Capital: Its Origins and Applications in Modern Sociology." *Annual Review of Sociology* 24:1–24.

Portes, Alejandro. 2003. "Conclusions: Theoretical Convergences and Empirical Evidence in the Study of Immigrant Transnationalism." *International Migration Review* 37:874–892.

Portes, Alejandro, Cristina Escobar, and Alexandria W. Radford. 2007. "Immigrant Transnational Organizations and Development: A Comparative Study." *International Migration Review* 41:242–281.

Portes, Alejandro, Patricia Fernandez Kelly, and William Haller. 2005. "Segmented Assimilation on the Ground: The New Second Generation in Early Adulthood." *Ethnic and Racial Studies* 28:1000–1040.

Portes, Alejandro, L.E. Guarnizo, and P. Landolt. 1999. "The Study of Transnationalism: Pitfalls and Promise of an Emergent Research Field." *Ethnic and Racial Studies* 22, 2:217–237.

Portes, Alejandro, W. Haller, and L.E. Guarnizo. 2002. "Transnational Entrepreneurship among Latin Immigrant Groups in the U.S." *American Sociological Review* 67, 2:278–298.

Portes, Alejandro, and Patricia Landolt. 1996. "The Downside of Social Capital." *The American Prospect* 26:18–22.

Portes, Alejandro, and Ruben Rumbaut. 2001. *Legacies: The Story of the Immigrant Second Generation.* Los Angeles: University of California Press.

Preibisch, Kerry. 2007. "Globalizing Work, Globalizing Citizenship: Community-Migrant Worker Alliances in Southern Ontario." In *Organizing the Transnational: Labour, Politics, and Social Change,* edited by Luin Goldring and Sailaja Krishnamurti (pp. 98–114). Vancouver: UBC Press.

Preibisch, Kerry, and Leigh Binford. 2007. "Interrogating Racialized Global Labour Supply: An Exploration of the Racial/National Replacement of Foreign Agricultural Workers in Canada." *Canadian Review of Sociology and Anthropology* 44, 1:5–36.

Preston, Valerie. 2009. *Immigrants and Homelessness: A Risk in Canada's Outer Suburb: A Pilot Study in York Region.* Toronto: CERIS. Retrieved 9 July 2009 [http://ceris.metropolis.net/research-policy/Homelessness/index.htm]

Preston, Valerie, Audrey Kobayashi, and Myer Siemiatycki. 2006. "Transnational Urbanism: Toronto at a Crossroads." In *Transnational Identities and Practices in Canada,* edited by Vic Satzewich and Lloyd Wong (pp. 91–110). Vancouver: UBC Press.

Putnam, Robert D. 1995. "Tuning in, Tuning out: The Strange Disappearance of Social Capital in America." *Political Science and Politics* 27:664–683.

Putnam, Robert D. 2000. *Bowling Alone: The Collapse and Revival of American Community.* New York: Simon & Schuster.

Qadeer, Mohammad, and Sandeep Kumar. 2006. "Ethnic Enclaves and Social Cohesion." *Canadian Journal of Urban Research* 15:1–17.

Rajiva, Mythili. 2006. "Brown Girls, White Worlds: Adolescence and the Making of Racialized Selves." *Canadian Review of Sociology and Anthropology* 43:165–183.

Rallu, Jean-Louis, Victor Piché, and Patrick Simon. 2005. "Demography and Ethnicity: An Ambiguous Relationship." Section II, Chapter 95 in *Demography: Analysis and Synthesis,* vol. 3, edited by Graziella Casseli, Jacques Vallin, and Guillaume Wunsch, pp. 531–550. Amsterdam: Elsevier.

Raper, Stan, and Kerry Preibisch (Stan Raper interviewed by Kerry Preibisch). 2007. "Forcing Governments to Govern in Defence of Noncitizen Workers: A Story about the Canadian Labour Movement's Alliance with Agricultural Migrants." In *Organizing the Transnational: Labour, Politics, and Social Change,* edited by Luin Goldring and Sailaja Krishnamurti (pp. 115–128). Vancouver: UBC Press.

Ratha, D. 2004. *Leveraging Remittances in Development.* Oslo: Second Plenary Meeting of the Leading Group on Solidarity Levies to Fund Development.

Ravenstein, Ernst G. 1885. "The Laws of Migration." *Journal of the Statistical Society of London* 48:167–235.

Ravenstein, Ernst G. 1889. "The Laws of Migration (Revised)." *Journal of the Statistical Society of London* 52:241–301.

Reitz, Jeffrey G. 1998. *Warmth of the Welcome: The Social Causes of Economic Success for Immigrants in Different Nations and Cities.* Boulder: Westview Press.

Reitz, Jeffrey G. 2001. "Immigrant Skill Utilization in the Canadian Labour Market: Implications of Human Capital Research." *Journal of International Migration and Integration* 2:347–378.

Reitz, Jeffrey G. 2005. *Tapping Immigrants' Skills: New Directions for Canadian Immigration Policy in the Knowledge Economy.* Montreal: Institute for Research on Public Policies Choices.

Reitz, Jeffrey G. 2007a. "Immigrant Employment Success in Canada, Part I: Individual and Contextual Causes." *Journal of International Migration and Integration* 8:11–36.

Reitz, Jeffrey G. 2007b. "Immigrant Employment Success in Canada, Part II: Understanding the Decline." *Journal of International Migration and Integration* 8, 1:37–62.

Reitz, Jeffrey, and Rupa Banerjee. 2007. "Racial Inequality, Social Cohesion and Policy Issues." In *Belonging? Diversity, Recognition and Shared Citizenship in Canada,* edited by Keith Banting, Thomas J. Courchene and F. Leslie Seidle (pp. 489–546). Montreal: Institute for Research on Public Policy.

Reitz, Jeffrey G., and Janet M. Lum. 2006. "Immigration and Diversity in a Changing Canadian City: Social Bases of Intergroup Relations in Toronto." In *Inside the Mosaic,* edited by Eric Fong (pp. 15–50). Toronto: University of Toronto Press.

Rekai, Peter. 2008. "Whose Marriage? Whose Convenience?" *Globe and Mail* (20 May), A17.

Rex, J. 1986. *Race and Ethnicity.* Milton Keynes: Open University Press.

Richmond, Anthony H. 1994. *Global Apartheid: Refugees, Racism, and the New World Order.* Toronto: Oxford University Press.

Richmond, Anthony H. 1997. "Multiculturalism and the Millennium: Global Perspectives." *Refuge* 15:8–11.

Riddell, W.C. 2009. "Recession." *The Canadian Encyclopedia.* Retrieved 24 March 2009 [http://www.thecanadianencyclopedia.com.ezproxy.library.yorku.ca/index.cfm?PgNm=TCE&Params=A1ARTA0006709].

Rimok, Patricia, and Ralph Rouzier. 2008. "Integration Policies in Quebec: A Need to Expand the Structures?" In *Immigration and Integration in Canada,* edited by John Biles, Meyer Burstein, and James Frideres (pp. 187–210). Montreal and Kingston: McGill-Queen's University Press.

Roberts, Barbara. 1988. *Whence They Came: Deportation from Canada 1900–1935.* Ottawa: University of Ottawa Press.

Robertson, Roland. 1992. *Globalization: Social Theory and Global Culture.* London: Sage Publications.

Robinson, David. 2007. "All Pain, No Gain: Canadian Labour in the Integrated North American Economy." In *Whose Canada? Continental Integration, Fortress North America, and the Corporate Agenda,* edited by Ricardo Grinspun and Yasmine Shamsie (pp. 259–276). Montreal and Kingston: McGill-Queen's University Press.

Ruhs, Martin. 2005. *The Potential of Temporary Migration Programmes in Future International Migration Policy.* Geneva: Global Commission on International Migration.

Rummens, Joanna A. 2003. "Conceptualising Identity and Diversity: Overlaps, Intersections, and Processes." *Canadian Ethnic Studies* 35:10–25.

Ryder, Norm. 1997. "Migration and Population Replacement." *Canadian Studies in Population* 24, 1:1–26.

Sacks, Jonathan. 2002. *The Dignity of Differences: How to Avoid the Clash of Civilizations.* London: Continuum.

Salaff, Janet W. 2006. "Different Crossings: Migrants from Three Chinese Communities." In *Inside the Mosaic,* edited by Eric Fong (pp. 227–256). Toronto: University of Toronto Press.

Sassen, Saskia. 1998. *Globalization and Its Discontents: Essays on the New Mobility of People and Money.* New York: New Press.

Sassen, Saskia. 2001. *The Global City: New York, London, Tokyo.* Princeton: Princeton University Press.

Sassen, Saskia. 2006. *Cities in a World Economy.* Thousand Oaks: Pine Forge Press.

Satzewich, Vic. 1988. "The Canadian State and the Racialization of Caribbean Migrant Farm Labour, 1947–1966." *Ethnic and Racial Studies* 11, 3:282–304.

Satzewich, Vic. 1989. "Racism and Canadian Immigration Policy: The Government's View of Caribbean Migration, 1962–1966." *Ethnic and Racial Studies* 21, 1:77–97.

Satzewich, Vic. 1998. *Racism and Social Inequality in Canada.* Toronto: Thompson Educational Publishing, Inc.

Satzewich, Vic. 2007. "Business or Bureaucratic Dominance in Immigration Policymaking in Canada: Why Was Mexico Included in the Caribbean Seasonal Agricultural Workers Program in 1974?" *Journal of International Migration and Integration* 8, 3:255–275.

Satzewich, Vic, and Nikolaos Liodakis. 2007. *"Race" and Ethnicity in Canada: A Critical Introduction.* Oxford: Oxford University Press.

Satzewich, Vic, and Lloyd Wong. 2003. "Immigration, Ethnicity, and Race: The Transformation of Transnationalism, Localism, and Identities." In *Changing Canada: Political Economy as Transformation,* edited by Wallace Clement and Leah Vosko (pp. 363–390). Montreal and Kingston: McGill-Queen's University Press.

Satzewich, Vic, and Lloyd Wong. 2006. *Transnational Identities and Practices in Canada.* Vancouver: UBC Press.

Saywell, Trish. 2003. "Cupid the Bureaucrat? Singapore Tries to Play Matchmaker." *The Wall Street Journal* (30 January), A8.

Schmidtke, Oliver, and Saime Ozcurumez. 2008. *Of States, Rights, and Social Closure: Governing Migration and Citizenship.* New York: Palgrave Macmillan.

Sejersen, Tanja B. 2008. "'I Vow to Thee My Countries' — the Expansion of Dual Citizenship in the 21st Century." *International Migration Review* 42:523–549.

Serbanescu, F., L. Morris, P. Stupp, and A. Stanescu. 1995. "The Impact of Recent Policy Changes on Fertility, Abortion, and Contraceptive Use in Romania." *Studies in Family Planning* 26:76–87.

Sharma, Nandita R. 2006. *Home Economics: Nationalism and the Making of "Migrant Workers" in Canada.* Toronto: University of Toronto Press.

Silvera, Makeda. 1989. *Silenced: Talks with Working-Class Caribbean Women about Their Lives and Struggles as Domestic Workers in Canada.* Toronto: Black Women and Women of Colour Press.

Simmons, Alan B. 1987. "Explaining Migration: Theory at the Crossroads." In *Explanations in the Social Sciences: The Search for Causes in Demography,* edited by J. Duchene (pp. 73–79). Louvain-la-Neuve: Université catholique de Louvain, Institut de démographie.

Simmons, Alan B. 1993a. "Latin American Migration to Canada: New Linkages in the Hemispheric Migration and Refugee Flow System." *International Journal* XLVIII, 2:282–309.

Simmons, Alan B. 1993b. "Canada and Migration in the Western Hemisphere." In *Dynamic Partnership: Canada's Changing Role in the Americas,* edited by Jerry Haar and Edgar Dosman (pp. 45–60). Miami: University of Miami.

Simmons, Alan B. 1994. "Canadian Immigration Policy in the Early 1990s: A Commentary on Veuglers and Klassen's Analysis of the Breakdown in the Unemployment-Immigration Linkage." *Canadian Journal of Sociology* 19, 4:525–534.

Simmons, Alan B. 1997. "Canadian Immigration and Nation Building: Social and Political Implications of Recent Trends." In *Re(Defining) Canada: A Prospective Look at Our Country in the 21st Century,* edited by R. Hebert and R. Theberger (pp. 43–70). Winnipeg: Presses Universitaires de Saint-Boniface.

Simmons, Alan B. 1998a. "International Migration in the Context of NAFTA." *Labour, Capital, and Society* 31:10–43.

Simmons, Alan B. 1998b. "Racism and Immigration Policy." In *Racism and Social Inequality in Canada: Concepts, Controversies, and Strategies of Resistance,* edited by Vic Satzewich (pp. 87–114). Toronto: Thompson Educational Publishers.

Simmons, Alan B. 1999a. "Economic Integration and Designer Immigrants: Canadian Policy in the 1990's." In *Free Markets, Open Societies, Closed Borders? Trends in International Migration and Immigration Policy in the Americas,* edited by Max J. Castro (pp. 53–69). Coral Gables: North-South Center Press, University of Miami.

Simmons, Alan B. 1999b. "Immigration Policy: Imagined Futures." In *Immigrant Canada: Demographic, Economic, and Social Challenges*, edited by Shiva Halli and Leo Driedger (pp. 21–50). Toronto: University of Toronto Press.

Simmons, Alan B. 2002. "Mondialisation et migration internationale: Tendeance, interrogations, et models theoriques." *Cahiers Quebecois de demographie* 31, 1:7–33.

Simmons, Alan B. 2005. *International Migration and the Millennium Development Goals*. New York: United Nations Fund for Population Activities.

Simmons, Alan B. 2008. "Why International Banks Became Interested in Migrant Remittances: A Critical Refection on Globalization, Ideology, and International Migration." In *Governing International Labor Migration*, edited by Hélène Pellerin and Christina Gabriel (pp. 60–78). New York: Routledge.

Simmons, Alan B., and Luis Carrillos. 2009. *Home and Heart: Identity Politics among Latino Youths in Toronto*. Toronto: Centre for Research on Latin American and the Caribbean (CERLAC), York University.

Simmons, Alan B., and Jean-Pierre Guengant. 1992. "Caribbean Exodus and the World System." In *International Migration Systems: A Global Approach*, edited by Mary M. Kritz, Lin L. Lim, and Hania Zlotnik (pp. 94–114). Oxford: Clarendon Press.

Simmons, Alan B., and Kieran Keohane. 1992. "Shifts in Canadian Immigration Policy: State Strategies and the Quest for Legitimacy." *Canada Review of Sociology and Anthropology* 29, 4:421–452.

Simmons, Alan B., and Dwaine E. Plaza. 1998. "Breaking through the Glass Ceiling: The Pursuit of University Training among African-Caribbean Migrants and Their Children in Toronto." *Canadian Ethnic Studies* XXX, 3:99–120.

Simmons, Alan B., and Dwaine E. Plaza. 2006. "The Caribbean Community in Canada: Transnational Connections and Transformations." In *Transnational Identities and Practices in Canada*, edited by Vic Satzewich and Lloyd Wong (pp. 130–149). Vancouver: UBC Press.

Simmons, Alan B., Dwaine Plaza, and Victor Piché. 2005. *The Remittance Sending Practices of Haitians and Jamaicans in Canada*. Toronto: Centre for Research on Latin American and the Caribbean (CERLAC), York University.

Simmons, Alan B., and Jean Turner. 1993. "L'Immigration Antillaise au Canada, 1967–1987: Contraintes structurelles et experiences vecues." In *Population, reproduction, societes: Perspectives et enjeux de demographie sociale*, edited by D. Cordell, Gervais Gauvreau, and C. Le Bourdais (pp. 395–418). Montreal: Presses de l'Université de Montréal.

Simon, Rita J., and Keri W. Sikich. 2007. "Public Attitudes toward Immigrants and Immigration Policies across Seven Nations." *International Migration Review* 41, 4:956–962.

Stafford, J., and B. McMillan. 1988. *Immigration and the Two Schools of Canadian Political Economy: A Report to the National Demographic Review*. Thunder Bay: Lakehead University.

Stalker, Peter. 2000. *Workers without Frontiers: The Impact of Globalization on International Migration*. Geneva: International Labour Organization.

Stalker, Peter. 2002. *The No-Nonsense Guide to International Migration*. Toronto: New International Publication.

Standing Committee on Multiculturalism. 1987. *Multiculturalism: Building the Canadian Mosaic: Report of the Standing Committee on Multiculturalism*. Ottawa: The Standing Committee on Multiculturalism.

Stark, Oded. 1991. *The Migration of Labour*. Cambridge: Basil Blackwell.

Stark, Oded, and E. Katz. 1986. "Labour Migration and Risk Aversion in Less Developed Countries." *Journal of Labour Economics* 4:134–149.

Stasiulis, Daiva. 1997. "The Political Economy of Race, Ethnicity, and Migration." In *Understanding Canada: Building the New Canadian Political Economy*, edited by W. Clement (pp. 141–171). Montreal and Kingston: McGill-Queen's University Press.

Statistics Canada. 2003. *Ethnic Diversity Survey: Portrait of a Multicultural Society.* Catalogue no. 89-593-XIE. Ottawa: Minister of Industry.

Statistics Canada. 2004. *Report on the Demographic Situation in Canada 2004.* Ottawa: Statistics Canada.

Statistics Canada. 2005a. *Longitudinal Survey of Immigrants to Canada: A Portrait of Early Settlement Experiences.* Ottawa: Statistics Canada, Special Surveys Division.

Statistics Canada. 2005b. "Population and Growth Components (1851–2001 Censuses)." Statistics Canada. Retrieved 26 March 2009 [http://www40.statcan.gc.ca.ezproxy.library.yorku.ca/l01/cst01/demo03-eng.htm].

Statistics Canada. 2006a. *Canada's Ethnocultural Mosaic, 2006 Census: Findings.* Ottawa: Statistics Canada. Retreived 16 March 2009. [http://www12.statcan.ca/english/census06/analysis/ethnicorigin/index.cfm]

Statistics Canada. 2006b. *Earnings and Incomes of Canadians over the Past Quarter Century, 2006 Census.* Catalogue no. 97-563 22. Ottawa: Statistics Canada.

Statistics Canada. 2007a. *Citizenship, Place of Birth, Sex, and Immigrant Status and Period of Immigration for the Population of Canada, Provinces, Territories, Census Metropolitan Areas, and Census Agglomerations, 2006 Census.* Ottawa: Statistics Canada.

Statistics Canada. 2007b. "Observed (1981–2005) and Projected (2006–2056) Population According to Three Scenarios." Statistics Canada. Retrieved 26 March 2009 [http://www.statcan.gc.ca.ezproxy.library.yorku.ca/ads-annonces/91-520-x/c-g/c-g1-eng.htm].

Statistics Canada. 2007c. "Observed (1981–2004) and Projected (2005–2056) Natural and Migratory Increase in Canada According to Scenario 3 (Medium Growth)." Statistics Canada. Retrieved 26 March 2009 [http://www.statcan.gc.ca.ezproxy.library.yorku.ca/ads-annonces/91-520-x/c-g/c-g2-eng.htm].

Statistics Canada. 2008a. *Merchandise Trade of Canada, December 2008.* Ottawa: Statistics Canada.

Statistics Canada. 2008b. "Estimated Population of Canada, 1605 to Present." Statistics Canada. Retrieved 26 March 2009 [http://www.statcan.gc.ca.ezproxy.library.yorku.ca/pub/98-187-x/4151287-eng.htm].

Stoffman, Daniel. 2002. *Who Gets in: What's Wrong with Canada's Immigration Program – and How to Fix It.* Toronto: Macfarlane, Walter & Ross.

Stoffman, Daniel. 2004. "Canada Is a Real Country: A Reply to Peter Li." *Journal of International Migration and Integration* 5:497–504.

Stouffer, Samuel A. 1940. "Intervening Opportunities: A Theory Relating to Mobility and Distance." *American Sociological Review* 5:845–867.

Suárez-Orozco, Carola, and M. Suárez-Orozco. 2001. *Children of Immigrants.* Cambridge: Harvard University Press.

Sweetman, Arthur. 2004. *Immigrant Source Country Educational Quality and Canadian Labour Market Outcomes.* Ottawa: Business and Labour Market Analysis, Statistics Canada.

Tejada, Juana. 2008. "Juana Tejada Timeline and Links." Retrieved 24 November 2008 [http://www.juana-tejada.info].

Thomas, Brinley. 1972. *Migration and Economic Growth: A Study of Great Britain and the Atlantic Community.* Cambridge: Cambridge University Press.

Timlin, Mabel. 1960. "Canada's Immigration Policy, 1896–1910." *Canadian Journal of Economics and Political Science* 26:518.

Toft, Monica D. 2003. *The Geography of Ethnic Violence: Identity, Interests, and the Indivisibility of Territory.* Princeton: Princeton University Press.

Turner, Jean. 1991. "Migrants and Their Therapists: A Trans-Context Approach." *Family Process* 30:407–419.

Turner, Jean, and Alan Simmons. 2006. "Transnational Resilience and Resistance: Key Concepts for Working with Refugees." In *Immigrant Families and Immigration: Therapeutic Work*, edited by Gonzalo Bacigalupe and Janine Roberts (pp. 6–22). Washington: American Family Therapy Academy.

Tusicisny, Andrej. 2004. "Civilizational Conflicts: More Frequent, Longer, and Bloodier?" *Journal of Peace Research* 41, 4:485–498.

UNDP. 2006. "Human Development Index." United Nations Development Programme. Retrieved 30 August 2008 [www.undp.org].

Ungerleider, Charles S. 2006. "Immigration, Multiculturalism, and Citizenship: The Development of the Canadian Social Justice Infrastructure." In *Identity and Belonging: Rethinking Race and Ethnicity in Canadian Social Society*, edited by Sean P. Hier and B.S. Bolaria (pp. 201–214). Toronto: Canadian Scholars' Press Inc.

UNPD. 2000. "Replacement Migration: Is It a Solution to Declining and Aging Populations?" United Nations Population Division, Department of Economic and Social Affairs. Retrieved 15 November 2008 [http://www.un.org.ezproxy.library.yorku.ca/esa/population/publications/migration/execsum.htm].

UNPD. 2006. "Population, Resources, Environment, and Development: The 2005 Revision Data Retrieval System." United Nations Department of Economics and Social Affairs, Population Division. Retrieved 10 March 2009 [http://unstats.un.org.ezproxy.library.yorku.ca/pop/dVariables/DRetrieval.aspx].

UNPD. 2007. *World Population Prospects: The 2006 Revision*. New York: United Nation Population Division.

UNPD. 2008. *World Population Prospects: The 2008 Revision Population Data Base*. New York: United Nations Population Division.

Van Oudenhoven, Jan P., Colleen Ward, and Anne-Marie Masgoret. 2006. "Patterns of Relations between Immigrants and Host Societies." *International Journal of Intercultural Relations* 30:637–651.

Verduzco, Gustavo. 1999. "El Programa de Trabajadores Agricolas Mexicanos Con Canada; Un Contraste Frente a La Experiencia Con Estados Unidos." *Estudios Demograficos y Urbanos* 14:165–191.

Vertovec, Stephen. 1999. "Conceiving and Researching Transnationalism." *Ethnic and Racial Studies* 22:447–462.

Vertovec, Stephen. 2009. *Transnationalism*. London and New York: Routledge.

Veugelers, John W.P., and Thomas R. Klassen. 1994. "Continuity and Change in Canada's Unemployment-Immigration Linkage." *Canadian Journal of Sociology* 19, 3:351–369.

Vézina, Hélène, Marc Tremblay, Bertrand Desjardins, and Louis Houde. 2005. "Origines et contributions génétiques des fondatrices et des fondateurs de la population Québécoise." *Cahiers québécois de démographie* 34:235–258.

Viccari, Ben. 2007. "Canadian Multiculturalism in Danger." Canadian Ethnic Media Association News Bulletin. Retrieved 20 March 2009 [http://canadianethnicmedia.com/?p=82].

Walcott, R. 1997. *Black Like Who? Writing Black Canada*. Toronto: Insomniac Press.

Walters, David, Kelli Phythian, and Paul Anisef. 2007. "The Acculturation of Canadian Immigrants: Determinants of Ethnic Identification with the Host Society." *Canadian Review of Sociology and Anthropology* 44, 1:37–64.

Wanner, Richard A. 1998. "Prejudice, Profit, or Productivity: Explaining Returns to Human Capital among Male Immigrants to Canada." *Canadian Ethnic Studies* 30:24–55.

Wanner, Richard A. 2000. "A Matter of Degree(s): Twentieth-Century Trends in Occupational Status Returns to Educational Credentials in Canada." *Canadian Review of Sociology and Anthropology* 37:313–343.

Wanner, Richard A. 2001. "Diagnosing and Preventing 'Brain Waste' in Canada's Immigrant Population: A Synthesis of Comments on Reitz." *Journal of International Migration and Integration* 2:417–428.

Wanner, Richard A. 2003. "Entry Class and the Earnings Attainment of Immigrants to Canada, 1980–1995." *Canadian Public Policy* 29:53–71.

Warman, Casey R., and Christopher Worswick. 2004. "Immigrant Earnings Performance in Canadian Cities: 1981 through 2001." *Canadian Journal of Urban Research* 13, 1:62–84.

Waslander, Bert. 2003. "The Falling Earnings of New Immigrant Men in Canada's Large Cities." In *Canadian Immigration Policy for the 21st Century*, edited by Charles M. Beach, Alan G. Green, and Jeffrey G. Reitz (pp. 335–372). Montreal and Kingston: McGill-Queen's University Press.

Waters, Malcolm. 1995. *Globalization*. London: Routledge.

Wayland, Sarah V. 2006. "The Politics of Transnationalism: Comparative Perspectives." In *Transnational Identities and Practices in Canada*, edited by Vic Satzewich and Lloyd Wong (pp. 18–34). Vancouver: UBC Press.

Wayland, Sarah V. 2007. "Transnational Nationalism: Sri Lankan Tamils in Canada." In *Organizing the Transnational: Labour, Politics, and Social Change*, edited by Luin Goldring and Sailaja Krishnamurti (pp. 55–66). Vancouver: UBC Press.

Weber, Max. [1922] 1978. *Economy and Society*, edited by Guenther Roth and Claus Wittich. Translated by Ephraim Fischof. Berkeley: University of California Press.

Weber, Max. 1949. *The Methodology of the Social Sciences*. Translated by Eduard Shils and Henry Finch. New York: The Free Press.

Weeks, John R. 2008. *Population: An Introduction to Concepts and Issues* (10th ed.). Belmont: Wadsworth/Thompson.

White, Patrick. 2009. "In Hard Times, Icelanders Look to Prairie Refuge." *Globe and Mail* (27 January), A9.

Wilkes, Rima, Neil Guppy, and Lily Farris. 2008. "'No Thanks, We're Full': Individual Characteristics, National Context, and Changing Attitudes toward Immigration." *International Migration Review* 42, 2:302–329.

Wilkinson, Lori. 2008. "Labor Market Transitions of Immigrant-Born, Refugee-Born, and Canadian-Born Youth." *Canadian Review of Sociology* 45:151–176.

Winter, Elke. 2005. *Max Weber et les relations ethniques: Du refus du biologisme racial a l'etat multinational*. Quebec: Les Presses de l'Université Laval.

Winter, Elke. 2007. "Neither 'America' nor 'Quebec': Constructing the Canadian Multicultural Nation." *Nations and Nationalism* 13:481–503.

Wolf, Eric. 1982. *Europe and the People without History*. Berkeley: University of California Press.

Wong, Fred. 1998. *Canada's Information Technology Sector*. Ottawa: Statistics Canada.

Wong, Lloyd, and Connie Ho. 2006. "Chinese Transnationalism: Class and Capital Flows." In *Transnational Identities and Practices in Canada*, edited by Vic Satzewich and Lloyd Wong (pp. 241–260). Vancouver: UBC Press.

Wong, Lloyd L., and Michele Ng. 1998. "Chinese Immigrant Entrepreneurs in Vancouver: A Case Study of Ethnic Business Development." *Canadian Ethnic Studies* XXX:64–85.

World Bank. 2006. *Global Economic Prospects 2006: Economic Implications of Remittances and Migration*. Washington: The International Bank for Reconstruction and Development/The World Bank.

Young, Margaret. 1998. *Canadian Citizenship Act and Current Issues*. Ottawa: Government of Canada, Law and Government Division. Retrieved 26 March 2009 [http://dsp-psd.tpsgc.gc.ca/Collection-R/LoPBdP/BP/bp445-e.htm].

Yuval-Davis, Nira. 1999. "The 'Multi-layered Citizen': Citizenship at the Age of 'Globalization.'" *International Feminist Journal of Politics* 1:119–136.

Zelinski, Wilber. 1971. "The Hypotheses of the Mobility Transition." *The Geographical Review* 61:219–249.

Zhang, Sheldon X. 2008. *Chinese Human-Smuggling Organizations: Families, Social Networks, and Cultural Imperatives.* Stanford: Stanford University Press.

Zlotnik, Hania. 1992. "Empirical Identification of International Migration Systems." In *International Migration Systems: A Global Approach,* edited by Mary M. Kritz, Lin L. Lim, and Hania Zlotnik (pp. 19–40). Oxford: Clarendon Press.

Zolberg, Aristide R. 1992. "Labour Migration and International Economic Regimes: Bretton Woods and after." In *International Migration Systems: A Global Approach,* edited by Mary M. Kritz, Lin L. Lim, and Hania Zlotnik (pp. 315–334). Oxford: Clarendon Press.

Zolberg, Aristide R., Astri Suhrke, and Sergio Aguayo, eds. 1989. *Escape from Violence: Conflict and the Refugee Crisis in the Developing World.* New York: Oxford University Press.

Copyright Acknowledgements

Index

"absorptive capacity," 72
Acadia, 52
acceleration, of migration flow, 116, 119–20
accents, 154
acculturation, 175, 176;
    concordant, 210;
    discordant, 210;
    selective, 209–11
Action Committee of Non-status Algerians, 111
Action Committee of Pakistani Refugees, 111
Act of Direct Passage, 56, 57
Adjustment of Status Program (1973), 111
admissibility, as determinant of immigration,
    115–16, 118, 120, 135
adult vs. child immigrants, 205–6, 208–11
affective criteria, 197
Africa: colonialism in, 35;
    fertility rates in, 227, 270;
    francophone countries in, 102;
    immigration from, 28, 54, 124, 134, 135,
      136, 154–55, 173.
    See also under individual countries.
Afro-Caribbean peoples, 187
AIC Limited, 8
Alberta, 55, 67, 82, 245;
    foreign workers in, 246–47
Algeria, immigration from, 110–11, 134
alternative conceptual frameworks, 29
ambivalence, 199
American Revolutionary War, 53, 54
Anderson, Benedict, 14–18;
    Imagined Communities, 15
anglophone immigrants, to Quebec, 102–3
Annual Report on Immigration (1958–59), 73
*Annual Report to Parliament on Immigration
    Levels*, 91
anti-Chinese riots, 48
anti-discrimination, 5, 68, 192
anti-immigrant sentiment, 41, 48, 71, 204,
    256, 270
anti-racism, 60, 63, 67, 68, 74–75, 180, 187, 196,
    199, 219, 263–64

anti-Semitism, 58
anti-sexism, 75
apartheid, "global," 136
Arab Association for Human Rights, 192
Arab Gulf states, migrants in, 121
Armenia, immigration from, 213
ascription, 197
Asia, immigration from, 7, 27, 28, 60, 124, 135,
    154–55, 173.
    See also under individual countries.
assimilation, 172, 175–76, 177;
    vs. integration, 172
"astronaut" family, 186
asylum seekers, 89, 105, 107, 256
attitudes toward immigrants, 214–20;
    changes in over time, 217–20;
    cross-national comparison of, 215, 216–17;
    urban vs. rural, 214
Australia, 14, 21, 22, 28, 35, 129, 173, 255;
    abandonment of Whites-only immigra-
      tion policy, 74;
    attitudes toward immigration in, 215;
    foreign-born residents in, 120–21;
    immigration from, 184;
    job exporting, 244
automotive industry, 67, 69

baby boom, 223, 228
baby bust, 223
Baie de Chaleur (Quebec), 50–51
"banana" stereotype, 204
Barbados, immigration from, 131
Barth, Fredrik, 199, 203;
    Ethnic Groups and Boundaries, 197
being and belonging, transnational, 169–93
Belgium, 102
Bell-Northern Research, 151
belonging, 15, 114;
    citizenship and, 188–91;
    ethnic, 17–18;
    global, 191–92;
    hybrid aspects of, 196;